The real thing

For Hugo and Horatia

Tanya Harrod

The real thing

essays on making in the modern world

Hyphen Press . London

Published by Hyphen Press, London, in 2015

The book was designed by Françoise Berserik, The Hague. The text was typeset and made into pages by Henk Pel, Zeist, and Robin Kinross, London, in Adobe InDesign. This text was output in the typeface TEFF Lexicon, designed by Bram de Does, Orvelte. The index was made by Robin Kinross. Proofs of the final pages were read by Jan Cumming, London. The book was made and printed in Belgium by Die Keure, Bruges, and bound in the Netherlands by Binderij Hexspoor, Boxtel

ISBN 978-0-907259-50-3

www.hyphenpress.co.uk

Contents

Preface

This is a selection of my writing from the mid-1980s to 2013 – mostly short essays and some longer pieces – published in magazines and newspapers. They are all, in different ways, about making things. They scrutinize areas of facture that generally go unnoticed by art critics and which are rarely considered by writers on design and architecture.

The shorter pieces are arranged under three headings – 'Visiting', 'Reading', and 'People'. They are not set out chronologically although the 'People' section orders its subjects by their dates of birth – from William Morris, born 1834, to Robin Wood, born 1965. In the other two sections the sequence is more poetically conceived – one topic leading to another. An article originally published in 2011 might be followed by one penned in 1990. I owe this ordering to Françoise Berserik, designer and co-editor of this book.

It works in part because the period covered by the book has a unity, in which Britain experienced fundamental change regardless of the government in power. From the 1980s a generously funded social democracy, marked by a degree of social equality, was gradually undermined by the relentless logic of neo-liberal economics. We became a nation of consumers as opposed to producers, moving from physical production to a service economy. The same period saw the startling expansion of Asian productivity, particularly that of China, and the emergence of pervasive computing and a networked world of infinite images that at times appears to outface the analogue world.

Our responses to a world where centres of manufacturing are constantly on the move, chasing economic efficiency, apparently careless of the effect on lives and communities emerges, therefore, as one area of investigation in this book. Some essays explore the rather more hermetic world of modern studio craft that I discussed more formally in my book *The crafts in Britain in the 20th century* (1999). Other articles record a new turn to craft that is less to do with the product and more to do with the process – craft as a form of activism. Quite a few pieces of writing take us abroad – to North America, to West Africa, to China, to Korea, and to Japan. Still other essays discuss artists like Picasso, Alexander Calder, and Isamu Noguchi but very much from the perspective of making.

Although much of this writing takes the road less travelled, I'd like to think that almost any reader will find much that is familiar. Robinson Crusoe, Le Corbusier, and Philip K. Dick, activities like knitting, playing computer games, and worrying about the environment – these are hardly obscure subjects. Distributism, puppetry, and Brazilian *gambiarra* might appear more of a puzzle, while technologies such as rapid prototyping, often described as three-dimensional printing, are now being much discussed at popular and specialized levels.

I hope that I communicate both a deep love and a deep distrust of the world we now inhabit. I've called this book *The real thing*, after an unsettling exhibition of Chinese art held at Tate Liverpool in 2007. Through writing about a catholic range of events, exhibitions, and books, and about the lives of individuals (including quite a few awkward customers working in relative obscurity) I have tried to address one important question: 'how can we be modern yet be true to ourselves?'

These writings first appeared in a variety of places, principally: *Crafts*, *The Spectator*, *The Independent* and *The Independent on Sunday*, the *Times Literary Supplement*, and *The Burlington Magazine*. My thanks go to my editors, especially Jenny Naipaul at *The Spectator* and Tom Sutcliffe at *The Independent*, for being open to ideas about making before the topic became fashionable. My thanks also to Geraldine Rudge of *Crafts*, who in 2003 trustingly gave me a column entitled 'As I please' (in homage to George Orwell). It continues to this day under the rubric 'Thinking Aloud' and with Grant Gibson as benign editor.

TH, October 2014

Pictures: acknowledgements and sources

We are glad to acknowledge the following copyright holders and others who provided pictures for this book.

Visiting

A cabinet of wonders

Coming out of Sheffield station, it is impossible to miss the cliff-like façade of the Park Hill housing estate. It was intended as a post-war social condenser, a city within a city, and is now in danger of demolition. Heading for the centre over the ring-road and away from this bold tribute to Le Corbusier, the traveller arrives at the Graves Art Gallery, filled with harmless paintings, the fruits of a mail-order fortune amassed by Alderman Graves. His was a handsome gift but an unremarkable one. The really startling collection, the Ruskin Gallery, is just around the corner.

John Ruskin's collection for Sheffield was never actually given to the city and still belongs to his Guild of St George. As a realistic project the Guild must be counted a failure. Probably Ruskin never quite believed he could found an ideal society anywhere in Britain, but nineteenth-century Sheffield, with its craft traditions, slums, smoke and inequalities must have seemed the place to start. But if the Guild's value was largely symbolic, his museum in Sheffield was real enough – first housed in a little cottage in Walkley, which he often visited, and then on a grander scale at Meersbrook Park. The collection has had its vicissitudes. After the war, just as the Hyde Park flats were going up, it was dismissed as irrelevant and put into store. Since 1985, however, it has been beautifully displayed in its new home in Norfolk Street. What Ruskin created was a museum with an argument and today these arguments seem as fresh as ever.

Nowadays we seem uncertain about the purpose of a museum. Ruskin had no such doubts. 'A museum is not a place of entertainment, but a place of education. And a museum is ... not a place for elementary education but for that of already far advanced scholars.' That sounds old-fashioned and exclusive – but is it? In the 1870s he was creating collections for two groups of 'far advanced' scholars. One was for Oxford undergraduates. The other was for the working people of Sheffield. That the two collections were similar and intended to be studied in the same way is suggestive. It is no exaggeration to say that their principal purpose was to foster a discontent with the present and a desire for change.

To do this Ruskin needed to show his audience the kind of things money could not buy. Therein lies his uniqueness as a collector. Ruskin was a wealthy man but he was not interested in *objets d'art*. Rather he wanted to introduce his students to the government of Venice, to the Gothic architecture of northern Italy, to the history of mosaics, to the structure of leaves and the pigmentation of birds' feathers. This meant that his museum had to be above all a museum of casts and copies. Today, most of us have a hunger for authen-

John Wharlton Bunney, 'Western façade of the Basilica of San Marco, Venice' (1877–82, oil on canvas).

ticity. We want to see the real thing, hence the tightly packed pilgrim crowds in the galleries of Europe. Ruskin, on the other hand, believed passionately in copies, because, paradoxically, they involved lengthy and thoughtful study. When he commissioned John Bunney to paint the West front of St Mark's (a task taking three years) or had casts made of a carving high on St Mark's central archivolt, or had water-colours made of St Mark's mosaics, he knew that he was giving the people of Sheffield something that most visitors to Venice would miss. His collection is filled with beauties that all our modern travelling and costly books of photographs tend to overlook.

But his museum is unique in another way. Just about the time he was putting it together, collections of art and of science were being separated. In London, the art stayed in the British Museum while the natural history went to South Kensington. Ruskin went back to a much earlier arrangement – the cabinet of wonders, what Francis Bacon had called 'a model of universal nature made private'. Geology was Ruskin's earliest love but he never isolated it from his later work. It went hand in hand with landscape painting and he geologized Turner, he geologized Mantegna.

So Ruskin's museum is different because of its juxtapositions. We learn about colour by comparing prints of humming birds with cases of brightly hued minerals. The devastating restoration of St Mark's is made vivid by the display of fragments of alabaster from its façade, literally the Stones of Venice. And the museum's curator, Janet Barnes, keeps Ruskin's extraordinary connective impulses alive by including contemporary art, putting a leaf sculpture by Andy Goldsworthy among the exquisite botanical studies made by Ruskin and his assistants. A sense is conveyed of a great unity of art and the natural world which today we seem to have lost.

The result seems remarkably modern while differing wildly from the Disneyland approach favoured by many museums today. For example, Ruskin loved crystals. When we enter his museum in Sheffield one of his finest specimens is displayed as the first object for us to meditate on. Paper and pencil are available for those who wish to draw it. The contrast with the Natural History Museum in South Kensington, where Ruskin spent many happy hours, is striking. Recently it hosted an extraordinary exhibition of giant crystals from Strasbourg: 100 years ago this awe-inspiring display would have attracted great crowds and would have appealed to artists and scientists alike. Today, probably because it was dubbed 'The Rock Festival' by the museum, with a stick of rock as its logo, most grown-ups managed to miss it. It is difficult to imagine what Ruskin would have made of the Natural History Museum today with its blipping and buzzing interactive displays. Certainly his little gallery in Sheffield (where drawing and botany, ornithology and geology, the crafts of missal illumination and mosaic, studies of clouds and electrotypes of coins, are exhibited together) suggests that museums of art and science were both impoverished when they were divided.

The Independent on Sunday, 1 April 1990

In 2001 the Ruskin Gallery: the Collection of the Guild of St George moved from its atmospheric gallery in 101 Norfolk Street to Sheffield's glitzy Millennium Gallery, at Arundel Gate. In 1998 the Park Hill flats were listed Grade II by English Heritage and have since been redeveloped by Urban Splash with two-thirds of the flats for private sale.

The language of things

'The Language of Things': exhibition at Kettle's Yard, Cambridge, 13 January to 11 March 2001

Much current work in both design and fine art seems to be responding to an existential problem – why make art at all in such a full world? There are so many odd haunting things around, why go further? A whole group of young designers – shortly to be seen at the Crafts Council show 'Industry of One' – have based their practice on the transformation of existing objects. And two memorable fine art shows, 'Craft' held at the Richard Salmon Gallery and at Kettle's Yard in 1997 and 'Thinking Aloud' curated by the sculptor Richard Wentworth at Camden Arts Centre in 1999 were, as much as anything, a response to the multiplicity of meanings that existing objects can embody. Just two examples – Wentworth included an item from a 1930s German toy soldier set. It is a bizarre little *objet trouvé*, an explosion reified in some kind of composite rubber, brightly painted yellow and red. And at the Richard Salmon Gallery there was Neil Cummings's strange replication of Gerrit Rietveld's famous Red Blue chair, rendered completely non-functional and unstable by being made in veneer and cardboard.

In the past artists represented objects through the genre known as still life. Not really at the cutting edge of artistic practice since Cubism, the still life suddenly seems important again as 'The Language of Things', now at Kettle's Yard, demonstrates. This elegantly selected show begins quietly enough with a couple of paintings by William Nicholson – the first, a sensuous play with objects and reflective surfaces, then a later, sparser study of pears, a plate, and a couple of knives painted in 1938. The genre, in its twentieth-century form, is pushed forward by William's son Ben Nicholson and by William Scott. Both were in touch with School of Paris painting but they present us with a peculiarly native response to the modern still life. They, and other St Ives painters, give us design reform based on the renunciation of ornament while continental artists like Morandi (six fine examples are included in this exhibition) concentrate on painterly representation and analysis.

The younger contributors to this show (all British save one) push the still life out of the painterly frame into sculpture and photography. A small piece by Rachel Whiteread sets the anxious tone as we try to read her reverse simulacrum of shelves of books. Tim Head and Ginny Read set up similar tensions by conspicuously failing to deliver the truths we expect of photography. Richard Wentworth re-educates the eye through the juxtaposition of everyday things. On one occasion in the past he paid a visit to an ironmonger to buy a galvanized bucket. The shopkeeper wrapped it in a brown paper bag. Struck by the absurdity of this action Wentworth went back the next day and bought a second bucket and created the eloquent little piece 'Two paper bags'. At Kettle's Yard there is his sculpture 'Profit and loss' in which another galvanized bucket half filled with water appears to float in a galvanized tub. Except – a sudden shock here – the surface of the 'water' in the tub and the unstable floating bucket turn out to be metal sheet.

Sculptural illusionism of this kind has mostly eclipsed the painterly *trompe l'oeil* in force and metaphysical content. Indeed most contemporary painters' ability to deceive appears limited. But the work of the young Spanish painter Manuel Franquelo at Kettle's Yard reminds us that illusionism of this kind can be majestic and disturbing. Franquelo – rather like his great seventeenth-century Spanish predecessor Juan Sánchez Cotán – so mimics the real that for a sudden shocking moment the painting casts doubt on the viewer's place in the world. This vertiginous illusion is achieved in part, I imagine, by the absence of a perspectival system with a single vanishing point. Norman Bryson's book of essays on still-life painting, *Looking at the overlooked*, provides the best elucidation of the strange logic of this area of still life.

When I visited the show there was plenty of evidence of the shocks caused by Franquelo's work, as viewers involuntarily reached forward to touch his three paintings – a naive and moving sight. Curiously enough I can hardly remember what he depicted in these works, all of which adopt the same format in which humble objects – things like a tape cassette, a pencil and pencil sharpener – are depicted on a narrow shelf. Like all the work in this exhibition, Franquelo's paintings reflect intelligently on the very nature of representation – and who could ask more of the visual arts?

The Spectator, 3 February 2001

The power of making

'Power of Making: the importance of being skilled': exhibition at the Victoria & Albert Museum, 6 September 2011 to 2 January 2012

Crowded, closely arrayed and hung, for objects also flow up the walls, 'Power of Making: the importance of being skilled' is worth seeing for many reasons. One must be to witness the level of pleasure among its visitors. As a show it evidently satisfies a yearning, even a palpable need, shared by a large, diverse audience.

'Power of Making' resembles a *Wunderkammer* or cabinet of curiosities in its determination to celebrate making in all its diversity. In the spirit of such collections the exhibits represent what the anthropologist Alfred Gell called 'the enchantment of technology' in which skilled facture excites wonder and awe. This 'enchantment' can take many forms. As a schoolboy, Gell was captivated by a miniature replica of Salisbury Cathedral made of matchsticks. As a sophisticated academic he became more interested in the visual power of Trobriand Islanders' canoe prows and in the art of Marcel Duchamp. But many of the objects in 'Power of Making' recall Gell's matchstick cathedral; they hold our attention by demonstrating an apparently magical mastery of technical difficulty. An over life-size gorilla made of metal coat-hangers, a set of pencils whose leads have been carved into micro sculptures, a ball gown made of dressmakers' pins, sugar sculpture, and a bicycle constructed in steam-bent mahogany make us smile with pleasure. Partly this is because as objects they articulate a disdain for the exigencies of time and money. Thus they have a political dimension, playfully undermining functionalist economics, creating disorder in the world of work.

More seriously, 'Power of Making' challenges the notion that manufacture has become a thing of the past in Europe and North America. Most of us assume, correctly, that the majority of our goods are made in factories in the Far East, probably situated in the Pearl River Delta of Southern China. And we are equally conscious that we no longer understand the internal workings of the products we buy and cannot fix them. There is little point in looking under the bonnet of a car these days. Cars come with their own software and a mechanic is more likely to tap at a laptop than use a monkey wrench. 'Power of Making' sets out to rectify this sense of helplessness by suggesting that we need not remain passive consumers. We can combine literacy and handwork; like Tocqueville's early American settlers we can read a newspaper and use an axe.

Things are emissaries and this is an exhibition of communicative objects. Some belong to the luxury trades – a dressage saddle, bespoke shoes from

John Lobb, a Watson Brothers shotgun. Some were made in situations of duress. Major Casdagli's sampler was created while he was a prisoner during World War Two. It is embellished with swastikas but Hitler is told to 'fuck off' in neatly cross-stitched morse code. Death is addressed in the shape of coffins, one woven from sustainable wicker, another carved in the form of a gleaming lion at Kane Kwei's famous workshop outside Accra. A prosthetic leg, artificial eyeballs, and an electronic prosthetic arm, combine high skill and formal beauty. Sophisticated technology is often abstractly beautiful and while we are spared the Rolls Royce engine of countless Council of Industrial Design exhibitions of the 1960s, we do have a sculptural curvaceous door panel for the Dutch car manufacturer Spyker, made in Coventry using an experimental hot-forming vacuum process.

One of the surprising arguments of the show is that pervasive computing has made it possible to learn and share skills, old and new. Ancient crafts like barrel-making and dry-stone walling, both represented, are finding new practitioners through countless micro-communities that operate as online networks, putting up short films of making processes on YouTube. This may seem paradoxical but then 'Power of Making' abounds in paradoxes, not least in the person of its curator Daniel Charny.

Charny teaches at the Royal College of Art, not in the School of Applied Arts, the obvious home for craftsmanship, but in the Department of Design Products. In the twenty-first century we might imagine product designers working away at screens using 3D digital software just as their predecessors honed technical drawings. But Charny's department is a place where a huge amount of making goes on, often using 'old' materials like wood and rubber and clay. While the students use computers, rapid prototyping machines, and sophisticated computer numeric controlled cutting machines, there is also an understanding that a good designer needs to do some making and tinkering. In that spirit, one of the nicest objects in the show is a majestic table and benches by the design team El Ultimo Grito. Made of cardboard and lacquered paper it looks, deceptively, like a lash-up, inviting us all to get out scissors and glue.

At the heart of the exhibition is a dream of democratized making, some of it technologically advanced. Charny includes some affordable 3D printers including Adrian Bowyer's RepRap, a machine that can manufacture its own parts to replicate itself. For the technophobic, 3D printers (also known as rapid prototyping machines) work from a digital file to print out objects, just as ordinary 2D printers produce texts and images. But instead of ink they print in resin or plaster or even clay. The online communities, whose shared knowledge has made these cheap printers possible, dream of every home becoming a manufactory. Need new shower curtain rings? Or a washer for a tap? Go online, download a digital design and print it out. There is a poetry about the idea of us all becoming homesteaders, no longer dependent on the dark satanic mills of anywhere for our goods.

Charny does not push this point. 3D printers take their place among over a hundred other remarkable objects that hover between art and craft, design and technology. As Danny Miller observes in an essay in the accompanying catalogue, the V&A is the proper venue for this show. The V&A was first conceived in 1852 as a Museum of Manufactures, open to all and free to students, with the populist purpose of improving industrial design. Gradually, as the nineteenth century wore on, it morphed into an encyclopaedic collection of historic fine and applied art. But 'Power of Making', with its eager audiences looking with wonderment and engaged delight at products and processes, goes some way towards recreating the atmosphere of the Museum's early days when a visit was intended to inspire hands-on production.

Times Literary Supplement, 23 September 2011

The real thing

'The Real Thing: contemporary art from China': exhibition at Tate Liverpool, 30 March to 10 June 2007

As Simon Groom, the co-curator of 'The Real Thing', points out, it is a golden time to be an artist in China, if only from a commercial point of view. Prices for contemporary Chinese art in the international auction houses have risen exponentially. But Groom goes on to suggest that the work that has been the most admired here and in the USA does the reputation of Chinese art a disservice. He has a point.

The West has a long history of coming to the art of other cultures with expectations that are inherently conservative and essentialist. For example, a current strand of interest in art from China (and Russia) focuses on easel painting that employs reassuringly academic mimetic skills to narrate ideological collapse. Thus the work of Wang Guangyi drops the logos of luxury Western brands into pastiche renderings of iconic revolutionary posters while Shi Xinning plays the meme game, inserting the figure of Mao Zedong into painterly representations of iconic occidental photographs – so we have Mao and Peggy Guggenheim sunbathing, Mao and the Queen Mother, Mao at the Yalta Conference. Such art certainly looks recognizably Chinese to anyone who once owned a copy of Mao's Little Red Book, but Groom would argue that it succeeds only because it confirms our expectations and prejudices.

There is nothing new about these sorts of power relations and they present non-Western artists with an impossible dilemma. Joining the international mainstream might seem to be the answer. But those who choose not to embrace some species of vernacular sensibility have always courted accusations of inauthenticity – be they late nineteenth-century Japanese Post-Impressionists or 1950s sub-Saharan Tachistes. And the boundaries of the art world continue to be policed. So we have the art critic Richard Dorment (writing in *The Daily Telegraph*) dismissing much of the work in 'The Real Thing' as conceptually unoriginal. In his view all that is on offer is a glimpse of exotic subject matter conveyed through strategies already explored by figures like Fischli and Weiss, Richard Long, Gillian Wearing, and Bill Viola. This seems an unimaginative assessment. The work on show in Liverpool, most of it specially commissioned, is extremely varied, but there is one overriding theme – the terror and strangeness of rapid, relentless industrialization. The strength of 'The Real Thing' lies in its documentary power.

Social change is now being explored in a multitude of ways in Chinese art. Last year's Shanghai Biennale, for instance, included work which appeared to recast some of the concerns of the English Arts & Crafts movement. China is, after all, living through an analogous industrial revolution that might yet throw up an oriental John Ruskin or William Morris. The first exhibits to greet the eye were retrospective – eight wooden models of historic Chinese pavilions and temples, constructed in the 1950s and 1960s and on loan from the architectural studio at Tongji University. A catalogue essay by one of the Biennale's curators, Zhang Qing, explained that the craftsman who made these beautiful objects, Xu Hesheng, came in for fierce criticism during the Cultural Revolution. Why, he was asked, did he not use nails to construct his models? He was denounced so fiercely for his traditional techniques that he committed suicide by thrusting a bamboo rod into his throat. The inclusion of the models, therefore, seemed partly political – a parable in which good craft practice becomes a matter of life and death. But the show also included plenty of other threnodic tributes to craftsmanship by young Chinese artists chosen by Zhang Qing. The strange Mindicraft group (Zhang Beiru, Ruan Jiewang, and Mak Yee Fun) seek to honour Ming and Quing craft skills, while Yan Jun recreates traditional Chinese furniture out of recycled heating pipes. Liang Shaoji's video, photography and timber installation 'Essence of Wood' mourns the ongoing demolition of vernacular architecture. Meanwhile another artist, Liu Jianhua, underlines the reality of present-day China. His piece piles up 30,000 low-cost objects made in Yiwu. This is a manufacturing town unfamiliar, I would guess, to most of us, but every day Yiwu exports 1,000 containers to the shopping malls of the West.

'The Real Thing' develops this engagement with the stresses of modernity rather differently, by taking us into factories, into depleted industrial and rural landscapes, and into homes, to explore the hopes and dreams of individuals caught up in China's extraordinary economic expansion. Wang Gongxin's video 'Our sky is falling' shows a peaceful, warmly-lit room with a father and son reading. But their books are suddenly swept up into the air and as the rest of the small family gathers in alarm the ceiling starts crumbling and floating down until finally they are left unsheltered in an empty landscape. It is beautifully filmed and the message is simple – nothing is fixed or stable in present-day China.

Wang Gongxin's work is frankly beguiling but there is plenty of grittier social documentation in this show. For instance Zhuang Hui reifies his memories of the 'East is west tractor factory' where he worked as a 16-year-old. Part of the factory with its hulking machinery has been perfectly replicated. Some hastily abandoned stools and lunch-boxes memorialize a horrific factory accident that occurred during Zhuang Hui's time there. But it turns out to be an eerie simulation, made of carved and painted polystyrene. The piece was fabricated in the very same tractor factory where Zhuang Hui worked as a boy, in the tool-making section where models of machine parts are sculpted for the mould-makers.

This seamlessness reminds us that, here in Britain, the culture and skills of factory work are fast disappearing. One wonders at the long-term cultural effect of living in a country dominated by white-collar services. After all, the artist and the industrial worker have certain affinities and a surprising number of post-war British fine artists had working-class parents who made 'things', albeit in factories not in studios. 'The Real Thing' suggests that in China the large pool of industrial workers informs the culture of Chinese art, as well as making it possible to realize the production of ambitious installation art quickly and relatively cheaply.

The resonances of this can be unexpected. For example Ai Weiwei has recreated an unrealized project – Tatlin's 'Monument to the Third International' – in glass and steel and crystal. It is a sophisticated piece of engineering demanding a huge workforce and was brought to completion in just four months. Admittedly it is not on the massive scale that Tatlin envisaged, but seeing it lit up and bobbing about like a life buoy in the dock in front of Tate Liverpool is a surprise, a kind of message in a bottle that reflects on the industrial histories of the Soviet Union, China, and Liverpool.

The vagaries of time are a hidden theme of this exhibition. In China goods (and art) can be manufactured at breakneck speed (as they were once in nineteenth-century Britain). Other areas of Chinese life suggest stasis of a particularly grim kind. Yang Fudong's 'East of Que village' is a video installa-

Cao Fei, still from video installation 'Whose utopia?' (2006).

tion that records the bleak lives of a pack of wild dogs and their village owners in Hebei province in North China. Just around the corner hang the documentary paintings of Yang Shaobin. '800 metres' depict coalminers at work
and at play. Loosely painted with a limited colour range and probably based
on photographs, they capture the backwardness of China's unregulated coal
fields, which supply 40 per cent of the world's coal and account for 80 per
cent of the world's mining fatalities. The atmosphere is 'awful but cheerful'.
In these dangerous surroundings Yang Shaobin records a lot of defiant humour.

These are political works of art in that they comment on injustices embedded in Chinese society and government. But one of the other charms
and surprises of 'The Real Thing' was to see art that is entirely playful, even
mannerist in spirit, and which could have been made anywhere by any gifted young person. Take Qiu Xiaofei's 'Art class' in which he creates a *trompe
l'oeil* assemblage of easels on which half-finished paintings are 'pinned', all
clustered round a plaster cast on a plinth, complete with rags and tubes of
discarded paint on the floor. It needs to be viewed with Qiu Xiaofei's touching text in which he remembers those first art classes when he was a 'country bumpkin' who wanted to realize 'my small adolescent dreams'. A young

Chinese aspirant artist listening to Guns N' Roses and dreaming of being a rock star hardly seems generically Chinese. But that is what is so refreshing. This universalism is taken a step further in Zhou Tiehai's camp presentation of three historic French desserts, completely invented by the artist but presented with a convincing faux history. It is a bizarre exercise in culinary scholarship that might seem like the last kind of art to come out of China.

But the finest piece in 'The Real Thing', by its youngest artist, addresses more serious concerns. Cao Fei's haunting video, 'Whose utopia?', reflects on the politics of work. It is not obviously directing criticism at the government, although seeing the barracks and bunk-beds where factory employees sleep on grimy pieces of cardboard is an eye-opener. The film is just as much about Western complicity with China as a stream of businesses move their manufacturing to the Far East, attracted by low wages. 'Whose utopia?' is set in the Osram lighting factory, long ago located in Hammersmith, and now, predictably enough, in the Pearl River Delta. It is organized theatrically into three acts, the first showing all the processes involved in making a whole range of light bulbs and fluorescent tubes. Much of the work is automated but there is a surprising amount of handwork involving delicate manoeuvres with lighting filaments. There is also a great deal of checking, also done by hand. The workforce is very young and very disciplined. The second part of the film interrogates their dreams and aspirations. A pair of women employees, one in a tutu and wearing white feathery wings, dance by the conveyor belt, while an older Tai Chi enthusiast shadow boxes his way down the aisles of workers. A boy dreamily plays his electric guitar while the relentless pace of production goes on around him. There is an extraordinary soundtrack that mixes music and the repetitive beat of automated production. In the final section Cao Fei trains her camera on individuals who gaze back steadily from their various work stations. The boy guitar players line up, their arms round each other, and a voice sings some fragmented lines, reminding us that this is a factory full of teenagers. It sounds romantic but it is in fact an unnerving film that tells us about factories everywhere, their monotony and their heartlessness.

Times Literary Supplement, 1 June 2007

The Omega project

'Beyond Bloomsbury: designs of the Omega Workshops 1913–19',
exhibition at the Courtauld Gallery, London, 18 June to 20 September 2009

A fresh look at the Omega Workshops under the rubric 'Beyond Bloomsbury' – can it be done when the painted furniture and screens, the famous Omega chair, and the textiles and rugs, are so familiar and have been so thoroughly researched? It is a brave decision by the Courtauld Galleries, given that the last two exhibitions to survey Roger Fry's early twentieth-century experiment – 'The Omega Workshops 1913–19: decorative arts of Bloomsbury' staged by the Crafts Council in 1984, and Tate Britain's millennium show 'The Art of Bloomsbury' in 1999 – were comprehensively panned. In 1984 Roy Strong (of all people) castigated Omega for its 'deadly lack of seriousness', arguing that a reappraisal was mistimed, the 1980s being a 'far more serious era' remote from 'such personal indulgence'. *Studio International* took a similarly moralistic tone, dismissing Omega because of the 'wilfulness' and the 'selfish motivations' that 'permeated the social and sexual life' of Bloomsbury. For *The Guardian*, Omega's bold brightness was simply un-English – 'as out of place in an English winter as a lemon yellow frock'. And in 1999 the reaction to Tate Britain's detailed survey of the paintings and the applied art of Bloomsbury was still more dismissive.

What is our problem with Omega? It was, after all, a bold attempt to give work to struggling young artists, admirers of continental Post-Impressionism, Cubism, and Fauvism. As a result the products of the Omega Workshops translated the most exciting European avant-garde art into textiles, furniture, ceramics and entire interior schemes. And, astonishingly, all this was mostly achieved during the First World War, which overtook the scheme after just one year. If the paintings that come under the Bloomsbury rubric often seem derivative, and, by the 1930s, just plain dull, then Omega's six years of existence must count as the group's visual success story. In addition, Omega was to have a major influence on the eclectic British modernism of the inter-war years. The textiles of Alec Walker's Cryséde, and of Phyllis Barron, Dorothy Larcher, and Paul Nash, would be unimaginable without the precedent of Omega. Its ceramics were all earthenware tin-glaze, but it was Roger Fry who first appreciated early Chinese ceramics and medieval British wares in a modernist spirit and provided a critical context for the new art form of studio pottery.

To dislike Omega is, perhaps, symptomatic of national self-loathing, inspired by anxieties about class, pleasure, 'abroad', and, as Christopher Reed has argued, sub-cultural political and sexual dissent. The Omega Workshops were transgressive – mixing fine art and design, using high art in a domestic context, decoratively. The hostility was articulated early, by a disgruntled Wyndham Lewis, and it was partly to do with gender expectations. Real men did not sit around, like Duncan Grant, in a 'curtain and pincushion factory' painting boxes. Reed, almost singlehandedly, has rescued Omega from this kind of condescension – in an essay of 1996 on Bloomsbury in *Not at home: the suppression of domesticity in modern art and architecture* and in his *Bloomsbury rooms* of 2004, Reed met the critics head-on, casting Bloomsbury's 'domestic modernism' and its bold experiments in living as a 'provocative early model of coalition' that blurred gender and sexual orientation 'to create rooms where Victorian moralism and propriety could be abandoned for a return to primal pleasures'.

Omega was one embodiment of the art critic and painter Roger Fry's generous social vision of art. Fry helped set up the Contemporary Art Society and National Art Collections Fund. He rescued *The Burlington Magazine* and he opened up our understanding of what art might be – African carving, the art of the Bushmen, Byzantine enamels, early Chinese ceramics, children's art, and the painting of Cézanne, were all examined on an equal footing. The idea that 'things' could be just as important as paintings or sculpture was something he had learned as an intense young man from Arts & Crafts figures like C. R. Ashbee. His dislike of 'machines' and high finish was an anti-industrial, Arts & Crafts prejudice, as was his interest in artists working together in something approximating a guild system. But he had witnessed the failure of C. R. Ashbee's Guild of Handicraft and the gradual ossification of the Arts & Crafts Exhibition Society. And most important of all he was in touch with Post-Impressionism and in 1910 staged 'Manet and the Post-Impressionists', after which, as Virginia Woolf observed, 'all human relations changed'.

It was a playful exaggeration but, in any case, Woolf provides an affectionate and witty account of the subsequent setting-up of Omega. In her biography of Fry we see the great man in action as a persuasive salesman: 'There were bright chintzes designed by the young artists; there were painted tables and painted chairs; and there was Roger Fry himself escorting now Lady So-and-So, now a businessman from Birmingham, round the rooms and persuading them to buy.' We also get her view of Omega craftsmanship: 'Cracks appeared. Legs came off. Varnish ran.' Some of the making was slapdash, although the rugs, printed textiles, and marquetry, were manufactured off-site, by professionals. But Omega would have been nothing without the young artists whom Fry set out to support. Figures like Duncan Grant, Vanessa Bell, Henri Gaudier-Brzeska, Wyndham Lewis, Frederick Etchells, Nina Hamnett and her husband Roald Kristian, George Turnbull, and many others, came and went; they were backed up by a stream of young Slade students, led by Winifred Gill, who eventually became manager of the shop and the workshop.

'Beyond Bloomsbury' has little new to tell us on a factual level. Judith Collins's scholarly work on Omega, back in 1984, remains unsurpassed. But the show does honour to technique and unlikely collaborations, showing sketches and objects side by side. The printing processes used in France to create Omega's remarkable linen textiles remain frustratingly mysterious, but we learn that Omega ceramics were mostly thrown while the flatware was made by jiggering, not casting as previously supposed. We discover more about who made what, about the odd, casual braiding of artists, amateurs, and commercial manufacturers. But it is the exhibition's approach to gender and to social and political context that helps convey some of the original excitement of the Omega project. Influenced by Reed's scholarship, with its broader cultural emphasis, we get to know shadowy figures like Winifred Gill, who is given proper recognition as a creative woman in her own right.

We may imagine that we are familiar with every shawl, screen, lily table, and artfully decorated Omega box. But 'Beyond Bloomsbury' also highlights the fact that during the First World War Omega was not just concerned with the applied arts. The house at 33 Fitzroy Square became a pacifist meeting-place. Avant-garde puppet shows were staged during Omega evening events, and, although the visual evidence for these has largely vanished, Grace Brockington's incisive essay in the exhibition catalogue gives a sense of the radicalism of Omega's evening discussions and performances. Winifred Gill reappears, making the puppets for Fry's Cambridge friend Goldsworthy Lowes Dickinson's pacifist play *War and peace*. Brockington writes of the 'performative and conversational forms' of resistance developed at Omega. The Workshop was in part an informal talking shop. Everyone wanted to go to Omega's evening meetings – from George Bernard Shaw to Arnold Bennett to Lytton Strachey to Ottoline Morrell – even if they had to put up with Fry's idea of improvised seating, sacks stuffed with straw.

Strangely, one of the best pieces of writing on Omega appeared in 1941, penned by Nikolaus Pevsner. But perhaps that is not so surprising. Pevsner wrote the article in *The Architectural Review* during the Second World War and it is a typically efficient piece of research, in the course of which he talked to Winifred Gill (inspiring some informative letters) and to many of the artists and collectors connected with Omega. A recent exile from Hitler's Germany, he may have particularly appreciated Omega's easy ebullience, and, as a relative outsider, he was not bothered by the accusations of elitism that bubble up in any discussion of Bloomsbury. He was particularly struck by Omega's prescience, arguing that its adaptation of the visual tropes of Cubism anticipated developments in the applied arts (particularly textiles) in France and

Germany by ten to fifteen years. He found it remarkable that what was to appear fashionable at the Paris International Exhibition of 1925 had been created in London as early as 1913.

Omega gave us home-spun Cubism and cushion covers instead of fine art heroics, long before what has come to be called Art Déco. And 'Beyond Bloomsbury' reveals how much more nuanced and exquisite are Omega's colour schemes and flat patterns – as nuanced and exquisite as the social and political milieu that made possible this remarkable experiment in art and design.

Crafts, no. 218, May / June 2009

Arts & Crafts

'International Arts and Crafts': exhibition at the Victoria & Albert Museum, London, 17 March to 24 July 2005 and 'The Art and Crafts Movement in Europe and America: design for the modern world': exhibition at Los Angeles County Museum of Art, 19 December 2004 to 3 April 2005

This year it will be possible to see two ambitious exhibitions devoted to a single design phenomenon. Superficially at least Wendy Kaplan's 'The Arts and Crafts Movement in Europe and America', initiated at Los Angeles County Museum of Art (LACMA), and 'International Arts and Crafts' curated by Karen Livingstone and Linda Parry at the Victoria & Albert Museum, are similar in scope. Both trace the Arts & Crafts movement from its origins in Britain (or more accurately in England) outwards to Europe, North America and (in the case of 'International Arts and Crafts') to inter-war Japan. In fact the two exhibitions (and their accompanying books) are very different.

To begin in London, 'International Arts and Crafts' is the third in a series of large-scale exhibitions mounted by the V&A. It follows 'Art Nouveau 1890–1914' (2000) and 'Art Deco' (2003), both of which stressed the global reach and rapid dissemination of a glamorous decorative arts style. Each worked well on its own terms despite the fact that a style-based approach invariably has a reductive tendency to float free from history, from ambient politics, and from the rich anecdotal evidence of the lives of artists and designers.[1] The Arts & Crafts movement is, however, most emphatically not a style but rather an attitude to ways of working, to designing, to exploring materials, and to practising as an artist in difficult times.

Each of us will have our own Arts & Crafts movement but most accounts begin in England in the 1880s, a period when pride and independence in work of all kinds seemed challenged and where there was widespread economic recession, above all in a fast emptying countryside.[2] In this situation a handful of artists and architects gave making processes special importance, inspired as much as anything by the writings and visual records of buildings, sculpture and landscape made by John Ruskin. His chapter on 'The nature of Gothic' in the second volume of *The stones of Venice* may have been more poetic than practical: his technological understanding was extremely limited. But Ruskin's basic premise, that work should be satisfying, created a social and aesthetic programme for the whole movement.

In its opening section on the movement's origins in Britain 'International Arts and Crafts' does a good job of presenting an array of significant and eye-catching objects. But from the outset something is missing, in the form of stories of individuals caught in a challenging historical moment and responding through the practical creation of things. Lives were changed by the movement and the idea of what it meant to be an artist was recast. As the movement gathers pace, we find a proliferation of research into materials and techniques that becomes increasingly more intense and, in some ways, anti-modern. The results are often remarkable and unexpected.

For instance Christopher Whall, a failed painter, began to use thick, uneven blown glass that seemed closer in spirit to medieval craftsmanship. His panel of St Chad in this exhibition looks entirely unlike the more conventional example of stained glass also included here, designed but not made by Selwyn Image. Whall gives us an arresting otherworldly combination of saturated colours and silvery whites and greens only arrived at because he attended to every step of the process himself – cutting the glass, painting, fixing. Then again, in the late 1890s a dreamy young man named Edward Johnston who had abandoned his medical studies, began to investigate the development of writing by studying early uncial and Winchester scripts. This exhibition includes a fine, if somewhat anomalous, example of his calligraphy and his design for the revolutionary sanserif alphabet still used on the London Underground. But we can only begin to imagine the impact of Johnston's researches. Thanks to him, calligraphy was taught in all art schools up until the 1960s while twentieth-century typography also owes him much. And the basis of all this seems at first sight archaic, to do with learning to use a reed or quill pen cut in a certain way. In an exhibition on the Arts & Crafts movement the extent of this kind of research and development somehow needs to be conveyed, perhaps by including photographs of workshops and studios, even by showing tools and materials.

Both Whall and Johnston contributed to the remarkable series of Handbooks on the Artistic Crafts edited by the architect W. R. Lethaby. He is absent from this exhibition, something that reminds us that art education does not get much coverage. And yet visually registering the movement's impact on education at all levels would, I think, have laid to rest the idea that it was a narrow elite affair in flight from the economic and social realities of modernity. As Peter Cormack has pointed out in a polemical article in *Apollo*, the Arts & Crafts movement in Britain was in reality a mass movement that dramatically affected art education both on a professional level at places like the Central School of Arts & Crafts, Birmingham School of Art, and the Royal College of Art, and at a semi-amateur level through bodies like the philanthropic Home Arts and Industries Association and the socialist Clarion Guild of Handicraft.[3] As Cormack's own research into the lives of stained glass artists reveals, the movement also enabled sizeable numbers of women to gain recognition as designers for the first time. Women are, of course, included in this opening section, with, *inter alia*, painted ceramics and calligraphy by Louise Powell, embroidery by her sister Thérèse Lessore, and, best of all, the great embroidered panels 'The progress of a soul' by the multi-talented Scot Phoebe Traquair. But it would have been helpful to have said more about the contribution made by women – and to have included one of the greatest artists to come out of the movement in Britain, the Irish stained glass artist Wilhelmina Geddes.

If 'International Arts and Crafts' seems to run scared from some of the central concerns of the movement we have to reflect that this is a difficult cultural moment in which to do the subject justice. We only have to read the reviews of 'International Arts and Crafts' that have already appeared in the 'quality' newspapers. They are positive, in a vulgar kind of way, but almost without exception dismiss the radicalism and idealism of the movement, particularly in its English, or British, context. There is much talk of 'the world-class naivety of the enterprise', 'born of bourgeois nostalgia and regret'. Faced with art critics whose ignorance of the decorative arts allows them to describe insular Arts & Crafts objects as 'lumpen and rustic' and as being inspired by 'that champagne socialist William Morris' this was indeed a brave exhibition to mount.

But perhaps it would have been braver still to have demolished these misconceptions by looking in depth at the movement in Britain alone. Astonishingly this has never been done. The North Americans have been luckier with two important exhibitions, 'The Arts and Crafts Movement in America 1876–1916' held at Princeton University Art Museum in 1972, and Wendy Kaplan's 'The Art that is Life: the Arts and Crafts Movement in America 1875–1920' in 1987, staged at the Museum of Fine Arts, Boston. It would have been daring to stick to the British story. It would also have been good to extend coverage of the British movement into the inter-war period. The introductory essay in the show's accompanying book appears to argue that the movement died in Britain, degenerating into '"craftwork" on a semi- or completely amateur basis'.[4]

With the British movement out of the way this exhibition charts a trajectory of development (in effect a modified Pevsnerian approach) that takes us first to North America. This is a wonderfully spacious section of the show and admirable in its generous scope. But we then hurry on into Europe, where Vienna and Budapest within the Hapsburg Empire and Russia, Norway, Finland, and Germany are visited in quick succession. Two countries not covered in the exhibition, the Netherlands and Sweden, are given essays in the book (even though the author of the essay on the Netherlands queries whether a Dutch Arts & Crafts movement can be said to have existed). That many of the themes touched on in the European section have already been explored by the V&A as recently as 2000 in its Art Nouveau exhibition may explain the rather disengaged nature of this part of the exhibition.

The final section of 'International Arts and Crafts' is devoted to Japan. It is a visual feast that will be unfamiliar to most visitors. But how does it fit into the story of the movement? As the authors of two of the essays in the accompanying book have argued elsewhere, the *Mingei* movement was profoundly elitist, led by a small self-appointed group of artists, including the British potter Bernard Leach.[5] The movement's theorist, Yanagi Sōetsu, saw himself as a sensei (master), guiding 'unspoilt' artisanal craftsmen whose work, he believed, should remain essentially anonymous. His way of thinking contrasts with the ideals of the Arts & Crafts Exhibition Society that from the start had made a point of giving credit to both the designer and maker of an object in their catalogues.

Then again, *Mingei* appears more inspired by modernist formalist aesthetics than by the social (and often socialist) concerns that underpinned the Arts & Crafts movement. After all, Arts & Crafts designers and educators like C. R. Ashbee and W. R. Lethaby saw pleasurable work and artistic agency as central to the movement. Yanagi had a very different view. He wrote approvingly of the primitive conditions in which the Korean potters laboured and speculated on the submissive reliance on tradition that enabled the boys who decorated Chinese Tz'u-chou wares to produce work of beauty despite their tears of boredom and exhaustion.[6] In the same spirit Yanagi was not too worried about the division of labour, provided it took place in a handcraft environment. This final section is hugely enjoyable, in part because of the inclusion of a splendid selection of vernacular craft of the type admired by the leaders of the *Mingei* movement. To end with Japan is a bold stroke – even if we may doubt whether it is correct to see *Mingei* as the last gasp of the Arts & Crafts movement.

The presence of Japan sharply differentiates the London show from Wendy Kaplan's tightly argued and impeccably chosen exhibition at LACMA. Many of the criticisms that I have made of 'International Arts and Crafts' can also be levelled at 'The Arts and Crafts Movement in Europe and America'. For instance there is little about education or about the exploration of materials and techniques. But this is a more nuanced show which begins with a map of Europe and the announcement of three over-arching themes – Art and Industry, Design and National Identity, and Art and Life – that are returned to throughout the exhibition.

The show opens with an elegant section that underlines the interlinked internationalism of the movement mediated through exhibitions, museum purchases, journals like *The Studio*, *Ver Sacrum*, and *Deutsche Kunst und Dekoration*, and the translated writing of key Arts & Crafts figures. A writing cabinet by C. R. Ashbee shares space with a chair by Charles Rennie Mackintosh. Both were shown at the eighth Viennese Secession exhibition of 1900 and the Mackintosh chair was purchased by the Viennese designer Koloman Moser for his apartment. A catalogue cover designed by George Walton for an exhibition of British Arts & Crafts held in Budapest in 1902 sits alongside a German translation of one of Walter Crane's lectures. If we had any doubts about the European dimension of the movement they are dispelled by these juxtapositions.

Kaplan has had fewer in-house objects to draw upon than her London colleagues – despite the generous donations made to LACMA by the collector Max Palevsky. The pieces in Kaplan's show may be more modest than the examples in London but each one counts and each adds to a gradually unfolding narrative that makes sense of the movement's transformation and development in nine European countries and in North America. Wisely Kaplan differentiates between the Arts & Crafts movement in England, Scotland, and Ireland. Each gets its own section with the result that the important Scottish architect Robert Lorimer is included, as are Wilhelmina Geddes and the Dun Emer Guild from Ireland. And we get a sense of the people who gave their lives to the movement. Within the national sections the show explores five Utopian art colonies in some depth – the Guild of Handicraft in Chipping Campden, Darmstadt in Germany, Gödöllő in Hungary, and the Roycrofters and the Byrdcliffe colony (both in New York State). The atmosphere of these places is conveyed through well-chosen photographs. We come face to face with Ashbee's young guildsmen, with the striking Mariska Undi and her studio at Gödöllő and with a crowd of privileged, artistically dressed New Yorkers enjoying a summer festival held by the craft community at Woodstock.

The accompanying book suggests that Kaplan worked in a strongly collaborative spirit with her contributors over every aspect of the show. It is concise, admirably designed and illustrated, and the check-list of objects is more informative than is usual. Each essay ties in closely to the exhibition. Thus the section on Belgium in the exhibition reflects Amy Ogata's innovative research on the decorative arts there and in France, reifying, for instance, her discussion of the implications of Henry van de Velde's zealous conversion from painting to craft and design.

So, there we have it – two Arts & Crafts exhibitions appearing at once, like London buses. Both exhibitions have strengths and weaknesses. The London show has more glamorous objects, particularly in the British section. It also has the surprise inclusion of Japan, including a skilfully recreated room setting designed by Yanagi and his friends for an exhibition in Tokyo in 1928. The LACMA show is more rigorous, more rationally worked out, and has a better organized publication. It seems, and this is important, to convey the idealism of the Arts & Crafts movement more convincingly. For an inexperienced traveller it might be the bus to take.

1. This need not always be the case. We only have to think back to the Council of Europe's *The age of Neoclassicism* of 1972, remarkable as much as anything for its catalogue, which could be held in the hand but which contained eleven ground-breaking essays, full entries for each object and full biographies for each artist.
2. See Jose Harris, *Private lives, public spirit: Britain 1870–1914*, Oxford 1993: chapter five on 'Work'.
3. Peter Cormack, 'A truly British movement', *Apollo*, April 2005, pp. 48–53.
4. Linda Parry & Karen Livingstone, 'Introduction' in *International Arts and Crafts*, London 2005, p. 10.
5. See Yuko Kikuchi, *Japanese modernisation and Mingei theory*, London 2004; Edmund de Waal, 'Homo orientalis: Bernard Leach and the image of the Japanese craftsman', *Journal of Design History*, vol. 10, no. 4, 1997, pp. 355–62.
6. Yanagi Muneyoshi, 'Buddhist idea of Beauty' in *The unknown craftsman: a Japanese insight into beauty*, Tokyo 1972.

The Burlington Magazine, June 2005

In 1931 the Empire Marketing Board Film Unit released the film *Industrial Britain*. Much of the footage had been shot by the great American documentary film-maker Robert Flaherty but he soon ran over budget and the film was finally put together by John Grierson and Edgar Anstey. It is one of the great inter-war British documentaries, but it inadvertently and strikingly reveals the extent of upper-middle-class ambivalence towards industrialization and towards the working classes. And although it is a film about industry it is in fact full of craft.

Partly this was because Flaherty chose to concentrate on the old skills that still existed within industry. He has been accused of practising salvage anthropology and certainly in his classic *Nanook of the North* (1920–1) Flaherty induced the Inuit to re-enact obsolete customs, just as in *Man of Aran* (1934) he persuaded the islanders to go to sea in small boats to hunt for basking sharks, a fishing practice they had long abandoned. But Grierson, the creator of the Empire Marketing Board Film Unit, clearly endorsed Flaherty's approach. The mood of *Industrial Britain* is elegiac. The opening shots move from a windmill, a spinning wheel, hand-loom weaving, corn stooks, a basket maker, and a ship in full sail, to grim chimney stacks and a scripted voice-over telling us: 'This is the world that coal has created.' But behind 'those industrial chimney stacks', reassuringly enough, we find 'that the spirit of craftsmanship has not disappeared'. Flaherty filmed extensive footage of a young potter throwing vases and much of this was used, the voice-over reassuring us that the young man at the wheel was working just as the Greek potters worked – 'making the same beautiful things using the same simple tools'.

Throughout *Industrial Britain* hand skills are emphasized. There are some extraordinary sequences showing men tapping iron furnaces and guiding the molten, flaming metal into moulds – a complex and dangerous operation. The film avoids the less visually satisfying industries. Women, employed in large numbers in repetitive or decorative work in textile manufacture and in the potteries, are entirely excluded. Light electrical goods, again employing women, are absent, as are assembly lines in general. Empire is referred to obliquely with shots of flying boats – 'we build for transport, for India and West Africa'. In effect we are shown an aestheticized version of nineteenth-century male industrial Britain with a heavy bias towards craft skills.

For the men and women who in various ways projected the image of Britain from the 1930s onwards, craftsmanship in the broadest sense was invariably invoked to reassure. This could be done in very different ways. In *Brief city*, the short film about the South Bank Exhibition made just before its closure in September 1951, the young Hugh Casson emphasized a British fondness for the domestic and small-scale. There was to be nothing bombastic or formal about the layout of the buildings at the South Bank. The emphasis was on picturesque pleasure, on humour and brightness and light. Indeed the grimy rail-track, pubs, and housing, just outside the exhibition space, were cleverly screened out. In this celebratory 'Story of Britain' the monotony and squalor of everyday life had no place.

The background to Britain's industrial base was surveyed in the complex displays in the Dome of Discovery – a building both technologically advanced and yet humane, its great supporting struts moving perceptibly in the wind. The actuality of industry was found in the Power and Production Pavilion where the main hall was arranged as a symbolic factory, with machinery weaving carpets, wrapping sweets and making biscuits. But there was plenty of craft activity in the pavilion too – with demonstrations of silversmithing and jewellery, instrument making, shoe making, paper making and glass blowing. As Ian Cox, the author of *The South Bank Exhibition: a guide to the story it tells* explained, machines had their limitations and there will always be 'craftsmen we cannot replace ... We are proud of these men; they are basic to our way of life, of which machines will never quite take charge.'

In any case, if visitors had taken Ian Cox's advice and followed the recommended circulation plan, they would already have encountered a good deal of craft, much of it by the most gifted women in the post-war British craft world. In the Country Pavilion there was Constance Howard's stump-work wall hanging 'The country wife', showing all the activities of the Women's Institutes. Another embroiderer, Margaret Kaye, with the basket maker Pat Tew, created a series of tableaux of rural crafts. Indeed craftwork fulfilled a multiplicity of needs at the South Bank Exhibition. In wall hangings by Howard and Michael O'Connell, textile craft helped narrate the 'story', just as the murals painted by artists like Graham Sutherland and Josef Herman were subsumed to narrative. Craft's chameleon, uncertain identity meant that even objects designed and made by a single person fulfilled many roles. For example, David Pye's carved bowls and platters appeared in several contexts – standing for traditional skill in the Country Pavilion, for Englishness in the Lion and Unicorn Pavilion and for good design in the Homes and Gardens Pavilion.

In effect craft crept into these various pavilions almost unnoticed. The handmade attracted little comment and officially the objects included in the pavilions were in large part intended to reflect the taste of the recently formed Council of Industrial Design. What seems to have happened is that the theme conveners and designers for individual pavilions found the CoID's Stock List of objects limited. For the South Bank Exhibition was not meant to be 'a trade show of British wares'. It was rather meant to tell 'one continuous interwoven story' of 'The Land and the People'. As we saw in the case of *Indus-*

The smithy in F. H. K. Henrion's Country Pavilion, South Bank Exhibition, 1951.

trial Britain, the artistically-minded upper middle classes saw craftsmanship as a symbol of inclusiveness. And in several pavilions the theme conveners set up a dialectic between old and new, past and future. These opposites reflected the ambivalence of the exhibition as a whole, which combined a neoromantic celebration of the land and of old skills with the promise of technological advance.

A flash point of aesthetic and ideological difference emerged in the Country Pavilion where F.H.K.Henrion set aside an area for a country smithy. He soon found himself in conflict with the Rural Industries Bureau who demanded more space for a fully modernized smithy complete with oxyacetylene torches and power tools. As they pointed out, the countryside was changing and 'a smithy showing merely a hearth and anvil would give entirely the wrong impression'. But arguably the 'wrong impression' was conveyed by much of the ostensible 'country craft' in the pavilion. For we find pots by Lucie Rie and Steven Sykes and turned bowls from Dartington Hall and from Robin Nance's workshop in St Ives – from, in fact, an imagined community of artist craftsmen and women dreamed up by Henrion.

Craft at the South Bank worked in mysterious ways, helping to project that temporary image of a classless, united nation which comes over so strongly in *Brief city*. That craft had no role to play fifty years later in the Millennium Dome was perhaps hardly surprising. This was not because craft had vanished but more because the Dome barely told a story. And its designers relied heavily on storyboards and banks of television screens rather than objects. The relative immateriality was a puzzle. Was it expense, a problem with security, or were three-dimensional objects simply deemed hopelessly uncool and museological? The creation of such a virtual exhibition was mistaken. The emphasis on consumption, in which, for instance, serious medical advances were ironized as an eerie journey through a gigantic body, was a mistake too.

Craft is a condensed way of suggesting that there is production as well as consumption, that work need not be an alienating affair. At the South Bank 1951 there were blacksmiths, cricket bat and ball makers, and gunsmiths working away. They drew crowds. We may smile at the thought of their rapt audiences, in trilby hats, suits and ties, the women in demure summer frocks. But at Greenwich last year a few potters sitting at their wheels might have provided much needed relief from the existential anxieties and the terrible sense of anomie provoked by the ersatz attractions in the Millennium Dome, a pale shadow of its predecessor in 1951.

Crafts, no.172, September/October 2001

Brief city: the story of London's Festival buildings (1952) can now be seen online at YouTube.

Crafts Lives at the British Library

'There is always one moment in childhood when the door opens and lets the future in.' Michael Cardew liked to quote this line from Graham Greene's novel *The power and the glory* and it made sense in terms of his own life. As a child he saw the last of the North Devon potters at work, an experience that shaped his sensibility decisively. We know this happened because he tells us in his autobiography. But not all makers write biographies, or write very much at all. Which is why the British Library's Crafts Lives archive is of such extraordinary value.

Crafts Lives is part of National Life Stories, one of the most ambitious oral history projects in the world. The art historian and sociologist Paul Thompson and the historian Asa Briggs set up National Life Stories in 1987 to 're-cord first-hand experiences of as wide a cross-section of present-day society as possible'. Since then it has initiated interviews covering areas as diverse as the fishing, steel and oil industries, the book trade, the lives of artists and architects and, more recently, craftspeople. The Crafts Lives project was set up in 1999 but got under way properly in 2004 when a full-time interviewer was employed. It is chiefly funded, like all NLS projects, from charitable and individual donations.

So what is a typical interview? All are at least eight to ten hours long, covering the interviewee's parents and grandparents and attending to their class background, schooling, jobs, relationships, leisure, daily life, political and religious views, and, of course, in the case of makers, their creativity. To do this kind of interview requires a relationship of trust and some interviewees have chosen to close their interviews for several decades so that they can speak with perfect frankness. Each interview provides a remarkable record of a life. All are available for listening at the British Library, many are transcribed in full and all have summaries that are searchable online. Ultimately all the recordings will be made listenable online.

In the case of Crafts Lives the life-story format means that there are now over one hundred accounts of the experiences of makers of all kinds, including potters, textile artists, glass artists, silversmiths, bookbinders, furniture makers, and jewellers. It is an extraordinary resource. Not surprisingly Graham Greene's observation turns out to be correct. For instance, makers and designers and artists tend to be sensitive to materials and processes from an early age. Some, like the lettercutter Ralph Beyer, grew up surrounded by the very best art, craft, and design. But equally a childhood marked by austerity can prove just as inspiring. Stuart Devlin talks movingly about the hard labour of pea picking as a child and how even that monotonous task had an aesthetic dimension. Aunts who worked in a textile mill and a great-grandfather who carved woodblocks for the textile industry float up in Michael Brennand-Wood's childhood and he reflects on genetic memory and its influence on his work.

It might be thought that a sound recording would not do justice to a visual artist. But articulating a making process or describing a finished work is revealing in itself. Listening to Walter Keeler describing the act of throwing a pot on the wheel or Tessa Clegg talking about the physical demands of glass blowing is a remarkable experience. Tacit skills are put into words. Crafts Lives interviews, like Artists' Lives and Architects' Lives, range widely and archetypal themes are played out – neophytes rebel against their teachers, careers are transformed by key encounters, moments of epiphany occur when a material, a skill, or a concept is fully understood.

So far the archive has concentrated on the 'studio crafts'. In future Crafts Lives might take in trade or rural crafts, or interview designers whose practice interrogates the politics of labour and making processes. Categories are less important than capturing these extraordinary stories in which individuals choose to go against the grain and, instead of simply working to live, live for their work.

For online access to National Life Stories, British Library Sound Archive: < www.bl.uk/nls >

Crafts, no. 235, March / April 2012

Planes of reality

Royal Society of Marine Artists: exhibition at the Mall Galleries, London, 30 October to 11 November 1991; Guild of Aviation Artists: exhibition at the Carisbrook Gallery, London, July 1991

John Worsley paints ships. He went to Goldsmiths School of Art, joined the Navy in 1939 and in 1943 was appointed an Official War Artist. He made numerous vivid sketches of shipboard life and later attempted more ambitious set-pieces – bombardments and landings in the grand sea-battle tradition.

After the war he was to concentrate on marine painting, becoming a staunch supporter and sometime president of the Royal Society of Marine

Artists. Though he has worked as an illustrator and as a commercial artist, his marine paintings belong somewhat uneasily to a tradition that goes back to Willem van de Velde and encompasses artists of the stature of Crome, Cotman, and Turner.

Like Turner, who was lashed to a mast to paint his famous snowstorm at sea, Worsley believes in the value of being on the spot. In his more commercial persona he has done purely nostalgic pictures – the Golden Hind clipping across a spumy ocean, for example. But in the main, Worsley will have been on the boat, witnessed the race, talked to the crew. However, while Turner was the hero of Ruskin's defiantly titled *Modern painters*, Worsley is in no sense a modern artist. His works and those of fellow members of the Royal Society of Marine Artists tend not to get reviewed in newspapers and are not found in histories of modern art. The Imperial War Museum, which owns his wartime work, would not purchase Worsley's paintings now, nor would the Tate or the Arts Council. Worsley is not too bothered – 'I'm too old' – and in any case has views on modern art that recall Sir Alfred Munnings at his fieriest. Abstract art gets short shrift – 'one of the biggest frauds in the art world, anyone can do it'. He has photocopies of Giovanni Papini's interview with Picasso in which the artist confesses to having pulled a fast one on a foolish public – an interview, incidentally, which Picasso scholars regard as the purest fiction.

One of his most ambitious pictures, now hanging in Norman Foster's Hong Kong and Shanghai Bank, depicts the Aberdeen Docks area of Hong Kong. Crammed with detail and sharp observation, this kind of art is often dismissed as illustration. It is in fact an extraordinary record, based on hours of studious sketching and photography on site. Worsley has a strong sense of duty about marine paintings which is fired by the belief that boats have to be depicted correctly. This was hardly something that bothered Turner, but the painted ships on Worsley's painted oceans are accurate – 'everything to do with the sea has to be practical'. And they're usually bought by clients for whom that accuracy is important – because they sail, because they won the race, because they own the boat. Of course twentieth-century artists have painted ships, but the boats tend to be abstracted components in a composition. For Worsley the ship is the thing, with rigging all correct and ropes wound clockwise. Similarly, the sea is not an opportunity for expressive bravura painting, but has to be caught with scientific accuracy. Worsley has evolved his own methods – a penknife dragged across a dark area will give the effect of broken sparkling water, dark horizontal clouds add to an impression of speed.

Worsley feels that the camera has a lot to answer for, that it has irrevocably changed art. But whereas photography's effect on avant-garde art has

Wilfred Hardy, 'Fourteen tons of thunder' (gouache, 1991, reproduced from a folded copy of *The Independent*).

been to free it from reportage, Worsley has gone the other way. He is bravely competing with the camera and using it to piece together an idealized simulacrum of life.

The Royal Society of Marine Artists is just one of many specialist artist groups. The Guild of Aviation Artists, whose annual open exhibition began last week, is a relative newcomer founded in 1971. John Worsley is doubtful about aviation artists. Whereas marine art can embrace any watery subject and may not even include boats, in aviation art the gleaming planes and helicopters invariably hold centre stage.

In fact, the Guild's exhibition has the unexpected effect of reminding us how tasteful and untroubling most avant-garde art has become. The show contains some startling little pictures that inadvertently and clumsily comment on the uneasy relationship between representation and reality.

Make your way to the Gulf War section – some forty pictures. Only one of these artists has been anywhere near the Gulf. Squadron Leader Mike Rondot was on active service during the war and his 'The longest minute' is billed in the press release as 'a very dramatic moment over Kuwait'. In fact it is a quiet, dryly meticulous illustration of two Jaguar jets against a poster-blue sky. The rest of the Gulf pictures are works of imagination, dominated by Guild's president Michael Turner's 'Gulf strike' – Tornados attacking an airfield at night, all flying shrapnel, spurts of flame and dark wings. The titles tend to be technical. 'Twenty Third TFG Gulf Victory' is a small painting of planes bombing tanks. A burning man is running away, but this is really a picture about the hardware – US planes, Russian-made tanks. There are pictures for the drawing-room – two Constable-inspired cloudscapes complete with soaring Tornados and Buccaneers. Others may be more suitable for the rumpus room – Ronald Wong's 'Laser surgery Iraq 1991' is held to be a very accurate depiction of Tornados and Buccaneers guiding bombs to target.

The exhibition also includes evocations of the First and Second World Wars, mostly painted by people too young to have experienced either. But it is the eager response to this year's war that seems so odd. Yvonne Bonham, the Guild's treasurer, is briskly practical. Given that the war was so recent and that the artists had limited time and reference material, she was pleased with the Gulf section. But such pictures would not find their way into the Imperial War Museum. The keeper of the department of art hopes no one imagines that these are the kind of pictures acquired for the museum's collection. Indeed, the thought of imaginary compositions based on the Gulf War makes her extremely angry.

The Guild artists work like eighteenth-century history painters – with much painstaking research into war literature and accounts of air battles. Photographs and videos as well as sketches are used. But history paintings were not only meant to depict events with archaeological accuracy. They were also meant to move the spirit, to point a moral. That is what the Guild misses out on. *Swoosh*, *zoom*, the blurr of wings, the belch of fire caught by careful research – he who dares wins. Flight should have inspired some sort of new art, though on the whole the patchwork literalism has been disappointing. Apart from Paul Nash's great Second World War paintings, Peter Lanyon is about the only major flight-inspired artist and he painted clouds, not planes. But anyone interested in social history, popular art, and the highways and byways of patriotism should visit the Guild exhibition.

The Independent, 23 July 1991

Undercover Surrealism

'Undercover Surrealism: Picasso, Miró, Masson and the vision of Georges Bataille':
exhibition at the Hayward Gallery, London, 11 May to 30 July 2006

There is an exhibition at the Hayward Gallery that should not be missed. 'Undercover Surrealism: Picasso, Miró, Masson and the vision of Georges Bataille' takes as its subject a short-lived magazine, *Documents*, published in Paris in 1929–30. To make a magazine the basis of an exhibition may not seem easy, but the show's curators have succeeded triumphantly by giving us objects of the kind illustrated and discussed in *Documents* and arranging them so as to convey the extraordinary visual juxtapositions that characterized each issue. It is a tribute to the magazine's afterlife that many of the exhibits may seem strangely familiar, part of a counter-cultural postmodernist canon. Images of flayed bodies (from Daniel le Bossu's *Nouvelles tables anatomiques* of 1673), gruesome police photos of slain gangsters (from *X marks the spot: Chicago gang wars in pictures*), Franz Xaver Messerschmidt's 'character' heads (exaggerated studies of human emotions), and Eli Lotar's tough photographs of the Paris abattoir at La Villette, characterize *Documents*. Francis Bacon was an early admirer but the *Documents* aesthetic has clearly been a primer for artists such as Damien Hirst and the Chapman brothers.

The subtitle of the show is somewhat misleading. While Picasso, Miró, and Masson are given plenty of space, they take their place alongside an extraordinarily eclectic range of material. *Documents*'s mix of high and low culture differentiate it from other inter-war art journals – though parallels can be drawn with the French magazine *Jazz* and the German journal *Der Querschnitt*. Perhaps the closest comparison would be with Le Corbusier's *L'Esprit Nouveau* which ran from 1920 to 1925 and which made its point through comparable pairings of images, scissored from the pages of all kinds of publications – so we get flower structures and factory chimneys, groups of tribesmen and the cool interior of Ozenfant's studio. Both *L'Esprit Nouveau* and *Documents* share a proselytizing intent.

Who chose the illustrations for *Documents*, some of which were specially commissioned? Most probably it was Georges Bataille. Most of his life he worked in the Coins and Medals department of the Bibliothèque Nationale, but he also wrote on a huge range of topics beyond numismatics. His most notorious work is *Story of the eye*, a dreamlike work of pornography. Reading Bataille requires strong nerves, but it is his attitude to the hierarchies of art that is of most interest to us. Bataille had a healthy contempt for the elevated status of fine art – he wrote: 'we enter art galleries as we do the chemists, seeking well-presented remedies for accepted sicknesses.' Even when he was

A modern master potter: M. Jean Besnard (left) in his workshop, *Documents*, no.4, 1930.

discussing an artist whom he admired, the qualities he found to praise were disturbing and unexpected. For instance in Picassso's art he identified incoherence, instability, and intellectual terrorism – high praise from Bataille! How important was painting anyway? Bataille threw down a challenge: 'I defy any lover of art to love a picture as much as a fetishist loves a shoe.'

The other contributors to *Documents* shared Bataille's intellectual universe. As Michel Leiris wrote in an article on Giacometti: 'almost all works of art are terrifyingly dull'. *Documents* set out to encompass art, archaeology, ethnography, and 'variétés'. Translated as 'variety', this subheading has a sense of popular rather than high culture and encompassed Hollywood musicals, cheap pulp thrillers, and semi-pornographic images. Bataille made a strange but persuasive link between Hollywood musicals and the extravagant cults and prodigal displays that he associated with pre-modern cultures. Musicals like *The Hollywood revue* seemed to him to mimic the processions, ritual offerings, and incantations of early religions. Hollywood was, he argued provocatively, a last remaining site of pilgrimage.

All this may seem remote from craft and making. But *Documents* had a strongly ethnographic dimension (while presciently challenging the whole idea of the detached white ethnographer surveying 'authentic' non-Western cultures), and so took in odd byways of European folk craft (passion bottles from Notre-Dame-de-Liesse, maypole dances, the folk inspired pottery of Jean Besnard) as well as a suggestive array of African and prehistoric material. It has been argued that the catholicity of visual sources in *Documents* owes something to the collections at the Cabinet des Médailles where Bataille was employed. It was much more than a collection of coins and medals, having originated as a royal cabinet of curiosities, with claims to being the oldest museum in Europe. It included all kinds of strange items – a cloak made from a whale's intestine, the vessel used by Christ to perform his miracle at Cana. No wonder Bataille dismissed routine art history. His interests and the interests of co-writers like Michel Leiris and Marcel Griaule took in a much richer world of things. It was a point of honour to defy the tastes of the typical wealthy collector of the inter-war period.

Documents rejected intrinsic value and authenticity. Bataille wrote: 'It is clear that the world is purely parodic ... that each thing seen is the parody of another, or the same thing in deceptive form.' That sounds like Barthes or Baudrillard, who were indeed greatly influenced by Bataille's thinking. For Bataille, images of dead flies on flypaper, and a gruesome row of severed cows legs leaning against a wall, took their place in his *musée imaginaire* alongside the greatest paintings of Picasso. Bataille concluded: 'What is really loved is loved mainly in shame.' His was an extreme position, but it opened up the visual world long before cultural studies and handbooks on 'the everyday' made such interests an academic orthodoxy.

Crafts, no. 201, July / August 2006

Middle English

Ewan Forster and Christopher Heighes, 'Middle English: a performance piece':
a play staged at the Art Workers' Guild, 10 April 2003

'Middle English', is described as a 'performance lecture' by its ingenious creators Ewan Forster and Christopher Heighes. It is the first play I have reviewed and will probably be the last. But then theatre rarely takes an audience so deeply into forgotten areas of architecture and lost vernacular craft. And it is not often that the skills of hurdle-making or road building are demonstrated on stage.

The play's subject is a building – Giles Gilbert Scott's Whitelands College (1930), hidden just off the A3 in Putney. Scott is better known for his Gothic Liverpool Cathedral, for Battersea Power Station (at the moment in a ruinous state), and for the former Bankside Power Station, now restored as Tate Modern. Whitelands is another largely forgotten masterpiece in monumental brickwork, its majestic Mayan terraces looking towards the North Downs. We gradually come to understand Whitelands and much else besides, through a poetic collage of film, text, slides, live music and, not least, objects.

Using a draw-knife in Ewan Forster and Christopher Heighes's 'Middle English: a performance piece', Art Workers' Guild, 10 April 2003.

By the end of the evening at the Art Workers' Guild the stage was filled with things – two halves of a rowing skiff, some ten large dolls houses, representing suburban sprawl, a cupboard, a row of hawthorn trees in pots as well as three hurdles, some split and shaved logs, coppicing tools, and a little patch of cobbled road. It is difficult to convey the atmosphere of this strange, brilliantly compelling event. In its surreal, melancholy didacticism it reminded me of Patrick Keiller's two films about Englishness, *Robinson in Space* and *London*. A comparison might also be made with Théâtre de Complicité, whose much larger team of writers and actors also move from arcane research into magical performance.

'Middle English' takes the form of an exam, a kind of bizarre General Paper that might easily have been sat by the young trainee women teachers at Whitelands in the 1930s. There are two fierce invigilators, Patrick Driver and Sarah Archdeacon, who also take on plenty of other roles, mostly otherworldly. The 'exam' disinters lost histories, of the relationship between Scott and Winifred Mercier, Whitelands' idealistic Principal, and of the role played by that strange admirer of the College in the 1880s, the art critic and social reformer John Ruskin. Indeed, this is a very Ruskinian play, echoing the great man's capacious, connective mind and his own strange 'performance lectures' in which he used lantern slides but also employed servants to carry evocative objects onto the lecture platform. Ruskin's doubts about modernity and the current neglect of his writings are paralleled by Scott's own ambivalent position. His greatest buildings have been victims of modernity's depredations, while his career as an architect is hard to fit into an evolutionary account of the Modern movement.

Altogether this was an evening of great enchantment, a threnody for lost ideals and tacit skills, for forgotten individuals and buildings. Language and roots of words are explored but, equally, there are many purely visual moments, as when an oak cupboard from Whitelands is opened to reveal an image of Scott's brickwork projected onto the interior. Out of the cupboard comes a miniaturized radio mast soon to be held aloft by an angel singing a Latin plaint. Throughout, there is music, by 'lost' English twentieth-century composers like Elisabeth Lutyens, Alan Rawsthorne, and Edmund Rubbra. Modernisms collide. As Forster and Heighes labour upstream in racing skiffs (this is a very physical play), the back projection (drawn as a series of *Boy's Own* cartoon strips) shows them rowing up the Rhine to visit Hilversum, with its famous Town Hall by Scott's mentor Willem Dudok. The two faux-innocents are also afloat in a world of cultural ironies. The Dutch town reminds us of the Hilversum dial position on old radio sets and in an earlier part of 'Middle English', after breakfast with her father, the young composer Elizabeth Lutyens secretly tunes in to Hilversum to hear her own radical Chamber Concerto no. 1.

The very next day I felt impelled to visit Whitelands College. Although the building seemed run-down and hemmed in by roads and houses, Forster and Heighes's extraordinary play made it possible to read it as a living space, a site for dreaming and learning. But those dreams are over. Later that evening I looked up Whitelands on the internet and learned that the College was to 'relocate'. The 'prime freehold site' has been sold to Crest Nicolson plc, who will carve 132 luxury apartments and a 'health and fitness facility' out of Scott's great building. In the grounds there will be a further 119 apartments, 50 townhouses, 18 semi-detached villas, and a concierge gatehouse.

This is the third Forster–Heighes theatrical event. All concern 'intriguing and neglected architectural sites'. Their next project takes the form of an installation at another Scott building, Liverpool Cathedral. Meanwhile 'Middle English' is expensive to stage and has so far only been seen by small audiences. Anyone with ideas for funding and venues for further performances should go to www.forster-heighes.org.uk.

Crafts, no. 183, July / August 2003

Forster and Heighes continue to examine the creeping privatization of British society by staging performances that take as their subject neglected or abandoned architectural sites once devoted to the public good. Like Whitelands College, educational buildings continue to be sold off to be redeveloped as 'luxury' flats.

Fired with passion

Stagily spotlit in the Great Hall at Aberystwyth Arts Centre, with cameras and tapes whirring, the Nigerian potter Asebe Magaji began to work with a solid cylinder of clay. This she punched into almost casually before scraping and pulling it up. The audience was attentive. It was difficult to resist the thought that she had been brought here – all the way from her small village – to reassure them, to show them that craftsmanship was not a marginal luxury everywhere, and that, yes, it was all right to go on making things by hand in an industrialized society. By now the basic structure of a large pot was revealed, the whole thing swaying outrageously as she added rough coils of clay, smoothing them swiftly into a thin wall. The shape was then bellied out with a scraper, while a couple of graceful pacing walks round the pot, manipulating a piece of cloth, created its elegant rim.

This Gwari technique, with all its bold directness, has frequently been described and photographed; but to see it done with such assurance was an extraordinary experience. The end result had a classical rightness: shoulder to rim, rim to base, shoulder to base revealed a natural sense of harmonic proportion. The pot was gradually decorated with rough striations made with a corn cob, with bands of horizontal lines and with areas of burnished ochre slip.

The next day Asebe Magaji and her fellow potter Asibe Ido fired a sizeable group of pots in a bonfire clamp in a field behind the Arts Centre. Again, there was an air of practised ease as they laid the circular bed of sticks that made the base of the clamp, balanced the pre-heated pots against each other, wedging them with sherds and covering them with a blanket of guinea-corn heads (brought, like the clay which Asebe used, from Nigeria) and straw. The firing was successfully completed in a mere hour.

For the whole weekend of the 1989 International Potters Camp, held ten days ago in Aberystwyth, the crowd of spectators gave off an almost palpable craving for some part of this skill wedded so firmly to certainty. Indeed, whenever Asebe Magaji began to work she was immediately surrounded by an oppressive crush of bodies, filming, photographing, and devouring her every action. At this international gathering she was undoubtedly the star. Yet the occasion wasn't one of mere voyeurism. The two women were surrounded by fellow potters, and tools were examined and clays discussed.

But Asebe Magaji's responses were strictly limited to the practical. Anything too remote from her own path was manifestly of little interest to her. After all, her pots were made with important specific uses in mind and their

Asebe Magaji decorating a hand-built pot.

beauty was a byproduct of notions of service. The pots from her village of Tatiko sell quickly in the market, outclassing the onslaught of plastic and enamel wares: there is a genuine demand for her work. And she maintains her standards in the context of the village, training her daughters to make pots amid the self-regulatory criticism of fellow potters. Still, it is difficult to know what to make of such an impressive tradition when it is presented to us as spectacle.

Large-scale events like the camp at Aberystwyth, egalitarian affairs at which technique is communicated by demonstration, are popular with potters. Perhaps these camps, with their concentration on process at the expense of ideas, suggest that potters are not part of the community of fine artists. But however odd, even laughable, such gatherings may appear to outsiders, the know-how paraded deserves respect. For they are continuing a painful recovery job, first undertaken at the beginning of this century when traditional and early industrial skills seemed likely to vanish without trace. Studio pottery was born out of a sense of loss.

Yet inevitably the idea of bringing people from a remote and 'authentic' culture to enact their craft provokes a sense of unease. Vague memories surface of photos of the British Empire Exhibitions between the wars, showing subject races brought to Wembley or Glasgow to make pots or weave in jaunty pavilions beside mock waterfalls. An inconvenient memory of colonialism hung about the whole weekend.

Whether we like it or not, part of our interest in a good deal of the material culture of the Third World goes back to a colonial moment when the more artistic servants of the Empire found their lives transformed by the vitality and creativity around them. For instance, the presence of Asebe Magaji and Asibe Ido at Aberystwyth can be traced back to the passionate response of the artist-potter Michael Cardew to West Africa. He chose to work there from the 1940s onwards in order to shake off the Arts & Crafts exclusivity which he found so repellent in England. Colonial rule gave him, ironically enough, a sensible context for his activities.

His pottery training centre for Nigerian men and women at Abuja was, he argued, a bridge between cultures, an intervening stage before industrialization. In fact it was pitifully like bringing coals to Newcastle, for he was surrounded by women like Magaji who without his wheels and kilns could fashion pots of great beauty and entire fitness to purpose. Being no fool, Cardew understood that irony and admitted, not so very secretly, that while he came in the guise of an educator he took more than he gave.

Throughout the weekend at Aberystwyth Asebe Magaji indicated with a quiet disregard that most of the cultural trafficking would be one way – from her to us. Cardew would have sympathized. Her certainty highlighted the plight of studio pottery. The strength of Asebe's work derives from the fact that it is not individualistic; she may be the best potter in Tatiko but all the potters of Tatiko are capable of good work. In honour of this anonymous tradition the modern studio potter invariably makes a respectful pact with the past. This can produce dull hybrids, but it also results in pieces of extraordinary beauty in which that sense of loss and a concomitant desire to make reparation are resolved and become art.

The Independent, 20 July 1989

What is folk art?

'Folk Archive: contemporary popular art from the UK': exhibition at the Barbican Centre, London, 12 May to 24 July 2005

What is folk art? It is usually defined as being made by 'the people' as opposed to academically trained artists. Its nineteenth-century admirers liked to emphasize that it was made for love, not money, and was therefore beyond vulgar commodification. It was heartening to think that in Sweden a young lover would carve a present for his wife-to-be while in return she would make and embroider him a linen shirt. As one Victorian collector explained, the results would be beautiful because 'The Peasant, perfectly unconscious of any Art principles, does instinctively the right thing'. But England, dominated by getting and spending, posed problems and it was acknowledged that English folk art was in short supply. Advanced farming methods meant that we lacked a landed peasantry with the time and the energy to weave and whittle in the long winter evenings. In any case the English 'folk' were uncertain guardians of their fragile traditions. Greyhound racing and pigeon fancying outfaced Morris dancing. Cecil Sharp and other collectors of traditional song found, disappointingly, that raucous music hall tunes were being sung in the remotest villages.

By the 1930s and 1940s the term 'popular art' seemed a more realistic term. The designer Enid Marx identified a vernacular tradition that had survived the industrial revolution and that had, in fact, drawn inspiration from it. For her popular art was 'hard to define though easy enough to recognize when seen'. It encompassed samplers, Staffordshire flatbacks, lustre wares, ships' figureheads, fairground decorations, farm wagons, sign-writing, gypsy caravans, bargees' art, horse brasses, tinsel pictures and other examples of printing such as broadsheets and chapbooks, patchwork and quilting – all relatively tasteful and eminently collectable.

Marx identified a marked decline in the surviving manifestations of popular art by the end of the Second World War: 'The "innocent eye" is disappearing' she declared. But the artist Barbara Jones was more forgiving towards the cruder, brasher examples of the genre. In her show 'Black Eyes and Lemonade' organized for the Festival of Britain in 1951 she included contemporary objects that Marx would have found impossibly vulgar – a fireplace tiled in the form of an Airedale dog and the famous Talking Lemon used to advertise Idris lemon squash.

What constituted a people's art was, and is, highly relative. By the late 1950s the Independent Group, meeting regularly at the ICA, had identified another vernacular that was rooted in American consumer culture and com-

George Bush and Tony Blair Sculpture, Stop the War March, London 2002.

pletely at odds with the insular vision of Enid Marx and Barbara Jones. But in general the focus shifted towards working-class art, taking in trade-union banners and creative activity directly linked to the industrial workplace. In 1994 Emmanuel Cooper's exhaustive *The people's art* offered this kind of politicized version of folk art, in which social inclusion was of more importance than Enid Marx's formalist 'forthrightness, gaiety and delight in bright colours'.

And now we have 'Folk Archive' – a touring exhibition of videos, photographs, paintings, drawings and objects put together by two artists, Alan Kane and Turner Prize winner Jeremy Deller. It reflects the concerns of many contemporary artists, being strongly documentary and ethnographic in spirit. Performance is given as much emphasis as collectable objects. Good taste and formalist aesthetics are set aside, even if Enid Marx's 'forthrightness' is echoed by Deller and Kane's search for work that is 'direct'.

There is no attempt to track an 'authentic' folk culture (though plenty of traditional rural festivals like the Egremont Crab Fair in Cumbria are covered). Nonetheless a powerful series of voices come through. There is much that is poignant about this show, and familiar too. What is crucial is that the cake decorations, roughly painted snack-bar signs, prostitutes' phone cards, personalized crash helmets, crop circles, Stop the War posters, all announce their home-made status. I think that much of this loud, humorous and crudely made material would have been beneath the notice of early aficionados of popular art. But 'Folk Archive' stands for something important – creativity outside an increasingly packaged and regulated culture industry. It is something, as Enid Marx observed, that is hard to define though easy enough to recognize when seen.

The Spectator, 16 July 2005

Beauty and foolishness

'20th Century Silver': an exhibition at the Crafts Council Gallery, 16 September to 7 November 1993, accompanied by a smaller show, 'The Chemistry Set'

Until the fifteenth century the bedroom, with its costly display of textiles, was the centre of a grand household – the most prestigious site for an interview with a person of influence. By the eighteenth and nineteenth centuries reception and dining rooms became the arena for power-broking, the former with a background of furniture and painting, the latter dominated by porcelain and silver. It was a shift from a shamanistic, queen bee kind of veneration of an individual to a more mercantile display of power through conspicuous consumption.

Today feasting lavishness is enjoyed by very few: livery companies, Oxford colleges, and state banquets are the main surviving patrons of the grandest art of the silversmith. In ordinary homes the kitchen is now the place where status and consumption are on display. No one can quarrel with the message conveyed by a newly installed Aga or a plethora of woks, waffle irons, and orange juice squeezers. In this context silver – usually in the form of salt-cellars and neglected napkin rings – languishes tarnished in a cupboard. Its glitter has effectively been replicated by stainless steel.

'20th Century Silver' therefore, held at the Crafts Council Gallery in London, holds out the promise of explaining the technical mysteries of the craft and throwing some light on how silver functions as an art form today. This is a beautifully mounted show with over a hundred pieces, ranging over the century and drawing on collections from all over Europe. It is limited to objects connected with the table. Trophies and sporting cups – among the most prestigious (and often most tasteless) examples of the silversmith's art – as well as church plate are excluded.

The show starts by addressing a modernist functional aesthetic, traced from the eighteenth century through to the beginnings of the Modern movement. Thus there is no rococo silver, and even Arts & Crafts work – including the wilful, strange designs of Henry Wilson – is seen as a preparation for the triumph of modernism. This is a rather old-fashioned approach to the history of design. It also makes the last part of the show seem anomalous. The selection of contemporary work show modernism's purity and logic to have been largely abandoned: ornamentalism reigns.

What is missing from this show is the how and why of an activity uneasily poised between trade and art, between Garrard the Crown Jewellers and C. R. Ashbee's Guild of Handicraft. The 'how' is important (and in fact covered in a handy Crafts Council guide, *Looking at silver*), because procedures like raising a flat piece of silver into the form of a bowl with specially designed hammers are far more mysterious to outsiders than, say, throwing a pot. Part of the hidden message of these objects must be the level of skill employed. The most readable part of the exhibition, a marvellous display of cutlery, is the most familiar. The language of knives and forks is one with which we all have an intimacy. The 'why' – the intricate relations between maker, designer and designer-maker, between trade and craft, between demand and supply – is not easy to convey in an exhibition and perhaps its curator Helen Clifford was wise not to attempt it.

Michael Rowe, 'Conditions for Ornament', no. 8: 'Conical vessel'
(1988, brass, tin finish, 28 × 52 × 22 cm).

What becomes plain, however, is that silver was a difficult medium in which to address certain modernist themes, above all the machine aesthetic of the 1930s. Inter-war painters and sculptors drew inspiration from simplified techniques and from the intrinsic qualities of wood and stone. Likewise the sleek, highly finished products of the machine were, and remain, an important design source for modern silver. Ironically, great skill was employed in order that a soft, malleable material should suggest the effects of highly engineered steel. In the ancient world metalworkers originated shapes and effects which were imitated in other materials, above all ceramics. During this century technology has left silver behind.

The most impressive pieces in the show do seem to express some quality of truth to silverness that matches direct carving in sculpture and a sensitivity to mark-making in painting. To seek such a quality is both an Arts & Crafts and a modern response and the objects that best exude ease with the material form part of a specifically English tradition exemplified by the post-war work of Robert Welch, Gerald Benney, and David Mellor. Their silver is modern with eighteenth-century roots, restrained, even modest. It is as near as we shall ever get to egalitarian silver. Studying such work has the odd effect of making Christopher Dresser, the undoubted design genius of nineteenth-century silver, seem hard, stylized and relatively insensitive to the medium. It also shows up recent silver, not least because the dominant aesthetic of the bulk of the show is one of simplicity and care for function. The most recent work of the late-1980s and the 1990s, therefore, seems willfully irrational. In the aesthetic chaos of the 1980s conspicuous display, unparalleled in the history of silver since the complexities of rococo, was unleashed. There are certainly some beauties here but also much foolishness.

Beauty and foolishness similarly co-exist in the accompanying exhibition, 'The Chemistry Set', which sets out to examine the use of patination and colouration by contemporary metalworkers. In 1982 Richard Hughes and Michael Rowe co-authored a seminal reference book entitled *The colouring, bronzing and patination of metals*. This show reveals the impact of their researches. Whimsical objects abound, but it is worth a visit simply to see one piece by Michael Rowe, part of a series entitled 'Conditions for ornament'. Anyone who ever doubted that objects could carry the poetic charge assumed to be the right of painting and sculpture should take note of this extraordinary work of art.

The Spectator, 2 October 1993

Sculpture / furniture

'Figuring Space: sculpture / furniture from Mies to Moore': exhibition at the Henry Moore Institute, Leeds, 18 January to 1 April 2007

This exhibition poses an apparently simple question – do sculpture and furniture occupy a similar role in the context of twentieth-century architecture? The show's curator, Penelope Curtis, works within a precise time-frame – 1930 to 1960 – but this could nonetheless have been a big, informative show that surveyed a neglected aspect of modernism. Instead the approach is poetic, using the work of Mies van der Rohe as a testing ground. As Curtis says, this is an 'intuitive and idiosyncratic' exhibition. We are reminded of the high seriousness of renaissance paragone discussions in which the relative merits of painting and sculpture were hotly debated and compared to architecture and to poetry.

'Figuring Space' opens dramatically, using the steep entrance ramp of the Henry Moore Institute to frame an 'eye-catcher' worthy of Stowe or

Rousham – a female *figura serpentinata* whose arms and hands seem to oscillate between welcome and dismissal. The sculpture looks oddly familiar and, indeed, turns out to be a plaster version of Georg Kolbe's 'Morning', the mysterious enlivening presence in Mies van der Rohe's German Pavilion for the Barcelona International Exposition of 1929. 'Morning' is best known to us through a haunting series of contemporary black and white photographs of the pavilion in which the sculpture appears both in actuality and is reflected elusively against the glass and marble of that extraordinary building. Since 1986 we have also encountered it as a cast bronze, glimpsed as we traverse the interconnected spaces of the exquisite reconstruction of Mies's iconic building. Seen here at Leeds we become much more conscious both of its scale (bordering on the monumental) and of the fact that in British terms 'Morning' is close in spirit to the New Sculpture of the late 1890s.

The first room of 'Figuring Space' concentrates on Mies's deployment of sculpture – both in actual buildings and in his plans and renderings. It was a focused interest for he limited himself to work by Kolbe, Wilhelm Lehmbruck (a close friend who had committed suicide in 1919), and Aristide Maillol. When we consider the breakthroughs and excitements of early twentieth-century sculpture this may appear a conservative choice for the pre-eminent architect of the twentieth century. But as recent revisionist exhibitions like 'Mies in Berlin' (2001) have demonstrated, Mies's modernism was more complex and perhaps less starkly 'modern' than the polemic presented by Henry-Russell Hitchcock and Philip Johnson in the 1930s and 1940s. In any case what was perceived to be modern sculpture in the early twentieth century bears little relation to the sharply delineated evolutionary canon that we admire today. To appreciate that the nude figure stood for something innovative in Germany of the 1920s demands that we cultivate a period eye and, more specifically, forget the respect accorded to figurative sculpture (and, incidentally, to the work of Kolbe) during the Third Reich.

One of the functions of sculpture in Mies's architecture was to articulate and inhabit space. His use of Lehmbruck's torso 'Girl turning round' helped link the discrete areas of the Tugendhat House (1928–30). Another cast of the same sculpture played a similar role in his Glass House, an installation for the glass industry for the 1927 Werkbund exhibition 'Die Wohnung unserer Zeit'. It could be said, perhaps mischievously, that inanimate objects – sculpture (and furniture) – were for Mies the ideal occupants of his interiors. And Mies's invariable use of just three sculptors recalls the limited range of objects Le Corbusier deemed permissible for modern living. These included carefully chosen furniture (after 1928, designed by himself and Charlotte Perriand), peasant pots, and kelim rugs. All appear regularly in the pristine photographs of Le Corbusier's inter-war villas, taken before their owners moved

Installation photograph of 'Figuring Space' showing Henry Moore's 'King and queen', 1952–3, and Ludwig Mies van der Rohe's Barcelona chairs (MR90), 1929.

in. Both figurative sculpture and vernacular craft may seem incongruous adjuncts to Modern movement architecture but their otherness was perhaps the point.

Curtis argues that Mies valued his chosen sculptures because they had a 'completely different pace', being 'thicker, slower and more opaque', functioning as a foil to the transparency of his architecture. But their inclusion, whether actual or as images in his photomontages, bring Surrealist aesthetics to mind – in which different, apparently irreconcilable realities were brought together, often through collage. Sculptures by Lehmbruck and Maillol continue to pop up as carefully cut-out photographs, placed without regard to scale in Mies's renderings of the 1940s. It is a choice that suggests an interest in the obsolete and the just-out-of-date, something Walter Benjamin identified as the 'extraordinary discovery' of Surrealism.

Mies's use of his own furniture designs is markedly less ambiguous than his deployment of sculpture. And the furniture itself fits neatly into the modernist mapping of modern art: if Mies's chairs bring sculpture to mind it is the recognisable avant-garde of constructed sculpture whose ultimate source was Cubism. The positioning of chairs and tables (shown on his floor plans for the German pavilion and the Tugendhat House) indicated the function of different spaces in what were essentially open-plan interiors. Thus the Barcelona and Tugendhat chairs were for sitting rooms and the MR and Brno chairs for study and dining areas. It seems that furniture and sculpture performed different tasks for Mies. Furniture was used to impose the architect's will. Sculpture created movement and even disorder – which perhaps explains why its use has until now been virtually ignored in Miesian studies.

Curtis pursues her analogic line of questioning obliquely and daringly in the second room of 'Figuring Space'. She sites two of Mies's Barcelona chairs on the corner of a black carpet – rather as they were positioned in the German pavilion in 1929. On the diagonal corner she places Henry Moore's bronze 'King and queen' of 1952–3. It is an entirely ahistorical gesture – over twenty years separate Mies's chairs and Moore's sculpture. But the juxtaposition sets us thinking. The Barcelona chairs are rescued from their present-day association with expensive office interiors and we are reminded of their original purpose, as modernist thrones for the King and Queen of Spain when they visited the pavilion in May 1929. We are made conscious that both furniture and sculpture are produced in multiples and, more importantly, can mean different things in different spaces. Moore's 'King and queen' is probably best known from dramatic photographs of the cast placed by Sir William Keswick high in a rocky field on his Scottish estate. Seen in 'Figuring Space' the royal pair appear smaller and more domestic – constitutional monarchs for a Welfare State. In contrast the Barcelona chairs seem more formal and magisterial, literally so – for they resemble the classical *sella curulis* reserved for magistrates and Roman rulers.

The final room of 'Figuring Space' pursues the sculpture / furniture analogy into the post-war period with two pieces by Charles and Ray Eames, the so-called director's chair and ottoman and their daring 'La chaise', together with Arne Jacobsen's famous Egg chair designed for the Royal Hotel in Copenhagen. They are set against an image of a rolling landscape, blown up to cover the back wall – reminding us of a pastoral view from a modernist *casa in villa* seen through a plate glass window. Again Curtis says more with less. The catalogue interrogates links with sculptural production: wire frames and plaster were used to develop the plywood forms of the Eames chair and ottoman while the Egg chair was also modelled in plaster at the design stage. The importance of Ray Eames's fine art background, as a student of Hans Hofmann, is also shown to be crucial. So too were new craft skills that came out of wartime industries – aircraft construction and the making of lightweight splints. All kinds of post-war visual synchronicities float up. Curtis pairs the Eames lounge chair and ottoman with Henry Moore's two-piece sculptures developed in the late 1950s. Where sculpture went, furniture followed. The asymmetry of Arp's sculptures of the 1920s also had a major influence on post-war design in many media, not least on the Eames's curvaceous fibreglass 'La chaise'.

What does seem indisputable is that the best post-war furniture – organic, curvilinear, and anthropomorphic – was well able to dominate and articulate space, convivially. It is possible to argue, as Curtis does, that furniture did the job of figurative sculpture by other means. Meanwhile, cast, carved and constructed sculpture was by the 1960s to be found either in the neutral space of the gallery or clumsily sited in public spaces, often as a symbol of corporate patronage and greeted with indifference or hostility by the general public.

'Figuring Space' is the kind of exhibition that leads us to reflect on the present. What is the relationship now? Furniture design has become unusually self-referential, chiefly sustained by quoting, parodying, and replicating the iconic designs of the last century. As for sculpture, the work of Damien Hirst appropriates cheap office furniture, the lees of modernism, to create macabre tableaux. Thus sculpture's relationship with furniture has become predatory rather than inspiring and sustaining.

Times Literary Supplement, 16 February 2007

Ian Hamilton Finlay in Luton

When Nikolaus Pevsner visited Luton in the 1960s, compiling his volume on Bedfordshire, he found it too dreary to recommend one of his famous peram-bulations. The centre of the city was in the process of being demolished, leav-ing the beautiful fifteenth-century church of St Mary's stranded in the traffic. Nearby, the Arndale Shopping Centre was to rise ringed by multi-storey car parks, a formidable negation of urban space.

Yet, as Pevsner observed, Luton, with its engineering and car industry, was a prosperous place. Lutonians, he concluded, were well-off but lacked visual responsibility. Perhaps Luton was too close to London to develop its own cultural identity. Prey to the worst excesses of post-war planning, it seemed destined to be known principally for its airport.

But this is a parable both of changing taste and civic pride. 'Luton's look-ing up', the town's new corporate logo tells us. Perhaps this is true. The bor-ough council has recently done something rather extraordinary for a town lacking visual responsibility: it has commissioned and just opened a garden designed by the Scots poet, sculptor, and neo-classicist Ian Hamilton Finlay.

If merely viewed as an example of local cultural ambition, this bit of pa-tronage certainly puts Luton on the art-world's map. The Kröller-Müller Mu-seum in the Netherlands has its Sacred Grove, the Max Planck Institute in Stuttgart has a generous sequence of Finlay's sculptures in a garden setting, but Luton's Stockwood Park has the only garden designed by Finlay in Great Britain, aside from the artist's own much-admired Stonypath in Scotland.

What we have at Luton, it must be emphasized, is not a sculpture park. Like Stonypath, it is a modern garden rooted in eighteenth-century land-scape theory, a place where planting, inscriptions, and carvings all work in harmony. The sculpture park is, on the other hand, a distinctly post-war phenomenon in which sculpture is placed – 'dotted around' is perhaps the appropriate phrase – out-of-doors, in order to preserve the integrity of sculp-tures that are not truly and wholeheartedly integrated into the landscape.

It was Henry Moore who priggishly reminded visitors to such places that they should not confuse the serious business of looking at sculpture with the distracting pleasures of nature and the general niceness of the park. The sculpture park idea was somewhat modified in the 1970s with more in-tegrated schemes like the Grizedale Sculpture Project, where artists worked on site, using locally won wood, like latter-day charcoal-burners. The results were pleasing but had no particular intellectual coherence.

The eighteenth-century ideal of a harmonious and meaningful blend of

Ian Hamilton Finlay, tree plaque carved by Nicholas Sloan, 1991.

planting, architecture, and sculpture – arguably the greatest art form to orig-inate in Britain – seemed alien to the twentieth century. Despite the valiant efforts of Geoffrey Jellicoe, Christopher Tunnard, and Sir Frederick Gibberd to create gardens, all that tended to be on offer in the public sector were those expanses of grass which Le Corbusier believed would evoke Virgilian dreams.

In fact the reality of this emptiness, windy and litter-strewn, fell short of the ideal. But on the other hand, occasional attempts to turn back the clock and emulate William Kent or Capability Brown on private estates have tend-ed to seem camp and meagre. This background makes Ian Hamilton Finlay's achievement all the more extraordinary. He is the one artist to have given a convincing continuity to the eighteenth-century landscape garden tradition. Yet his garden at Stonypath is in no sense a pastiche: it is emphatically mod-ern and concerned with present pleasures and present woes.

The garden at Stockwood is not Stonypath: it is simpler cent, a series of gentle tributes to nature and the healing po cal language of architecture. Finlay has taken a much-publi the Terror, in the writings of Saint-Just, in the graphic symb ture of the Third Reich, and he has employed this material in a fashion which many find painfully incomprehensible. He is also fond of Erwin Panofsky's classic essay on Poussin's 'Et in Arcadia ego' in which the art historian analyses the aphorism and discerns the painting's darker meaning. Such things are not found at Stockwood: there is no dark presence in this Arcadia.

'I sing for the Muses and myself' is the hortatory carved inscription that greets us at the entrance to Stockwood. The stone tablet hangs from a tree, like a *trompe l'oeil* inscription in a painting, signalling that we are entering a garden that is also a representation of an ideal landscape. The ground does not rise and fall picturesquely; there are at present no pools or rills, although those may come. Though the garden contains six pieces by Finlay it is hardly a Rousham or a Stowe. Yet even with the regular stream of planes flying in low, bound for the airport, it evokes the spirit of such places.

The garden will not be ready for some years, but it is a remarkable site and likely to become more beautiful and complex as the years pass and the ivy, willows, laurels, and yews grow up to confound and conceal. It stands, like much of Finlay's work, as a true collaboration between the artist, his carvers, and lettercutters, and above all with Luton's gifted Master Gardener, Robert Burgoyne. The garden belongs very much in the world of exemplary local authority public art commissions, passed by committees, multi-funded, part of new cultural initiatives, and so on. Yet it is difficult not to adopt the language of Alexander Pope when discussing it. This seems immediately paradoxical though, in an ideal world, it would not be.

In many ways Stockwood Park and its fortunes neatly sum up the changing image and aspirations of Luton: the handsome Georgian house demolished in the 1960s, the stables and gardens neglected, a change of heart in the conservation-minded 1980s, the stables rehabilitated, and the opening of a craft museum. None of this entirely explains either the genesis of the Ian Hamilton Finlay commission or how the borough council came to have a Master Gardener happy, indeed delighted, to interpret Finlay's drawings in the manner of Claude Lorraine.

The Independent, 25 April 1991

The garden flourishes as part of the renamed Stockwood Discovery Centre, London Road, Luton LU1 4LX.

pet sweepers, old mangles

'Design, Miroir du Siècle': exhibition at the Grand Palais, Paris, 19 May to 25 July 1993

Karl Marx was not a design historian but no other writer gives more vivid, intense accounts of modern 'things', nor has better described a great textile mill or the misery of a brick field or the enigmatic nature of commodities. 'To discover the various uses of things is the work of history', wrote Marx in the first volume and on the first page of *Das Kapital*. He would have been fascinated by this show.

'Design, Miroir du Siècle' covers 150 years of design and contains over 1,000 objects, some by now being withdrawn by anxious, conservation-minded owners. The public enter through an aircraft passenger tunnel and bridge into a scaffolded space in the Grand Palais – the glass and iron building itself evidence of the technological confidence of the last century. Appropriately, discomfort and a feeling of intense alienation is the principle reaction to this attempt to examine the modernisms that make up modernity.

'Design, Miroir du Siècle' starts off quietly enough with a small selection of well-crafted early cameras, push-bikes, and telephones, but as we walk through time up the hall there is an intensification of objects. Christopher Dresser silverware, Thonet bentwood furniture, Singer sewing machines fight for space with carpet sweepers, old mangles, and rusty egg whisks. All, whether of great or small value, are treated democratically, being placed unceremoniously on a grey, rather dirty-looking carpet. The show looks like a flea market or, quite literally, the sale of the century.

Plaques set into the floor announce modern discoveries – 'Aspirin 1852', 'Powdered Milk: 1855'. A backdrop of vastly enlarged photographs trace the development of industrialization from a pastoral image of English ironworks set among green fields circa 1860, to sheds filled with massive Linotype machinery, to lines of unemployed men and women, right up to the sanitized new technology that dominates first-world working environments today. If this were not enough, there is an incessant aural background of recorded sound ranging from an insistent squeak mushrooming out of a little microphone placed by a carpet sweeper of 1900 to the buzz and panic of voices selling shares at the height of the Wall Street crash. Decade by decade objects are packed more tightly until we reach the present day – a dense sea of miniaturized computerized bibelots – technology encased in postmodern styling, all rounded edges and pastel shades.

The show is full of the sights and sounds of destruction, mapping industrial expansion obliterating European folk culture at the beginning of the nineteenth century, and going on to undermine the arts and crafts of the rest

View of the exhibition 'Design, Miroir du Siècle'.

of the world. The whole experience is deeply fatiguing – almost a manifesto for de-industrialization or revolution, designed to induce in most visitors a strong sense of misery and loss.

Museum curators were horrified by this show, above all by the casual way in which 'things' were jammed side by side and labelled in the baldest, briefest fashion. But I can think of no other exhibition that gives such a strong sense of the experience of being modern and that reminds one so forcibly that to be truly modern must always mean, at least in part, being anti-modern.

The Spectator, 26 June 1993

1916

1950

1960

1994

Detroit downtown streetplan figure-ground diagrams by Richard Plunz.

Visiting Detroit

I had put myself forward when Mark, the Cranbrook archivist, mentioned a trip into Detroit. Mark loves three things – his archive, George Booth, the newspaper magnate who founded Cranbrook Academy of Art in 1925, and Detroit. Mark warns me that the day might be disturbing and perhaps distressing. He sounds like the voice-over flagged before violent television programmes. I feel pretty confident. After all I've visited Belfast and we are not heading for a war zone, just a run-down city.

'Detroit was once called the Paris of the Great Lakes', said Mark. All the way down East Jefferson Avenue he points out surviving apartment blocks and grand houses where in his teens he had dated girls or been to parties. Mark is about 50 and can remember Detroit before it became a ruin. On the skyline, eye-catching, we glimpse a gigantic building, all its windows blank, quite isolated and alone. As we drive closer we see a sweeping iron and glass canopy under which cars would set down passengers. The glass is shattered and cracked but the glamorous curves remain. This is the shell of the Michigan Central Railway Station built by Warren & Wetmore, the same architects who designed the Grand Central Station in New York. It was one of three majestic station termini in Detroit. Now there is only a tiny Amtrak building, built meanly out of breeze-block.

For most of our long hot day we stayed in the car, partly because we were seeing a lot and partly because it was clearly too dangerous to do otherwise. Mark started off in high spirits but by the afternoon he became melancholy. We drive past some gates leading into a scruffy park. His voice cracks a bit. 'Yeah, here is George Booth's home in Detroit – and you see he left it and a lovely garden to the city and what did they do but pull it all down.' Only the gates remain, dusty litter-covered grass and, beyond, small box-like houses – prefabs, only a step up from trailers, all painted peach. A brick pergola survives, vineless.

We stop outside another neglected building. 'And this', says Mark, with a kind of sad satisfaction, 'was the home of the Detroit Arts and Crafts Society set up by George Booth.' No one associates Detroit with North America's Arts and Crafts movement, not least because no one much wants to come to Detroit to research Booth's munificent patronage. We pass the Freer House where Whistler's gold and blue Peacock Room was housed in its own wing before being moved to Washington. Now it is surrounded by desolation. Further down the street the sights are even sadder, just the odd wood-frame house with no windows, or a couple side by side, their top floors and roofs torched. Pheasants roam the grassy emptiness of Detroit. This is the city at the end of the world, after some mass catastrophe, a gassing or bombing, when people had to begin at the beginning with – what? Basket weaving perhaps.

Block upon block of houses has been demolished or burnt down, leaving brown grass, dust and the scraps of litter that float lazily in the warm spring air. There is no public transport to speak of – just the occasional bus and a tiny 'people mover' in the business district; it does not connect to anything but goes round and round on its own trajectory. No public phones in sight, no taxis and no police. That evening I look at some building density plans. In 1853 you see the city emerging in the south, following Augustus Woodward's scheme for sweeping circular terraces. By 1916 Detroit is a major city on a grid extending north. By 1950 it is even more built up. The final plan covers the same area in 1994. Where has the city gone? Large parts have been rubbed away carelessly, rendering a readable layout hieroglyphic.

Detroit is the ultimate modern city, the mo-town where mass labour was first divided into countless idiotic tasks. 'The man who puts in a bolt does not put on the nut; the man who puts on the nut does not tighten it', decreed Henry Ford. In Detroit we can see what went wrong when an economic monoculture based on the automobile industry collapsed and those with wealth, including George Booth, abandoned the city.

On the way back to utopian Cranbrook we stop at the Eleanor and Edsel Ford House on Grosse Point alongside Lake St Clair. This sixty-room mansion was inspired by the vernacular architecture of the Cotswolds. I remember that the construction of the roof was supervised by a Gloucestershire craftsman named H. J. Gooding. He travelled from England by ship with his tools and thousands of split stone slates from the Eyford quarry, carefully packed in boxes. In the late 1920s, Fordism seemed a wonder to a countryman like Gooding. As he recalled, his American workforce all arrived at Grosse Point in their own cars.

Crafts, no. 189, July / August 2004

Memory-work

In 2003 Neil Brownsword began interviewing some of the most highly trained employees at Wedgwood's factory at Barlaston. The resulting videos record master mould-makers, turners, an ornamenter, a figure-maker, a pitchure mould-maker, and a pâte-sur-pâte decorator at work.[1] All were using skills that go back at least one if not two centuries. The tone of the interviews is decidedly elegiac as the craftsmen reflect on their apprenticeships, on the disappearance of family-run firms, and on the shrinkage of the workforce in the ceramics industry. Most of the interviewees are men, reminding us that an informal system of gender segregation still operates in the industry; men tend to have the best-paid jobs and the ones that are deemed highly specialist.

The project took place against a backdrop of redundancies at Waterford Wedgwood, the result of both increased automation and the use of CAD / CAM technologies at the design stage and the relocation of production to the Far East. We overhear a mould-maker describing how workers from Stoke are sent out to China to train people who will then take over their jobs for lower wages. With some satisfaction a pitchure mould-maker notes that all attempts to automate his job have so far ended in failure. A turner demonstrates the exquisite action of a fluting lathe of a kind designed in the late eighteenth century and never improved upon. He doubts if a computerized tool could do the job better or faster. Several interviewees talk of a tacit knowledge of clay that is only acquired through long experience. Neil Brownsword's films testify to a pride, even a joy, in labour that may be peculiar to the ceramics industry. When J. B. Priestley went on his *English journey* back in 1933 he was keenly struck by the high craft standards and by the happiness of the 'brisk and contented' workforce in the Potteries, the collective name for the Six Towns of which Stoke-on-Trent is the most famous.[2]

Neil Brownsword grew up in Newcastle-under-Lyme, near Bradwell Woods, famous for its iron-rich clay known as Etruria marl. This was where the Dutch silversmiths John and David Elers settled in 1693, experimenting with salt-glaze and producing a red unglazed ware decorated with sharply moulded relief patterns. Brownsword's grandmother and many other relations worked in ceramics factories, while his mother had a collection of Royal Doulton and Coalport figurines that, as he grew older, both intrigued and repelled him. It seemed natural to go into the industry and in 1987, aged 16, Brownsword went to Wedgwood on a Youth Training Scheme to train as a tableware modeller. He was there for two years, picking up a range of skills including relief modelling and graphic design.

This experience was to prove profoundly important. His career as an artist can be read as an extended and varied meditation on the area in which he grew up and on the decline of its pottery industry over the past twenty years. His work also interrogates the nature of skill and its uncertain and contingent relationship with creativity.

As a very young man Brownsword began to react in his own way against the division of labour in the industry. He chose not to specialize and, as far as possible, tried to gain an understanding of each phase of the production process. In 1989 he left Wedgwood to embark on a foundation course that took him on to study ceramics at the University of Wales at Cardiff and at the Royal College of Art, graduating in 1995. The early part of his career as a studio ceramicist has been well documented. He was strikingly successful, being given a residency and a solo show at Stoke-on-Trent Museum and Art Gallery a year after graduating.

The work he made at that time was figurative, much of it concerned with his boyhood friends and their lives in a town in decline, where jobs were dead-end and where the only release was a culture of drink and drugs. His figurative pieces with their urban vernacular titles – 'Not tonight', 'Don't let the little head rule the big head', and 'She wants your junk' – combined disturbing subject matter with a remarkable sensitivity to his material. Brownsword's former tutor Alison Britton has noted his remarkable 'ceramic articulacy' and at first it was employed to narrate tales of emotional confusion and despair.[3] He collaged an archaeology of broken shards, casts taken from scrap moulds, bits of kiln furniture, clay pipes and recycled sprigging to create punkish descendents of the figurine. These could be read on two levels – as sardonic social commentary and as a tender response to a material with a rich and complex history.

By the late 1990s Brownsword had tired of his figurative pieces, despite their positive reception. In 1999 he took up a fellowship at the European Ceramic Work Centre (EKWC) and in the creative atmosphere engendered by its visionary founder-director Xavier Toubes he began to work rather differently. As a ceramicist who writes, Brownsword has described his shift in interest with some eloquence.[4] Residencies generate stories of artistic progress and EKWC is no exception.[5] Brownsword experienced the kind of epiphanies that neatly condense ideas about creativity. One crucial turning point took place early in the residency during a return visit to Stoke. He saw factories being summarily demolished and he began to photograph these scenes of destruction, conscious that a whole industrial world was fast disappearing. He visited the City Museum at Stoke-on-Trent and the Gladstone Pottery Museum, and photographed old tools, defunct tile presses and print beds, and saggars and kiln props.

Neil Brownsword, glazed trivets with drip trays from 'Salvage Series', 2005.

Brownsword started to think about Stoke in more abstract terms – as a place that could be represented not by images of its people but by something subtler, by the interaction of the workforce and their materials. The Pottery towns are built on top of what is known in the trade as 'shraff', the waste from ceramic processes. The generous studio space at EKWC allowed Brownsword to begin an open-ended investigation into forming, decorating and firing clay. He began mixing clay intuitively and playing with all aspects of forming. Moulds took on a symbolic importance. He made an array of objects that when exhibited at EKWC on low plinths suggested the post-industrial landscapes and shraff-filled sub-strata of the Potteries area.

The ruination of a former hive of happy industry is at the heart of Brownsword's latest work. It combines research and filming in the Wedgwood factory and a body of new ceramics which we see in this exhibition. The project has in part been driven by the demands of a practice-based doctoral degree. But it is safe to say that it is a line of enquiry that Brownsword would have pursued anyway. He has become Stoke's Pindar through his documentation of the Wedgwood workforce and through installations that seek to dramatise the evanescent traces of processes that may in the future be performed by robots or, through inexorable globalization, by workers outside Europe.

In a great factory like Wedgwood perfection is demanded of the final product. As the first Josiah Wedgwood wrote to his partner Bentley, 'I will make machines out of men'. But Brownsword has chosen to honour the workforce by seeking out signs of human touch that occur inadvertently. These are to be found among marginal discarded things - in the props and spurs that are pinched by hand, in the strips of clay left after turning and in rejected wares thrown into the scrap trucks. Many bear the 'the momentary imprints of the operator's hand'.[6] Brownsword writes of his project: 'It became an obsession to use up every bit of unwanted clay in the hope that out of that nothingness something would be created.'

Much recent art is characterized by recycling and re-presenting what already exists. Take, for instance, Tracey Rowledge's gold-tooled binding for an early edition of James Joyce's *Ulysses*. The intense network of lines reproduce a ballpoint scribble on a piece of card that Rowledge found in the streets near her studio. Rowledge takes the most forlorn, casually abandoned scraps of paper – examples of what she calls 'a poignant moment in time' – and transmutes and reprocesses this material with high skill into permanence.[7] Similarly, the sculptor Rachel Whiteread is attentive to existing objects in a slightly different way. It is absence, not-thereness, which interests her and she goes to great lengths to cast negative spaces – the inside of a house, a room, a bath – in a variety of materials. No process could convey more clearly an iconography of memory and of loss. This kind of work is about process, about procedures for making art in difficult times, art in a full world.

Whiteread's sculpture is particularly close in spirit to Brownsword's recent researches. Casting has been a central activity in ceramics for centuries. But Brownsword concentrates on the negative spaces and on the discarded detritus of the casting process, recuperating them and using them as the basis for new work. For instance, traditionally, when a mould is damaged a cast is taken from it and then the cast's hollow cavity is filled with plaster – a process known as plaster-lining. The plaster supports and keeps the cast moist while it is being remodelled. Once repaired a new mould can be taken from the cast. But it is the obscure plaster-lining that Brownsword chooses to celebrate, revealing as it does a ghostly, blunted image of the cast object that it supported. Similarly Brownsword is fascinated by the detritus of semi-automated handle-making and by the chain-like clay structures that are created by a worker's repetitive action of removing the clay plug that forms in the opening of hand-poured moulds.

This is a form of memorializing that only an artist with a real knowledge of the industry and its skills could undertake. As a result, the men and women who are and were employed in the Potteries will be a privileged audience, even if the formal beauty of this exhibition will speak directly to a broad public. But Brownsword's traces, relics, and souvenirs impel us to think seriously about a fast-vanishing world of work . Brownsword is not drawn to the nostalgia that underpins much studio pottery. Instead he recaptures threatened skills through shards, fragments, and waste materials, and by revisiting a range of industrial processes. Relocation out of Europe and the old dream of the autogenic factory are the future for the ceramics industry, which is one reason why Brownsword's 'memory-work' is so important. But his work is important also because it expands our understanding of ceramics as an art form and as a protean, mysterious material.

1. Neil Brownsword's original video campaign was complemented by further interviews under the auspices of the National Electronic & Video Archive of the Crafts (NEVAC) in February / March 2004.
2. J. B. Priestley, *English journey: being a rambling but truthful account of what one man saw and heard and felt and thought during a journey through England during the autumn of the year 1933*, London: William Heinemann, 1934, pp. 205–34.
3. Alison Britton, *The fine line: revelations in clay*, in *Neil Brownsword*, City Museum and Art Gallery, Stoke-on-Trent, 1996.
4. See his doctoral thesis: Neil Brownsword, 'Action-reflection: examining the evolution of process and concept through personal ceramic art practice', 2006, Buckinghamshire Chilterns University College. This discusses exhibitions and projects subsequent to his EKWC residency that are not covered in this essay.
5. On residencies see pp. 138–43 below.
6. See Neil Brownsword, 'Action-reflection', chapter 5.
7. Tanya Harrod, 'Made by renunciation: the bindings of Tracey Rowledge', in: *Ripe*, London: Crafts Council, 2000, p. 48.

Written for the booklet accompanying 'Neil Brownsword: collaging history', an exhibition at the Potteries Museum & Art Gallery, Stoke-on-Trent, 23 April to 19 June 2005

Cold War craft

'Cold War Modern: design 1945–1970': exhibition at the Victoria & Albert Museum, 25 September 2008 to 11 January 2009

'Cold War Modern' is a brave show that looks at how art, design and architecture were shaped by the Cold War. It could have been a superficial exercise in retro-chic but instead its curators have unearthed remarkable material that illuminates the tensions and overlaps between East and West, as each sought to demonstrate a superior modernity. There are things you might expect to see – like a Trabant car and a section on the controversial 1953 competition for a monument to an unknown political prisoner, administered by the ICA with covert backing from the USA. There are oddities like the Soviet film *Cherry town* (1962) with music by Shostakovich, peopled with dancing young couples singing the praises of public housing. A fascinating section is devoted to the American National Exhibition held in Moscow in 1959, giving a sense of the lush post-war consumer culture that was put on display for Soviet citizens. There are also surprises like the small display of Czech glass and a wall hanging by the Polish tapestry artist Magdalena Abakanowicz.

'Cold War Modern' is a technologically driven show. Although it examines how men and women related to objects and got consumer satisfaction on both sides of the Iron Curtain, the space and the arms race are central to the visual focus of the show. But seeing the handful of examples of applied art included in 'Cold War Modern' reminded me of their strange position in Eastern Europe.

The lowly position of the crafts had its advantages. The genre was assumed to be ideas-free. The comprehensive show 'Czech Glass 1945–1980: design in an age of adversity' held at the Museum Kunstpalast in Düsseldorf in 2005 showed how artists turned to craft in the form of glass in the 1950s in order to avoid censorship. As the artist Karel Wünsch explained: 'Art was used as ideological propaganda for the regime. We were lucky that glass was useless for this purpose. We could make abstract drawings in glass because, for the regime, glass was not art ... It is wonderful that in any regime you can find a way for creation.'

Paradoxically, because Czech glass was given this freedom, it turned out to be useful to the Communist regime. The Czechs had already made a big splash with their glass display at the Brussels Expo '58 – René Roubíček showed a daring glass sculpture 'Mass–form–expression' while Jan Kotík, banned from exhibiting his paintings, contributed a large, highly idiosyncratic stained glass installation, 'Sun, water, air'. 'Cold War Modern' includes Stanislav Libenský and Jaroslava Brychtová's haunting 'Zoomorphic stones', inspired by cave paintings, also shown at Brussels. A year later the Russian authorities, worried about the impact of the American National Exhibition, turned to Prague for help. The result was a Moscow show of Czech glass so dazzling that it went some way to diverting attention from the American way of life on display on the other side of town.

This creative freedom had its limits. In 1970 Stanislav Libenský and Jaroslava Brychtová's 'The river of life' was a major attraction at the Osaka Expo. This monumental, cast glass sculpture represented flowing water, human forms – and the footprints of army boots. The artists' not so subtle allusion to the destruction of Czech hopes following the Prague Spring was noticed and they were both expelled from the Communist Party.

Jaroslava Brychtová and Stanislav Libenský, 'The river of life', glass sculpture on display at Expo '70, Osaka, 1970.

The relative freedom of Czech glass contrasted strikingly with the restraints that informed fine art. But there was more to it than that. Czech glass and Polish textiles were in advance of anything being done in the rest of Europe and North America. The well-illustrated catalogue of the first Lausanne Tapestry Biennale held in 1962 records the avant-garde contributions made by the five women exhibitors from Poland. Their work stood out because it pushed the boundaries of tapestry beyond the slightly folky, figurative approach inspired by Jean Lurçat favoured by almost all the other exhibitors.

Magdalena Abakanowicz went on to become world famous, but in that Lausanne show she was the first among equals together with Ada Kierzkowska, Jolanta Owidzka, Wojciech Sadley and Anna Śledziewska. These women transformed the discipline, paving the way for a new ambitiousness in textiles. In general, the marginality of craft worked to its advantage in Eastern

Europe. It was less vigorously policed because of hierarchies that go back to the renaissance. The whole story of craft behind the Iron Curtain, which might also include Hungarian ceramics of the 1960s, ought one day to be told.

Crafts, no. 215, November / December 2008

Sculpture in the home

'Sculpture in the Home: restaging a post-war initiative': an exhibition at Leeds Art Gallery, 2 October 2008 to 4 January 2009

'The sculptor must come out into the open, into the church and the market place, the town hall and the public park; his work must rise majestically above the agora, the assembled people'.[1] Herbert Read's hopeful vision for public sculpture just after the Second World War was, to an extent, realized in the 1950s. There were substantial sculpture commissions for the South Bank Exhibition of the Festival of Britain while the more enlightened local education authorities, Hertfordshire and Leicestershire in particular, spent heavily on art and craft, commissioning sculptures for individual schools. Sculptures were bought for the New Towns and the Arts Council organized open-air exhibitions of sculpture in collaboration with the London County Council in 1948, 1951, and 1954, and in 1949 with the Glasgow Corporation. These included British and Continental work, both academic and progressive. Perhaps the heterogeneous choice of sculptors lacked a sharply defined artistic position. Nonetheless, the exhibitions stood for humanistic values such as citizenship and the family and, in effect, replaced a public sculpture with commemorative, memorial or religious functions. The artist who came to exemplify these values most successfully was, of course, Henry Moore.

The temporary open-air shows at Battersea and Holland Park and at Kelvingrove Park in Glasgow were initiatives without precedent. But there were twentieth-century antecedents for another example of Arts Council patronage that sought to democratize the appreciation and consumption of sculpture. The four 'Sculpture in the Home' travelling exhibitions of 1946–7, 1950–1, 1953–4 and 1958–9 are partially reconstructed in a fascinating exhibition at the Henry Moore Institute in Leeds: 'Sculpture in the Home: restaging a post-war initiative'.

The Arts Council's decision to show sculpture in the context of a domestic interior, alongside textiles, furniture and wallpapers can be traced back to the room settings organized by the Arts & Crafts Exhibition Society (particularly the Domus section of the remarkable 1916 show organized at Burlington House by Henry Wilson). Fine and applied art were also exhibited together by the inter-war Red Rose Guild and during the 1920s by the British Institute of Industrial Art and in the privately financed 'Industrial Art in Relation to the Home' held at Dorland Hall, Lower Regent Street in 1933. But two exhibitions held at the Zwemmer Gallery in 1932 and 1933 come closest to the 'Sculpture in the Home' series. 'Room and Book' organized by Paul Nash, and a follow-up show 'Artists of To-day', included small sculptures by Henry Moore, Gertrude Hermes and Barbara Hepworth, all of whom were subsequently included in the 'Sculpture in the Home' series. Alongside were paintings by Paul Nash, Ben Nicholson, Eric Ravilious, and David Jones, textiles by Phyllis Barron, Dorothy Larcher, Enid Marx, Edinburgh Weavers and Ben Nicholson, pottery by Bernard Leach and William Staite Murray, lights by Best & Lloyd and furniture by Serge Chermayeff, Pel and Gordon Russell. These two remarkable exhibitions were not purely about sculpture. Instead they presented an integrated modernism – what Nash saw as 'a universal and definite twentieth-century style'.[2]

Although there was overlap between the Zwemmer Gallery exhibitions and the 'Sculpture in the Home' series, in important respects they were different. The little catalogues published by the Arts Council for 'Sculpture in the Home' did not list the accompanying furnishings. The ideal of 'combined arts' that inspired the Arts & Crafts movement and which continued to characterize inter-war British modernism was, therefore, lost. So too was the gaiety and idiosyncrasy of the Zwemmer shows. Like the Homes and Gardens pavilion at the 1951 South Bank Exhibition the 'Sculpture in the Home' shows were profoundly paternalistic, seeking to influence and elevate popular taste. On tour in the provinces 'Sculpture in the Home' was redisplayed in different configurations, sometimes with historic furniture, as at Wakefield Art Gallery in 1946, or, as at the Manchester Cotton Board in 1950, with spindly indoor plants and gay pictorial batiks by Michael O'Connell. But the default setting was 'contemporary' and relatively austere. It was the very antithesis of 'the rich full life' described by Richard Hoggart in his contemporaneous *The uses of literacy*. Hoggart wrote (with a mixture of nostalgia and unease) of the 'sprawling, highly ornamented, rococo extravagance' of working-class taste, with its 'plastic gewgaws and teapots shaped like country cottages'.[3]

We get a sense of the domestic settings proposed by the 'Sculpture in the Home' exhibitions from a few surviving photographs and drawings and from the lists of furniture and textiles provided by the Council of Industrial Design. The furnishings used came from the Council's Stock List drawn up

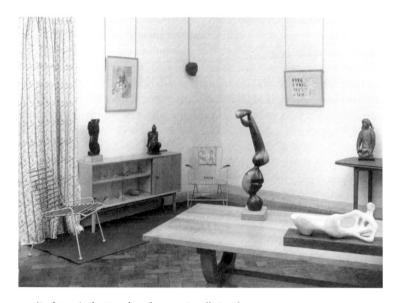

'Sculpture in the Home' London 1950, installation shot.

for the Festival of Britain. The emphasis was on 'simple lines, careful choice of timber and fabrics, attention to finish and detailing and generally a decent well-bred elegance'.[4] The Henry Moore Institute and Robert Burstow, the author of a useful accompanying pamphlet, have made a valiant attempt at recreation – finding sculptures included in the original shows (above all those of 1950 and 1954) and deploying them with suitable furniture by Robin Day for Hille, W. H. Russell for Gordon Russell and Neil Morris for H. Morris & Co Ltd.[5]

But even if taste at all levels was gradually changing in the 1950s as banisters were boxed in, panelled doors covered with hardboard and cornices and ceiling roses removed, the 'well-bred' modern furniture propagandized by the CoID was relatively expensive and so too were small sculptures. Those shown in the original 'Sculpture in the Home' exhibitions were priced between £250 and 10 guineas. Still more expensive pieces, like Henry Moore's 'Family group' and his 'Rocking chair', were loaned from wealthy collectors like Robert Sainsbury and from Moore himself. So while the exhibitions were well attended and did something to publicize younger artists, and in particular younger women artists like Hetta Crouse, Helen Meyer, and Rosemary Young, they did not succeed in finding a popular audience for progressive small-scale sculpture.

A footnote to this would surely be Colin Painter's equally brave attempt to domesticate sculpture in his 'Close encounters of the art kind' project of 2001–2. Colin Painter positioned sculptures by Tania Kovats, Langlands & Bell, Sarah Lucas, Richard Wilson, and Bill Woodrow in six 'ordinary' households who were asked to live with each sculpture for a month. In the average home the striking objects selected by Painter were invariably rendered invisible as just another knick-knack. As his documentation revealed, the sculptures were only properly recuperated at the Victoria & Albert Museum in an exhibition that chronicled the project. The project underlined the truism that the home is often a dangerous environment – for individuals, but also for things. The 'Sculpture in the Home' exhibitions, however, chose to set aside the messy reality of day-to-day living. As a result, the sparse, muted room settings reconfigured at Leeds seem like an exotic utopian experiment.

1. Quoted (at p.135) in Richard Calvocoressi, 'Public sculpture in the 1950s', in Sandy Nairne & Nicholas Serota (ed.), *British sculpture in the twentieth century*, London: Whitechapel Art Gallery, 1981.
2. J. E. Barton, *Room and book*, London: Zwemmer Gallery, 1932, p.4.
3. Richard Hoggart, *The uses of literacy* [1957], Harmondsworth: Penguin Books, 1958, p.143–4.
4. Quoted (at p.174) in Scott Oram, 'Constructing contemporary' in Susie McKellar & Penny Sparke (ed.), *Interior design and identity*, Manchester: Manchester University Press, 2004.
5. Robert Burstow, *The 'Sculpture in the home' exhibitions: reconstructing the home and family in postwar Britain*, Leeds: Henry Moore Institute, 2008.

The Burlington Magazine, vol.150, no.1269, December 2008

Down among the gamers

'Game On: the history and culture of videogames': an exhibition at the Barbican Gallery, London, 16 May to 15 September 2002

Can a computer game be beautiful? Are games an unrecognized art form? Should we know and revere the names of games designers, artists, musicians, and programmers? The answer to these questions posed by the Barbican curators must be a resounding 'no' – but that does not prevent 'Game On' from being a fascinating exhibition.

Beauty comes and goes rather early in 'Game On' in the form of the first computer game ever played on a monitor. *SpaceWar!* was invented in 1962 by an MIT researcher named Steve Russell and was played by computer scientists on a giant mini-computer called a PDP-I. Little white spaceships dash about a black screen avoiding a white cross at the centre. This is a game that looks as pure as an animated Suprematist painting. *SpaceWar!* is extremely difficult to play and here the unique atmosphere at this exhibition becomes apparent.

You will find yourself among friends. Indeed, you will feel part of a community, in effect logged on. Never mind that it is a community of boys and men, with the men in particular looking peaky and unwashed. They could not be more helpful and friendly, surprised perhaps to find themselves away from their lonely bedrooms where they spend nights and days gaming on and off-line, reading cyberpunk novels and dreaming of virtual girlfriends. It is not an entirely male audience. The first friend I made was a white-haired American lady gamer with whom I played *Pong* and who later tried to explain the mysteries of *Myst*. Anyway, it was reassuring to find that hardly anyone seemed able to play *SpaceWar!*

The first part of 'Game On' is devoted to historic games – which in this world takes us back only to the 1970s and 1980s. Early arcade games like *Space invaders* and *Donkey Kong* seem unbelievably innocent today. Playing *Donkey Kong* we first encounter an under-pixelated little character called Jumpman, the *fons et origo* of Super Mario. Today he has been plumped out with sophisticated 3D graphics but there was much collective nostalgic sighing over his low-resolution earlier self, just as everyone was touched by the clunky early games consoles – the black and white tacky plastic of the Magnavox Odyssey and the fake wood veneer of the Atari 2600. These objects still seem like lovable toys. They were given or thrown away when we became older but now are unbearably evocative of a time and place. Sadly however, as far as I was concerned, this Proustian encounter with things past was a high point.

Much depends on what is defined as a game. Zapping small moving objects, bouncing along avoiding sudden drops and small beasties, playing simulated ball games, or racing on a pretend track – these comprised the classic early games. They could be played endlessly but they had a pleasing take-it-or-leave-it quality. Failed to reach Level Four? Throw down the controls and leave the room! More recent games may be infinitely more sophisticated but they lack that irresponsible magic. What is now needed is a games reform movement, to restore a computing version of truth to materials to the games world.

The contemporary game has introduced several very unplayful elements. These include 3D cinematic realism, imposed narrative, and moral smugness, reminding us of the embarrassing fact that a high proportion of gamers are reasonably well-off grown-ups. For instance, the employment of expensive 3D animation makes games production very expensive. It is also inherently ungamelike. Just a few moments playing *Tomb raider* makes one long to

In the beginning: gamers playing *Pong*, the world's second commercial video game, mid-1970s.

be watching a feature film. What a lot of work it is manoeuvering Lara Croft round those snowy Mayan caverns. But at least Lara allows us an element of fantasy. She resembles a toy, albeit an eroticized one, and although she brandishes two pistols there isn't too much blood. But *Max Payne*, an exquisitely rendered wireframe 'undercover cop with nothing to lose', takes us into an unbelievably drab virtual world of underground car-parks, bathed in excessive amounts of gore.

The old games were rather simple – based on completing tasks speedily. But so-called adventure games, resource management games, and, worst of all, the numerous role-playing games are predicated on complex narratives that aspire to educate and improve the player. They are also unbelievably time-consuming as players get to know improbable worlds full of kitsch neo-classical or gothick architecture (*Myst*) or struggle to 'develop their characters' (*Asheron's call*). Responsibilities are shouldered as players decide where to put the sewage system (*SimCity*), or whether to allow Jed to date Jeff, or whether Gail's budget will stretch to a new cooker (*The Sims*). In Japan the role-playing element appears to have got completely out of hand. Over-worked Japanese schoolboys have no time to meet girls and prefer dating games like *Tokimeki memorial* to the real thing. The dating games bossily teach that the wrong sorts of interests will result in rejection. Those who succeed are rewarded with the softest of soft porn.

What a funny old postmodern world we live in. Of course, games are of huge interest to the military. At the Institute for Creative Technologies the

US army has enlisted the talents of the games development industries in a five-year project to advance the state of immersive training simulation. This will enable soldiers to 'experience the sights, sounds and circumstances they will encounter in real-world scenarios'. Meanwhile the September 11 terrorists probably honed their skills with 'flight sims' like Microsoft *Flight simulator*. Game on, indeed.

The Spectator, 8 June 2002

Three-dimensional scribble syndrome

'Autonomatic': exhibition at Metropolitan Works, London, March 2007

In the early days of cinema crowds flocked to see pictures that literally moved, in which people juggled, danced, marched, and sneezed. Historians of cinema categorize these early snippets of film as 'the cinema of attractions' – no narrative was necessary because the wonder lay in the technology. In his book *Snap to grid: a user's guide to digital arts, media and cultures* Peter Lunenfeld coins the term 'media of attractions' to describe many of the artefacts of new media. They enchant us because of their novelty, just like those early films. Thus, in the field of digitally-led design and craft much of the interest centres on its arcane technologies. These include data capturing and its artistic transformation – by softwares and by rapid prototyping machines and by computer numeric controlled milling machines. Novelty underlines much of what I've come to call the '3D scribble syndrome' – in which part of the fun derives from an understanding of the complex digital history of the object. Thus, the medium becomes the message or, more accurately, the narrative.

The syndrome was much in evidence at a fascinating exhibition held in March at Metropolitan Works by Autonomatic, the 3D digital production research group at University College, Falmouth. Take, for instance, the work of Tavs Jørgensen. He is a trained ceramicist, formerly a production thrower at Dartington Pottery and he showed some handsome glass bowls that were pleasing enough. It was, however, their backstory that made them seem extraordinary. Jørgensen used a tool called Microscribe that records the shape of an object and translates this information into a CAD file. It is normally used for reverse engineering and industrial inspection. But Jørgensen employed Microscribe as a freehand tool to draw circles in the air. These digital lines were then translated into a laser-cut collar of stainless steel that in turn was placed in a kiln with a disc of glass on top. The glass slumped over

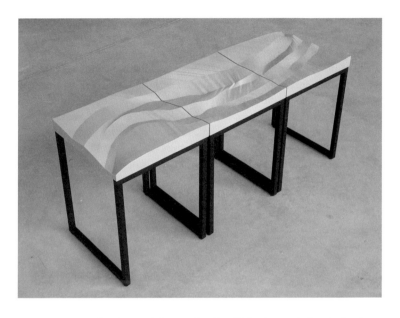

Tavs Jørgensen, 'Motion seats': three stools with milled resin seats designed using the Shapehand TM motion capture glove, 2006.

the steel collar to create a bowl whose irregular edge carried the memory of Jørgensen's original freehand 'drawing'. Is it important to know the design genesis of these bowls? The answer seems to be 'yes'. An understanding of the convoluted creative path taken by Jørgensen adds an undeniable interest to the final object. Similarly Autonomatic's patterned tea towels look attractive but they become even more desirable when we learn that the patterns are derived from motion-capturing the movements of a hand drying up a cup. It is as if digital practice has its own iconography and its own materiality.

This is very much the view of the American digital artist Casey Reas who argues that softwares should be regarded as materials with different qualities, like oak as compared to walnut, or rigid as opposed to flexible. Do we relate to softwares in this emotional way? The work of Paul B. Davis, recently on show at Seventeen (17 Kingsland Road, E2), suggests we do. He handcrafts obsolete video games cartridges to create large, projected wall pieces. In 'Five in one' Davis presents five hacks of Nintendo's *Super Mario* that use the game's basic building blocks to create video art-works. One airy piece is made up of the clouds that float through Mario-land, another shows all the constituent clunky icons of the game in fast-moving psychedelic rows, a third gives us a solitary Mario – 'Now I just stand here silently among data that grows cold'. The reactions of other visitors to the gallery were ecstatic – they were immersed in a nostalgic technological sublime.

To craft and recycle old data requires a sophisticated understanding of programming. But a digital vernacular can be found in the online world of Second Life – 'a 3D world where everyone you see is a real person and every place you visit is built by people just like you'. Here we find Second Lifers working to make all manner of ornamental objects that have been described as a form of digital folk craft. There is a commercial side to Second Life – you can buy objects, clothes, and houses – but mostly people are working for free. Second Life is not notable for elevated taste but it is full of handicraft made by true amateurs, putting in long hours, provoked into creativity by the media of attractions at its most accessible and seductive.

Crafts, no. 207, July/August 2007

Why don't we hate Etsy?

I used to give a lecture on the 1920s and 1930s entitled 'Why do we hate the crafts?' The answer was simple – they did not make economic sense in an age of multiple production. The great designers of the Arts & Crafts movement were caught between the cheaper processes offered by industry and sweatshops and the 'Dear Emily' amateurs who could lavish unlimited time on their work. By the 1930s making things by hand came, in any case, to seem morally reprehensible. As Herbert Read declared in his design polemic *Art and industry*, handwork lacked 'economic and practical justification'. And for Read in 1934 the economic law was 'absolute and healthy'. But the distaste that figures like Read felt for the inter-war craft movement also flowed from the fact that craft objects were unstable, unsatisfactory commodities with a tendency to confuse categories. The inter-war crafts were rich in objects that hovered between commodities and gifts and which looked like necessities physically – in the form of simple bowls or plainly made furniture – but in fact operated more like luxuries.

This taxonomic confusion had not gone away, as we discover when exploring Etsy, the online marketplace for buying and selling things handmade. Etsy is an enormous virtual craft fair which charges makers 20 cents to illustrate an object and which takes 3.5 per cent of the final sale price. So far most Etsy makers (and buyers) are North American, but this is changing. The site is wonderfully easy to navigate with items grouped under obvious head-ings like ceramics, glass, furniture, etc. But it is also searchable under a range of tag words – from 'spirit doll' to 'fibre craft' to an all-embracing 'everything else'. Visitors to the site can also shop by colour and can even commission a bespoke piece by going to the site's Alchemy space.

But the fact that there have been articles in *BusinessWeek*, the *Financial Times*, *Forbes*, *The New York Times* and *The Boston Globe* charting the success of Etsy does not mean that the financial establishment has embraced 'craft-ism'. Etsy is of interest to financial journalists because it has attracted large amounts of venture capital, not least because of the charm and charisma of Rob Kalin, Etsy's youthful founder. And Kalin is peddling a DIY dream that clearly goes down well with Etsy users who are 96 per cent female and pre-dominantly in their early thirties. The site comes across as wholesomely ide-alistic – on a mission to reconnect makers with buyers and enable people to earn a living making things. 'Our vision is to build a new economy and pre-sent a better choice: Buy, Sell, and Live Handmade.'

Etsy, therefore, does everything it can to encourage a sense of a crafting community by endorsing blogs and links to social networking sites and by setting up forums and chat rooms. It has been a huge success – with a mem-bership of more than 900,000 and a turnover of $6 million in April 2008 alone. Its rapid expansion has been linked to all kinds of virtuous causes – from environmental concerns to a desire to bypass Walmart globalization and, perhaps, most important of all, to our deep-seated need to connect around a virtual village green.

But, in fact, environmentally friendly craft is better represented in *Make* magazine, whose articles concentrate on heavy-duty grunge-tech recyling projects. *Make* products are worlds away from the goods that are traded on Etsy which, overwhelmingly, can be categorized as giftware – or even clutter. Indeed, many of the items on offer recall the home industries movement of the nineteenth century. But instead of poker-work, chip-carving and quill-work we find handmade soap, glass beads, and knitted iPod cosies.

Why don't we hate Etsy craft? Etsy rhetoric exploits a dream, that of giv-ing up a day job to pursue an autonomous life of craft. Thus, the archetypal Etsy object – even when crudely made or merely customized – suggests in-dividual freedom, the ownership of tools and a world of unalienated labour. It is all a delusion, of course, a perfect example of what Marxists call 'false consciousness'. Although firmly embedded in capitalism at its most venture-some, Etsy simultaneously offers a latter-day gift economy, promising dura-ble personal relations in a world where these appear to be in short supply.

A secret history of clay

'A Secret History of Clay: from Gauguin to Gormley': exhibition at Tate Liverpool,
28 May to 30 August 2004

'A Secret History of Clay: from Gauguin to Gormley' is intended to be ground-breaking, to change the way in which we look at art. It challenges the neglect of clay, in particular fired, glazed clay, by art critics and art historians. It is a hopeful exhibition which argues that artists are now turning to ceramic's messy materiality in reaction against the increasing virtuality of our digital culture. In this brave new world Grayson Perry's 2003 Turner Prize, bestowed upon a room full of pots, signifies a change of heart, an abandonment of the fustian hierarchies that have marginalized ceramics. But 'A Secret History of Clay', for all its polemical intent, tells a rather familiar story in which clay-work made by artists is seen as inherently more interesting than anything made by men and women who put ceramics at the centre of their artistic endeavour. Studio pottery, an artistic discipline born in the early part of the twentieth century, is almost excluded. 'A Secret History' includes eighty male artists and a handful of women – no Ruth Duckworth, no Viola Frey, no Anne Kraus, no Maria Martinez, no Beatrice Wood, no Betty Woodman, no Ladi Kwali, no Gwyn Hanssen Pigott, no Dionyse Carmen, no Lucie Rie, no Alison Britton, no Carol McNicoll. These names are probably unfamiliar – because the real secret history is that of studio pottery where women rank as equals. Nonetheless, despite its essential conservatism 'A Secret History' is a pleasurable exhibition. Although we may have seen much of this work in specialist books, artists' forays into clay, and indeed into any kind of applied art, are invariably excluded from art historical discourse.

The show opens with 'Fountain', Marcel Duchamp's famous ready-made of 1917. To be quite accurate, what we see is a version of 1964, one of several authorized by Duchamp after the lost 'original' of 1917. For Simon Groom, the exhibition's organizer, 'Fountain' encapsulates a central problem. It is one of the most recognizable icons of twentieth century art. It is also made of ceramic, a fact that Groom believes has been 'conceptualised out of existence'. While it is true that for most people Duchamp's urinal is not primarily seen as a specifically ceramic work, there are more important reasons for making 'Fountain' a curtain raiser to 'A Secret History of Clay'. The show is dominated by vessels of various kinds, revealing that artists find the medium's family of shapes engaging at a deep level. In effect jugs, platters, and vases operate very much like ready-mades, offering a repertoire of familiar forms – as Kenneth Silver once pointed out in an illuminating essay on Picasso. Ceramics therefore have the capacity to act as inspirational *objets trouvés*, ripe for re-representation.

Making pots also once stood for a radical anti-academicism, an alternative to the stranglehold of easel painting and sculptures perched on pedestals. In 'A Secret History of Clay' this daring rejection of mainstream art is made manifest by Paul Gauguin's haunting hand-built vases, by a monumental gesturally decorated pot and platter by the Danish artist Thorvald Bindesbøll, and the Fauves' engagement with tin-glaze decoration in the form of some glowing colouristic experiments by Georges Rouault and Maurice de Vlaminck. Much of this exhibition turns on anti-academicism and its perils. Gauguin did not do well out of his foray into ceramics and was bitter about the way in which the public appeared to prefer safer kinds of experimentation in the pure forms of Auguste Delaherche's handsome neo-oriental pots. Matisse, weakly represented in 'A Secret History', learned new colouristic freedoms and new ways of organizing space from decorating pots but his ceramics were and remain little discussed. Like Matisse, Picasso used ceramics to investigate painterly and sculptural space, returning with playful magnificence to ideas first addressed in his domestic scale sculpture 'The glass of absinthe' (1914). But, notoriously, the post-war ceramics of Picasso and of Joan Miró were summarily dismissed by an institutionalized avant-garde led by North American critics and curators.

Gravitas is evidently an issue. Serious play is hard to capture for all time. Take the ceramic activities of the CoBrA group in the 1950s. Ironically, the energy comes over best in photographs – of impromptu outdoor exhibitions, of Asger Jorn driving his scooter over a bed of clay to create a mural. The outcomes look a bit stranded at Tate Liverpool, even if the intense chaotic quality of CoBrA ceramics stood for everything that was lacking in the encroaching technocracy and warrior politics of the Cold War. But perhaps it is clay's protean identity that has proved problematic. 'A Secret History' includes expressively modelled sculptures by Lucio Fontana, reminding us that when Fontana showed Brancusi one of his polychrome ceramics in 1937 he was told that glazed, fired clay could not be sculpture. And indeed at that date it must have seemed the antithesis of direct carving or of truth to materials. Fontana's extraordinary ceramic output is only becoming as well known as his famous cut and slashed canvases because of the diminution of those surprisingly persistent formalist standards.

'A Secret History' brilliantly registers the messy fluidity of clay and the way in which it demands our performative engagement. Midway through we encounter three great piles of oil clay, 'Phase of nothingness' by the Japanese artist Nobuo Sekine, there for our pleasure, inviting our touch. The exhibition does not include the more conventional modern Japanese masters of ceramics – Hamada Shoji or even Rosanjin – but demonstrates that even at their most iconoclastic Japanese artists possess a heightened sensitivity to

Jim Melchert, 'Changes' performance piece, Amsterdam, 1972.

the medium. But the unforgettable image of Kazuo Shiraga naked and wrestling with a pile of clay in 1955 is matched by the American Jim Melchert's haunting video of his 'Changes' performance piece (1972) in which he and his companions dipped their heads in liquid clay and sat about while it dried into a series of melancholy masks. Such activities suggest that ceramics demand visceral commitment; another video of 2002 records a day spent by the young artists Roger Hiorns, Mark Titchner, and Gary Webb in a studio fighting it out with a ton of clay.

In a final underlit space 'A Secret History of Clay' addresses the spectre that haunts our appreciation of ceramics – that of a Victorian twilight zone of figurines and garnitures, of cake stands and of dusty souvenirs half-glimpsed behind glass-fronted cabinets. A job lot of Victorian furniture ironically frames ceramics by Cindy Sherman, Jeff Koons, Francis Upritchard, and James Turrell. As an environment it works well for Upritchard's array of car-boot sale stoneware to which have been added sinister animalier lids. Edmund de Waal's modernist variant on the eighteenth-century porcelain room looks less happy in this setting and it is too tasteful to do justice to Grayson Perry, Sherman, and Koons's historicizing exuberance. It is an odd finale, a return of the repressed that reminds us that Freud's 1917 essay 'The uncanny' is now required reading for curators.

The exhibition's subtitle – 'from Gauguin to Gormley' – suggests a visit to Antony Gormley's 'Field' on the floor below. It is one of several versions, this one made in North America. It is always moving to contemplate Gormley's sea of little manikins but, a rarely raised question this, what about the workers? 'Field' in all its variants, is made by, typically, co-opted OAPs, housewives, and children. But they are not there to express themselves, rather they are given the chance to experience the pleasures of mass production by hand. So 'Field' is almost an anomaly in the context of 'A Secret History of Clay'. It is not as humane as it looks and it is entirely remote from the anarchic, spontaneous engagements that characterize the rest of this thought-provoking exhibition.

Draft of a review published in the *Times Literary Supplement*, 23 July 2004

Bernard Leach as an artist and designer

'Bernard Leach: concept & form': an exhibition at the National Museum & Gallery, Cardiff, 10 July to 10 August 2003

This exhibition gathers together over 180 pots, drawings, etchings, furniture designs, and jewellery by the twentieth century's most famous studio potter, Bernard Leach.[1] Curated by Emmanuel Cooper, it coincides with the publication of Cooper's biography *Bernard Leach: life & work*, which gives us a very full sense of Leach's day-to-day existence, his hopes and aspirations, his complex family arrangements, and his gradual rise to fame after the Second World War, culminating in his appointment as a Companion of Honour six years before his death in 1979.[2] Yet as a biographical subject Leach remains elusive. This is not for lack of material; Cooper has made full use of Leach's extensive archive now housed at the Crafts Study Centre at the University for the Creative Arts. But anyone using this archive will immediately be struck by its hermetic quality and will need to face the problem of providing a context for Leach's artistic activity, which from 1911 was primarily focused on a new visual discipline, that of studio pottery.

The studio pottery movement has not yet been integrated into histories of twentieth-century design or of fine art. In part this is because the movement, as it developed, became a victim of its own success. After the Second World War, inspired as much as anything by Leach's extraordinarily influential *A potter's book* (1940 and many reprintings), scores of young men and women turned to ceramics. To take up pottery in the 1950s was one of the pleasures of peace, a compensatory activity after years of war. By the late

1960s middle-class potters, mostly art-school trained, dominated a craft renaissance that culminated in the setting up of the Crafts Advisory Committee in 1971. Potters had their own society, the Craftsmen Potters Association (founded 1957) and their own magazine, *Ceramic Review* (founded 1970). To a large extent, the discipline turned in on itself.

But in about 1911, when Leach attended a *raku-yaki* party in Toyko and decided to learn more about ceramics, to become a potter was an unusual choice. It was also inherently radical, being part of a more general attempt by young artists both to confront the challenge of modernity and to distance themselves from academic art. At that early date studio pottery needs to be seen in the context of other craft-based activities such as direct carving in stone and cutting bold woodblocks to print paper or textiles. In part, making technologically imperfect pots was an anti-modern response to new processes and new materials, to what D.H. Lawrence called 'the tragedy of ugliness that appeared to characterize the industrialized world'. Pottery came to stand for a species of elemental simplicity. Thus the potter's wheel was no mere tool but rather an instrument for experiencing what Leach's rival in the inter-war years, William Staite Murray, called 'rhythmic plastic growth and form'[4] in which a pot was 'born not made'.[5]

Bernard Leach's background was privileged and colonial. He was discouraged from becoming an artist, but attended the Slade from 1903 to 1905, then unwillingly worked for the Hong Kong and Shanghai Bank, breaking free in 1908 to study at the London School of Art where he was taught by Frank Brangwyn. At Cardiff there is a touching self-portrait painted in 1904, when Leach was 17, in which he presents himself as a Pater-esque young aesthete. A range of Leach's early drawings, water-colours, and etchings reveal his debt to Brangwyn but also suggest careful study of artists like Samuel Prout and John Sell Cotman. In those early years he was friendly with the painter Henry Lamb and attended the meetings and exhibitions of Vanessa Bell's Friday Club.

In 1909, inspired by memories of early childhood years spent in Japan with his grandparents, Leach set sail for Yokahama, reaching Tokyo in April. His plan was to teach etching. Through some serendipitous introductions he made contact with an elite group of artists, writers, and thinkers based in Tokyo and there he absorbed avant-garde European developments at long range. He also began writing for English-language publications in Japan, arguing for a combination of Eastern and Western values that he believed would spark off 'the greatest development in the history of human society'. This kind of thinking was not unusual in the first decades of the twentieth century and could have led Leach in any number of directions. Indeed, Leach spent some time in China, under the spell of Alfred Westharp, a more sophisticated East/West synthesizer who was later to run an experimental board-

Bernard Leach, Shoji Hamada, and Sono Matsumoto at the opening
of Leach and Hamada's joint kiln, Mashiko, Japan, 1934.

ing school in northern China, where aristocratic students wore shorts and
were encouraged to reject materialistic Western values, do handicrafts, and
play an active part in running the school.[6]

In the end pottery emerged as the best symbolic medium for Leach's
ideas. 'Concept & form' includes examples of the uncertain experimentation of the early years and the powerful, if uneven, work made on his return
to England in 1920. The finest of these first pieces made at his pottery in St
Ives, Cornwall are massive slipware platters inspired by Thomas Toft, but
decorated with haunting images culled from his years in the East – elaborate
well-heads, sketchy willow trees, horses eating seaweed on the beach, the
Tree of Life. He also experimented with stoneware, often carving patterns
and images through slip in a fashion inspired by Chinese Cizhou wares. But
Leach soon came to feel that his art was undervalued in England, a complaint
that retrospectively seems unjustified. Leach, his rival William Staite Murray

and Leach's pupils Katharine Pleydell-Bouverie, Norah Braden, and Michael Cardew exhibited frequently and were flatteringly reviewed. The economics of their situation did not really add up – running a pottery is a good deal more expensive than painting domestic-sized pictures or even carving relatively small pieces of sculpture. Nonetheless, their work was purchased by adventurous collectors.

What is striking is how often studio pottery was compared to sculpture, particularly in the late 1920s and early 1930s. More research needs to be done in this area but at least one patron, George Eumorfopoulos, bought early oriental pots, directly carved sculpture and modern stoneware pottery in abundance.[7] Critics, too, frequently made the connection between modern pots and modern sculpture. As Herbert Read pointed out, thrown pottery exemplified 'pure form' to a marked degree. Charles Marriott, the inter-war art critic of *The Times*, pointed out as late as 1943 that there were no British artists to compare with Brancusi, but 'pottery is, precisely, abstract sculpture'.[8]

Ironically Leach's most convincing monumental pots were made after the Second World War, many thrown by William Marshall to his designs. The technical problems that had beset his pottery in its early days were also resolved, in part by his son David. There is a fine array of this late work at Cardiff, exemplifying the 'Sung standard' that Leach came to prefer over other ceramic influences. But post-war sculpture in its various phases had little in common with studio pottery either visually or philosophically. A moment of synchronicity was over. And in the wake of Edward Said's transformative study *Orientalism*, Leach's oft repeated, essentializing identification of a passive East and a dynamic West has come under hostile scrutiny.[9] But the pots, especially the more awkwardly made inter-war examples, still stand for a strain of avant-gardism that for a few brief years put craftwork at the heart of English modernism.

Unfortunately 'Concept & form' does not include the rich holdings of Leach's pots in Japan which include pieces made on an important return visit paid by Leach to Japan in 1934–5.[10] These reveal that Leach worked with greater fluency and confidence with the support of Japanese artisans and technicians. He also experimented with a variety of media in Japan, designing furniture, textiles, and room settings. Leach disliked British 'Cotswold' furniture. An interesting, curvilinear three-legged chair made to Leach's design in about 1918 was included in 'Concept & form''s first venue, Penlee House Gallery & Museum, and a couple of intriguing drawings of Chinese-inspired tables may be seen at Cardiff.

1. 'Bernard Leach: concept & form' was toured by Penlee House Gallery & Museum to the Brunei Gallery, SOAS, London and to the National Museum & Gallery, Cardiff until August 31, 2003.

2. Emmanuel Cooper, *Bernard Leach: life & work*, London: Yale University Press 2003.

3. D. H. Lawrence, 'Nottingham and the mining country' (1929) in Alasdair Clayre (ed.), *Nature & Industrialisation*, Oxford: Oxford University Press, 1977, p. 389.

4. W. Staite Murray, 'Pottery from the artist's point of view', *Artwork*, vol. 11, no. 4, 1925, p. 201.

5. See Tanya Harrod, *The crafts in Britain in the 20th century*, London: Yale University Press, 1999, p. 38.

6. See Gabriele Goldfuss, 'Les tribulations d'un sinophile dans la Chine républicaine: le musicien et pedagogue Alfred Westharp', *Etudes Chinoises*, vol. 12, no. 2, 1993; Guy S. Alitto, *The last Confucian: Liang Shu-ming and the Chinese dilemma of modernity*, Los Angeles: University of California Press, 1987.

7. See Malcolm Haslam, 'Freedom beyond sculpture: early collectors of English studio pottery', *Country Life*, 5 June 1986, pp. 1605–7; Helen Long, 'The unobtrusive collector', *The Antique Collector*, September 1991, pp. 88–91; Penelope Curtis, 'Barbara Hepworth and the avant-garde of the 1920s', in Penelope Curtis and Alan G. Wilkinson (ed.), *Barbara Hepworth: a retrospective*, London: Tate Gallery, 1994.

8. Charles Marriott, *British handicrafts*, London: The British Council 1943, p. 33.

9. See Edmund de Waal, *Bernard Leach*, London: Tate Gallery, 1998.

10. For work by Leach in Japanese collections, see Oliver Watson's exemplary catalogue *Bernard Leach: potter and artist*, London: Crafts Council, 1997.

The Burlington Magazine, vol. 145, August 2003

Heroes with feats of clay

'Ray Finch and Winchcombe Pottery': exhibition at Contemporary Ceramics, 7 Marshall Street, London, 1 to 29 September 1990; 'Ewen Henderson: sculptural and other pots': exhibition at Galerie Besson, London, 5 September to 14 October 1990

In 1953 the Edinburgh Festival saw the first staging of T. S. Eliot's *The confidential clerk*. In one of the oddest passages in an admittedly curious play, the wealthy financier Sir Claude Mulhammer starts talking about art and his fondness for paintings and sculpture. But he goes on to argue, at great poetic length, that his real love is ceramics. In his view it is the greatest of the visual arts:

> 'Most people think of china or porcelain
> As merely for use, or for decoration –
> In either case, an inferior art.
> For me, they are neither 'use' nor 'decoration' –
> That is, decoration as a background for living;
> For me they are life itself. To be among such things,
> If it is an escape, is escape into living,
> Escape from a sordid world to a pure one.'

Eliot was not being merely eccentric or whimsical when he set down this speech in praise of pottery. He was, after all, a director at Faber & Faber, which had published Bernard Leach's pioneering *A potter's book* as well as the great series of monographs on oriental ceramics edited by Sir Harry Garner. Eliot, in 1953, was in fact merely reiterating the pre-war modernist consensus that had led Herbert Read to hail pottery as 'pure art ... plastic art in its most abstract essence'. In the 1930s ceramics were often compared to abstract sculpture and it did not seem strange that the potter William Staite Murray exhibited alongside Barbara Hepworth and Ben Nicholson in the exclusively abstract exhibitions run by the 7 & 5 Society, a group of avant-garde artists.

Ironically Eliot's play coincided with the end of an informed interest in ceramics in the art world. After the Second World War large numbers of practically minded men and women, inspired by Leach's *A potter's book*, decided to lead the simple life. Ceramics became a mass movement stronger on idealism than on aesthetics. Throughout the 1950s and into the 1960s and 1970s, it made sound economic sense to produce large quantities of handmade stoneware for everyday use and in the process a whole tradition of non-functional ceramics, from Tang figurines to Art Pottery, was set aside. Only a very few production potters were able to combine genuine beauty with utility. Meanwhile in the London art schools there was an opposition camp of potters working sculpturally – but they were undone by the brown mugs. A serious critical audience had disappeared and writing about contemporary ceramics ceased to be on the art critic's agenda.

The fine art world has continued to take a narrow view of the potter's role. Potters should make proper pots rather like Ray Finch who is now showing at Contemporary Ceramics in Marshall Street. Finch is indeed one of the most distinguished of the post-war functional potters, heading a team at Winchcombe in Gloucestershire which, for example, supplies Cranks with their immensely worthy tableware.

His present show consists of big pieces – great bowls, jugs and platters. It is handsome stuff but Finch would be the first to agree that his pots do not quite have the mysterious presence that activated the work of Michael Cardew or Staite Murray before the war. lt is undoubtedly part of that tradition, and technically it is probably of a higher quality, but it does not cry out to be compared with painting and sculpture.

Nonetheless, some contemporary pottery needs to be seen in a fine art context. Ewen Henderson is showing some twenty pieces at Galerie Besson, ranging from tall vase shapes to small tea-bowls, forms that owe more to a landscape of megaliths than to vessels. The immediate effect is of a group of objects, remote in time and geography, that activate the space around them just like the best sort of sculpture. Like good sculpture, they have a multi-

Ewen Henderson, 'Sculptural and other pots', Galerie Besson, London, 1990.

plicity of viewpoints. They demand to be studied at length and each view – all multilateral surfaces and dark voids – yields up new surprises.

But one can only push the sculptural analogy so far. It would be idle to pretend that it is possible to come cold to work like this – without any knowledge of the history of ceramics – any more than it is possible to appreciate contemporary art without some background knowledge. The tea-bowls, for instance, allude to a particular Japanese premise that a seemingly humble object can give a powerful aesthetic charge and should appeal to both sight and touch. Nearly all potters espouse a modernist version of *Japonisme* simply because Japan has a tradition of meditating on ceramics with unusual seriousness. Again our appreciation of the landscape surface of Henderson's work is heightened by some understanding of ceramic technique, in particular the risky magical transformation which takes place during the firing process.

There may be yet another sticking point for many people. Western art, despite the hiccup of abstraction, is firmly rooted in literature and narrative. Most pots have no easily understood narrative content. They are, as Herbert Read was aware, marvellous examples of pure form. This self-contained remoteness, which Eliot's Sir Claude found such a challenge, has come to appear problematic. There is a famous story about a student talking to the eminent designer David Pye. The student said that ceramics did not excite him at all. 'Did it ever occur to you,' asked Pye, 'that their function might be to calm you down?'

The Independent, 26 September 1990

Ceramics in Italy

'Terra Incognita: Italy's ceramic revival', exhibition at the Estorick Collection, London, 30 September to 20 December 2009

This is the most exciting ceramics exhibition to appear in London since the late Ewen Henderson's 'Pandora's Box' was shown at the Crafts Council Gallery in 1995. But it is very different in scope and context from that show. The anxieties that came to obsess Henderson as a ceramicist, and which he sought to lay to rest through curating a show of work that chimed with his sensibility, simply were not an issue in twentieth-century Italy. 'Terra Incognita: Italy's ceramic revival' is a superlative group of Italian ceramics from the early 1930s up until the early 1960s (part of the Bernd and Eva Hockemeyer collection of Italian art). The show is aptly titled – this is largely unknown territory despite the magnificent array of Lucio Fontana clayworks that were included in his Hayward Gallery retrospective in 1999.

Fontana is well represented in 'Terra Incognita', beginning with two pieces of 1931 that immediately suggest the daring variousness of his approach. 'Venere' is a roughly modelled slab of clay, the figure of Venus created in low relief with rough finger-strokes and casually incised lines and an encircling of green pigment. We know that Fontana rejected what he called the 'slavery' of bronze and marble. If 'Venere' demonstrates his determination to do away with the formality of carving and casting to achieve something more elemental through a direct engagement with the messy, changeable *matière* of clay, the other work of 1931, a lovely classical glazed clay head of 'Medusa', underlines his versatility. Fontana could just as easily control clay conventionally to make something analogous to a clay sketch for a formal sculpture.

But Fontana, for all his genius, is not the whole story. In the same room as these two early pieces there is a vase by Pietro Melandri whose ceramic workshop experimented with maiolica and with lustres. Melandri's vase, alive with fish, starfish, and octopi, quotes the decorative language of Minoan Cretan jars but is enriched with another tradition – of Persian and Hispano-Moresque lustre. Melandri would have described himself as a potter while

Leoncillo Leonardi working on 'Partigiana Veneta', 1954.

Fontana emphatically did not: 'I am a sculptor not a ceramicist. I have never turned a plate on a wheel nor painted a vase. I detest lacy designs and dainty nuances.'

Nonetheless there was an easy interchange and a network of support that made Fontana's experimentation possible. The beguiling figure of Tullio Mazzotti (of the Fabbrica Giuseppe Mazzotti at Albisola) was a key figure and the little coastal town of Albisola became a fulcrum for ceramic experimentation, particularly after the Second World War. But the 'movement' in ceramics can be mapped all over Italy. In Rome we find Leoncillo Leonardi, whose 'San Sebastiano bianco' (1962) stands as another remarkable tour de force of expressiveness, roughly painted with slips and enamel, at its heart a gash of raw clay. Leoncillo kept a diary in which he recorded: 'The handprints in the clay create a sweetly animated surface like the wind over wheat fields.' Writing like this is to be treasured.

We are in an exhilarating territory, which appears to have drawn inspiration from sources as old as clay itself. Fausto Melotti's tribute to Fontana of around 1948 is a primordial 'vase' made up of a lattice of lumps of clay clothed in a dark glaze. A vase of 1954 by the painter Emilio Scanavino is roughly gouged with *art informale* marks and splashed and poured slips and glazes. In Britain this turn to prehistory and to archetypal symbols floated up in the sculptor Eduardo Paolozzi's interest in 'primitive art, micro-zoology, the natural patterns formed by organic objects, and Picasso in all his periods' and in turn was passed on to ceramicists like Gordon Baldwin, Ruth Duckworth, Gillian Lowndes, Ian Auld, and, rather later, Ewen Henderson. But their freedoms were both hard won and circumscribed by their position in a 'craft' world.

The 'c' word has understandably been overlooked in most previous discussions of Italian ceramics; what went on in Italy has little in common with the studio pottery movement in Britain as it developed from the 1920s – even if both were markedly anti-industrial projects. Most writing on Fontana, for instance Sarah Whitfield's essay 'Handling space' in her Hayward Gallery catalogue (1999), fails to explore his work from an informed ceramic perspective. In his *Twentieth century ceramics* Edmund de Waal makes a start by positioning Italian ceramics and in particular the work of Fontana in a global context that takes in Picasso at Madoura, Joan Miró's collaborations with Lloréns Artigas, and Isamu Noguchi's colloborations with the maverick potter Rosanjin. Now we can go a step further. The complex linkages between Italian artists and an indigenous tradition of small ceramic workshops are explored in a book by Lisa Hockemeyer, the curator of 'Terra Incognita' (with an essay by Italy's pre-eminent design historian Gillo Dorfles). At the time of writing, the book was at the printers, but it will be the first publication to tease out the complexity of 'craft' in the context of Italian ceramics – not in a reductive sense but as a mythologically inspired engagement with material, with process, and with fire and metamorphosis.

Crafts, no. 221, November / December 2009

Why shouldn't a pot be as beautiful as a painting?

'The Raw and the Cooked: new work in clay': exhibition at the Barbican Art Gallery, London, 8 July to 5 September 1993

Three vessel shapes have been roughly carved and sliced out of solid greyish clay. Their creator, Tony Cragg, an aesthetician of waste and garbage, has always maintained that sculpture's principal responsibility is to give greater resonance to things and materials. His poetic piece is a modest resolution of this aim and one of the best things in a show full of beauty. 'The Raw and the Cooked', at the Barbican in London, attempts something difficult, the dismantling of hierarchies by showing the work of potters and sculptors side by side.

'Why should not a porcelain vase be as beautiful as a picture?' asked the potter Bernard Leach in 1911. He was then a young painter and etcher living in Tokyo, a member of a set of wealthy Japanese intellectuals and artists passionately absorbed by the European avant-garde but also engaged in a process of inverse orientalism through a study of Zen aesthetics, the cult of tea, and the vernacular arts of Korea. Soon after posing his question Leach read Clive Bell's *Art*. There he found an outline of modernism in which Sung vases, Chartres, Mexican sculpture, Giotto frescoes, and the paintings of Piero, Poussin, and Cézanne stood together on an equal footing. All great art, Bell argued, had a 'universal and eternal' appeal and could be appreciated without special knowledge or the experience of connoisseurship: 'If the forms of a work of art are significant, its provenance is irrelevant.' The democratization of art outlined by Bell was generous to all the world's art and put spontaneity and truth to materials before the relentless trade skills of the nineteenth-century art world. Bell's ideas filled Leach with hope and reflected his catholic experiences in Japan. Why should not a porcelain vase be as beautiful as a picture?

This was one of modernism's more fragile constructs. For a springtime-period, hand-block printed textiles, monumental pots carrying abstract marks, and directly carved sculpture represented some kind of unity of art, craft, and design. Artists turned their eyes to everyday objects, to 'things'. For instance, in a letter of 1924 detailing influences on his work, the poet Rilke put his intimacy with Rodin and his love of the work of Cézanne in second place. The real decisive encounters had been with artisans – watching the repetitive work of a rope-maker in Rome and of a potter in a small village by the Nile. And ceramic in the 1920s, with its marvellous tactile potential and its therapeutically enclosing brand of formalism, appeared an inclusive art that synthesized high art, archetypal shapes, and the repetitive actions of Rilke's humble Nilotic potter.

Since those first optimistic decades of the twentieth century, ceramics, defined narrowly as 'craft', has been caught uneasily between two modernisms – the modernism of fine art, uncertain and chaotic, and the Modern movement in design with its disciplinary certainties. If today the art of ceramics is mostly buoyed up by a devoted amateur following and by a discerning band of collectors, it nonetheless remains isolated. Fine art critics tend to be wildly misinformed, invariably taking pottery as an exemplar of qualities like skill and tradition. The exhibition at the Barbican is, therefore, cause for rejoicing. The great potters of our time are on show in the company of a handful of sculptors in a gallery firmly associated in the minds of the public with mainstream art activities. In fact the contribution from the fine art world seems a little thin – apart from Tony Cragg's handsome tribute made

Angus Suttie, 'Pot', earthenware, 1989.

at that epicentre for boundary crossing, the European Ceramic Work Centre in the Netherlands. Bruce McLean, surrounded by so much grave beauty, emerges as a *pasticheur* whose foray into ceramics looks coarse. Antony Gormley's 'Twenty-four hours', a scuttling Ascent of Man almost topples over into another vulgarity, one of ideas rather than workmanship. Other unclassifiable artists prove more interesting. Bryan Illsley, jeweller/painter/creator of collaborative books, Stephenie Bergman, painter/textile artist/ironic apron-maker, and Jacqueline Poncelet, potter turned sculptor, all in different ways understand something about clay at a profound level.

And there are problems with this show which are mainly to do with this particular *fin de siècle*, a time of retrenchment and artistic caution. There is a marked conservatism of ambition in which clay is tamed rather than allowed to declare its inchoate, messy qualities. Looking through a catalogue of a comparable show put on fifteen years ago, 'State of Clay', images of excess and optimistic sculptural experimentation abound.

At the Barbican, on the other hand, there is a good deal of well-made, well-mannered commentary on ceramic history. In pieces by Richard Slee,

Carol McNicoll, the late Angus Suttie, and Philip Eglin, this commentary attains a kind of anarchic playful seriousness that is rich in the kinds of elevated ironies we associate with mannerism. At its least successful such self-reflexive work can seem genteel.

Perhaps the greatest satisfactions in this exhibition are provided by artists who in different ways allude to early modernism, to a period when the pursuit of pure form stripped away historicism. Simplicity equals strength. There is Ewen Henderson with his towering megaliths, Gordon Baldwin's remarkable marriage of abstract painting and sculpture, and Gillian Lowndes's spare carapaces. There is Sara Radstone's austere minimalist stoneware and the work of young Lawson Oyekan whose tall, casually built vessels celebrate freedom and spontaneity.

Finally there is Gwyn Hanssen Pigott. She is the one potter in the show who belongs to that functional world, represented at its best by the porcelain of David Leach or Joanna Constantinidis. Hanssen Pigott has grouped a series of porcelain bottles, bowls, and beakers into austere tableaux. The idea, a *trompe l'oeil* commentary on the relationship between art and its objects, sounds familiar enough. But the simplicity and assurance of her work suggest, as much as anything in this show, those absolute, Platonic ur-shapes and objects that underpin all attempts to recuperate purity in the visual. Faced with Hanssen Pigott's work and that of Baldwin, Henderson, Radstone, Lowndes, and Oyekan, we can ask again, this time with more confidence, why should not a porcelain vase be as beautiful as a picture? Why not, indeed?

The Independent, 15 July 1993

Talking to Reginald Reynolds Amponsah

One of the strangest interviews that I've ever conducted was with a distinguished Ghanaian politician, Reginald Reynolds Amponsah. Over the phone, when I was arranging the interview, I asked him if he still made pots. He laughed and said no, that had all been a long time ago. This is his story.

He was a clever young man who managed to get a place at Achimota, an élite school set up in 1926 by the British colonial government in what was then the Gold Coast. He had planned to study law or perhaps to train as a teacher. He was extraordinarily likeable and soon formed friendships with the more eccentric and charismatic teachers on the Achimota staff. There was the sculptor Herbert Vladimir Meyerowitz and his brilliant anthropologist wife Eva, Harry Davis and his wife May, both with remarkable practical ceramic skills and, strangest of all, the 40-year-old Michael Cardew, a classicist famous for the beauty of his slipware, who had arrived in West Africa almost by accident in 1942. Between them they decided that young Amponsah should become a potter. Initially he was to be apprenticed at a large tile and brick works that Meyerowitz had set up near the school, and then he was to go to England to the art school at Stoke-on-Trent.

This was not a career that many educated young Gold Coasters would have relished, but Amponsah was persuaded by his mentors that a life devoted to Arts & Crafts would be worthwhile. He did go to Stoke and then on to the Royal College of Art. But he did not become a potter. While at the Royal College he became involved in the independence movement and was already corresponding with Kwame Nkrumah, another former Achimotan. Amponsah went into politics. He soon lost faith in Nkrumah and as an opposition MP was imprisoned for seven years by his former ally. He might have been in prison longer had Nkrumah not been toppled by a CIA-backed coup in 1966. During those years in prison the great park at Achimota and the tile works at Alajo and the prankish notices pinned up by Cardew in Latin must have seemed extraordinarily remote.

I went to Ghana and Nigeria to follow in the footsteps of Michael Cardew and as a result learned a good deal about the British Colonial Administrative Service in both countries during the 1940s and 1950s. In West Africa the British liked to think of themselves as benign paternalists, ruling indirectly through local chiefs and emirs, keen to uphold local customs and institutions. As Anne Phillips points out in her marvellous book *The enigma of colonialism: British policy in West Africa*, 'British colonial practice seemed to pride itself on retarding rather than hastening change, drawing on the values of feudalism rather than those of capitalism'.

The encouragement of craft activity was part of that pattern of rule. It was believed that West Africa should not modernize too fast and that large-scale industrialization should be kept at bay, allowing small industries to evolve, as it were, naturally. Northern Nigeria, with its indirect rule through emirs, was the most feudal 'unspoiled' part of British West Africa and that is where in the 1950s Cardew set up his Pottery Training Centre, a few years after he left Ghana.

As a colonial project the Pottery Training Centre generated a wealth of minutes, reports, and accounts that are by turns hilarious and heartbreaking. The scheme was romantically anti-capitalist. For instance, orders for pots were regularly turned down. The main market for the Centre's high-fired stoneware was the expatriate community, but Cardew saw no reason to

Achimota Cooler Unit apprentices, September 1942: Reginald Reynolds Amponsah (front row, third from the left), flanked by Michael Cardew and Harry Davis.

pander to their whims. Flower vases were in demand but Cardew respected the apprentices' preferences for tackling teapots, beakers, and bowls. Certain often-requested items were ruled out: 'Posy Rings, Toby Jugs, Bird and Fish Ornaments *et hoc genus omne*'.

Cardew's Training Centre still exists, renamed the Dr Ladi Kwali Pottery. But pots are not made there and the buildings are in ruins. The pottery has a Soviet air with a sizeable workforce paid by the government to do nothing. But Cardew's dream lives on in a limited way through the energy of a few committed individuals. There is the Maraba Pottery near Kaduna, run by Umaru Aliyu, and Stephen Mhya's beautiful Bwari Pottery at Bwari near the capital Abuja. At Bwari I bought a jug that bore an eerie resemblance to Cardew's best work.

There is craft and craft. Today in Nigeria the real handwork explosion is to be found in the multitude of small furniture and metal workshops that line the roadsides on the outskirts of every town. The design vocabularies are astoundingly eclectic. Bulgy leather sofas jostle with dining chairs of Arts & Crafts austerity and Bierdermeier bedsteads, while metal doors, grilles, and fences range from functionalist to unrestrainedly baroque. There is a popular market for this 'craft'. In particular the plethora of metalwork, along with the private security firms that protect the compounds of the rich, answers a vital need. In the extraordinary city that is Lagos, the artist Olu Amoda makes doors and grilles that reflect on this state of affairs and on the economic imperatives that drive him, somewhat unwillingly, to create functional works of art. He calls them 'Doors of Paradise' – because they protect paradisiacal interiors that the majority of Nigerians can only dream of.

Crafts, no. 197, November / December 2005

Where to see *Mingei* in Japan

Mingei was a neologism coined in 1925 by the Japanese philosopher and art critic Yanagi Soetsu and his two potter friends Kanjiro Kawai and Hamada Shoji to describe a family of objects that they collectively admired and which they feared would cease to be made in the face of rapid industrialization. The European equivalent of *Mingei* (from *minshuteki kogei* – 'art of the people') would be folk or popular art, while the *Mingei* movement as it developed between the wars had a good deal in common with the Arts & Crafts movement in late-nineteenth-century England. But there were striking differences that become apparent once inside Yanagi Soetsu's Nihon Mingeikan (Japan Folk Crafts Museum) in West Tokyo. The building alone is worth a visit as an antidote to the hallucinatory high-rise neon skyline of trendy Shibuya and Shinjuku. Since the museum opened in 1936 the chic little suburb of Komaba has sprung up around it, making its oya stone and wattle and daub walls, its magnificent timber interior inspired by the vernacular farmhouses of Japan and sweeping stone tile roof, look especially romantic and incongruous.

The Mingeikan is not an ethnographic collection in the spirit of Skansen in Sweden or the Folk Crafts Museum outside Oslo. It is more selective and, though dedicated to handwork, it is informed by a modernist spirit. *Mingei* objects are plainer and starker than anything produced or admired by the Arts & Crafts movement at its height in the 1880s. Yanagi Soetsu belonged to the avant-garde Shirakaba group of writers and intellectuals and he wrote one of the first major studies of William Blake as well as passionately admiring Cézanne and German Expressionism.

The folk art he collected testifies to the beauty of everyday objects in Japan and inter-war colonized Korea. There are deerskin fireman's jackets with stencilled crests, casually drawn *otsu-ye* paintings sold at Otsu to pilgrims, emblematic carved shop signs, cast-iron kettles, and massive sculptured blocks of wood carved into hook shapes from which these kettles were suspended. One real surprise are the objects from Britain dotted about the mu-

'Jizaikake' (kettle hanger), zelkova wood, Edo period (nineteenth century), Hokuriku region.

seum – a selection of Windsor chairs, a couple of long-case clocks, medieval jugs and country slipware and embroidered samplers, as well as weaving and ceramics by inter-war craftsmen and craftswomen like Ethel Mairet, Michael Cardew, and Bernard Leach.

Bernard Leach is, of course, the link. He lived in Japan from 1909 until 1920 and was a close friend of all the *Mingei* leaders, especially Yanagi and Hamada. Although he subsequently became something of a bore about Japan, writing in a cloudy mystical way about the union of East and West, it was there that he found real artistic fulfilment and where he never lacked patrons and admirers. And the Mingeikan forms the starting point for a *Mingei* trail round Japan full of surprises and delight.

First go north to Mashiko (best reached by car, though a train and a bus will take you there) to see the remarkable Mashiko Reference Collection housed in a group of beautiful thatched traditional buildings bought and reassembled there by Hamada in the 1930s. Hamada collected an extraordinary group of objects from all over the world – Pueblo baskets, Persian bowls, Korean moon jars, Aboriginal art, English gate-legged tables, and, of course, a group of Windsor chairs. Another fascinating *Mingei* museum is attached to the Sakuma family pottery, and there is also the Mashiko Ceramic Art Centre which has fine displays of work by most of the local potters.

Heading south to Kyoto, Kanjiro Kawai's house is maintained faithfully as a museum by his daughter and granddaughters. It is deeply atmospheric, as if Kawai had just walked out of the door, and bears witness to that shared, distinctive *Mingei* taste – more massive wooden kettle hooks collected for their sculptural beauty, a Korean stove, and carved shop signs mixed in with bamboo furniture and Cubist brass tobacco-pipes designed by Kawai, together with a selection of his radical calligraphy and his curious faceted pots. The house is in the potters' quarter of Kyoto and as with Hamada we get the sense of an intellectually minded artist turning away from his privileged background to lead the simple life.

Finally the fine Ohara Museum of Art in the pretty town of Kurashiki (about an hour by train from Kyoto) devotes one or two rooms each to Leach, Hamada, Kawai, to the potter Tomimoto Kenkichi (who subsequently repudiated *Mingei*), and to the faux-naïve print maker Shiko Munakata and the textile designer Keisuke Serisawa. Ohara Magosaburo was an idealistic textile magnate who also paid for the construction of Yanagi's Mingeikan in Tokyo. Although there are plenty of other *Mingei* collections to see in Japan, the wheel comes neatly full circle in Kurashiki.

The Spectator, 8 May 2004

Orientalizing in Korea

A report on the World Ceramic Exposition 2001, Kyonggi Province, Korea

As design and fine art become increasingly globalized, countries as diverse as Norway and South Korea are employing the crafts to convey a sense of a positive, individualistic national and regional identity. Of course Norway has a strong history of using both craft and site-specific art in this way – from her spectacular contributions to the Chicago World's Fair in 1892–3 and the Paris Exhibition of 1900, up to the impressive recently completed Artscape Nordland sculpture project and the exhibition Norwegian Contemporary Ceramics seen at the Ceramics Millenium Congress held in Amsterdam in 1999.

But the most impressive example of craft taking centre stage in the projection of national and regional identity must surely be this year's World Ceramic Exposition 2001 (WOCEK) held in Kyonggi Province in Korea. The Exposition, which was on the scale of a nineteenth-century World's Fair, did a remarkable job of conveying the complex nature of modern Korea. In the late 1920s Herbert Read pointed out that ceramic 'was so fundamental, so bound up with the elementary needs of civilization, that a national ethos must find its expression in this medium'. So it proved. From August to October 2001 it was possible to see sixteen major international ceramics exhibitions, documented by handsome and cheap catalogues at three separate exposition sites at Ichon, Yoju, and at Kwangji. And the thinking behind the choice of these sites was sophisticated. The exposition was held not in the capital, Seoul, but in the 'pastoral countryside'. Kyonggi Province might indeed seem to be a provincial place but in a postmodern world the marginal and the local have a new importance and the organizers argued that 'through ceramics the direct interaction from the peripheral to the center, from the local to the world, is achieved'.

Nonetheless, an invitation to speak on 'the vessel' at a ceramics symposium planned as part of the exposition seemed challenging. Was it a subject? What could I contribute? But as I worked away on my paper – which looked at early twentieth-century attitudes to the handmade in general and the changing taste for Chinese and Korean pots in particular – I realized that my vision of Korea was shaped by my ignorance and was limited to a range of iconic objects and accompanying writing mostly penned by inter-war visitors to Korea, in particular the British potter Bernard Leach and the Japanese arts-and-crafts theorist Yanagi Soetsu. I knew that to admire the exquisite celadons of the Koryo period (936–1392) and the more rugged wares made during the increasing decline and isolation of the Choson period (1392–1910) was the mark of a finely tuned ceramic sensibility. Indeed they were the very objects I sought out in the Victoria & Albert Museum and the British Museum as being the most beautiful examples of the potters' art, whether from east or west. But why was that so?

As I reflected on this matter of taste the early twentieth-century plight of Korea came very much alive. The historian Stefan Tanaka and the design historian Yuko Kikuchi have analysed how early twentieth-century responses to Korean culture were partly predicated upon a Japanese historiography that established an intellectual basis for the Japanese annexation of Korea in 1910. In their response to Korea, as Korean scholars have pointed out, we find Leach and Yanagi employing 'the aesthetic of colonialism'.

Leach paid at least two visits to Korea, in 1918 and 1935, in the company of Yanagi Soetsu, whose brother was a member of the Japanese administration in Korea. Leach and Yanagi's shared taste was shaped by modernism in the visual arts, but their taste reminds us that modernism's canon of ideal objects, which included objects as diverse as African carvings, Chinese carpets, and Korean ceramics, was almost invariably a by-product of political and economic intrusions into other cultures underpinned by colonial adventures. Leach chose to see occupied Korea as a creative Eden. He found the inhabitants 'spontaneous and trusting', making pots and other craft objects 'naturally'. Yanagi concurred with his enthusiasm, especially admiring Choson *punch'ong* stoneware and contemporary examples of *hakeme* or brushed slip, which were, in his view, 'healthy', not 'sickly or nervous like much of modern civilization'.

Leach and Yanagi's attitude to Korean ceramics, both historic and contemporary, in the context of the society that produced them was troubling. The endgame of their joint philosophy, that the best work is produced in the most difficult physical and economic conditions, suggests the paradoxical nature of twentieth-century taste. An admiration for elusive qualities like integrity and authenticity can translate into a blindness to political and social injustice. The ceramic vessel, particularly the Korean ceramic vessel, inadvertently came to function as the ideal embodiment of Leach and Yanagi's vicarious desires.

These were the sorts of themes that I touched on in my paper and they were brought into sharper focus when I arrived in Korea. It became clear that the production and consumption of ceramics was certainly one way into a nation's history, particularly a nation like Korea. Of course not all the WOCEK exhibitions were about Korean or Eastern ceramics. For instance, the First World Ceramic Biennale International Competition will be an important ongoing event. This year the extraordinarily generous first prize went to the Anglo-Nigerian Lawson Oyekan. A show of Contemporary World Ceramics was impressive, if over-dominated by American work. And displays mounted by members of the International Academy of Ceramics and by North America's NCECA seemed familiar, even parochial. The real marvel was the six major exhibitions of oriental ceramics – 'World Ceramic Heritages: the East', 'North-East Asian Ceramic Interchanges', 'Ancient Chinese Pottery', 'Korean Contemporary Ceramics', 'Korean Traditional Ceramics', and the Onggi exhibition – a celebration of the traditional large storage jars of Korea.

The historic exhibitions inevitably sparked off reflections. For instance, in the seventeenth and eighteenth centuries, while the Chinese were producing technically refined elaborately decorated wares, Korean Choson porcelain of the same date was roughly thrown and decorated with the freest of brushwork. What could one make of a ceramic culture that to our eyes got better and better as the society in which it was produced collapsed into economic recession and isolation? And what of ceramics as an art form now – what was its place in technologically advanced modern Korea? These paradoxes were addressed in the symposium, in particular in fine papers given by

Unpacking the climbing kiln at the World Ceramic Exposition, Kyonggi Province, Korea, 2001.

the historian Bang Byung-sun and by the ceramic scientist Koh Kyongshin; these swept aside the kind of Leachean essentialism that still characterizes much Western writing about historic Korean ceramics. But to underline that ceramic identity was very much a live issue, the potter Lim Moo-Keun gave a controversial paper attacking the decadence of contemporary American ceramics and the intellectual depredations of postmodernism. The 'total fiasco' of Communism was condemned too and Professor Lim called for a new kind of specifically Korean ceramics based on Christian values. Lest this seem too odd, we could set against it some of the celebratory papers placing clay at the centre of the intellectual universe which only American-based ceramicists seem able to write. Then there was the editor of *American Ceramics*, Ronald Kuchta, with a talk on the ceramics market in the USA that ended with slides of some of North America's wealthiest collectors posing among their pots in their various lush homes. He was preceded by Professor Wang from the Palace Museum in Beijing who gave a scholarly, austere paper on exports of

Chinese porcelain to Europe during the late Ming and early Ching dynasties. But somehow the conference worked, despite the odd pairings and the extreme difference of the discussants' responses. Men and women from China, Japan, the Netherlands, Norway, Great Britain, Korea, Switzerland, Italy, Finland, and Australia in the conference room at Ichon ended up talking about the nature of tradition, global technological interchange, eighteenth-century luxury debates, cultural difference, modernism, representation and, timely this, the limitations of terms like Orient and Occident. This was cultural exchange at its best. Perhaps the real surprise was that craft – in the form of ceramics – was able to throw such a powerful light on such a complicated range of issues.

Crafts, no. 174, January / February 2002

The flourish of wood and iron

'David Nash: sculpture 1971–90': exhibition at the Serpentine Gallery, London, 8 June to 21 July 1990; 'Julio Gonzalez: sculptures and drawings': exhibition at the Whitechapel Art Gallery, London, 15 June to 5 August 1990

First, the poster. It is a lush colour shot of a fantastical arboreal scene, something you might stumble upon in a fairy tale. A sculpture is being made, or rather charred, in a little bonfire in the glade of a forest. David Nash, famously, lives in Gwynedd, north Wales, and is an acknowledged nurturer of woodland, creating landscape art through cutting and planting schemes. He is the man who appears to have the enviable gift of making sculpture through good husbandry.

For instance, since 1976 he has been working with 'Ash dome' in the Vale of Ffestiniog: 22 ash trees in a 30-foot circle, which are being trained to form a ceiling over the enclosed space. It is just one of a number of literally growing projects which Nash regularly visits to maintain or tend in many parts of the world. Therefore a measure of our interest in and instinctive approval of Nash seems to have to do with the idea of an ordered rural existence. Nash is, as it were, standing in for a whole class of long-vanished artisans who had a harmonious relationship with the natural world – the charcoal burner, the wheelwright, the forester. Hand in hand with that nostalgia goes a recognition of the traditional skill or craftsmanship in the sculptures themselves.

It is not really possible to use wood sensibly without understanding its qualities. In one of the most luminous bits of art-historical sleuthing of re-

David Nash, 'Comet ball', elm, in the process of being made, 1990.

cent years, Michael Baxandall has demonstrated how the limewood sculptors of south Germany understood the especialness of the particular wood that they used. For example, wood is unstable and can shrink and crack radically as it dries, a phenomenon known as starshake. The Renaissance limewood sculptors adapted their figurative forms in such a way as to accommodate these fractures, making art of extraordinary freedom and flourish.

Some of Nash's sculptures turn this knowledge on its head. In 'Cracking box', he goes out of his way to reveal and display starshake, using hearts of wood roughly pegged together; its powerful charge arises mainly from the revelation of wood's natural energy and changeableness. Other of Nash's sculptures are even more direct. They are essays on the curvature of branches, what John Ruskin called 'the dryad's waywardness'. In effect, these let the tree do the work: Nash's intervention is kept to the minimum.

The earliest piece in the show at the Serpentine Gallery, 'Table with cubes' of 1970, demonstrates another preoccupation: with the sculptural presence of utilitarian objects. Here Nash is indebted to Brancusi's sequence of carved solid cups and bits of furniture. 'Table with cubes' is a youthful sculpture, a *paragone*-like response to the painterly still life, but the more recent 'Ancient table' is a monumental thing, functioning as a table for a race of giants or gods. Concentrating on these allows us to forget his distractingly Green credentials and appreciate his strength as a sculptor. 'Ancient table', the interlocking 'Emperor of China' and the 'Nature to nature' series deserve particular attention. They show that Nash's marvellous art is strongest when he, not the tree, does the talking.

Nash has always been an inspirational figure in the craft world but the relationship between fine art and the crafts is notably uneasy. Take Julio Gonzalez, regarded as a pivotal figure in twentieth-century sculpture. His background as a decorative metalsmith and jeweller is usually regarded with some ambivalence: either he is seen as having 'freed' himself from it, or signs of his craft origins are censured. Significantly, the work now on show at the Whitechapel fails to include any examples of his applied art; the spell must not be broken.

What we do know is that in 1928 Picasso created a series of sculptures in Gonzalez's studio with his fellow countryman's help. Subsequently, Gonzalez apparently asked Picasso's permission to continue to work using the sculptural language of their collaboration and Picasso assented. The rest is history, inspiring indirectly our own Anthony Caro and a whole school of St Martin's-trained sculptors.

Nonetheless, there is something odd about the Picasso story. Only in Gonzalez's studio did Picasso make metal sculpture of such excellence. In wood, paper, and in the general area of collage, Picasso was of course his own man. He must have encouraged Gonzalez to collage in metal; but his plaster and cast bronze sculptures look heavy by contrast with the pieces like the great 'Women in the garden', which he made with Gonzalez. Gonzalez and the kinds of materials he had in his studio were clearly crucial to Picasso's achievement as a sculptor in metal.

Whatever the nature of the indebtedness, Gonzalez went on to develop elements of their shared vocabulary into something rather different. The large 'Woman with a mirror' at the Whitechapel Art Gallery uses very much the same light-hearted codes as Picasso for hair and sexual parts. But then there is his 'Seated woman' of 1935 and his 'Harlequin' and the head called 'The tunnel': all are ostensibly figurative but use sheet metal and iron rods to emphasize the industrial origin of each part. Austere and majestic, these great pre-war sculptures still sing to us.

Welded sculpture might seem like an archaic activity to many of the young sculptors graduating this summer. They may prefer to meditate on the work of the German Harald Klingelhöller upstairs at the Whitechapel. His constructions make the most of the aesthetics of emptiness and anonymity. This school of the discarded kitchen unit, of corrugated cardboard, and cheap mirror glass makes Nash and Gonzalez seem, in different ways, wildly romantic and in love with art. Their sculptures spring up from a base or sit firmly on a surface, declaring themselves to be special and therefore exemplary. And that seems, for the time being at least, an old-fashioned kind of statement.

The Independent on Sunday, 24 June 1990

Robert Marsden

The gallery has become an environment, a place where sculptures comment on the links between sculpture and furniture and architecture. Five large forms are the core of Robert Marsden's installation entitled 'Stark reality'. They have been constructed for this space. But the group is also a proposal for a sculpture series to be realized in another material. For someone as sensitive as Marsden to the qualities of different metals this is a brave decision. Marsden wants the group to be constructed in stainless steel and Cor-Ten weathering steel. What we see here has been made, practically enough, out of laser-cut mild steel sheets bolted onto MDF panels. These are, therefore, interim objects. But what they emphatically are not are up-scaled versions of Marsden's smaller work.

Robert Marsden's table-sized sculptures are very different. They are all of a piece, sequential, and they are conceptually, technically and materially perfect. Perfection suggests ease and suavity. But Marsden's work is invariably unsettling. High finish and sureness of construction are combined with a structural logic that the eye cannot quite take in. Marsden offers spatial information that goes back on itself. Practically every one of his small to

Robert Marsden with 'Bessemer's closed cups', patinated brass, 1998 (on shelf) and 'Asides', aluminium and patinated brass, 2005 (on table).

medium sculptures suggests some heavy mathematics in the form of complex algorithms being set out in three dimensions. It would be natural to assume that a computer-modelling program played a part in the facture of these pieces – until we reflect that Marsden's 'Curve' series got under way in 1984, when only a handful of artists were engaging with the digital realm. And, in any case, when we look more closely it becomes clear that there is no ghostly software at work behind the scenes. Rather, a Marsden sculpture is completely self-determining and sovereign, while at the same time presenting us with immensely skilled artisanal work of the kind that has increasingly been stripped out of industrial labour. Tellingly he once described himself as an 'abstract light engineer'.

Marsden has made some of the most remarkable small sculptures of our time. They run in series that employ different materials (brass sheet, sawn aluminium, rusted mild steel block, bolted mild steel sheet) and different constructional techniques and they set out to solve very different visual problems. Small sculptures demand to be held or at least touched and each series offers entirely different sensuous experiences. Much of Marsden's work, therefore, comments on the denial of artisanal skill – in industry and also by artists themselves as they turn from artistic technique to a much more generalized activity – to what the art historian John Roberts has called 'social technique'. A rejection of artistic handwork was a revolutionary strategy in the early twentieth century. Now it has become an orthodoxy and, as a result, Marsden's way of working appears unusual, challenging and, increasingly, a radical model of authorship.

But Marsden has an understandable and intermittent desire to scale up. I have only seen these new works in his studio, crammed in and awkward – very unlike the small sculptures carefully positioned throughout his austerely beautiful house on the two floors above the studio. These big pieces work in pairs or as conjoined mirror forms. Pairs are usually meant to reassure, suggesting balance and symmetry. They are central to decorative art and furniture production. And pairs, sequences and suites are equally to be found in modern sculpture, and invariably produce a similar classical atmosphere of calm. But pairs also generate tension and excitement – in that they often are not exactly alike. They echo rather than mirror each other. The effect of the 'Stark reality' installation is, as I write, unknowable. But as Marsden's title suggests, unease may prevail. Each construction looks like an industrial object, though we have no idea of its purpose. On closer acquaintance the group appears carefully, even painstakingly made. Like Marsden's small sculptures, therefore, they comment on productive labour. But their real purpose is to create an environment – of pairs that are not quite pairs. Marsden does not give much away, but he has spoken of 'trying to convey a sense of not knowing, like looking into deeper sea'. Marsden's work operates at the extreme end of a modernist tradition and his marine image tells us what it is like to be there.

Published in a leaflet accompanying 'Robert Marsden: new work', exhibition at the Barrett Marsden Gallery, London, June to July 2009

The power of puppets

There is the living world – of people, animals and plants – and there is the world of things. But inanimate objects can have lifelike qualities. In part we vivify them by desiring them as commodities. They have social lives, histories, good times and bad, living it up as desirable treasure, or consigned to an attic or a junk shop, waiting to be rediscovered. In a famously strange passage of *Das Kapital* Marx tries to make sense of the power of commodities: 'The form of wood, for instance, is altered if a table is made out of it. Nevertheless the table continues to be wood, an ordinary, sensuous thing. But as soon as it emerges as a commodity, it changes into a thing which transcends sensuousness. It not only stands with its feet on the ground, but, in relation to all other commodities, it stands on its head, and evolves out of its wooden brain grotesque ideas, far more wonderful than if it were to begin dancing of its own free will.' This is a striking way of explaining the paradox whereby in capitalist societies objects are treated as if their value was inherent – rather than due to the labour expended on their creation. But what is especially memorable is the distinctly fairy-tale quality of Marx's language, reminding us of stories of supernatural metamorphosis, above all of Pinocchio, the marionette carved out of wood who comes alive.

Puppets and marionettes exert a strange power because they are animated things, halfway between the living and the object world. I am not sure that art or craft commentators have paid enough attention to puppetry – which, after all, synthesizes carving and constructional skills, architecture in miniature and theatre. And yet puppets were a key part of avant-garde activity in the early twentieth century, not least because they offered an alternative to the fustian realism of Edwardian theatre. But although artists like Alexander Calder, Kandinsky, Oskar Schlemmer, and Sophie Taeuber-Arp designed and made puppets, today the genre is almost entirely associated with children's entertainment. Recently, however, puppets, in combination with live actors, have been used to remarkable effect in theatre. The most striking example was the Royal Shakespeare Company's production of *Midsummer night's dream* (2005) in which the changling child was represented by an entrancingly beautiful puppet, thus making sense of Oberon and Titania's passionate tug-of-love quarrel over the boy.

Earlier this year the RSC and Islington's Little Angel Theatre staged their ground-breaking production of Shakespeare's erotic love poem *Venus and Adonis*. This featured both stringed marionettes (for an exquisite opening scene) and Japanese *bunraku* puppets. These are one-third life-size with each puppet being manipulated by three black-clad puppeteers in full view of the audience. But far from spoiling the theatrical illusion – in which Venus falls

William Simmonds and Eve Simmonds, marionettes of Flora and two fauns photographed c.1936.

unrequitedly in love with the youthful huntsman Adonis – the presence of the puppeteers lent a special charm to the performance, provoking all kinds of existential reflections on free will and individual agency.

The Little Angel Theatre, under the artistic direction of Steve Tiplady, is the place to see innovatory adult puppetry. The phrase sounds like an oxymoron, like 'ceramic sculpture' or 'textile artist'. In fact the concern about status that bedevils the craft world is mirrored by similar anxieties about the seriousness of puppetry. It is an angst that was amusingly explored in Spike Jonze's film *Being John Malkovich* – which incidentally included some magical marionette scenes. By taking over the body of John Malkovich, puppeteer Craig manages to raise the status of his art form. Once Malkovich appears to speak up for puppetry other Hollywood stars rush to follow suit and suddenly and hilariously puppets become cutting edge.

Puppet theatre and the crafts overlap in an obvious way because puppets are highly crafted objects. They both also form part of a lost or hidden story of modernism that is slowly being recuperated and which is attentive to modernism's Janus-faced synthesis of the archaic and the avant-garde. And that is where the craft of puppetry belongs – being at once elite and popular, vernacular and progressive, and with the potential to enchant, unsettle, and surprise us.

When Henry Moore wanted to make clear that he thought Eric Gill's sculpture dull and unadventurous he compared it to knitting. Times have changed and knitting has become fashionable, hence the Crafts Council's delightful exhibition 'Knit 2 Together'. There is, however, a strange feeling of déjà vu about all this. Remember the barefoot California boy Kaffe Fassett, dubbed by Sir Roy Strong the 'genius of the knitting needle'? There was a knitting renaissance back in the 1980s. Fassett had plenty of imitators with the result that a small knitwear business or an exciting yarn shop came to epitomize the brighter side of Margaret Thatcher's enterprise culture. But fashion is fickle. By the 1990s time had run out for shapeless waistcoats knitted in all the colours of the rainbow.

The more recent reinvention of knitting has been less about product and more about performance. It is currently dangerously cool to go out and knit publicly, with, for instance, Cast Off, aka the Knitting Club for Boys and Girls. They have held knit-ins in a variety of unlikely places – on the Circle Line, in the American Bar of the Savoy Hotel, and in Tate Modern. They were summarily ejected from the Savoy even though they were smartly dressed and ordered expensive cocktails. It was feared that the click, click of needles would annoy other guests. The sight of young men knitting was seen as faintly shocking also. So, there we have it. Knitting can be subversive. That Cast Off's knitting invasion of Tate Modern did not go down particularly well reminds us that back in the 1970s nothing annoyed unreconstructed male art critics more than the use of domestic skills like knitting, along with crochet and embroidery, to disrupt the categories of high and low art and the distinction between amateur and professional artist.

Of course there has always been a secret history of modern art that took in the domestic sphere. We only have to think of Matisse's fondness for textiles and of Eduardo Paolozzi's activities as a wallpaper designer. At present there is a lot of art about which aims to explore the familiarity and strangeness of the domestic interior and of domestic objects and craft processes. Maybe the Crafts Council should have looked at this phenomenon on a broader front – with pots by Grayson Perry, shoes by Jordan Baseman, and rag rugs by Ben Hall. As it is, the effect of visiting 'Knit 2 Together' is slightly risible. It is as though some cultural commissar had decreed that henceforth all art must be made with 4-ply wool. But on reflection, why not? 'Knit 2 Together', consciously or unconsciously, sends up a lot of avant-garde strategies.

Freddie Robins, 'How to make a piece of work when you are too tired to make decisions', 2005.

Instead of setting off on a self-important walk like Richard Long, Celia Pym knitted her way round Japan, producing a 24 metre long record of her trip in blue yarns that she bought on the journey. Instead of charring and destroying books like John Latham, Stephanie Speight has shredded books with a fettucine machine and knitted them into a scarf-like hanging entitled 'In the beginning was the word'. Grids? Look no further than Françoise Dupré's mathematical arrangement of cake boards on which are pinned brightly coloured spirals of French knitting. Duchampian games of chance? Freddie Robins, the show's co-curator, offers 'How to make a piece of work when you are too tired to make decisions', in which knitted 'actions' are decided by a throw of the dice.

Some of this work is disturbing, like Susie MacMurray's 'Maidenhair', a fragile rope of human hair. Kelly Jenkins's giant machine-knitted wall pieces parody the graphics of the sex industry – its phone cards and chat-line adverts in the language of purl and plain – 'Steamy live needle action', etc. It is an amusing but strictly one-line joke. The most powerful piece in the show is by the Japanese artist Takehiko Sanada. He has created a little flock of sculptures, each knitted from a single fleece spun into thread by the artist. What sets them apart is a very Japanese sensitivity to the qualities of the fibre that is not so apparent elsewhere in the show.

But the idea of imposing knitting's soothing algorithms on some of the leading artists of our time is strangely attractive. Think how satisfying a knitted 'Angel of the North' would be and how modestly impermanent. Perhaps it is time for a moratorium on making – except, that is, with needles and a ball of wool.

The Spectator, 19 March 2005

The fine art of icing

'The Sugared Imagination: an art and a trade': exhibition at the Usher Gallery, Lincoln, 24 June to 6 August 1989

'The Sugared Imagination' reveals a whole new art form for the jaded, with its own journals, books, guilds, its own elevated practice and populist tendencies, its own amateurs and professionals, and its own hierarchies and jealousies. So far as I know its practitioners have never received an Arts or Crafts Council grant. It flourishes – disguised partly as a trade and partly as housework – without the benefit of prescriptive criticism and without the attentions of arbiters of taste. I mean, of course, the butterfly virtuoso art of cake icing. This delightful exhibition was created by Dr June Freeman, a crusader-like sociologist dedicated to doing justice to the creative activities which will forever elude the museums and which will continue to be ignored by the arts establishment. She has given us knitting and quilting and now cake decoration. In an odd sort of way she is a subversive figure, taking the pretensions of the craft world and turning them upside down, revealing extraordinary levels of skill in the most unexpected of contexts.

In the past the genius of the confectioner was highly valued. This was partly because from the fifteenth century onwards elaborate table decorations were an important aristocratic art form, a crucial display of power and style at feasts, weddings and diplomatic encounters. Whole exotic worlds with figurines, temples, palaces, and parks were moulded in miniature from sugar, wax and, by the eighteenth century, from porcelain. Today only the remnants of porcelain table decorations survive to hint at the lavishness of these ephemeral displays.

But by the nineteenth century the extravagant use of sugar ceased to

Cover of the catalogue.

suggest princely generosity – the extraction of sugar from sugar beet meant it had become a cheap source of energy for the very poor. In addition table decorations lost their complexity. The ceramic figurines of the grand service quit the table and ended up forlornly stranded on the mantelpiece. At about the same time the sugary skills of the confectioners retreated onto iced cakes. Once firmly fixed to a cake, icing ceased to be a modeller's material comparable with wax or clay. But a new skill – piping – developed in the nineteenth century. Piping – 'ornamental cord-like lines of sugar on cakes' (OED) – is more like three-dimensional calligraphy than anything else and can range from delicate skeins to robust swags and scrolls. Chilling accuracy is much prized among the icing elite. It is surely one of the great unsung skills – here today, chopped and consumed tomorrow.

From the start the decoration of cakes seems to have been architectural in inspiration – the three decker wedding cake was supposedly based on the spire of St Bride's, Fleet Street. Those appalled by modernism in architecture will be happy to discover that the Modern movement has passed cake decoration by. Nonetheless, in the historical section of the show, with cakes reproduced from Schulbe's trusty classic *Advanced piping and modelling*, we witness a slow falling off or failure of nerve as we pass from the vibrant confidence of the Victorian cake to the fussy uncertainties of the 1950s and 1960s. Just now a highly skilled reticent approach seems fashionable.

Dr Freeman investigates many intriguing cake byways – the manly military cake, the first night cake, and the *Twelfth Night* cake made annually for the Drury Lane Theatre in memory of Robert Baddeley, a stage-struck pastry cook befriended by Garrick. Then there is the exuberant Afro-Caribbean contribution in the form of Beryl Alexander's freestyle coronation cake in pink and white. June Freeman includes a section mischievously entitled 'Exploring a new medium'. In order to get her grant from the Crafts Council to put on this exhibition she had to invite some 'proper' artists to decorate cakes. Naturally none attempted piping. Some did not rise to the occasion at all. The excessive use of small plastic toys was a cop-out, Peter Blake! Spitting Image did rather well with a Margaret Thatcher tenth anniversary cake, and Judith Duffey gets high marks for her 'Devil's food cake'. But the best cakes were the work of the professionals, a new band of heroes and heroines: Julie Suter, Robert Robertson, senior lecturer in bakery at Glasgow College of Food Technology, and stalwart R. H. Lorimer of the Army Catering Corps, who boldly and treasonably collaborated with Spitting Image and who made his own elegiac cake commemorating his 22 years of army service.

The Spectator, 14 October 1989

The writing on the wall

'The Spirit of the Letter: a celebration of lettering and calligraphy in Britain today': exhibition at the City Museum and Art Gallery, Portsmouth, 12 September to 12 November 1989

When it comes to lettering, everyone is an expert; most of us intuitively respond to the message of a particular typeface. Edward Johnston's sanserif type for the London Underground (1915) still strikes an efficient modern note amidst the dirt and gloom. Similarly the Faber book-jackets, designed by Berthold Wolpe in the 1960s, employing his own typeface Albertus, convey a sense of literary energy and creativity. So do the Gollancz wrappers of the 1930s and beyond with an audacious mixture of typefaces printed on glaring yellow paper.

Twentieth-century artists as diverse as Klee, Miró, Jackson Pollock, and Mark Tobey, inspired by the apparent freedom of oriental calligraphy, have invented new alphabets and made abstract art with letter shapes. The neo-Romantic poet and painter David Jones drew on an eclectic range of writing styles to create a whole series of semi-private painted inscriptions. Artists

Stone carver and lettercutter Alec Peever in his studio.

like these, however, whose influence on lettering has been a liberating one, are not to be found in 'The Spirit of the Letter' at Portsmouth City Museum and Art Gallery. This is essentially a crafts- and design-based exhibition that does not attempt to give a European or transatlantic overview. Still, while it does not pretend to be comprehensive, 'The Spirit of the Letter' manages to provoke many questions about the protean and varied role of lettering, from typography to bravura calligraphy, from public inscriptions to computer-generated letterforms.

Calligraphy – which literally translates as 'beautiful writing' – bears the same relationship to typography as post and lintel architecture does to the classical orders. Purists would argue that type cannot be intelligently de-signed unless the creator understands the calligraphic origin of the thin and broad parts of most typefaces. Certainly Johnston, Wolpe, and Eric Gill, the authors of some of the finest modern typefaces, possessed considerable writing or inscriptional skills. On the other hand, Stanley Morison, responsible for the typographic identity of *The Times* in the 1930s, was not an adroit pen-man – he simply had an unerring eye for good typefaces and strong compo-sition. The same might be said of Neville Brody whose typography for *The Face* owes more to computer-operated typesetting than to calligraphy. Unac-countably, he is absent from this exhibition.

'The Spirit of the Letter' pays a good deal of attention to the vellum/scribe/fine-penmanship side of the lettering question. Here, the problem is as much to do with content as with form. Whose words deserve expensive risk-taking with black inks, gold leaf, and vellum? At Portsmouth Museum, Lilly Lee creatively amplifies a passage from Machiavelli's *The prince*, inscribing a chilling statement in a bold agitated hand. But many calligraphers inhabit a gentler world and are happy to embellish prettily texts of staggering banality.

Arguably this problem of content lies at the heart of the whole lettering question. It is an abstract art, which we nonetheless consume as readers rather than as connoisseurs of pure form. And when it comes to content, the key public commission since the war must be the eight New Testament inscriptions in Basil Spence's Coventry Cathedral. Whatever else may be said about the Cathedral's architecture and its glass and its sculpture, no one would dispute the success of Ralph Beyer's contribution, known as the 'Tablets of the word' and cut in Hollington stone on a grand scale. Beyer's background is cosmopolitan and his sources have always been varied – German expressionist typography, early Christian inscriptions in the catacombs, the art of David Jones. The texts themselves are inspirational, but Beyer's lettering style for this commission, which treated each letter as a piece of incised sculpture in its own right, greatly adds to their declamatory power.

Are we likely to see anything on the scale of the Coventry commission again? In general the public commissions that have provided work for our artist craftsmen and women have, since Coventry, tended to be bland and factual. Which means that the talents of such fine lettercutters as David Kindersley, Richard Kindersley, Bryant Fedden, Sarah More, Tom Perkins, Alec Peever, David Holgate, Michael Harvey, and many others are being underused. It is partly up to them to break free of their role as craftsmen and craftswomen working to order, and to surprise us, as Ralph Beyer consistently does, with lapidary writing that operates as a literary form with a sculptural presence.

The career of the Scottish artist Ian Hamilton Finlay demonstrates what can happen when secular public inscriptions go beyond the formulaic. He has elevated inscriptions to a new seriousness because the wording of his own work is not bland and ranges from the delphic to the painfully controversial. The public inscription, like public sculpture, is in a tricky political position today. The way forward may be a modest one. 'Poems on the Underground', that much-loved project developed with the London College of Printing, suggests the realistic possibilities for uplifting collective reading. In these days of decline in public provision, these little posters are perhaps the best we can hope for.

The Independent, 10 October 1989

How to get money

'Small Show, Huge Talent': exhibition at 9 Hillgate Street, London, 26 to 28 January 2008

In December 1981 the painter Howard Hodgkin gave the William Townsend Memorial Lecture at the Slade School of Fine Art. His title was 'How to be an artist', but he pointed out that the full title should really have been 'How to be an artist in England', because a career in England was, he believed, 'more difficult, more traumatic and probably more fraught with absolute certainty of failure than in any other country'. Grim words – and Hodgkin went on to attack art schools as places cut off from art and to attack artists who turned to teaching because it was a safe option. Finally he announced that he was going to talk about money 'because if you are wondering how to be an artist, the most important thing of all is that you should be paid for doing it'. Money meant affirmation and reward for a lonely, arduous activity, and Hodgkin argued there was nothing wrong with an artist wanting money and plenty of it. Many in the audience were shocked at this apparently mercenary vision; but Hodgkin was right.

The crafts have always been short of money. In some ways this has largely been a problem created in the twentieth century. As the crafts turned against many unpleasant aspects of modernity, makers also turned against the luxurious end of the applied arts in favour of a kind of neo-primitivism – both in ideas and materials. The result is that the complexity and strangeness of much recent craft goes unrecognized.

So how to get money? The best sort of money, as Hodgkin makes clear, comes from the committed collector who buys your work. This is money with no strings attached that can enable the artist or maker to live a free life. Sadly, however, most of the money that is available to both artists and makers is hedged about with restrictions. Perhaps the most dispiriting way to get money is to fill in a complex form for some kind of 'practice-based research' that will be carried out in association with a college of art. Here, the artwork has to be envisaged in advance of its creation for the purpose of peer-reviewed selection. The 'project' will need a theoretical underpinning and it will have to signal in advance that the work/research will be, on some obvious level, innovative. There are plenty of other restrictive ways to get money – teaching, of course, which drains an artist in ways he or she may not realize, public commissions bristling with local needs that must be answered and the artist's residency where the maker or artist is uprooted and often turned into a kind of performing bear that makes art.

So perhaps it is time to praise the people who really keep the visual arts afloat and free. These are the committed collectors and the collectors who go

Tomáš Gabzdil Libertíny holding his Honey Comb Vase, beeswax:
conceived 2005, realized 2006–10, edition of 7.

a step further and become proselytizers and organize exhibitions, write and
otherwise support the artists they admire. I was thinking of this when I went
to 'Small Show, Huge Talent', a pop-up exhibition in an empty house in Hillgate Street in Notting Hill Gate. It was only on for a few days in January but it
will have had an impact far beyond its transitory appearance in a temporary
space.

It included Joris Laarman's use of digital technology to create 'Heat-
wave' – modular rococo radiators cast from polyconcrete – and his sculptural
'Bonechaise' cast in polyurethane resin. This high technology sat playfully
alongside Tomáš Gabzdil Libertíny's vases, made by a process he calls 'slow
prototyping'. A construction of wax sheets is introduced into a beehive and,
gradually colonized, creates a vase that is, in effect, the cunning work of bees
and is also a wry comment on the slickness of current consumerism. Pieke
Bergmans collaborates with glass technicians at Royal Leerdam Crystal.
Molten glass vessels are placed on iconic chairs and stools where they settle,
doing damage. There is a strange little film of the process on YouTube and
the resulting objects – Glass Viruses – are surprisingly majestic.

This was just some of the work in 'Small Show, Huge Talent'. And of
course it had been organized by Janice Blackburn. It had all the character-
istics of a Blackburn intervention – in particular young exhibitors who are
hard to categorize. Were they artists, designers, or makers? Then there was
the exhilarating mix of materials and aesthetic approaches and the fact that

unless you were very *au courant* these would be new names and new work. And you may be sure that these makers felt excited and honoured to be selected by Blackburn, who has a track record of extraordinary shows in unexpected places. But she also, and this is important, collects. And she encourages other people to collect. She understands the importance of money without strings, money for freedom.

Crafts, no. 211, March/April 2008

Our past remade in China

Monday 5 June 2010
Flying into the darkness the clouds begin to look artistic. We land at Guangzhou at 10 pm. It is hot, humid, and late, but the campus of South China Normal University bustles with students. Banyan trees line the avenues. I am in China, land of my dreams.

Sunday 6 June
We set off early for Foshan under a heavy, humid sky, through an area of gated communities – high and low rises of great luxury, sporting columns, pediments, incongruous cornices, and roof gardens. 'For the rich', explains Lai Fan, my unnervingly clever student interpreter.

We are going to meet Wei Hua, a ceramic artist who works in two large studios in stripped-out factory buildings. Foshan is undergoing a classic artist-led urban regeneration. A businessman owns the buildings in which Wei Hua works, together with the surrounding surviving traditional streets. Everything has been turned over to craftwork and pretty restaurants. Wei Hua has given the area atmosphere – with handsome outdoor tile installations and an extraordinary waterfall wall made up of hundreds of urinals, hand-basins and lavatories over which water gushes. The effect is funny and impressive. His gallery-sized work quotes the crowded figurative roof decorations of Foshan temples. He makes hollow rectangular blocks and presses semi-relief figures into them – gods, philosophers, and sometimes, incongruously, Chairman Mao – all slightly squashed and blurred as if pressed by the weight of history.

He takes us to see a friend – Pan Bolin – renowned for hyper-realistic ceramic eagles, tigers, mythological figures, legendary scholars, Buddhas, and, even, a Mother Teresa. We enter his grand studio to find him and his

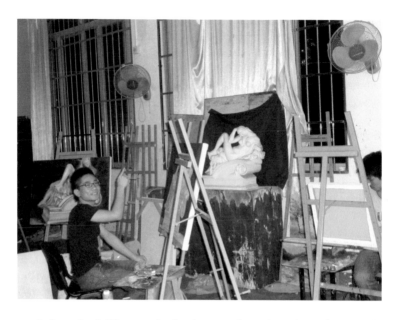

Student at South China Normal University, Guangzhou, painting from a plaster cast of Michelangelo's 'Night' in 2010.

assistants grouped theatrically around a large ceramic sculpture of three monkeys. 'Why is the Mona Lisa more famous than my work?' he asks, only half-humorously. Pan Bolin has a global clientele.

Monday 7 June

Today is our factory visit. Anyone visiting China would want to see the workshop of the world up close, just as informed visitors to England in the nineteenth century put a tour of Manchester or Birmingham high on their list. We are going to Autolite Electrical Ltd. Like many new Chinese factories, it is set incongruously in deep countryside, amid fields of maize, fish ponds, and duck lakes. Suddenly we arrive at a set of retractable metal gates and are welcomed into a meeting room by one of the managers.

Later – having dutifully studied their array of sensor lights, and after a long lunch – we walk through the air-conditioned design studios onto the assembly line floor. It is like stumbling upon a fifth-form electronics class. But these schoolchildren are unusually well-behaved, silent and working very hard – soldering bits onto circuit boards, checking them, assembling plastic casings, carrying out final tests, and packing. It is very hot. Down in reception more young people are arriving, prettily dressed boys and girls all clutching forms. The 2,000 workers at Autolite Electrical live on site in barrack-like dormitories. The management try to temper their isolation and possible homesickness with a dance floor, karaoke, and table-tennis tables.

Tuesday 8 June

While factories churn out low-cost lights for export, skills and exquisite sensibilities are everywhere apparent. Buying a calligraphy brush or making dumplings is taken very seriously indeed. The humblest workman carries an elegant thermos of hot water infused with medicinal herbs.

I spend a day in the University's art department. The studios are full of casts after Michelangelo – David's head, Moses, Dawn, and Dusk from the Medici chapel. From drawing and painting from casts they move on to life drawing and an extensive study of oil-painting techniques. Copying is central to their training. A student in the Chinese traditional painting department shows me his copy of a large classical Chinese painting. It took him a year to complete. Most students are adept at calligraphy – both formal and free. When I go back in the late evening the students are still hard at work.

The art department degree show opens in the afternoon and I discover that when these students turn to video or installation art they appear incapable of ugly or banal work.

Later a conference gets under way, followed by a trip to Yunnan. But Foshan, the lighting factory lost in the countryside, and the Guangzhou undergraduates working late into the night all hang in my mind. A philanthropic millionaire, a fashionable *animalier* sculptor, factories edging into the countryside, fledgling artists working from casts: this is the future (as China alarmingly appears to be) but it is also the nineteenth century – our past.

Crafts, no. 226, September / October 2010

Makonde and David Mutasa

'Makonde: wooden sculpture from East Africa from the Malde Collection': exhibition at the Museum of Modern Art, Oxford, 2 April to 21 May 1989; 'David Mutasa: sculpture': exhibition at 198, Brixton, London

Contemporary African artists have difficulty in promoting their work in the West. The great collections favour historic art made for ritual purposes, squirrelled out of Africa and displayed formally without the context of the shrine, dance, or the wayside. In this way the objects fit neatly into our notions of modernism and, in the USA at least, are often an adjunct to holdings of modern paintings and sculpture from which the contemporary art of Africa is noticeably absent. Yet in this century numerous new art forms have sprung up in African countries – the most naive often gaining our approval (wire toys, sign painting), while others are suspected of tourist or airport art tendencies by arbiters of taste who do not know urban Africa.

Certainly Makonde carvings have their airport forms but the majority of Makonde artists have catered for the consumerism of the First World without losing their artistic integrity. Migrants from the south who moved up into what is now Tanzania, Makonde sculptors early in this century spontaneously began to make pieces that were quite different from the art of their forefathers. The question is: were the Makonde responding solely to the desires of their Western customers by giving them the kind of art that seemed 'African'? The phenomenon is a baffling one. Certainly they abandoned their traditional materials and took to carving in dark hardwood. Europeans preferred its lasting qualities and, absurdly enough, seemed to expect carvings made by Africans to echo the colour of their skin. The carvings deploy both naturalism and the grotesque, both being thought appropriate by First World purchasers. Similarly a Western desire for major art is satisfied by the gigantism of some of these pieces. But on the other hand the Makonde remained completely artistically independent, refusing to repeat work or to take exact orders from traders and middlemen.

The fine collection at the Museum of Modern Art, Oxford, was brought together in the 1950s and 1960s by a husband-and-wife team – Moti and Kanchan Malde. Wherever possible they bought direct from the sculptors and were able to record the narratives depicted in the carvings. The sculptures fall into three main groups. The *binadamu*, literally 'children of Adam', are naturalistic depictions of local people, the kind of art made to oblige the traveller the world over. Nonetheless *binadamu* are not toylike or quaint; the Makonde seem incapable of unimaginative carving. In the 1950s an extraordinary new art form was invented: *shetani* – the depiction of the spirits that inhabit their myths and legends. *Shetani* carvings are semi-abstract, with a look of biomorphic Surrealism about them, springing up into rococo curves which swell disturbingly into limbs and facial details. Later innovations include *ujamaa* – images of brotherhood and unity, which are towering piles of figures carved out of single columns of wood. In Tanzania and Mozambique *ujamaa* is a politically powerful concept and these sculptures have an important national significance.

David Mutasa's work is very different. He belongs to a school of Zimbabwean stone carvers which is now several generations old. There are carvings in the great Zimbabwean ruins but the tradition appears to have been dead

The Makonde artist Pilis Mpwesa with one his carvings, mid-1960s.

for centuries. In the 1940s a few settlers and educators like Thomas Blome-field and Frank McEwen set up informal stone-carving workshops. The carving has gone from strength to strength and is a powerful art form in modern Zimbabwe.

Mutasa is perhaps not the greatest of these carvers but no one can doubt his craft skills in handling intractable stones like serpentine and verdite. Like many East African artists he has had a brush with airport art in order to finance his work as an independent sculptor. At 198 (a new gallery at 198 Railton Road, London SE24, dedicated to showing work by black artists) he shows semi-abstract pieces and vivid and naturalistic portrait heads.

Zimbabwean carving is not well known in this country but the reasons are not straightforward. Of course the art world is narrow, despite its much-vaunted internationalism, and it is generally unsympathetic to non-Western cultures while often blatantly borrowing from them. And Mutasa is in many ways out of step with the British sculptors of his generation who prefer to work with cheap, low-grade recycled materials, and who, ironically enough, are attracted by the bricolage techniques which can be found in the folk art of many developing countries. In contrast, Mutasa's sculptures have a glamorous, highly polished finish. The materials he employs have a precious air. This sets him apart even from British sculptors who have returned to direct carving.

Nonetheless, the fact that he is exhibiting in London is very important. He has found his place in the black British community and is carrying out a major commission for Lambeth. But that should not prevent him from taking part in debates with his British contemporaries about his loyalty to sculpture-on-a-plinth – an art form most young sculptors have turned away from. For one thing, Mutasa's approach makes it possible for him to take on public commissions. Very few British sculptors seem able to respond to these openly and without irony.

The Spectator, 15 April 1989

The black British artist and curator Eddie Chambers launched a ferocious attack on the Makonde exhibition in *Art Monthly* (no. 129, September 1989), accusing the Museum of Modern Art in Oxford of showing 'exotic bric-a-brac' and urging the gallery to seek out 'Africa's truly modern art'. This sparked off a debate that raged in *Art Monthly*'s pages over the next few months. The search for a truly African art continues, largely orchestrated by European and North American curators. David Mutasa, the Zimbabwean stone carver, completed his commission for Lambeth Council with National Lottery backing via the Arts Council. 'First child' stands on the Brixton Road. It was damaged by vandals within a few weeks of its unveiling.

Brian Clarke, glass artist

Stained glass belongs to an older world. It is, as Brian Clarke acknowledges, a beleaguered art form whose future hangs in the balance. Yet, paradoxically, since the 1920s glass and the idea of transparency have been crucial components of progressive architecture. As the German architect Arthur Korn explained in 1929:

> 'It is now possible to have an independent wall of glass, a skin of glass around a building: no longer a solid wall with windows. Even though the window might be the dominant part – this window is the wall itself, or in other words, this wall is itself the window. And with this we have come to a turning point.'[1]

Korn was describing the use of plate or sheet glass, but transparency has had a poetic as well as functional role in modern architecture. Bruno Taut's fantastical 1914 Glass Pavilion, his subsequent writings on sublime architecture in *Alpine Architektur* of 1919 and the discussion he initiated between architects under the rubric 'Die Gläserne Kette' (The glass chain) suggest that transparency also stood for mythic longings, a neo-Gothic sensibility.[2] On the other hand, transparency was central to the lightness and openness of Le Corbusier and Mies van der Rohe's experiments with the interpenetration of inner and outer space, which were intended to foster new ways of living. Montage, film, photography, and electronic and digital media have also figured in the architectural conception of transparency.[3]

If postmodern architecture rejected transparency in favour of fake solid walls and classically proportioned window openings, interest in transparency has now never been greater or more sophisticated in its expression – as, for instance, in the work of the Japanese architectural partnership SANAA and the accompanying writings of Eve Blau.[4] Glass and transparency are now all-pervasive elements of architectural practice and theory. But, to paraphrase Korn, the fact that invariably the window is the wall and the wall is the window means that ambitious architecture has ceased to provide a literal frame for traditional stained or architectural glass. Brian Clarke is one of the few architectural glass artists to have confronted this problem head-on.

The question of framing, as Glenn Adamson has pointed out in his book *Thinking through craft*, is usefully discussed in Jacques Derrida's essay on 'The truth in painting' in the context of the carved or gilt frame that traditionally surrounds a painting. The frame emphasizes the autonomy of the art-work by creating a visual caesura. The frame is therefore what Derrida calls a 'supplement', but he goes on to argue that the painting needs the frame, to screen out visual distractions, as much as the frame needs the painting. The perversity of the Derrida model helps us adjust our understanding of the role of stained glass in pre-modern architecture.[5] The building holds in place and valorizes its glass just as a frame holds and valorizes a painting. In some instances, at Chartres Cathedral for example, it could be argued that even a building can function as the supplement.

Many of Clarke's most dramatic designs are conventionally framed – traditional glass and lead inserted into openings in solid walls. It is a way of working he does not intend to relinquish. The Gothic Cistercian abbey church of Fille-Dieu at Romont in Switzerland, beautifully glazed by Clarke in 1996, is just one example of his mature style. Other, earlier, commissions responded to early industrial and commercial architecture – as with his contribution to the refurbishment of Joseph Paxton's Thermal Baths at Buxton (1984–7) and his creation of a stained glass roof to span a street of arcades in Leeds (1989).

But the greatest challenge is presented by the transparency of modernist

When glass is everywhere how does an architectural glass artist
h any degree of autonomy? The answer, in Clarke's case, has been
is way of working and turn to new materials and techniques. If
stained glass has obvious affinities with painting, Clarke's work for Norman
Foster at both the Al Faisaliah Complex in Riyadh (2000) and the Pyramid
of Peace at Astana, the new capital of Kazakhstan, suggests IMAX cinema or
monumental digital projection. His remarkable effects are achieved using
three laminated layers of float glass, each printed with enamel glass paint in
a different colour using a dot matrix. The result is daring and scenographic.
In the case of the Pyramid of Peace, whose apex is entirely glass dominated by
the yellow and green of the Kazakhstan flag overlaid with hugely scaled-up
fluttering doves, the cinematic effect is intentionally overwhelming, and has
drawn comparisons with Powell and Pressburger's filmic heaven in *A matter
of life and death*.[6]

This is glass unbound but it also serves to remind us of the complex
role of glass in modernist architecture. The writings and utopian drawings
of Bruno Taut, in which glass aspires to the monumental and the sacred,
form a sharp contrast to situations where glass lets in light, both actual and
metaphoric, to create a new openness. Foster and Clarke's collaboration in
Kazakhstan belongs firmly to the sacred strain in modernism's use of glass –
appropriately enough, given the cult of personality associated with Kazakhstan's President and his ambitious plans to debate world peace and the pro-
motion of faith and human equality in the very chamber glazed by Clarke. In
the end, therefore, this is not glass unbound. Kazakhstan has a poor human
rights record, and Clarke's frame here is an uneasy one, ideologically speaking.[7]

Clarke is an artist who paints and draws obsessively and continually. It
is therefore unsurprising that he has also undertaken glass projects that are
non-collaborative and literally free-standing. 'Lamina', shown in 2005 at the
Heddon Street Gagosian Gallery in London, develops Clarke's use of laminated glass combined with photographically generated imagery. Once again
the imagery and effect appear strikingly cinematic, in this instance bringing
to mind the work of the film-maker Patrick Keiller, whose un-peopled films
reflect on Englishness using lengthy single camera shots of foliage, complete
with ambient sound. Clarke's oak leaves and glimpses of cerulean printed
onto a curvilinear, undulating plate glass wall that spills out of the gallery
onto the street draws on a similar pastoral impulse. And as visitors walk
round the piece, altering the play of light, 'Lamina' shares territory with digital interactive art works while making most of them appear formulaic and
clunky.

Brian Clarke, 'Lamina', triple laminate float glass and dot matrix, 2005.

'Lamina' shares the wondrous quality of the best interactive digital art – by figures like Simon Heijdens – and, like Heijdens's work, can be fruitfully viewed as a form of magical technology.[8] The anthropologist Alfred Gell has written of the 'enchantment of technology' and of 'the power that technical processes have of casting a spell over us'.[9] For Gell – in search of a theory of art that bypassed art-world aesthetics – great art is defined by its transformative technical power. Gell's writings on the magical quality of technology appeared in the 1980s. They now appear prophetic of developments in fine art. Thomas Heatherwick's Seed Cathedral for the Shanghai Expo, Annie Cattrell's remarkable attempts to capture breath, the human heart, and diaphanous clouds, and Lu Shengzhong's monumental wall pieces made of scissored paper all have the quality of technological sublime that fascinated Gell. Like 'Lamina' they each in different ways enable us 'to see the real world in enchanted form'.

1. Quoted (at p. 286) in Adrian Forty, *Words and buildings: a vocabulary of modern architecture*, London: Thames & Hudson, 2000.

2. See Rosemarie Haag Bletter, 'The interpretation of the glass dream: Expressionist architecture and the history of the crystal metaphor', *Journal of the Society of Architectural Historians*, vol. 40, no. 1, 1981, pp. 20–43.

3. See Sergei M. Eisenstein, 'Montage and architecture', *Assemblage*, no. 10, 1989, 111–31.

4. Eve Blau, 'Tensions in transparency. Between information and experience: the dialectical logic of SANAA's architecture', *Harvard Design Magazine*, no. 29, 2008–9, pp. 29–37.

5. See the discussion in Glenn Adamson, *Thinking through craft*, Oxford: Berg, 2007, pp. 11–13.

6. Hugh Pearman, 'Architecture: one steppe beyond', *The Sunday Times*, 3 September 2006.

7. These thoughts on modernist use of glass are informed by Lutz Koepnick, 'Redeeming history? Foster's dome and the political aesthetic of the Berlin Republic', *German Studies Review*, vol. 24, no. 2, 2001, pp. 303–23.

8. See *Decode: digital design sensations*, London: Victoria & Albert Museum, 2010.

9. Alfred Gell, 'The technology of enchantment and the enchantment of technology' in *The art of anthropology: essays and diagrams*, London: Athlone Press, 1999, p. 163.

2012; commissioned for an as yet unpublished book of essays on Brian Clarke

The artist in residence

In 1949, the American poet Elizabeth Bishop was staying at Yaddo, a large country house in Saratoga Springs, New York. She was an artist in residence, freed from worldly cares and therefore able to put her creative gifts to their fullest use. But it did not quite work out like that, and she wrote unhappily to her friend the painter Loren MacIver: 'The people are mostly rather young and ebullient and I was never any good at horse play, even when I was as young as they are. A couple of the youngest boys I like quite well but god, are they intense, and a new poem appears about every hour.' A week or so later, she wrote to the poet Robert Lowell, 'I haven't been able to "work" at all so spend most of my time very pleasantly sitting on the balcony blowing bubbles.' On a later visit, she broke down completely and went on a drinking spree. She found the whole experience 'extremely lonely'.[1]

Artists' residencies can take many forms and are usually not as luxurious or as cut-off as at Yaddo. In Britain, an artist in residence is far more likely to be parachuted, alone, into an urban community to teach, lecture, conduct workshops, contribute to local regeneration projects, and in general be available, as well as making a body of new work. Such residencies stand for a democratization of the visual arts, forcing the artist to interact with local communities and people who may well be critical of, or indifferent to, artistic activity.[2] But artists' residencies can be a strikingly generous form of modern patronage, designed to bring artists together, to remove them from quotidian cares. In the case of visual artists, residencies can offer improved technical possibilities or a chance to work in an entirely new medium, as at the European Ceramic Work Centre at 's-Hertogenbosch, the Netherlands,[3] and at the Pilchuck Glass School in Stanwood, Washington, or at the Xerox Corporation's Palo Alto Research Center where artists are given the opportunity to form creative relationships with computer scientists.[4]

The residency phenomenon as we know it today seems, in the USA at least, to have come into being in the early twentieth century, perhaps as an off-shoot of summer schools like the Chautauqua Institution and the Alfred Summer School. But its antecedents can be traced back further. If we see the residency as a chance for an artist to work uninterruptedly and to expand intellectually, then parallels might be drawn with the opportunities offered to court artists from the Renaissance onwards. In seventeenth-century Italy, a generous patron might have granted an artist a salary over and above payment for specific works of art. In addition, the artist was often encouraged to travel and visit other collections at the patron's expense.[5] The enforced intimacy of life at court could, however, prove restricting as well as enabling. Perhaps, therefore, the first artists' residency proper appears in the 1660s, when winners of the French Prix de Rome were given the chance to live at the Académie de France in Rome and to engage in the study of the antique.[6] The scholarship came with strings attached. Traditionally one of the duties of a 'pensionnaire' was to create a steady supply of copies – both casts and paintings – to send back to France. The Prix de Rome was discontinued in 1968, though young French artists are still sent to Rome to the Académie's Villa Medici. British scholarships to Rome also continue to this day, even if they are no longer predicated on a study of Classical or Renaissance sculpture and architecture.

Many residencies, however, follow a rather later exemplar, seeking instead to recreate something of the experience of nineteenth-century rural artists' colonies. These aimed for what the art historian Nina Lübbren has called 'creative sociability' in remote unspoilt surroundings geographically removed from the demands of the art market.[7] Artists' colonies tended to be self-generating: the artificially created colony at Darmstadt funded by the Grand Duke Ernst Ludwig von Hessen in 1899 had a relatively short-lived existence. But although residencies are artificial constructs, like artists' colonies they provide the illusion of respite from the stresses of today's highly commodified art, craft, and design world. That the whole experience is meant to be the antithesis of normal domestic life reminds us that the home and family life has long been seen as the enemy of avant-gardism and indeed of utopian writing and thought.[8]

Residencies may have utopian ambitions but they are rarely set up in an entirely disinterested spirit. The exceptions are few. The enticingly named Akademie Schloss Solitude in Stuttgart insists that its participants will experience time in 'a different, qualitatively better way' and that a stay there 'may perhaps not bear fruit until much later'.[9] Similarly, the European Ceramic Work Centre prides itself on not demanding an exhibition at the end of each resident's stay. Nonetheless, as the writer Lorette Coen noted of the Centre: 'Nothing is imposed here; it's the place itself that makes demands.'[10] But many residencies are deliberately organized as creative pressure-cookers that are intended to push an artist's work forward then and there. Thus they often end with a group exhibition and a party, as at the Triangle Workshop in New York State. As Anthony Caro, Triangle's co-founder, explained in 1984: 'since it all exists on a shoe string, we depend on the generosity of a lot of the people who come to the party.'[11]

A group residency can be a challenging experience. Tales abound of humid North American summers, claustrophobic studios, tick-infested woods, uncongenial companions, uncomfortable accommodation, problems with materials, visitations from unsympathetic critics, late nights, and heavy drinking. A residency can, however, be a chance to reinvent both one's art and personhood. As Keith Roberts noted in a diary kept at the Triangle Workshop in the late 1990s: 'Now wear my Banesto hat at will, backwards, forwards, whatever, and everyone thinks I've always worn it in the studio. And here's the thing, there is no history, no precedent, so your work can be whatever you wish it.' Roberts felt daunted by the sculptors: 'Many look like heroes who might throw steel around as easily as cardboard.'[12] Artists' residencies are often characterized by physical activities: kiln building, wood-firing, and constructing steel sculpture. Making on a far bigger scale and throwing aesthetic caution to the winds are often central to the residency experience.

Sometimes, usually in smaller workshop situations, artists can be actively forced to make in new ways. At a mini-residency held at West Dean in England in the 1990s, the silversmith, sculptor, and jeweller Onno Boekhoudt denied a group of distinguished silversmiths the use of any but the simplest tools. Materials were restricted to clay, tissue paper, and sheet silver to challenge and disrupt hard-won skills.[13] At the other end of the spectrum, usually in the area of traditional craft, there are residencies that actively discourage innovation. A good example would be the workshops run at the Indian Crafts Museum in Delhi. Artisans are invited from all over India to work and to hone their skills. But collaborations and experimentation are not seen as desirable outcomes.[14]

There can be no doubt that group residencies provide an antidote to creative loneliness, enabling artists who work in geographic or intellectual isolation to come together. The forays by an artist like Picasso into print-making or ceramics fulfilled an analogical companionable goal. His creativity as a potter serves to remind us that residencies are invariably predicated on the production of art. So what happens when the actual making of art-works loses its intellectual purchase and artists turn to research projects in which activities such as painting, drawing, potting, or sculpting play little or no part?[15] Terry Atkinson, a founder member of Art & Language, the artists' group in England, has written an account of his visit in 1987 to Emma Lake, Canada, that reads like the death knell of the artists' residency. He arrived with a suitcase full of theoretical texts but was soon to deplore the lack of 'discursive exchange'. He found a culture of making upheld by 'modernist certainties'.[16]

Making is central to craft practice and, despite the urgent search for a theoretical underpinning for crafts, it seems unlikely that this will change. This is in part why the Wood Turning Center's International Turning Exchange in Philadelphia has proved to be so successful over the past decade. Making is put on display for the benefit of all. Many residencies offer artists individual studios, but the logic of a woodworking shop makes that kind of privacy impossible and undesirable. Thus at a Turning Exchange residency, the kind of tacit skills that are so characteristic of craft practice are readily and generously shared. But for a craft genre that has not had the kind of critical attention that has been paid to ceramics or textiles a residency like Turning Exchange has a further importance.

Both artists' colonies and residencies generate anecdotes. What the art historian and critic Michael Baxandall called 'the critico-mythic anecdote' has been used from Vasari onwards to situate artists and their achievements.[17] The art world is no longer intimate in the way that Vasari's Florence was intimate, but the late nineteenth-century artists' colony and the twentieth- and twenty-first-century residency generate anecdotal narratives that neatly condense ideas about creativity and artistry. Anecdote, an 'episode from the secret life' of an artist, serves to disrupt the grand narratives of progress that characterize conventional art history, including monolithic accounts of modernism which exclude the applied arts.[18] Anecdote and story telling, as Nina Lübbren argues, need to be rehabilitated in order to write more nuanced art history.

International Turning Exchange residencies throw up a great range of stories as well as objects. The material is multi-layered and exceptionally well documented – through the participants' responses to detailed questionnaires and through accounts of each residency published in the magazine *Turning Points*. Significantly, a photojournalist or scholar records each residency – and often learns wood-turning in the process. This body of writing generates recurring themes that have distinctly critico-mythic qualities.

142

Epiphanies occur when residents see new art or visit important collections. There are arcadian encounters with nature and periods of despair and loneliness. Often there is cathartic change, a shift to less functional or physically larger work, a move away from utility towards poetics, a narrative of progress. Some anecdotes are more mysterious, such as when an accident leads into a new way of working or when a respected fellow artist brings gifts that carry veiled meanings.

Some accounts of the Turning Exchange residencies recall the intense individualism of post-war modernism in New York.[19] Personalities clash but result in intense friendships and mutual aid. Discussions continue far into the night. Other accounts recall the vivid intimacies of Vasari's *Lives of the artists*, like the moment when Todd Hoyer and Hayley Smith worked on a piece together (a collaboration that led to marriage); when Gordon Peteran 'performed' wood-turning with a pencil sharpener and a pencil, with exquisite, if ironic, skill; or when Remi Verchot burst on the scene in 1999, only 19-years-old but brilliantly mature. As in Vasari, the scene is animated by the presence of proud and knowledgeable patrons and by scholars and connoisseurs. One decorative arts historian associated with the Turning Exchange, Edward S. Cooke, has provided an account of wood-turning that sets forth its high status as a polite technology practised by princes, its decline through association with the industrial revolution, and its recuperation during the craft renaissance of the 1970s. The scholarship is impeccable. Cooke also gives us a gripping narrative that satisfyingly concludes in an expansive present.[20]

A residency is an artificial construct but individual residents have experiences that are vivid and sometimes life-changing. Residencies may encourage new work and new ambitions. They also generate narratives that belong to the long history of artists' anecdotes. Dealing as they do with heroics, comedy, irony, and romance, these narratives need to be handled with caution.[21] But they are also a resource, deepening our understanding of how artists represent themselves and providing insights into what it means to be an artist.

1. Elizabeth Bishop, *One art: letters*, edited by Robert Giroux (1994), London: Pimlico, 1996, pp. 187, 193, 216.
2. For examples, see *Artist in and out of industry: residency schemes: the long-term effect on four artists*, Middlesbrough: Cleveland County Museum Service, 1985; 'Studios International: residency schemes home and abroad', *Alba*, 1988; *Riverscape: four international artist residencies*, Middlesbrough: Cleveland Arts, 1993.
3. There are many associated publications, but see *Tony Cragg: In camera*, Eindhoven: Van Abbemuseum, 1993.
4. Craig Harris (ed.), *Art and innovation: the Xerox PARC artist-in-residence program*, Cambridge, Mass.: MIT Press, 1999.
5. Francis Haskell, *Patrons and painters: art and society in Baroque Italy* (1963), New Haven: Yale University Press 1980, pp. 7–22; Martin Warnke, *The court artist: on the ancestry of the modern artist*, Cambridge: Cambridge University Press, 1993.

6. Jean-Baptiste Joly, 'About the necessity of residential centers in the contemporary context of art', talk given 4 May 1996, < www.resartis.org/en/activities__projects/meetings /general_meetings/1996_-_dublin/jean-baptiste_joly/ >.

7. Nina Lübbren, *Rural artists' colonies in Europe 1870–1910*, Manchester: Manchester University Press, 2001, pp. 17–36; Jean-Baptiste Joly, 'About the necessity of residential centers' (see note 6).

8. Christopher Reed, 'Introduction', in Christopher Reed (ed.), *Not at home: the suppression of domesticity in modern art and architecture*, London: Thames & Hudson, 1996.

9. Guiding principles of the Akademie Schloss Solitude. See also < www.akademie-solitude. de/en/institution/guiding-principles/ >.

10. Alexander Brodsky & Ilya Utkin, *The portal*, 's-Hertogenbosch: Europees Keramisch Werkcentrum, 1994.

11. Anthony Caro et al, 'Triangle Workshop: a discussion between Anthony Caro, Barry Martin, Mali Morris, John Gibbons and David Koloane', *Art Monthly*, no. 74, March 1984, p. 6.

12. Keith Roberts, 'Diary: Triangle Workshop' (Keith Roberts private archive).

13. For a similarly disruptive project in the craft area see Andreas Fabian & Simone ten Hompel, *A field of silver – silver in a field*, London: London Metropolitan University, 2002.

14. Paul Greenough, 'Nation, economy, and tradition displayed: the Indian Crafts Museum, New Delhi', in C. A. Breckenridge (ed.), *Consuming modernity*, Minneapolis: University of Minnesota Press, 1995.

15. See, for instance, *Capital: a project by Neil Cummings and Marysia Lewandowska*, London: Tate Publishing, 2001.

16. Terry Atkinson, 'From the lake of the swamp' in John O'Brian (ed.), *The flat side of the landscape: the Emma Lake artists' workshops*, Saskatoon: Mendel Art Gallery, 1989, pp. 62–7.

17. Michael Baxandall, 'Doing Justice to Vasari', *Times Literary Supplement*, 1 February 1980, p. 111.

18. Ernst Kris & Otto Kurz, *Legend, myth, and magic in the image of the artist* (1934), New Haven: Yale University Press, 1979, p. 10; cited in Lübbren, *Rural artists' colonies* (note 7 above).

19. For a critical account of this 'heroic' modernism, see Alex Potts, 'Autonomy in post-war art, quasi-heroic and casual', *Oxford Art Journal*, vol. 27, no. 1, 2004, pp. 43–59.

20. See, for example, these articles by Edward S. Cooke: 'Wood in the 1980s: expansion or commodification?' in Davira Taragin (ed.), *Contemporary crafts and the Saxe Collection*, New York: Hudson Hill Press, 1993; 'Turning wood in America: new perspectives on the lathe' in T. Turner (ed.), *Expressions in wood: masterworks from the Wornick Collection*, Washington: University of Washington Press, 1997; 'Turning and contemporary studio furniture: an uneasy relationship', in *Papers from the 1997 World Turning Conference*, Philadelphia: Wood Turning Center, 2000; 'From manual training to freewheeling craft: the transformation of wood turning, 1900–79' in *Wood turning in North America since 1930*, Philadelphia and New Haven: Wood Turning Center / Yale University Art Gallery, 2001.

21. This list comes close to the basic 'emplotments' which Hayden White sees as informing the writing of narrative history. See Hayden White, *Metahistory: the historic imagination in nineteenth-century Europe*, Baltimore, MD: Johns Hopkins University Press, 1973.

Written for *Connections: International Turning Exchange, 1995–2005*, Philadelphia: Wood Turning Exchange, 2005.

Reading

Unpacking my library

Rainy March is a good time to stay quietly indoors and tidy up and rearrange my books. This is not a straightforward task. An interest in the crafts demands adventurous book collecting because the subject itself has hardly begun to generate a literature of its own. So although I have sections devoted to ceramics, textiles, glass, metalwork, and so on, it would be a dull library that was simply made up of titles on the applied arts. In fact it is the peripheral books, which only just touch on the world of the handmade, that are the most inspiring. They include Peter Wollen's *Raiding the ice box: reflections on twentieth-century culture*, Christopher Reed's edited book of essays *Not at home: the suppression of domesticity in modern art and architecture*, Pat Kirkham's biography *Charles and Ray Eames, designers of the twentieth century*, Bruce Adams's *Rustic cubism: Anne Dangar and the art colony at Moly-Sabata* and Marshall Berman's *All that is solid melts into air*. Each challenges conventional histories of twentieth-century art and design, and all, in different ways, allow space for something that we might call 'craft'.

They share shelf space with a small but choice group of texts by anthropologists, starting with Alfred Gell's *Art and agency* and his book of essays, *The art of anthropology* with its two essential articles, 'The technology of enchantment and the enchantment of technology' and 'Vogel's net: traps as artworks and artworks as traps'. Arjun Appadurai's *The social life of things* is another indispensable, with two particularly fine essays by Brian Spooner and C. A. Bayly on oriental rugs and on the Indian *Swadeshi* movement. Then there is Mary Douglas's classic study of consumption *The world of goods* and James Clifford's bold reframing of ethnography, travel writing, and art history in *The predicament of culture*. If we are interested in craft we are bound to attend to anti-modernism in all its varied forms. For many artists and designers an improved future was shaped through the study of the past or of geographically remote cultures. Thus we need books on tourism (Dean MacCannell's classic *The tourist*), books on artists' colonies (Nina Lübbren's *Rural artists' colonies in Europe 1870–1910*), and the vast literature that comes under the rubric of post-colonialism and orientalism. Everyone has favourite texts in this area but two of mine are Anne McClintock's *Imperial leather* and Marianna Torgovnick's impassioned *Gone primitive*. Another crucial text has to be Daniel Miller's 'Primitive art and the necessity of primitivism to art', to be found in Susan Hiller's *The myth of primitivism*.

Then there is the category of experiential books by makers, designers, and those who have closely observed making. There is a surprising amount to be learned about making processes in Marx's *Capital*, particularly on the

148

uncanny way in which industrial machinery replicated the actions and forms of hand tools. But George Sturt's *The wheelwright's shop* heads the experiential list, followed by Dorothy Hartley's remarkable *Made in England*. Anything by Le Corbusier is worth reading, but especially *The decorative art of today* and the English edition of the notebooks he kept on his *Voyage d'Orient*. Norman Potter's *What is a designer* and *Models & constructs* introduce us to a most unusual design intelligence, while Michael Cardew's autobiography *A pioneer potter* and his highly technical *Pioneer pottery* outclass anything else in the ceramic field. Robin Wood's *The wooden bowl* touches the same heights in the context of wood-turning, along with Fred Smeijers's *Counterpunch*, an extraordinary book that looks afresh at the now arcane craft of punchcutting.

Finally, poets and novelists win an honoured place on my shelves if they attend to the world of objects or the making of objects. Their writing functions as inspiration, providing a reason to go on looking. Thomas Hardy wrote some haunting 'object' poems – like 'The convergence of the twain' in which he describes the building of The Titanic while in sinister parallel:

'as the smart ship grew
In stature, grace and hue,
In shadowy silent distance grew the Iceberg too.'

There are old favourites like Wallace Stevens's 'Anecdote of the jar' and new discoveries like James Schuyler's homage to the potter Andrew Lord in his *Last poems*. The great Elizabeth Bishop is another fine thing poet. Here are two lines from her tough little poem 'The Bight':

'The frowsy sponge boats keep coming in
With the obliging air of retrievers'

The passage in my copy is marked in a way that would horrify a bibliophile, by turning down the corner of the relevant page, just as I've so marked the chapter entitled 'A chair' in D.H. Lawrence's *Women in love* and the ninth of Rilke's *Duino elegies*. Thing-sensitive literature is an endlessly expanding field, but I'll end with Defoe's *Robinson Crusoe*. Defoe deals poetically with tools, simple shelters, and the creation of pots and baskets. Crusoe's attempt at boat-building can stand as a warning to all makers. After labouring for several months Crusoe discovers that his boat is too heavy to drag down to the water, testifying to 'the folly of beginning a work before we count the cost, and before we judge rightly of our own strength to go through with it'.

Crafts, no.199, March/April 2006

I am not sure why I did not mention Walter Benjamin, who gave me the title of this piece. Esther Leslie's brilliant essay 'Walter Benjamin: traces of craft' shows where to look in Benjamin's writings. It is reprinted in Glenn Adamson (ed.), *The craft reader*, London: Bloomsbury/Berg, 2010.

Writing *The crafts in Britain in the 20th century*

The crafts – it would be difficult to think of a subject with a more fragile and compromised identity. Conversations would go like this: 'So what exactly is your design book about?' 'Well, it's a study of the crafts actually, the hand-made in the twentieth century in Britain, a sort of wide-ranging social history ... a remapping of visual culture.' But the word craft would already have had its electrifyingly negative effect – 'The crafts – you mean macramé and that kind of thing.' Further explanations – that I was writing a book which showed how the crafts were bearers of dreams and ideals, standing for, variously, English modernism, an arcadian de-industrialized England, democracy in all the arts, and post-war contacts with advanced art in Continental Europe – would fade on the air. And worryingly my book begins with an ending. William Morris and the Arts & Crafts movement tower over any discussion of modern handwork. Morris's career got under way in the 1860s; the Arts & Crafts movement was given a name and a public identity with the founding of the Arts & Crafts Exhibition Society in 1888. Morris and the men and women in the movement left behind a powerful set of buildings, objects, and interiors, together with an important body of writing. Everyone knew that around 1914 the movement fizzled out and lost its way.

Of course this was far from being the case. But art and design historians still tend to present the reader with an evolutionary, baton-passing view of visual culture in which movement leads on to movement, progressively. My book adopted a different approach and probably could only have been written at this postmodern moment when faith in human progress and perfectibility is at an all-time low. In the book I chose to watch the crafts over the century, watch as the crafts endlessly redefined themselves, and redefined their various practices in relation to fine art, design, modernism, education, patterns of consumption, class, politics and all sorts of currents in social and cultural history.

The crafts – from ceramics to silversmithing, from stained glass to hand-block printing – emerged as having multivalent and constructed personae, and it is this shifting identity which makes them so absorbing. Craft could encompass blind ex-servicemen making nets just after the First World War at the philanthropic workshops set up by the charity St Dunstan's, miners' wives in the Rhondda Valley making quilts under the aegis of the Rural Industries Bureau in the Depression of the late 1920s, and hand-block printed textiles designed and made by Phyllis Barron for the Duke of Westminster's yacht Flying Cloud in the early 1920s. Any definition of craft could also take in a good deal of handwork in industry and surviving vernacular craft such as hurdle-making or basketry. After the Second World War the situation becomes, if anything, more complex.

Many themes are explored in the book but one of the most important and captivating is the relationship of the crafts to English modernism and feminism between the World Wars. (Things are rather different in Scotland, as I try to indicate.) In England, creative men and women alike subscribed to an adaptation of Continental modernism, and, in terms of this English modernism, hand-block printed textiles, highly textured weaving, and austere stoneware pots were at the adventurous end of the design world in the 1920s. In the area of textiles, in particular, women were the pioneers, part of a forgotten history of modernism dominated by hand-processes.

In fact the crafts provided an important creative space and income in a time of social and economic stasis for women in general. The major gain in the early part of the century, the admission to the franchise, led to few other advances for women. The proportion in the professions moved very little; it was no higher in the early 1950s than it had been in 1914. The crafts in effect operated for women as a 'third space' between the better defined activities of fine art and design. Not surprisingly a marked number of inter-war women makers never married – a characteristically modern decision being made for the first time in those years. Many made their lives with other women, devotedly. They formed strong networks, with each other and with women patrons and retailers. Wealthy women like Margaret Pilkington and Dorothy Elmhirst created opportunities – in Elmhirst's case by commissioning work, and in Pilkington's case through involvement in exhibiting societies and above all through her creation of the Red Rose Guild of Artworkers in 1921. The main retail outlets for inter-war craft were run by women.

But an unmarried status has consquences. It is striking how few letters and archives associated with inter-war women makers survive. The papers of male makers, like those of male artists, designers, and architects, were carefully preserved by their wives and children. But the nieces and nephews of many women makers saw no reason to honour the memory of an eccentric deceased aunt who wove, or made pots or stained glass windows. Where archival material survives, personal letters have often been carefully filleted out. All we have are fragments – like Katharine Pleydell-Bouverie and Norah Braden's more intimate letters to Bernard Leach, with their records of tiffs between lovers, visits to exhibitions, books read, and battles with materials. What we can discover of the untramelled, buoyant lives of these women – financially independent, creative, cultivated, quarrelsome, and loving – suggests that the special freedom conferred by staying outside the conventionalities of marriage was central to their creativity.

Inscribed in the activities of these inter-war women modernists are stories of liberation. Take Elizabeth Peacock. She had remained a semi-invalid at home until 1916, when, at the age of 36, she suddenly defied her family and joined Ethel Mairet's first workshop at Shottery in Stratford-upon-Avon. Suppose she had lacked the courage? Radclyffe Hall's novel of 1924, *The unlit lamp*, sets out one possible outcome. The heroine Joan is too fearful to leave her tyrannical mother and ends her days caring for a capricious mentally handicapped old uncle. Peacock's life story worked out better. She moved with Mairet to Ditchling and found a life-long companion in Molly Stobart, the daughter of a local landowner. By 1922 Molly's family had built them a home, 'Weavers', and provided a smallholding at Clayton, under the South Downs, with Peacock's brother contributing a workshop across the yard. She became quietly famous. King Faisal of Egypt bought her lengths of handwoven cotton. Her shawls and dress lengths were bought by Schiaparelli. She was also ambitious artistically; the sequence of eight monumental banners commissioned by Dorothy Elmhirst for the utopian community at Dartington Hall, woven from 1930 until 1938, suggest her genius for abstract design on a large scale.

The chameleon crafts take the curious writer in many directions – into utopian communities and small half-forgotten political parties, into remarkable wartime propaganda exercises like the exhibition of 'Modern British Crafts' sent by the British Council to the USA in 1942, into the South Bank Exhibition of the Festival of Britain, where the crafts were used to illustrate themes as diverse as good design and the British character. In the 1970s the crafts stood for, variously, the counter-culture and individual freedom, while its crossovers into conceptual art were celebrated by the newly formed Crafts Advisory Committee. By the 1980s the crafts reinvented themselves again, as Thatcherite 'small businesses' and as providers of corporate craft for the lush foyers of Nigel Lawson's 'enterprise culture'. And the 1990s? Undoubtedly quite another story, but one which is bound to be similarly emblematic of the desires and anxieties of the decade.

The Independent, 10 February 2000, and *Crafts*, no. 162, January / February 2000

152

The apprentice

Martin Gayford, David Kindersley, & Lida Lopes Cardozo Kindersley, *Apprenticeship: the necessity of learning by doing*, Cambridge: Cardozo Kindersley, 2003.

'Letters grow. It is not a stroke with a little bit stuck on. A letter begins from itself. That is what I call "home-going". The problem is that everything I tell you, and all that you have to draw and know will be invisible. When a serif "looks" home-going you have overdone it. It must have the "feel" of an upturn, not the look. The same for the whole serif – it has to look a straight line, yet in order to make it look straight you cannot make it straight. There is no such thing as a straight line in the cut capital alphabet that we are going to learn. In order to make it look straight it has to be slightly curved.'

This is the remembered voice of the lettercutter David Kindersley, vividly recalled by his widow and former apprentice Lida Lopes Cardozo Kindersley.

Just now apprenticeships in the so-called creative and cultural industries are being encouraged and discussed, mostly under the aegis of the government funded Creative and Cultural Skills, part of the Learning and Skills Council. This autumn will see the launch of Creative Apprenticeships, described as 'the first officially recognised apprenticeship framework for the creative and cultural industries'. There was a successful trial run in the summer of 2007 and EMI, Sage Gateshead, the Institute of Field Archaeologists, the National Trust, and the Royal Opera House, have supported the scheme from the outset. The Crafts Council, as one might expect, has also been involved.

But although the crafts might seem the obvious place for learning by doing there is no database of makers who are willing to offer apprenticeships – although the Art Workers' Guild is working on such a project. But it appears that few individual makers are willing formally to come forward. Typing 'apprenticeship' into the Crafts Council's own website yielded just three search responses – James and Tilla Waters, who served apprenticeships with Rupert Spira, the Prince's Foundation for the Built Environment (which runs a Building Crafts Apprentice scheme), and the Cardozo Kindersley Workshop, publishers of *Apprenticeship: the necessity of learning by doing* – the source of my opening quotation.

It is both instructive and moving to read Lida Kindersley's beautiful little book *Apprenticeship*. Opening with a helpful short history of the topic, the art historian Martin Gayford observes that, in the case of the visual arts, techniques have become so personalized that there is little practical knowledge to pass on – and the same might be said of the work of many makers. Idi-

The Cardozo Kindersley Workshop cutting the Churchill Archives inscription in situ, Cambridge, 2002.

osyncratic methods of facture are their signature. As Gayford points out, formal education lasts much longer than in the past and, increasingly, academic qualifications are seen as the only recognized way of gaining knowledge.

Although phrases like mentoring and work experience are bandied about, they suggest something less demanding – on the part of teacher and pupil – than apprenticeship in the traditional sense. It is not possible, nor even desirable, to go back to 'traditional' trade apprenticeships – which were often ways of employing the young cheaply and educating them exceptionally slowly. But it is surely the duty of gifted makers to feel positive about passing on their skills in a studio environment. Yet when Lida Kindersley spoke about this moral imperative at the Art Workers' Guild in 2000 she got a mixed reception.

The simple fact is that most craft studios are one-person affairs that could not afford to pay an apprentice wages. Ironically, the paid apprenticeship is more likely to flourish in areas remote from the crafts. Young doctors serve apprenticeships in hospitals after qualifying. Young accountants learn on the job while studying for their exams. So have the crafts become too marginal or too individualistic to offer that kind of education?

Certain crafts, often those to do with building conservation, seem to lend themselves to an apprenticeship. Lettercutting is another candidate, supported, for instance, by the Lettering & Commemorative Arts Trust which funds yearly apprenticeships. It is a great art form that demands absolute technical confidence and mastery. Lida Kindersley's book ends with a description of her team of five cutting an inscription at the Churchill Archives Centre in Cambridge. 'Everyone gave their best and was bravely hammering straight into the Portland stone wall. Any mistakes made would affect all of us; there was no room for correction if a mistake is made.' That at least three of those hammering were apprentices suggests the extraordinary nature of this kind of education.

Crafts, no. 214, September / October 2008

Making art work

Patsy Craig (ed.), *Making art work: the Mike Smith Studio*, London: Trolley, 2003

'I think my think and then I make my think.' For Eric Gill this remark made by a small child seemed to get to the heart of creativity, as well as being the sharply practical antithesis of most musings on art. Gill was good at realizing his 'think' in a range of media. He was only defeated by one project – a plan hatched with Jacob Epstein for a Stonehenge of monumental figures to stand somewhere in the Sussex countryside. This was abandoned not for practical reasons but because of a mysterious, if predictable, quarrel between the two men.

Gill was, in most technical respects, a traditionalist, even a neo-primitive. But innovative art often demands innovative practice, which is why the history of art is littered with ambitious unfulfilled dreams. Sometimes the solution is simply to ask a fellow artist for help. Thus, just as Michelangelo sorted out Sebastiano del Piombo's perspective, initially at least Anthony Caro got assistance with welding from fellow sculptors like David Annesley. There are endless examples of this kind of co-operation. In other areas, for instance bronze casting or print-making, there has been a tradition of division of labour whereby artists could turn to professional technicians and fabricators.

But in certain circumstances the facilitator of an artist's ideas can end up feeling undervalued while, in turn, the artist may be unwilling to acknowledge collaborative help. I do not imagine that the workforce that cast Barbara Hepworth's 'Single form' in 1964 at the Morris Singer foundry felt anxious about matters of authorship. Foundries have existed for centuries and their function is well understood. But Dicon Nance, as the carver of many of Hepworth's sculptures in stone, was less happy with his role. Her stone sculpture was predicated on an early-modern endorsement of direct carving and Nance, sometimes working from a rough sketch, often felt he should have got more credit for his input. In quite a different cultural context, the highly skilled granite carvers of Mahabalipuram in India who worked for the British sculptor Stephen Cox in the 1980s felt similarly unregarded.

Issues of authorship and intentionality can be very complex. In his provocative book *Art and agency* the late Alfred Gell shows art to be a series of social relationships between objects and persons. Some objects, for instance Chinese cloudstones, author themselves. They are recognized rather than made by artists. Sometimes the patron is the author, as arguably was the case with Louis XIV's creation of Versailles. Sometimes the owner works on the object, as when a Volt sorcery devotee sticks pins into a wax image of an enemy. By removing their sole agency, Gell's approach ought to appeal to contemporary artists. It is, after all, commonplace to reject the idea of festering obsessively in a studio, making. Instead, many artists see themselves as akin to film directors or curators, always on the move and more likely to use a laptop than a paintbrush. Taking the practice of Marcel Duchamp or Andy Warhol's Factory as a model, evidence of individual touch or mark-making are to be avoided at all costs.

Patsy Craig's book *Making art work: the Mike Smith Studio* suggests, however, that most artists cling passionately to their authorial status and that relations between ideas and outcomes have never been more problematic. Mike Smith is an artist turned fabricator. His clients since the 1980s read like a checklist of prominent Young British Artists. His workshop made, *inter alia*, Damien Hirst's tanks and vitrines, Darren Almond's series of clocks, Mona Hatoum's Brobdingnagian kitchen equipment, Michael Landy's people-chipper-shredder, and Rachel Whiteread's 'Monument' for Trafalgar Square. As this list suggests, each commission demands that Smith learn a whole new set of constructional skills in order to enable these artists to go beyond simply thinking their think. Understandably, therefore, in a series of discussions with the artists who have used Smith's expertise, interviewer William Furlough often refers to collaboration and authorial negotiation. But, almost without exception, such ideas are fiercely resisted by the artists. As Alex Hartley puts it: 'I use Mike as a tool like every other tool'. He goes on to say 'he's going to piss artists off if he starts claiming their work'. The aim of *Making art work* was presumably to recognize Mike Smith's undoubted contribution to the British art scene. But only Darren Almond and Cerith Wyn Evans are willing to give Smith credit for anything much more than practical artisanship. So the book is also a fascinating series of portraits of a group of contemporary artists. That they emerge as ungenerous and egotistical but also plagued by self-loathing and doubt only adds to its interest.

Crafts, no. 187, March/April 2004

Lurking anxiety and a sense of loss

A. S. Byatt, *The children's book*, London: Chatto & Windus, 2009

This is an extreme moment for the idea of 'craft'. A fashionable topic at a conceptual level, its viability and context as an art form is uncertain and obscure. What has caused this sudden collapse of confidence? One reason may be the fact that as a form of visual modernism, studio craft (as opposed to handwork in general) has always thrived as an oppositional activity, as a kind of reserve of anti-modernity. There was the factory and the large commercial workshop and, by contrast, the studio – a place of free creativity, a place to re-examine the politics of work, to look forward and to look back. As Britain became, increasingly, a service economy that dialectic was undermined.

An acute analysis of the political domain of craft is part of the project of A. S. Byatt's latest novel *The children's book*. It opens in 1895, the year of the trial of Oscar Wilde and ends in the trenches and mud of the First World War. This is, as far as I know, the first historical novel to honour the dreams and aspirations of the Arts & Crafts movement and it succeeds in offering an uncannily accurate account of advanced artistic and literary society at the turn of the last century. Figures like the artist and designer Walter Crane and the architect C. R. Ashbee had social lives that were strikingly similar to the milieu described by Byatt: bohemian, high-minded, politically adventurous, child-centred, socially concerned, and caught up in a multitude of interlinked causes – psychical research, theosophy, suffrage, anarchism, anti-vivisection. *The children's book* is heavily researched, a mass of material presented foursquare, relentlessly. But somehow it succeeds – as a haunting account of the lurking anxiety and the sense of loss that characterized the late Victorian and Edwardian age.

Part of that feeling of loss was to do with old skills and ancient craft. Byatt makes two activities central to the story – puppetry and ceramics – and she brings out the reparative nature of their revival and the poetry of their respective technologies. Benedict Fludd is a maker of aesthetic ceramics, working alone, living in poverty with his wife and children. He is a sinister figure, but his pots, wonderfully described, appear to be a mixture of William De Morgan's lustres, Bernard Moore's *flambé* glazes, and the glittering beauties of Eltonware. Fludd takes on Philip Warren, self-educated, hiding and sleeping overnight in the South Kensington Museum. He is hungry for an education in art and on the run from a lowly job in the grimy, smoky Potteries. On occasion Byatt gets her glazes and frits a bit mixed up but on the whole she provides a marvellous account of ceramics as art and as science and of the risks faced by the solitary innovator. As Fludd explains 'failure with clay is more complete and more spectacular than with other forms of art'.

Byatt is also a brilliant exponent of puppetry, an art form that appears all through the book, metaphorically mirroring the way in which her characters manipulate and are manipulated. She invents Anselm Stern, a puppeteer from Munich, perhaps based on the Viennese artist and puppeteer Richard Teschner. Stern is in flight from the plodding realism of mainstream theatre. He is inspired by Kleist's inspirational essay 'On the marionette theatre' and he is a member of the politicized Munich avant-garde, together with Frank Wedekind and his cabaret, the Elf Scharfrichter. Both the pottery and puppets get their strength and inspiration by looking backwards and looking outside Europe. They stand for the anti-modernity that was central to being modern circa 1900.

Like all good historical novels, *The children's book* causes us to reflect on the present. These days the word craft does not carry with it a sense of mourning for the lost domain that so haunted the Edwardians. But a reversion to making singlehandedly can still pack an ideological punch. Take Thomas Thwaites, who recently decided to build an electric toaster by digging up raw materials, processing them, and forming them into a handcrafted equivalent of an item that costs £3.99 at Argos. The result, Thwaites acknowledges, is absurd: an electrical appliance that sets out to disavow the infrastructure on which it relies, 'a domestic product produced on a domestic scale'. The potters, puppeteers, and political activists of *The children's book* would not have found it beautiful, unlike the electrical lighting that so awed them at the 1900 Paris Exhibition. But on a political and poetic level some of them would have understood the implications of Thwaites's project. To reiterate, at one end there is still the factory (and now a world of throwaway goods) and, by contrast, there remains the studio – a place of free creativity, a place to re-examine the politics of work, to look forward and to look back.

Crafts, no. 220, September/October 2009

After writing this I went with Glenn Adamson to interview A. S. Byatt about *The children's book*. The delightful result can be read in *The Journal of Modern Craft*, vol. 4, no. 1, 2011.

Concrete and curlicues

Alexandra Harris, *Romantic moderns: English writers, artists and the imagination from Virginia Woolf to John Piper*, London: Thames & Hudson, 2010

In 1934 Herbert Read published *Art and industry*: a primer that set out principles for good industrial design. The most important discussion of the topic to appear in Britain in the inter-war years, it was also a defence of abstract artists as the most likely creators of the pure forms required for machine-made multiple production. Read looked to Germany for many of the product illustrations in *Art and industry* and was helped in this by the émigré constructivist László Moholy-Nagy. But Read also included exemplary images of Sung dynasty Chinese pots, a vernacular Windsor chair, and eighteenth-century British glass and silver.

This turn to pre-industrial prime objects was not a sign of a particularly British conservatism. In continental Europe architects and designers also valued the vernacular and 'earliness'. There was nothing monolithic about visual modernism in the first half of the twentieth century; faced with the messy, commercialized vulgarities of modernity, modernism was often 'anti-modern'. Designers and architects as different as Adolf Loos, Le Corbusier, and Berthold Lubetkin were all inspired by the past and the vernacular present, by peasant pottery, primordial log cabins, and Islamic carpets.

In 1936 Herbert Read's adventurous mind and psychoanalytic interests led him to endorse Surrealism, editing a collection of essays to accompany the International Surrealist Exhibition held in London that year. And in Alexandra Harris's remarkable *Romantic moderns* we meet Read in yet another incarnation, as a Yorkshireman who claimed to be 'by birth and tradition a peasant', the editor of two anthologies of prose and verse – *The English vision* and *The knapsack* – that stressed a rooted Englishness.

Romantic moderns is not about British design, nor does it focus on the left-wing politics that underpinned the technological romanticism and drive for scientific planning during the 1930s. Instead Harris charts a 'passionate, exuberant return to tradition' among a loosely linked group of writers and artists just before and during the Second World War. Her argument depends, in part, upon a creative misreading of the Modern movement as a dismayingly functionalist programme that rejected history and tradition, seeking a *tabula rasa* devoid of national or local identity. With John Betjeman and John Piper in mind she asks whether it 'was a betrayal of the Modern movement to be in love with old churches and tea-shops; was this a case of giving up and going home?' It is a simple enough question that is belied by the sophisticated analysis that follows.

The font at Toller Fratrum: photograph by John Piper, 1936.

Harris's insights are based on a close, imaginative reading of collaborations and connections mapped through friendships and unlikely encounters. Her book is full of vivid snapshots, telling detail, and beguiling loose ends. Her acute period eye presents 'an elastic kind of England, a bit seedy and very stylish, full of contrasts and odd pairings, and all the better for that'. Read's move from industrial design to Surrealism suddenly appears less strange and, as Harris points out, Read claimed the movement for England, invoking Edward Lear and Lewis Carroll and finding 'all the ingredients' of the surreal in the Pre-Raphaelites. In England, the insular and the avant-guarde were intertwined.

In a fold of the South Downs, the artist Peggy Angus entertained Moholy-Nagy together with Eric Ravilious, whose Cubism was braided with the wood engravings of Thomas Bewick. *The Architectural Review*, edited by Angus's husband J. M. Richards, featured both 'concrete and curlicues', with articles on the latest architecture jostling with studies of chromolithography and the lavish taxonomy of Edwardian pub interiors. Myfanwy Evans and

John Piper edited her avant-garde journal *Axis* from the kitchen table of an old flint-walled farmhouse. From this deep England John Piper studied the aerial photography of archaeological sites, seeing these images as nativist abstraction while the Norman carvings on the font at Toller Fratrum in Dorset appeared to anticipate the 'bigness and strangeness' of Picasso's figuration. With such riches, Europe could be ignored. As Laurence Binyon put it: 'There was no need to invoke Cézanne for Cotman was there to show the way.' Pure abstraction came to seem sterile.

All this is familiar but has never been told quite so acutely and well. Harris also charts a darker struggle with objects and interiors played out in literature, in Virginia Stephens's flight from Palace Gate in Kensington to emptier rooms and brilliantly fragmentary writing; and through Elizabeth Bowen's unnervingly claustrophobic interiors where her characters live, as the young heroine of *The hotel* observes, 'under the compulsion of their furniture'. Meanwhile the author's ancestral home Bowen's Court, with its bare four-square rooms, suggested a means of escape through a return to the past. The eighteenth century offered an alternative that was both insular and pan-European, old but proto-modern.

The Georgian Group, set up in 1937, brought together modernists and antiquarians in flight from Victorian historicism and the debased Arts & Crafts Tudorbethan of the suburbs. But, as Harris shows, this 'elastic' pursuit of national identity also allowed for a Victorian afterlife. In *Orlando* Woolf represented the nineteenth century as a black cloud while Roger Fry saw repression and conformity in Victorian upholstery and busy ornament. But Fry also predicted the period's imminent rediscovery by a younger generation. Evelyn Waugh, Betjeman, Cecil Beaton, and Edward Bawden reified their anti-modernism by admiring wax fruits under glass domes, lush narrative paintings and Arundel prints. Obsolete objects became markers of aesthetic freedom.

A passion for rediscovery, collecting, and reframing, and a desire to recuperate forgotten areas of the national culture took many of the characters in *Romantic moderns* map-reading and exploring, orientalizing on home ground, seeking out the lost rose garden and the decayed manor house at the end of the abandoned drive. *Romantic moderns* investigates a literary, topographical, and architectural search for a lost domain made more urgent by war. Harris brings a sympathetic eye to what can be read as compensatory home-making, taking in Beaton's Ashcombe, Stephen Tennant's Wilsford, Lord Berners's Faringdon, and Waugh's Piers Court. (The Sitwells' Renishaw might be classified as a 'readymade', an inherited house crowded with history.) Harris identifies both the modernity and the archaism of aesthetes in fancy dress, characterizing Beaton and his friends as 'silver-suited futurists' who also aspired to be eighteenth-century squires.

But in the troubled 1930s home-making could take many forms. For right-wing organic farmers like Rolf Gardiner and Lord Lymington home became a work camp, a rural retreat peopled not with Bright Young Things dressed as nymphs and swains, but with unemployed miners being reintroduced to the land. Home was the parish and village, not the city. When Kenneth Clark set up 'Recording Britain' to provide work for artists during the war, the result was an archive of water-colours of ancient churches, country houses, follies, popular art and craft processes. It was as if England had never had an industrial revolution.

Romantic moderns closes with an afterword in which Alexandra Harris visits the Victoria & Albert Museum in 2006 to see the exhibition 'Modernism: designing a new world, 1914–1939'. She, like other commentators at the time, wondered at the paucity of English contributions. She thinks of Frederick Etchells, Le Corbusier's English translator, conserving country churches. Surely this too was part of the modernist story? Yes and no. The Modern movement, for better or worse, stood for low-cost housing and affordable well-designed goods. The crunch came after the Second World War, when Britain faced the challenge of urban rebuilding and rehousing on a mass scale. The results were often contingent and shoddy, which was unsurprising. As *Romantic moderns* demonstrates, many of the best minds had spent the previous three decades on a creative journey elsewhere.

Times Literary Supplement, 14 January 2011

Revivals!

Janet Kardon (ed.), *Revivals! Diverse traditions, 1920–1945: the history of twentieth-century American craft*, New York: Abrams and the American Craft Museum, 1995

Revivals! Diverse traditions, 1920–1945 accompanies the second exhibition in a major American Craft Museum project to document the history of twentieth-century craft in America. Eight volumes and exhibitions are planned. The first volume, *The ideal home, 1900–1920*, appeared in 1993, while a third volume, *Craft in the machine age, 1920–1945: European influence on American modernism*, will appear this year. Each is beautifully illustrated and includes essays, a catalogue, and checklists of makers, scholars, curators, and institutions relating to the crafts. It is difficult not to be awed by the scale, ambition, and generous funding of this immense project.

This volume deals with a very specific area of craft activity – the survival and revival of craft among Blacks, Hispanics, American Indians and

Appalachians in the inter-war period. It also analyses the fashion for Colonial Revival (seventeenth- and eighteenth-century) styles in architecture, furniture, glass, metalwork, and ceramics. It therefore concentrates on matters of regionalism, on crafts as practised by distinct racial groups and, in the case of Colonial Revival, on the ways in which objects were created to endorse a specifically White, Anglo-Saxon, Protestant image of America.

In addition, because the Depression dominates the period, all the essays deal with the surprising number of 'New Deal' programmes to encourage craft activity as either an economic resource or as a therapeutic panacea, or both. *Revivals!* does not focus on artist craftsmen and women whose work was characterized by innovation and a heightened consciousness of contemporary developments in art and design, although they appear in its pages as enablers and teachers. (They will be documented in volume 3.) The book deals with marginalized groups and the ways in which they retained and adapted craft activity in the face of cultural homogeneity. The Colonial Revival may appear to sit oddly in this company, but these essays chart all kinds of cultural shifts and insecurities. Among the dominant group in inter-war American society – the wealthy East Coast WASPs – continuing waves of European immigration came to represent a challenge to their values. Thus Colonial Williamsburg, funded by John D. Rockefeller, was intended to teach the 'patriotism, high purpose and unselfish devotion of our forefathers'. The buildings and interiors of the old capital of Virginia were 'restored'. Makers in eighteenth-century costume worked at its forge, in its cabinet-making workshop and pewter shop. That one of Williamsburg's best craftsmen, Max Rieg, had trained at the Bauhaus strikes an ironic note. Williamsburg – a 'living' museum – was the antithesis of the modern urban world that Bauhaus students had been trained to serve and reform.

Most of the craft activity which is recorded in *Revivals!* was outside the dominant culture, though WASP-culture's philanthropy exercised an important influence, both artistic and economic. The New Deal's Federal Art Project (FAP) commissioned craftwork to create jobs, as did bodies as various as the Department of Indian Affairs and the National Parks Service. For instance, the Forest Service and FAP joined forces to build Timberline Lodge, a luxurious stone and timber ski hotel which involved several hundred makers –including wood-carvers, smiths, weavers, rug makers, and furniture makers – all working in the pioneer style favoured by wealthy holiday makers. The pioneer values inherent in Appalachian crafts also attracted philanthropic and commercial attention. The Appalachian folk were regarded as pure Anglo-Saxon and Celtic stock, and, as such, a cultural resource to be studied, encouraged and preserved.

But the 'New Deal' also sponsored American Indian crafts with the for-

Hosteen Klah with one of his large sand-painting textiles.

mation of the Indian Arts and Crafts Board in 1936, while Hispanic crafts were supported by FAP projects in New Mexico. The least regarded of the marginal groups were the Black Americans. Whereas inter-war enthusiasm for American Indian craftwork was fuelled by a vision of an indigenous Edenic past that existed before the arrival of white settlers, such ideas could not be applied to Blacks. Their brutal history (more tragic, even, than that of American Indians) suggested little likelihood of surviving craft traditions. The focus of liberal interest in the 1920s was on the Harlem Renaissance, an urban phenomenon in which an efflorescence of Black literature, fine art, music, and modern dance owed nothing to rural Southern roots (and concomitant craft activity). But, as the book reveals, there were Black makers – even if their pottery and quilting, for instance, appears to owe little to any African tradition. Basketry was believed to be the only craft inherited from the community's African forebears. Women basket makers in South Carolina proved particularly imaginative, artistically and commercially, adapting designs to modern uses and selling their work independently along the newly constructed Highway 17.

In fact, success came to marginal groups not through adherence to 'tradition', but through 'authentic' technique, backed up by creative relations with non-marginal institutions and individuals. Thus Maria and Julian Martinez had crucial relationships with archaeologists and curators; their work subtly combined renewed tradition (based on a distant past illuminated by archaeology) and current modern movements in applied art. Hybrids of great beauty came out of these odd cultural transactions. Hosteen Klah, the Navajo medicine man, translated his sand-paintings into weavings, encouraged by an anthropologist and a wealthy Bostonian patron. As a weaver he was already an ambiguous figure – 'nadle', a word that translates as 'transformed' – a male who wore woman's dress and practised a woman's craft and so had access to two worlds.

Not surprisingly some of the most interesting objects illustrated in *Revivals!* are profoundly ambiguous. They certainly have no real equivalent in inter-war British crafts. Our revivals and survivals – mainly in pottery and textiles – were much more timid. Our philanthropies during the Depression were meagre and, where they occurred, far more regimented. *Revivals!* tells an important part of the American craft story and suggests why American crafts in general developed along such bold, daring lines after the war, inspired, as much as anything by the rich racial and cultural mix recorded here.

Crafts, no. 133, March / April 1995

After the appearance of *Craft in the machine age, 1920–1945: European influence on American modernism* in 1996 this fine series was abandoned. A shame, partly recompensed by the appearance of Janet Koplos and Bruce Metcalf's *Makers: a history of American studio craft*, Chapel Hill: University of North Carolina Press, 2010. But *Makers*, while impressive, lacked the expansiveness of Janet Kardon's project.

Folk nationalism

Kim Brandt, *Kingdom of beauty: Mingei and the politics of folk art in imperial Japan*, Durham, NC: Duke University Press, 2007

Every now and then a book comes along that sweeps away fondly held preconceptions and long cherished opinions. This had been the effect (on me at least) of Kim Brandt's *Kingdom of beauty: Mingei and the politics of folk art in imperial Japan*. For some time the jury has been out on *Mingei* – a twentieth-century anti-industrial movement that sought to confer value on folk or popular art and craft. The design historian Yuko Kikuchi's *Japanese modernization and Mingei theory* of 2004 showed how the leaders of *Mingei* essentialized the folk and their humble artefacts and sought to put folk craft to the service of nationalism. This might not seem very grave – it's similar to the turn to folk art in the nineteenth century by Finland, Hungary, and Norway as they sought a visual identity in their struggle for national independence.

Mingei comes to us with both light and shade, mediated through the potter Bernard Leach and his presentation of the thoughts of the movement's intellectual leader Yanagi Soetsu. Published in 1972 in a translation by Leach and Mihoko Okamura, Yanagi's *The unknown craftsman* became a bestseller in counter-culture circles and is still in print. *Mingei* certainly has plenty of visual credibility. Yanagi, the potters Hamada and Kanjiro Kawai and their associates had unerring taste in their pursuit of folk art objects. It was a taste educated by modernism and it led them all through the 1930s to seek out formally powerful objects – traditional firemen's coats with stencilled crests, handsome sculptural carved wooden pot-hangers, cast-iron teapots, and a wealth of regional folk pottery, some of the most beautiful examples coming from occupied Korea.

Occupied Korea sounds a warning note here, for as Kim Brandt argues in *Kingdom of beauty*, *Mingei* grew out of Yanagi's 'discovery' of Korean arts and crafts. But it was a discovery that depended on, and indirectly helped validate, the Japanese annexation of Korea from 1910 to 1945. Casting the Koreans as innocent and childlike and dependent on elevated Japanese taste to identify their ceramic masterpieces helped endorse Japanese imperialism. That seems like a bad start for an iconic, highly spiritualized movement, but worst was to come. Kim Brandt looks at the role of *Mingei* during the Second Sino-Japanese War of 1937–45 when Japan conquered large parts of China and began to plan a visual programme for all its oriental possessions within what was dubbed 'the Greater East Asian Co-Prosperity Sphere'. *Mingei* took a disturbing turn in occupied China with the setting up of the People's Renovation Society led by Yoshida Shoya, a friend of Yanagi and a keen *Mingei* proselyte. In 1940 Hamada, Yanagi, and Kawai flew to Beijing to see a show of Chinese handicrafts carried out under Japanese guidance. A Japanese article of 1941, entitled 'Crafts movement in combat regions', described teaching Chinese boys the intricacies of vegetable dying and rug making, noting 'it was no ordinary labour to put them [these boys], with their stubborn character and opposition in their hearts, on this new path'. Chinese visual culture was to be reconfigured – right down to dress, dealt with under the rubric Asian Development Dress. As late as 1943 Hamada was giving design advice in a Chinese pottery factory.

There is little visual evidence of these activities – which were contemporaneous with rather more frightful experiments being visited on the Chinese. After the war, *Mingei* survived as a movement, honour intact. In 1952 Hamada and Yanagi were honoured guests at the International Conference of Craftsmen in Pottery and Textiles held at Dartington Hall in Devon, a celebration of the humanistic value of craft. The event was able to take in British colonial interventions in West Africa without missing a moral beat. Yanagi spoke twice – on both occasions suggesting, more or less, that Japanese aesthetics might serve as a model for Europe and for North America. Yanagi also told his audience about Korean pottery – naïve, simple, rough, healthy, and decorated in ways that 'one may with reason call childish' and with 'no trace of intellectual consciousness … to be detected in them'.

Mingei has had an extraordinary trajectory. It started out as an idiosyncratic arts and crafts movement spearheaded by one powerful personality, was co-opted to the service of Japanese imperialism, and ended up associated with objects and craft philosophies that remain greatly admired in the USA and Britain. Yet in Germany and Italy the idea of 'folk craft' was besmirched by its similarly totalitarian associations. Why not *Mingei*? After the Second World War *Mingei* was rehabilitated with occupying America's blessing – as evidence of the pacific, democratic artistry of the Japanese people. Kim Brandt shows how it became naturalized as timeless and characteristically Japanese. Amnesia set in fairly quickly – helped by the fact that by 1949 China was a Communist state and therefore beyond the pale.

Crafts, no. 217, March / April 2009

The corrosion of character

Richard Sennett, *The corrosion of character: the personal consequences of work in the new capitalism*, London & New York: Norton, 1998, and Richard Sennett, *Respect: the formation of character in an age of inequality*, London: Allen Lane, 2003

Craft is probably most regularly (and reductively) discussed in one particular context, that of its relationship to the fine arts. The tone is invariably one of frustration in which the crafts seem discriminated against by the fine art world. Sometimes, though, the old hierarchies are declared obsolete. 'Forget mung beans and basket weaving' – here we could equally list lentils, macramé, brown mugs, and knitting, the stuff of countless similar headlines – 'Craft is the new fine art'. 'No it's not, stupid', might be a reasonable response to that particular example of neophilia which appeared in *The Observer* this February.

In fact, craft is now being debated in contexts that bypass the art/craft debate and have more in common with late nineteenth-century musings on the politics of work – issues addressed by figures like John Ruskin and William Morris.

Take, for instance, Malcolm McCullough's *Abstracting craft: the practiced digital hand* (1996). It is a wonderful book but the vision of craft it presents, that of patient artisanal practice, might seem remote to all but a few contemporary makers. As McCullough declares, 'Craft remains skilled work applied towards practical ends'. Craft practice is invoked by McCullough to humanize the world of New Media, in particular the hard, hard work of programming and of confidently using CAD systems. Making an analogy with craft suggests a world of personal post-industrial satisfactions. It is a comparison that may lose some of its force as computing becomes easier to master and more interactive. But strikingly McCullough's perception of craft is a traditional one, exemplified by an illustration of the *Mingei* potter Hamada Shoji throwing a pot on a wheel.

Ideas about patience, long practice, and skill similarly inform the perceptions of the sociologist Richard Sennett. Craft values are central to his two most recent books *The corrosion of character: the personal consequences of work in the new capitalism* (1998) and *Respect: the formation of character in an age of inequality* (2003). Sennett sees craft as an alternative to the endless self-reflexiveness of contemporary life. His vision of craft is informed by his youthful training as professional cellist, a career cut tragically short by a botched operation on his hand.

Some of his ideas, to do with the politics of work, belong to a genre of elegiac anti-industrial writing that can be traced back to the eighteenth century and even earlier. In *The corrosion of character*, however, he writes movingly of how new post-industrial working practices based on flexibility, here-and-now organization, and short-term contracts damage people's sense of self, making it harder for them to construct life stories with a sense of cumulative achievement. Skills won through long experience appear to count for nothing. In many instances work is no longer legible to the workforce – they can neither mend the machines they use nor fully understand the processes of production. As a result identities are eroded. Sennett manages to combine theoretical musings on the writings of Diderot, Rousseau, and Adam Smith, with descriptions of vivid encounters with men and women bruised by employment today – from the rootless young engineering consultant Rico to Rodney Everts, a baker whose craft knowledge was made meaningless by the introduction of computerized bread-making technology.

Respect: the formation of character in an age of inequality gives craft a still more important role. Sennett argues that craft, defined as 'doing something well for its own sake', bestows inner self-respect. Sennett grew up on a deprived social-housing estate in Chicago in the 1950s. In that environment learning to play the cello gave him a sense of self-worth. He had 'the anchor of a demanding art'. Craft can be an anchor and also a shield. Sennett goes on to analyse the consequences of living in a world that singles out comparatively few for recognition and where, as a result, respect is in short supply. We may live in a meritocracy, he argues, but the endless assessing and judging of our potential can be crueller and more wasteful than the *ancien régime*'s hierarchies, where privilege was inherited rather than earned.

Sennett offers a surprising solution to the problem of inequality and its harsh socio-economic consequences: 'The best protection I'm able to imagine against the evils of invidious comparison is the experience of the ability I've called craftwork, and the reason for this is simple. Comparisons, ratings, and testings are deflected from other people into the self; one sets the critical standard internally. Craftwork certainly does not banish invidious comparison to the work of others; it does refocus a person's energies, however, to getting an act right in itself, for oneself. The craftsman can sustain his or her self-respect in an unequal world.'

In the writings of Sennett, what he calls 'craft-love' takes centre stage. It defends us in a cruelly competitive world where an obsession with charisma and stardom has become, in Sennett's view, uncivilized. But like McCullough, Sennett conceptualizes craft in a very particular way. It might seem heartening that one of the most acclaimed sociologists writing today has put craft at the heart of his thinking. But his interpretation illustrates the slippery nature of the term. Sennett's 'craft' stands as the antithesis of 'the new fine art'.

Crafts, no. 188, May / June 2004

Craft without politics

Richard Sennett, *The craftsman*, London: Allen Lane, 2008

The sociologist Richard Sennett has already given craft, both as concept and practice, a promising resonance in books like *The corrosion of character* (1998) and *Respect: the formation of character in an age of inequality* (2003). There he identifies craft as an antidote in a world of post-industrial working practices that serve to damage the dignity of the individual, making it harder to construct life stories with a sense of cumulative achievement.

So it was with real excitement that I began reading his latest book *The craftsman*, expecting a magisterial recasting of our ideas about craft, written with David Pye's rigour but within an expanded intellectual field. I was not disappointed by its scope. *The craftsman* operates on a broad front – moving effortlessly from discussions of the impact of collectivization on material culture in Soviet Russia to the development of the mobile phone. There is analysis of the implications of Computer Aided Design for architecture, the problems of knowledge transfer in the Stradivari workshop, and the difficulties experienced by doctors and nurses in a National Health Service dominated by an audit culture. There are marvellously vivid passages in which Sennett describes and theorizes his engagement with things, places, and processes – as he negotiates the Peachtree Center, a soulless plaza development on the outskirts of Atlanta, sets about cooking a chicken, or reflects on piano technique. But at times *The craftsman* reads as one of those theory-of-everything books like Malcolm Gladwell's recent bestseller *Blink*. As with Gladwell, Sennett is good at turning complex ideas and research into narratives that take the reader by the hand. But in the process something accurate and grounded can be lost.

The craftsman is a profoundly humane book that seeks a better world in which individual effort is honoured and recognized. At its heart is an idea of craft seen from an Enlightenment perspective. Sennett writes with insight about the illustrations to Diderot and d'Alembert's *Encyclopédie*, which honoured manual labour and elucidated the complex techniques of making, step by step, visually. But although no one has written better about the post-industrial workplace, labour historians might smile at Sennett's thoughts on the potential for creative relationships between the worker and 'the machine'. He tends to overlook labour's helplessness in the face of capital and as such *The craftsman* lacks a recognizable political core. It is utopian in a peculiarly North American way. And there is something odd about a book that sets out to look at 'the thing in itself' but which pretty much bypasses the discipline of design history. At best this means that Sennett writes with a beguiling sense of wonder about, say, Gehry's interactions with the fabricators of the titanium cladding of the Guggenheim Museum at Bilbao. At worst we end up wondering what he knows of the design debates of the early twentieth century in which terms like 'type-form' (a term that Sennett uses particularly freely) were coined.

Parts of the book are devoted to describing making processes in some detail. Sennett is keenly aware that craft's importance has been marginalized because its tacit knowledge cannot easily be made explicit. He would agree with W. R. Lethaby's assertion that 'Culture should be thought of as not only book-learning, but as a tempered human spirit. A shepherd, ship-skipper or carpenter enjoys a different culture from the book-scholar, but it is nonetheless a true culture.' But when Sennett writes about the making of pottery or bricks (for instance) it becomes clear that his tacit and technical understanding is fairly limited. And why not! Mine is also. But what he is attempting in part is a meditation on making that draws ethical and philosophical conclusions from those very processes. And that requires an intimate familiarity with a range of crafts of the kind that a David Pye could effortlessly provide. In the end this emerges as a thrilling, flawed book that will fascinate and madden any practitioner in equal measure.

Crafts, no. 210, January / February 2008

David Pye (1914–93) was a designer, a tutor at the Royal College of Art, and a wood-turner. He wrote a small masterpiece, *The nature and art of workmanship* (1968), which did much to clarify thoughts on craft, partly by avoiding the term altogether.

Philip K. Dick's 'The variable man'

'The radio, and the telephone and the movies that we know
May just be passing fancies and in time may go.'
George and Ira Gershwin, 'Our love is here to stay'

Someone should write a book about the crafts and science fiction. Craft usually floats up in that sub-genre of sci-fi, the catastrophe novel. Society is stripped of the technology that we all take for granted and sometimes – as in H. G. Wells's *The war in the air* (1908), a world destroyed by aerial bombardment – this step backwards is presented as being for the best. Wells's book ends with a return to the essentials of life, to the way of the peasant since time immemorial and to craft: 'They loved and suffered and were happy'.

A plot that tracks a reversion to an agrarian craft-based existence works as a critique of the present. In Cicely Hamilton's *Theodore Savage: a story of the past or the future* (1922) a brutalized tribal society emerges after gas warfare. The eponymous hero, an upper-middle-class civil servant, painstakingly learns to weave baskets, to hunt, and to till the soil. His efforts are contrasted with those of Ada whom he takes as a wife. She turns out to be 'a thoroughly helpless woman; helpless after the fashion of the town-bred specialist, the product of the division of labour'. While his background of walking holidays and country pursuits enables him to survive, Ada is doomed as 'a parasite, a minor product of civilisation, machine-bred'.

In catastrophe novels like *Theodore Savage* craft is a vital tool for survival. Science fiction that maps a technological sublime tends only to include hand skills as an exotic hangover. In H. G. Wells's *A modern utopia* (1905) a bearded sandal-wearing Luddite is blind to the scientific and social perfection of a state ruled by high-minded Samurai. He is presented as an irrelevance, as are the small group of Rastafarians who have managed to keep out of the Matrix in William Gibson's *Neuromancer* (1993). While their handmade ramshackle space station Zion smells of cooked vegetables and ganga, the Rastas contribute nothing to the cool logic of cyberspace. But in Philip K. Dick's remarkable time-travel short story 'The variable man' (1953) craft takes a central position in an unexpected exploration of tacit knowledge.

The action takes place on Terra, Earth in the year 2136, ravaged by a series of nuclear conflicts. The planet is hemmed in by the Centauran Empire with whom Terra has long been at war. Peter Sheridov, a Polish scientist, is working on a bomb that will finally destroy the Centaurans. But if Terra is technologically advanced, hand skills have been completely lost. Nothing is ever fixed or mended and when the laboratory robots fail to complete the bomb's wiring, Sheridov is stumped. Enter Thomas Cole, a handyman from the year 1913, sent a millenium ahead in a time-travel mix-up. Sheridov immediately recognizes Cole's special power: 'He knows nothing. It's not in his head, a form of learning. He works by intuition – his power is in his hands, not his head. Jack of all trades. His hands! Like a painter, an artist.' Cole wires up the bomb, turning it into a harmless hyperdrive that will enable Terreans to travel beyond Centauria and colonize other solar systems. This removes the motive for war and Terra becomes a freer, more humane society.

Science fiction has an eerie way of ventilating contemporary anxieties. What might have seemed unlikely in 1953, when 'The variable man' appeared, has become a reality. We mostly don't know how to fix things and we are increasingly dependent on systems that we don't fully understand. Plenty of thinkers have seen the Doomsday scenario as an important reason for preserving pre-industrial skills. In 1926 the design commentator John Gloag warned against intensive division of labour, predicting that in the event of a cataclysmic world war we would be unable to survive a reversal to stone-age conditions. It is a line of thought that continues to have traction, and we are set to wondering how we would manage if everything familiar was stripped away, if craft became a dire necessity.

Crafts, no. 230, May/June 2011

Distributism

What is Distributism? It's an economic and political philosophy whose obscurity can be ascribed to its links with the Roman Catholic church and with a cluster of reactionary inter-war figures, in particular with G. K. Chesterton. Yet it has influenced various 'third way' and stakeholder policies set out by Tony Blair and by the present Coalition government and it is still a live force today.

Distributism started out as a very British movement. It was in part inspired by a papal encyclical of 1891, *Rerum novarum* (Of new things), which attacked both communism and rampant capitalism and called for a fairer distribution of property and of the means of production. Leo XIII wrote *Rerum novarum* partly at the instigation of Cardinal Manning who, in turn, was appalled by the condition of the poor in late nineteenth-century Britain. But it was Hilaire Belloc's *The servile state* (1912) that got Distributism as a movement under way. Much of the book has a prophetic ring. Belloc argued that a symbiotic relationship was developing between socialism and capitalism in which 'those who do not own the means of production shall be legally compelled to work for those who do'. The state would take up the slack with various forms of welfare, leaving the owners of capitalist enterprises free to put their shareholders first.

From the start Distributism opposed commercial banking and was in favour of credit unions. It favoured existing mutuals in the form of co-operative societies, friendly societies, and building societies. It also singled out the crafts and artisanship as a model for the individual ownership of the tools of production. The Distributist journal *G. K.'s Weekly*, founded in 1925, urged its readers to favour small shops, and to buy handmade locally-crafted goods. Inspired by the Dominican monk Father Vincent McNabb, Eric Gill and Douglas Pepler formed the Distributist Guild of St Joseph and St Dominic at Ditchling in Sussex in 1920, a highly successful craft co-operative that survived until 1989.

Meanwhile the Catholic church has continued to make craft-friendly and anti-capitalist pronouncements. Pope Pius XI's encyclical of 1931, *On the reconstruction of the social order*, is still worth reading, with its penetrating discussion of the innate selfishness of the free market. And after the Second World War Pius XII praised the intimacy of the craft workshop as a model for employment: 'Craftworkers, then, are a picked militia for the safeguarding of social peace and for the renewal and prosperity of the national economy.' Most recently Pope Benedict XVI's *Caritas in veritate* of 2009 looked to ways of 'civilizing the economy'.

Against all the odds Distributism lives on. Its most convincing current exponent is Race Mathews, a former Australian Labour MP whose book *Jobs of our own* (1999) sets out the arguments for a philosophy whose aims and ideals are more challenged than ever. Who would have predicted, for instance, that so many friendly societies and other co-operative organizations would be taken over and dismantled by predatory de-mutualizers? Or that banks would flagrantly abuse our trust?

Mathews gives two examples of Distributism in practice. The Antigonish movement of Nova Scotia flourished in the 1920s and 1930s. Led by two Catholic priests, initially it set up co-operatives in the face of the industrialization of fishing. It spread through the Maritime Provinces, creating credit unions, retailing co-operatives, agricultural co-operatives, and a self-build housing movement. The Antigonish movement failed in the 1980s. But Basque-based Mondragón in Spain, also priest-led, has grown from a co-operative paraffin stove factory using hand tools in 1956 into a conglomerate with several hundred firms owned by their workers.

The Mondragón Co-operative Corporation sounds as competitive as any other business enterprise. But its business model does not recognize common practices such as predatory buy-outs, asset stripping, and relocation outside Europe to avoid higher wages. It is ruled by the Distributist principle of subsidiarity, which means that the smallest unit is served by the corporation, not the other way round. Mondragón is not specifically craft-centred but it is worker-centred. Everything about it suggests the trust and intimacy of the small workshop, writ large.

Crafts, no. 231, July / August 2011

According to the BBC's Tom Burridge (14 August 2012 < www.bbc.co.uk/news/world-europe-19213425 >) and *The Guardian*'s Giles Tremlett (7 March 2013) Mondragón is surviving the catastrophic economic recession in Spain surprisingly well.

Let's save the world

Alex Steffen (ed.), *World changing: a user's guide to the 21st century*, New York: Abrams, 2006

It had a beautiful cover, showing the earth mostly in shadow, photographed from NASA's Apollo 4 spacecraft in 1967. The *Whole earth catalog*, a guide to alternative living and 'personal power', was first brought out in 1968 by Stewart Brand, a well-educated, wealthy drop-out. With its subtitle 'access to tools' the *Catalog* listed all the reading matter and equipment for a communard lifestyle outside the 'system' – the military-industrial complex made more fearsome for young Americans by the escalating war in Vietnam and constant threat of the draft. 'Tools' were broadly interpreted and, from the start, Brand was interested in systems and networks and, by extension, in digital technology. As Fred Turner points out in his book *From counterculture to cyberculture: Stewart Brand, the whole network, and the rise of digital utopianism* (2006) the *Catalog* included the fringed deerskin jackets favoured by the communards as well as the cybernetic musings of Norbert Wiener and the latest calculators from Hewlett-Packard.

Now we have *World changing: a user's guide to the 21st century*. Although it is far more stylishly presented it has a good deal in common with the *Catalog*. There are the same sections devoted to 'shelter' and to 'community' and the same libertarian distrust of state intervention. But it is the ways in which *World changing* differs that are of greatest interest. The *Catalog* was ahead of its time on ecological matters but overall the solution offered was an unrealistic one – a retreat from modernity and urban life, even if that life was to be lived in a technologically advanced geodesic dome. That is why the *Catalog* was full of information on woodworking tools, basket making, weaving, leatherwork, log cabin building, wood-stoves, and so on. Despite its prescient interest in cybernetics, the *Catalog* now seems curiously ruralist and isolationist. *World changing*, on the other hand, is all about global politics and global sustainability and pays serious attention to the third world and its cities.

Ironically, the emphasis on craft in the *Whole earth catalog* helped give the term a bad name. Candle-making and macramé came to stand for everything that was depressing about the counter-culture's engagement with the handmade. *World changing*, on the other hand, throws out the looms and potters' wheels in favour of the very latest Green high-tech. For instance, its section on architecture focuses on zero-energy housing, on light structures for refugee camps, and on ways of saving water. Instead of the hands-on romanticism of the *Catalog*, *World changing* offers sensible consumerism alongside plenty of DIY advice. So we have Emma Wolfenden and Tord Boontje's recycled Transglass and Jurgen Bey's hay and resin compostable garden chairs for

Droog Design. A small section called 'Craft it yourself' also concentrates on recycling while some of the most exciting sections are scientific – with discussions of nanotechnology, and Green computing.

World changing is peculiarly American in its optimism. Its editor Alex Steffen claims that it should be possible to 'redesign our personal lives in such a way that we're doing the right thing and having a hell of a good time'. Whether we can have all this gain without pain is a moot point. The only other model, which happens to involve a craft revival of a sort, is irredeemably grim. It is set out by James Kunstler in *The long emergency* (2005), a series of reflections on what will happen when what he calls the 'oil fiesta' is over.

Kunstler writes with some satisfaction of a future in which local food production will become a priority, in which cities like Los Angeles built on the edge of deserts will vanish as unsustainable, in which 'real' skills such as farming, animal husbandry, and carpentry will gain status while other professions (public relations, writing books) will disappear altogether. In fact Kunstler's new world order, in which a multi-tool becomes man's best friend, is a doomsday version of the more Luddite sections of the *Whole earth catalog*. The cheery Green-lite of *World changing* seems infinitely preferable to a life of hard craft that few of us, Kunstler excepted, would relish. We can only hope that the *World changing* geeks prevail.

Crafts, no. 204, January / February, 2007

A larger moose is better

Jake Tilson, *A tale of 12 kitchens: family cooking in four countries*, London: Weidenfeld & Nicolosn, 2006

In flight from uninspiring Edwardian food, the potter Bernard Leach was calmed and delighted by 'a clear soup in a lacquer bowl' served on his arrival in Japan in 1909. In many ways the early studio pottery movement acted as critique not just of industrially produced ceramics but also of the extraordinarily complex family of shapes – cake stands, centrepieces, ice pails, tureens for soups and vegetables, finger bowls, sauce ladles, grape scissors, sweetmeat boxes, and decanters – that characterized the ritualized dining habits of the upper middle classes. Such objects went hand in hand with cooking of a peculiarly depressing kind.

Turning away from industrial Wedgwood, Roger Fry's Omega ceramics were inspired by the simplicities of Mediterranean vernacular pottery

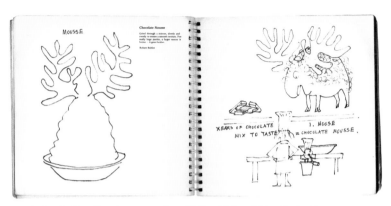

Robert Buhler, Chocolate mousse from *The Royal College of Art cookbook*, 1980.

with its splashed tin-glaze decoration. New ceramics meant different food. Fry and other Bloomsbury figures looked south – to the lovingly described daubes in Virginia Woolf's *To the lighthouse*. Others turned to the warmth and kindness of English country slipware and as a result favoured traditional dishes like fish pie, carrageen puddings, and junket. Leach took the oriental route. At the St Ives Pottery Leach's workforce survived on rice and on what passed for Japanese or Chinese cooking.

Perhaps the first British artists to braid design and eating habits were the leading figures in the Arts & Crafts movement. For William Morris the ideal interior was a kitchen in a country farmhouse; his utopian novel *News from nowhere* is full of simple meals eaten off rustic earthenware plates. W. R. Lethaby, too, was keen on country housekeeping. He took the trouble to draw a Northumbrian loaf, made in a twisted plait, and he sketched wooden butter pats for stamping butter in the form of leaves, wheat ears, and tulips. What is certain is that artists and designers are usually good cooks. They are strong on luxurious austerity.

Artists' recipes can be robust. They are often simple. Surprisingly, considering the circles in which she moved, Alice B. Toklas's famous *Cookbook* contains only one recipe provided by a French artist. But this was Francis Picabia's dish of eggs, in which eight eggs are very slowly scrambled with half a pound of butter. The whole process takes at least half an hour. Then there is the film-maker Jean Renoir's *Renoir, my father*, which must be one of the few biographies to provide a detailed, realizable recipe – for Renoir *père*'s favourite *fricassée* of chicken. It is wonderfully precise and very delicious. Like Morris and Lethaby, Renoir found most contemporary glass and tableware pretentious, and he liked plain food – grilled meat, *pot-au-feu*, potatoes baked in the ashes.

The love affair of artists, makers, and designers with the kitchen continues into the present. The Royal College of Art cookbook of 1980 is an offbeat treasure. Sadly its more recent successor – published in 2002 – suggests a serious falling off in the College's collective culinary skills, with the best recipes being provided by the college chef. But the 1980 collection has masterpieces like Eduardo Paolozzi's *spaghetti al aglio*. This is nothing more than spaghetti with a sauce made of slowly cooked onions and garlic; if Paolozzi's instructions are carefully followed it is unbeatably good. The painter Robert Buhler's recipe for chocolate mousse is another gem, though perhaps not a pudding we should take too seriously: 'Grind through a mincer, slowly and evenly to ensure a smooth texture. For really large parties, a larger moose is better – it goes further.'

And now we have the artist, typographer, and designer Jake Tilson's *A tale of 12 kitchens: family cooking in four countries* – a recipe book, an autobiography, and a work of startlingly original graphic design. It began life as www.the-cooker.com, Tilson's wild and wonderful website that allows users to wander the globe 'ordering' breakfasts, lunches, and dinners, experiencing the sights and sounds of cafés and restaurants from Tokyo to New York to Bombay. Taking as his motto R. D. Laing's assertion that 'the map's not the territory, the menu's not the meal', Tilson has designed an episodic book that traces all kinds of gustatory geographies – a childhood in Notting Hill and Wiltshire, student days in Paris, a whole Scottish dimension after marrying the ceramicist Jennifer Lee, Italy, visits to Manhattan Island, the East Coast, the West Coast and down Mexico way.

A tale of 12 kitchens is animated by Tilson's idiosyncratic typefaces and is illustrated with a small museum of packaging – from Marmite jars to sardine cans, to maple syrup in a log-cabin tin. Stainless-steel counter-tops, large slotted spoons, deep fryers, and napkin rings bought second-hand in California are lyrically described. Back in Peckham Tilson triumphantly constructs a tortilla press from three pieces of wood. And there is, of course, an array of wonderful recipes – a Proustian memory bank of meatballs, spiced eggs Baghdad, fried cucumbers, salt duck, haggis and neeps. Tilson's book is a beguilingly original monument to the pleasures of cookery – as craft, art, and design.

Crafts, no. 202, September/October 2006

Proustian mail order

Manufactum is a German mail order catalogue whose aim is recuperative. It offers tried and tested objects, a high proportion of which were designed in the first half of the twentieth century or just after the Second World War. Many items, like a selection of carbon steel knives from Solingen in Germany, involve a considerable amount of handwork. This is not, however, a collection of craft objects. Manufactum offers quantity-produced goods. But these are chosen on the basis of a very particular set of passions and prejudices marked by a heightened concern with materials and processes.

Thomas Hoof, the somewhat mysterious figure behind Manufactum, is a modernist whose taste would mesh effortlessly with that of Adolf Loos or Le Corbusier. Indeed, Hoof shares many of the design obsessions set out in the latter's *L'Art décoratif d'aujourd'hui*. He admires well-made luggage, good mass-produced glass and china and functional (pre-digital) office equipment. These were all what Le Corbusier called 'type-objects' or 'beautiful tools', objects that displayed classical qualities of durability, usefulness, and beauty. Hoof also shares the great man's obsessive concern with domestic hygiene. 'Never undress in your bedroom. It is not a clean thing to do', commands Le Corbusier, while Hoof bossily tells us never to put recently worn shoes into a closed wardrobe: 'Shoes should always be aired after use'.

In *L'Art décoratif d'aujourd'hui* Le Corbusier was attacking the overwrought aesthetics of the Paris 1925 exhibition. Hoof, on the other hand, is grappling with the rise of electronics and the information revolution, the triumph of polymers based on petrochemicals, and the built-in obsolescence of practically all manufactured goods. Hoof hates these developments. He can be amusingly savage about details that tend to be overlooked. For instance, scissors, in his view, 'have sunk to a pitiable state'. This is because the blades are invariably riveted, making them impossible to unscrew and sharpen. Worse, 'some rivets are disguised as screws on one side'. Hoof offers heavy-duty multi-purpose scissors with screwed blades made in Sheffield by William Whiteley & Sons: 'one of the few companies not yet resigned in the face of the flood of cheap goods'. Manufactum's offer to sharpen any cutting tools bought from them at cost price is a serious one, reminding us that knife-sharpeners stopped calling door-to-door some twenty years ago.

Hoof is also dismissive of beeping electronic clocks, kitchen and personal scales, and all goods dependent on environmentally damaging batteries. Manufactum offers older alternatives – the Winder personal weighing machine, mechanical scales that have been manufactured in Italy for over fifty years, and the Mauthe wall clock, made in the Black Forest, with its Hermle escapement clockwork and quiet, pleasant tick. When it comes to plastic, petroleum-based plastics are forbidden. Bakelite and melamine win Hoof's approval as does celluloid with its distinctive scent of cellulose and camphor. Hoof recommends the Officina Mechanica Armando Simoni pen whose body is carved out of a solid block of celluloid. It is light and pleasant to hold because celluloid, we are told, swiftly assumes the user's body temperature and as a result the hand does not sweat.

Touch, weight and smell are important to Hoof. He writes lyrically of roughly textured linen towelling from Finland, of the reassuring weightiness of a 1.5 kilogram cast-iron sellotape dispenser, and about the seductive 'marzipan-like aroma' of Coccoina paper glue. Hoof's is a familiar multi-sensory aesthetic informed by a keen sense of loss. His vivid descriptions of endangered skills and abandoned materials and his search for authentic things run like a thread through much modernist writing and thought. As Marshall Berman has pointed out, 'to be fully modern is to be anti-modern'. Hoof certainly fits that descriptor. But the Manufactum catalogue cannot be dismissed as a mere exercise in nostalgia: it is too sharply specific and technically informed. Read Hoof on the ubiquitous dishwasher's negative influence on kitchen-ware, on the virtues of carbon steel over stainless steel for kitchen knives, and on forged rather than rolled steel for garden tools.

Nonetheless, Manufactum objects are potentially souvenirs, poised to spark off involuntary memories, transporting their consumers back to a certain time and place. Swiss, German, and French customers, in particular, are guaranteed serendipitous encounters – with the Gutenberg Gummier Stift, the Caran d'Ache Fixpencil, and the legendary 'Moleskine' notebook. Sadly, we British may have fewer Proustian moments. Although we are presented with objects that, almost without exception, are still being made in Europe, in small workshops that have kept flexible specialization alive in the face of mass production, very few Manufactum products come from Britain. Hoof's catalogue may take a passage from John Ruskin's *Unto this last* as its opening epigram, but it also reminds us that as a nation we have failed to respect and maintain artisanal skills.

Crafts, no. 185, November/December 2003

Mysterious Thomas Hoof no longer runs Manufactum but has his own manufacturing and publishing firms that continue to develop his high standards.

Tech-tinkering from Newcastle to Nairobi

Once associated with painstaking tile grouting and step-by-step guides to wallpaper hanging, DIY has gone electronic and robotic. It's a phenomenon that links back to the so-called 'polite science' of the eighteenth century and which resurfaced in the 1950s as a less elite activity among makers of crystal radio sets, balsa wood model planes, and homemade loudspeakers.

This tinkering, technological brand of craft is best experienced at the Maker Faires organized and created by *Make* magazine. Celebrating 'the Do-It-Yourself mindset', the first Faire was held in 2006 in San Mateo, California, while the first British Faire was organized in March 2009 in Newcastle. It should be just possible to catch a Mini-Faire scheduled for 3 September at the Brighton Dome, but for a full-dress experience, the committed need to travel to New York's Hall of Science for the weekend of 17–19 September.

The ethos of Maker Faires is driven by the rhetoric of *Make* magazine: 'Maker Faire offers the opportunity for us to see ourselves as more than consumers; we are productive; we are creative. Everyone is a maker and our world is what we make it.' Inspiring words, a play on Eric Gill's idea that 'the artist is not a special kind of man but every man is a special kind of artist'. And there is no doubt that the experience of a Maker Faire is pretty unforgettable. If there is an aesthetic it might be summed up as the *Whole earth catalog* meets Terry Gilliam's *Brazil* meets the early days of Nigel Coates's NATO meets steampunk.

Nineteenth-century technologies of pin-hole cameras and Tesla coils jostle with digital software. Recycled materials, simple mechanics, and an open-source culture make for some extraordinary objects – a rideable fire-breathing horse was the big attraction at Newcastle 2010. Giant motorized cupcakes and a car embellished with singing, dancing fish and lobsters suggest that in the USA Maker Faires come even bigger, better and more eccentric.

Maker Faires are also a major presence in Africa but while the Anglo-American Faires are intended to be a non-commercial celebration of amateurism, humanizing technology, in Africa they have a far more serious intent. They are the brainchild of Emeka Okafor, a leading Anglo-Nigerian thinker whose blogs Timbuktu Chronicles and Africa Unchained set out his aim of creating a maker philosophy in the continent.

Africa is rarely discussed in terms of manufacturing – indeed during the colonial period value-adding production was actively discouraged. The colonial powers saw Africa as providing raw materials for manufacture that would take place elsewhere. Meanwhile the colonial educational system bestowed all the status on white-collar work. African countries are still being

Maker Faire Africa, Lagos 2012, Urine-powered generator created by Duro-Aina Adebola (14), Akindele Abiola (14), Faleke Oluwatoyin (14) and Bello Eniola (15). One litre of urine produced six hours of electricity.

exploited for raw materials and technical and manual work still has a low status. Paradoxically there is a huge economy centred on rubbish dumps, scrapyards, and backstreet repair shops. Making happens but it is trapped in an unrecognized informal sector.

Through Maker Faire Africa (which is independent of the *Make* magazine franchise) Okafor hopes to encourage entrepreneurial manufacturing. The serious young men and women interviewed at the 2010 Nairobi Faire were mostly concentrating on low-energy, low-cost products. Sixty of them are featured on Maker Faire Africa's Match-a-Maker scheme, which aims to pair young innovators with venture capitalists. So instead of heading to New York to marvel at biofeedback clothing and mad steampunk pyrotechnics it might be more worthwhile to visit the American University in Cairo on 6 and 7 October for the third Maker Faire Africa. This will present making at the sharp end, not as a form of arcane entertainment but as a project to recuperate what colonialism discouraged and which neo-colonialism continues to frustrate.

Crafts, no. 232, September / October 2011

Rapid prototyping: the right tool for our time?

Back in 2000 Ron Arad, with his usual clarity, set out a taxonomy of making processes. There was wasting or cutting, forming or moulding, assembling, and finally, growing. By 'growing' Arad was referring poetically to rapid prototyping (RP) or 3D printing. At his V&A retrospective there was a 3D printer in action. Visitors clustered round it, hypnotized by the busy industriousness of the printer head moving back and forth. It was all very exciting. Now, eleven years on, 3D printers have become ubiquitous in college art and design departments.

But a debate is developing. On the one hand there is a wired constituency that envisages a future in which every household owns a cheap 3D printer to make spare parts, one-offs, and short runs of objects. We can make our own stuff and save on expensive transportation costs. We will have a replicator economy; and more than that. With simple-to-use haptic softwares we will all be free to design on screen and then print out the exotic results.

There is no doubt that 3D printing is a transformative tool for complex customized technology. Individualized prosthetics can stand for a multiplicity of worthwhile applications. But it seems probable that most households will not buy a 3D printer. Aesthetics aside, the energy consumed during the printing process will always make mass production the greener alternative. 3D printers will have their specialized uses. At a household level they should attract a sizeable percentage of hobbyists. They won't follow the trajectory of home computers or mobile phones. I promise.

The Crafts Council touring show 'Lab Craft' is, however, very much a celebration of the artistic possibilities of rapid prototyping. The results are both interesting and disappointing. At the moment, however, the 'look' of an object printed in 3D appears to captivate design pundits and curators. The V&A recently bought 'Fractal table II', designed by WertelOberfell. It is 3D printed, its configuration mimicking the fractal growth patterns found in nature.

But when 'Fractal table II' was first unveiled in 2008 a little storm blew up on the Dezeen magazine site. First reactions were positive – 'just beautiful!', 'the perfect use of RP!' 'the coolest thing', and so on. But a critical note soon crept in – 'just because something can be made, it doesn't mean it should be'. The main gripe was that it was ecologically unsound to use RP technology to make something large and decorative – 'as wrong as oversized shoulder-pads were in the late 80s'. Dezeen's angry bloggers had a point. The use of RP to print out a table suggests the strangeness of the 3D printer as a tool.

3D printers make highly crafted objects that will never compete with

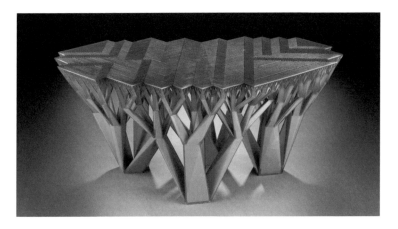

'Fractal table II', 2011, epoxy resin, built by stereolithography; hollow structure filled with polyurethane. Designed by WertelOberfell (Jan Wertel and Gernot Oberfell) with Matthias Bär, for MGX by Materialise, Leuven (manufacturer).

mass production. Nonetheless they are the tool for any job, even if we miss the sharpness produced by a cutting tool and notice that RP 'grown' products lack the logical limitations associated with vacuum forming or moulding. I have called RP machines 'tools' but in fact they sit uneasily in tool history. They are not what the designer Rickard Whittingham calls 'task focused objects'.

When Whittingham set his graduate students on Northumbria's Designers in Residence scheme a project called 'A Tool for Daily Life', he got a remarkable response. Tribute was paid to wheels and axles, to wedges and to planers. There were witty investigations of rasping files, and of pencils as multi-tools. Clearly designers still like tools even if they don't collect them or pour over reference books like Salaman's famous tools *Dictionary*.

There is one book that should not be missed by anyone even vaguely interested in tool history. H.J. Massingham's *Country relics* of 1939, beautifully illustrated by the artist Thomas Hennell, has just been reissued by its original publisher Cambridge University Press. Its reappearance is timely, reminding us of the rich variety of historic tools, each of which was the precise tool for a specific job.

Crafts, no. 234, January / February 2012

It's unwise to make predictions but I stick to the idea that the household 3D printer won't become commonplace. Even as I write this, doubts creep in: 'There is no reason anyone would want a computer in their home', said Ken Olson, president, chairman and founder of Digital Equipment Corp., in 1977.

Craft conviviality

Back in the 1970s the inspirational Austrian polymath Ivan Illich wrote a series of books that interrogated our assumptions about education, energy and transport, work and technology and, indeed, our very conceptions of progress.

Take his commentary on technological development, *Tools for conviviality*. Warning against the passivity of consumerism, *Tools for conviviality* reads as freshly today as it did in 1973. Illich argued that consumerism deprives us of conviviality: 'People need not only to obtain things, they need above all the freedom to make things among which they can live, to give shape to them according to their own tastes and to put them to use in caring for and about others.' He went on to explain 'I choose the term "conviviality" to designate the opposite of industrial production. I intend it to mean autonomous and creative intercourse among persons and the intercourse of persons with their environment.'

Illich believed that most modern tools (and tools could encompass institutions like health services) lacked conviviality. While he saw telephones, handwritten letters, and most hand tools as emblematic of freedom and creativity, what Illich feared was the systematization of everyday life. Within a systematized world the distinction between tool and user is eroded. Both are commandeered into 'the system', forced to work in specific ways.

Although Illich's book has barely affected the remorseless march of systematization in education, the workplace, and government policy, we are now seeing a groundswell of dissent, an active search for conviviality in everyday life. Illich would probably have listed small shops as tools for conviviality, especially a small shop that aims at restoring making skills, and which sells convivial tools and reconnects us with the creation of materials and the rituals of process. Which is a good enough description of Prick Your Finger, near Bethnal Green Tube Station in East London, run with self-deprecating zeal by Rachael Matthews and Louise Harries.

It is a yarn shop with unexpected add-ons – spinning and dyeing on the premises, plenty of specially spun British yarns, exotic up-cycled yarns, knitting needles, buttons, crochet hooks, embroidery silks, darning mushrooms, and much more. There is a library of vintage patterns and a small bookshop. Radical art jostles with skill-based evening classes. The WI meets hacker culture, and vice versa. There is something slightly unnerving about listening to Matthews and Harries talk eloquently about breeds of sheep and the qualities of different wools, sounding uncannily similar to legendary inter-war figures like Margery Kendon, Ella McLeod, and Elizabeth Peacock, whose researches into yarns and techniques were regarded at the time as being comparable to Cecil Sharp's attempt to collect and revive English folk song.

Matthews and Harries are a whole lot more fun than those redoubtable spinners, weavers, and dyers of the 1930s. Matthews was the founder of Cast Off, aka the Knitting Club for Boys and Girls, which conducted a series of subversive public knit-ins: invasions of the Underground, Tate Modern, and, in 2004, the American Bar at the Savoy, from which the knitsters were summarily expelled. Matthews has also written two books, *Knitorama* (2005) and *Hookorama* (2006), zany how-to guides that manage to teach complicated skills amusingly and painlessly. In the same spirit, while Harries and Matthews appear the very embodiment of light-hearted anarchy, their manifesto for Prick Your Finger is strikingly serious about the empowerment that comes from making stuff:

'We Believe ...

In making your own reality.

In making your own clothes.

In making sure earth's resources aren't squandered today,

leaving nothing for our futures.

In making our own yarns.

In making old skills and new technologies work together in harmony.

In making for the love of creation.

In making instead of throwing away.

In making it possible to live a thoughtful and creative life,

even when it seems impossible.

In making chaos.

In making love not war.

In making a stand.'

It is hard to quarrel with that. Illich would have loved their strange, beautiful shop made out of salvaged wood. It's about the most convivial place imaginable.

Crafts, no. 236, May / June 2012

Prick Your Finger is to be found at 260 Globe Road, Bethnal Green, London E2 0JD.

The future is handmade

Iftikhar Dadi (ed.), 'The future is handmade: the survival and innovation of crafts', *Prince Claus Fund Journal*, no. 10a, 2003

The Dutch ceramicist Babs Haenen recently sent me the tenth number of the *Prince Claus Fund Journal*, 'The future is handmade: the survival and innovation of the crafts'. The Fund supports a number of challenging core themes including 'recording slavery', 'truth and reconciliation', and 'creating spaces of freedom'. 'Craft survival and innovation' has joined these as an ongoing topic to be explored through conferences, publications, and exhibitions. 'The future is handmade' is particularly interesting because its essays make a strong case for interpreting the term craft in the broadest possible terms. It also pays a lot of attention to craft activity in the so-called Third World.

'The future is handmade' reminds us that, although we live in a multicultural society, the British craft world is intensely parochial. Third-World craft has been quietly ignored through subscribing to a form of political correctness that goes right back to 1974 when Marigold Coleman, the then editor of *Crafts*, attended the World Crafts Council conference in Toronto. She felt uneasy about the whole event, especially its international exhibition 'In praise of hands'. There, traditional / folk craft was given generous space, raising all sorts of guilt-drenched issues for Coleman. On the one hand she noted that the 'Traditional crafts elbowed their way to the front, triumphant and delightful but drowning out everyone else and unbalancing the exhibition'. But as she watched a Mexican in regional dress 'working away' she reflected on 'the reasons for his work, the validity of its content, the alternatives open to him and the buying power of his remuneration after others have taken their cut'. In those far-off days she saw rapid industrialization as the solution to Third-World poverty, envisaging factories in sub-Saharan Africa massproducing 'penicillin or powdered milk'.

But craft-based or artisanal activity elsewhere should not be ignored simply because it may appear 'inauthentic' or exploitative in its production or because it is made by the disadvantaged. The essays in 'The future is handmade' by art historians, anthropologists, curators, and artists from Nigeria, Indonesia, Mexico, South Africa, Costa Rica, China, and India, draw on postcolonial theory to demonstrate the extraordinary hybridity of craft practices outside Europe and North America, their links with formal and informal economies, their creation of agency and identity for individuals and groups, and their capacity to disrupt distinctions between high and low art, and between fine art and design.

Many of these essays document the eclecticism and responsiveness to consumer demand of Third-World makers as well as suggesting how contin-

Nadín Ospina, 'Casa de Xólotl', carved stone, 2001.

gent the idea of craft really is. For instance, Iftikhar Dadi argues that cheap toys made in Pakistan using recycled plastic and hand-operated plastic-moulding machines can be viewed as a species of urban craft. The moulds are made in backstreet metal foundries and finished by hand – thus allowing an extraordinary variety of fast-changing designs. If more tourists visited Pakistan these plastic toys would surely already be collected; it is only a matter of time before an entrepreneurial individual will start buying them up for export, reframing them as a species of ethnicity alongside toys made out of wire and recycled sheet metal. We like these kinds of things and want to possess them, such is our hunger for commodity diversification. But as we purchase them we reflect, meanly, 'I bet this cost much less in Karachi', or, more piously, 'I wonder how much of this cash is going to the actual maker'. All the more reason, therefore, to engage seriously and creatively with this area of craft. For instance, it would be valuable to see an exhibition of so-called tourist art from around the world that analysed the variety of political economies in which this mostly handmade work is produced. After all, nothing puts our range of essentializing orientalisms on display more dammingly than our taste for these kinds of souvenirs.

'The future is handmade' is full of illuminating essays but one in particular made me smile. In 2001 – note the date – the Columbian artist Nadín Ospina put on an exhibition of carved stone sculptures and ceramics in San José, Costa Rica. At first glance the exhibits looked pre-Columbian and they were displayed as if they were museum pieces, boutique-lit in an otherwise darkened room. But on closer examination they did not represent Ehecatl or Quetzalcóatl but Mickey Mouse and Donald Duck. Just over a year later two British artists, the Chapman Brothers showed their 'Family collection'. This played exactly the same trick on the innocent viewer, presenting what appeared to be a fine collection of African sculptures as a critique of a certain fast-food outlet. But of course Ospina's exhibition made its point more powerfully because he was commenting on his own culture – one that is rich in pre-Columbian sites yielding museum objects that are part of the modernist canon but which is also subject to overwhelming cultural bombardment from North America. The fact that the exhibits were made for Ospina by stone carvers and ceramicists who normally cater for mass tourism's appetite for 'authentic' souvenirs only made his humour darker.

Crafts, no. 190, September / October 2004

Theatres of memory

Raphael Samuel, *Theatres of memory: past and present in contemporary culture*, London: Verso, 1995

This is a maddening rag-bag of a book, under-edited and full of repetitions. But, as one might expect from a founder of History Workshop, it is creatively combative – attacking received notions of what constitutes 'proper' history while also sniping at the deconstructivist activities of cultural theorists.

A good deal of Raphael Samuel's *Theatres of memory* is devoted to areas of enthusiasm and enterprise which historians would dismiss and which exponents of cultural studies would analyse in a distinctly negative spirit. He looks at the ways in which the past is viewed and consumed at a popular level – through the activities of amateur historians and archaeologists, the heritage industry, 'period' films and television series, through various kinds of conservation, including what Samuel calls 'retrofitting' or 'reperiodizing' our homes. In particular, he takes issue with the 'heritage baiters', who have suggested that heritage is an unhistorical term. For them it is a symptom of national decline, part of a top-down plot designed both to sanitize and anaesthetize the past, and a branch of Tory consumerism in which the past is commodified.

Theatres of memory is a celebration of the ways in which we use the past to enrich the present, playfully, often inaccurately, but with enthusiasm. Much of this is done through the recovery and rediscovery of objects. Samuel suggests that activities as diverse as architectural salvage, metal detecting, and steam rallies contribute to our understanding of the past far more directly than the archival researches of historians. In an interesting section entitled 'Retrochic' he tracks the gradual collapse of post-war faith in modern design and architecture in favour of what he calls 'retrofitting'. Samuel makes no value judgements about this shift in sensibility. Indeed, he is enthusiastic about the ways in which, at a private level, home owners have sought to create utopian space and a sense of warmth, softness and enclosure. He sympathizes with the restoration (often extremely well researched) of period features such as dado rails, ceiling roses, and fireplaces (frequently bought as salvage to replace those ripped out in the 1950s and early 1960s).

There is a good deal on the crafts in this book. In open-air museums, living exhibits – blacksmiths, saddlers, and candlemakers – work before fascinated audiences. 'Heritage' building has led to a revival of traditional brickmaking. From the evidence of Samuel's book it is this aspect of craft practice which has a real appeal for the general public, because it contributes to the expanding popular passion for engaging with history using the evidence of objects.

Samuel is inclusive about the practice of history which he defines as an activity, not a profession. He argues that its practitioners are legion – the writers of historical whodunnits, the animators of *The Flintstones*, the creators of *Blackadder*, collectors, librarians, players of early musical instruments. He describes the term 'heritage' as 'a nomadic term, which travels easily, and puts down roots – or bivouacs – in seemingly quite unpromising terrain'. It is, he argues, a term 'capacious enough to accommodate wildly discrepant meanings'.

In fact, heritage is a word rather like the term craft. Craft is a multivalent word, suggesting both the high seriousness of responsible artistic endeavour and whimsical self-expression. It can be used to suggest skill. It can equally be commandeered in the guise of the 'handmade' to make attractive the purest commercialism. As Samuel observes: 'To follow the range of handmade goods advertised in the Sunday colour supplements, on offer at the gift shops and galleries, or displayed at the home furnishers, one might have imagined that the economy had reverted to pre-industrial times.'

Why is the word 'handmade' so seductive when stamped on a jar of jam or a box of fudge? 'Handmade' fudge stands for something accessible and feeds into a widely held belief that the past, however fantasized and idealized, was better than the present. Samuel sees this tendency (which peaked in the 1970s and 1980s) as the reverse of escapist or sinister. Instead, he regards it as healthily symptomatic of cultural dissidence. Heritage, as he argues it, is a rich arena for cultural playfulness and exploration. The giftware produced by the successful firm, Past Times – the current catalogue includes a medieval leather purse, reproduction Celtic crosses, and Pugin cushion kits based on 'sketches now in the Victoria & Albert Museum' – is as worthy of our attention and informed interest as ostensibly more serious attempts to engage with the past.

I think there is a lot to be said for 'heritage baiting' – its effects on civic design, for instance, have been disastrous – but this is a fascinating book. It serves as a kind of model for a history of the crafts – in part because of the extraordinarily varied source material recorded in Raphael Samuel's marvellous footnotes. In his pursuit of history as a social form of knowledge, he cites magazines like *Do It Yourself* and *Country Homes*, property ads in the broadsheet newspapers, and conversations with marine archaeologists, parish priests, and the manager of Blacks, a louche retro-Georgian drinking club in Soho. One chapter is even tellingly entitled 'Unofficial knowledge'. Certainly, trying to piece together the craft story and rescue it from the more powerful discourses associated with design and the fine arts requires similar exploratory trips into 'unofficial' terrain, where oral history jostles with all manner of printed ephemera as well as with an elusive array of objects.

Crafts, no. 136, September / October 1995

Quarrymen's vernacular

'Llechi cerfiedig Dyffryn Ogwen' / 'The carved slates of Dyffryn Ogwen', Amgueddfa Cymru / National Museum Wales, Cardiff, 1983

Slate quarrying has long been carried out on a small scale in North Wales. Near most farm settlements in Gwynedd an abandoned quarry can be found which provided the slates to roof the farm and its outbuildings. But between 1780 and 1850 another way of life was to intrude upon the farming community. With the enclosure of Crown lands entrepreneurs, usually from outside Wales, began to exploit the rich Cambrian slate belt in response to the vastly increased market for roofing slates. In 1780 fifty-four men worked as quarrymen in Gwynedd. By 1880 this number had risen to 14,000.

Two years ago the National Museum of Wales in Cardiff mounted a remarkable exhibition entitled 'The Carved Slates of Dyffryn Ogwen'. It was the result of the researches of the Llandegai and Llanllechid Archaeological Society and in particular was due to the discoveries of Gwenno Caffell, the author of the exhibition's excellent catalogue.

In 1977 Gwenno Caffell came across a damaged slate face down in a field near her home in Tregarth on which was carved a simple stylized arrangement of leaves, stems, and flowers. It appeared to be the lintel for a fireplace but at that stage she knew of only one other example – a quite elaborately carved slate in the Museum of Welsh Antiquities in Bangor, thought to be a unique piece carved by the singer and composer John Parry. But her curiosity was excited and she asked everyone who made deliveries to houses in the Ogwen area (which is dominated by the Penrhyn Quarry) to look out for similar slates.

Gradually she and the Society were able to build up a picture of a lively vernacular craft, rooted in the local community, which had flourished among quarrymen from about 1820 to 1840. Since 1977 the Society has recorded some 600 carvings, many still in situ around fireplaces and there are reports of similar, usually less sophisticated, carvings found in other quarrying areas of North Wales.

Most of these carvings are inscribed with dates. The earliest, 1823, and the latest, 1843, coincide with the massive expansion of the workforce in the Penrhyn Quarry. Many houses were built by the quarrymen themselves and the carved fireplace slates must have been an important embellishment to their homes. The slates are massive, usually with a 2.5 m by 0.5 m horizontal slab and two rather smaller uprights. The skills involved in decorating these relatively large surfaces had no connection with the quarryman's usual skills nor was there any earlier tradition of decorating wooden beams over farmhouse fireplaces.

The aristocrats of the quarries were, and still are, the men who work with great speed and grace in the quarry shed splitting the blocks into thin *llechi* using a broad but thin chisel exactly aligned with the slate's grain. In her great book *Made in England* Dorothy Hartley describes how 'some of the old workmen develop a wonderful sense of touch and balance and split true to a hair with a very light blow exactly placed. The curious slender strength and balance of the slate workers' tools are also shown in the very characteristic and structural quality of all slate designs.' Dorothy Hartley was the first to record the type of design that quarrymen made on slates and her discoveries were expanded by the poet and designer Arnold Rattenbury in his fine exhibition 'Ardudwy' mounted at Coleg Harlech in 1975. But their researches only hinted at the richness of carvings associated with fireplaces. The grandeur of the Ogwen slates bears little relationship to the houses in which they were found. The most elaborate slates that the Society has discovered, the astronomical slates of Bryn Twrw, were made in 1837 for the humblest type of farmhouse by Thomas and William Jones, 'quarrymen and farmers'. These are uncharacteristic in that the uprights illustrate complicated astronomical data given to the carvers by the self-educated mathematical genius John William Thomas who was to become Supervisor of Greenwich Observatory. The undermantle slate shows the signs of the zodiac carved with great wit and artistry and there is no reason to suppose that it was not entirely the invention of the two quarrymen.

Although motifs recur, ranging from characteristic concentric circles to a variety of freehand styles, it seems certain that none of these carvings were made commercially but rather that they were the work of large numbers of individual quarrymen, like the Jones brothers, and created for their immediate family and hearth.

Gwenno Caffell believes that techniques from wood-carving were adapted to carve slate. This was confirmed by the discovery of an old quarryman's tool kit which included a brace and a number of multi-toothed bits that were almost certainly used to carve the concentric circles. Nonetheless the fact that each carver appears to have approached the problem presented by the slate surface afresh explains the variable quality and success of the carvings. Though most of the designs are incised, there is a beautiful example of a relief carving. One very lovely design of a ship is scarcely visible because the carving is far too shallow. Some of the grandest designs are the simplest and made up of the concentric circles that Dorothy Hartley recorded. These appear in some form on practically all the slates and, as Gwenno Caffell points out, have a resemblance to prehistoric cup and ring marks. They also have affinities with the raised bosses with encircling rings that decorate much Bronze Age metalwork. But such resemblances are almost certainly fortuitous and really serve to highlight the strange parallelism in all decorative design, regardless of period and region. The varied and intricate borders made up of zig-zags, hoops, circles, or parallel lines also draw on these universal motifs. Plant forms appear regularly but they are rarely truly naturalistic. The floral form is one of the oldest and most widespread of decorative motifs. Though on some slates the plant grows in homely fashion out of a pot its representational function seems secondary. This tendency to abstraction perhaps explains a fascinating recurring form that appears to be a meld of a swastika and floral motif.

But much of the freehand carving is clearly representational and depicts houses, churches, wine glasses, ships, and neatly notated music. The Menai bridge, which was opened in 1827, appears on several slates. The way in which borders, objects and inscriptions are arranged can occasionally seem reminiscent of samplers but most slates have a far stronger sense of visual unity.

Thomas and William Jones, detail of the astronomical slates of Bryn Twrw, 1837, showing the eclipse of 1836 and Halley's Comet.

The music recorded on slates reminds us of the acknowledged breadth of the quarrymen's interests throughout the nineteenth century. Gwenno Caffell is keenly aware of this (she is the granddaughter and great-granddaughter of quarrymen) and her descriptions of her great grandfather's intellectual range – 'He was a poet, a geologist, an archaeologist, an antiquarian, a botanist – he was really quite good on ferns' – sound more like that of a rural parson than of a quarryman who rose at five, walked to the quarry, worked a ten hour day, and walked home again.

Quarrymen at Penrhyn Quarry set up self-help groups to study music notation and Gwenno Caffell wonders whether art or geometry were also studied: how else to explain the confident and masterly way in which the designs articulate the large surfaces they adorn? But few of these slates reveal any knowledge of primers on ornament or draughtsmanship. The carvings did not appear to have any real uniformity of style nor did they become an acknowledged byproduct of quarrying like the carving of slate fans. The craft appears to have been killed off by changing domestic fashions. By the mid-century the mills and mason's yards began to turn out deeply carved, highly finished slate fire-surrounds which must have made the carvings look old-fashioned and many existing carvings were disguised by marbling effects.

Perhaps because the slate carvings were home-based they were never celebrated or discussed. They are still little appreciated, and one of the Society's tasks is not only to record examples but to encourage owners to conserve and care for their surviving slates. The fire-surround and fireplace is often removed when a house is modernized and Gwenno Carrell has sad tales to tell of slates being taken out and smashed.

These carved slates owe much of their beauty and dignity to the very poverty of visual sources available to their executants. It has often been argued that the development of the decorative arts during the nineteenth century was bedevilled by too much visual information. Certainly, the quarrymen of Dyffryn Ogwen for a brief period drew on certain universal motifs and arranged them in a fashion that offered a remarkably satisfying logic of vision.

Crafts, no. 72, January / February 1985

Object lessons

Edmund de Waal, *The hare with amber eyes: a hidden inheritance*, London: Chatto & Windus, 2010

Netsuke are Lilliputian carvings designed to be worn. Peeping over a kimono's sash, they were an exquisite adjunct to fashionable male dress in Japan from the seventeenth century until the Meiji restoration. They functioned, modestly, as a toggle, threaded with a cord tightened with a bead, from which hung useful objects like tobacco pouches, sake flasks, and boxes containing seals or medicines. But when Japan decided to Westernize intellectually, industrially and sartorially, a great many objects lost their function almost overnight – most obviously Samurai armour and swords and sword fittings, but also elaborate brocade robes and sashes and the whole world of *sagemono* or 'hanging things', suspended chatelaine-like and secured by a netsuke.

Deprived of a functional context, netsuke were swiftly re-commodified. Whether made of a rare wood or of ivory or horn, they are designed to be smooth and delightful to the touch. Most are beautifully balanced, ready to stand unsupported on a flat surface as miniature sculptures – of animals, fruits, erotic couplings, bundles of kindling, *multum in parvo*. They are also the ultimate sculpture in the round; an exquisite miniaturized wild boar or tiger might on its underside be carved with plants or patterns and carry a signature. For the European *grand amateur* netsuke became short-hand for Japan, for pre-industrial labour and a whole world of playful craft. They offered endless scope for research into attributions, a deliciously fraught task given Japan's culture of the copy. By the early twentieth century these toggles had travelled a long way, functionally, geographically, and culturally.

When in 2005 the ceramicist Edmund de Waal inherited 264 netsuke ('a very big collection of very small objects'), he was confronted with an unsettling history of diaspora. He could have ignored the back-story, or dined out on it, or written up 'some Mitteleuropa narrative of loss'. But the netsuke, like magical things in a fairy tale, began to act upon him. The result is *The hare with amber eyes*, a self-questioning, witty, sharply perceptive book, shaped as series of journeys into European culture and its world of goods.

The search for de Waal's netsuke begins in late nineteenth-century Paris. He is descended from Charles Ephrussi, whose family were then the biggest grain-exporters in the world. The trading and banking networks of *'les rois de blé'* extended all over Europe but it seems that young Charles's gifts were recognized and he was allowed to stay out of the bank and the Bourse. Emerging as a collector of Renaissance art in his early twenties, he became the proprietor of the *Gazettes des Beaux Arts* and a significant patron of the Impressionists. De Waal argues with some passion that Ephrussi was the most likely model for Swann in Proust's *À la recherche du temps perdu*. He is a presence in Renoir's 'Le déjeuner des canotiers', back turned, strikingly formally dressed. It was Charles who bought de Waal's 264 netsuke, en bloc from the dealer Philippe Sichel. They were part of a larger collection of Japanese *objets d'art* that Charles shared with his mistress Louise Cahen d'Anvers. As small, tactile objects housed in his enfilade of rooms in the rue de Morceau, they stood for a fashionable collecting mania and, also, for a love affair.

As de Waal takes us in and out of libraries and museums and on flaneurial wanderings through Paris, a darker theme emerges. Charles purchased paintings by Gustave Moreau and Renoir's jealous reaction – 'Jew art' – sets the scene for Vienna, where the netsuke were sent in 1899 as a wedding present for Charles's nephew Viktor and his bride Emmy. There are many remarkable insights in *The hare with amber eyes*, not least de Waal's brilliantly nuanced account of the eroticized nature of French Japonisme. But a central haunting theme is European anti-Semitism, and its endgame in Austria in the 1930s.

In the Palais Ephrussi on the Ringstrasse, Viktor and Emmy lived as aristocratic, titled Jews, loyal to the Emperor in a city of unparalleled wealth and culture, whose neurasthenic anxieties are beautifully caught by de Waal. The netsuke lost some of their aesthetic traction in the staid marble and gilded interiors of the Palais. They ended up in Emmy's dressing room. Her children played with them while her maid helped dress the Baroness for another glittering evening. These children grew up and went away – intellectual Elizabeth (Edmund de Waal's grandmother) to Vienna University, and then to America, France, and to England. Gisela went to Spain and Iggie to Hollywood, where even his telephone number – Eldorado 5-0050 – hinted at a new, unbuttoned happiness.

Viktor and Emmy faced Hitler's Anschluss alone. Their story is a familiar one but by concentrating on the world of things, not least the netsuke in their velvet-lined vitrine, de Waal tells it afresh. The Ephrussi collection was picked over by the Nazi 'Property Transactions Office'. As catalogues were drawn up all over Vienna, art historians (Aryans only) came into their own. Punctilious scholarship accompanied persecution, terror, and suicide. Like the faithful servant in a tale by the Brothers Grimm, Emmy's maid Anna hid the netsuke in her mattress, handing them all back safely to Elizabeth after the war. In 1947 Iggie took the netsuke 'home' to occupied Tokyo. His lover Jiro left them, in turn, to de Waal – whose own fascination with Japan had begun during a boyhood apprenticeship with the austere potter Geoffrey Whiting.

The hare with amber eyes is rich in epiphanic moments but one stands out. Faced with the 'absurdly big' Ephrussi mansion in Vienna, de Waal reflects that he could 'turn away, cross the road, take the tram and leave this dynastic house and story alone'. After all, his great uncle Iggie and his grandmother Elizabeth, like many of their generation, decided on selective amnesia. In the same spirit, de Waal's father, who has a charming walk-on part, gives him a few letters and some playful drawings of the family that turn out to be by the Secessionist artist Joseph Olbrich. They are brought across London, incongruously, in a plastic bag. 'How could you possibly not know you had this?', de Waal asks. But in émigré flats and houses, from Teddington to Hampstead, there was a lot of post-war forgetting. A discreetly hung Schiele drawing or a Wiener Werkstätte lamp might be the only clue to a vanished world. De Waal, however, decided to 'get it right, go back and check it, walk it again'. And by writing objects into his family story he achieves something remarkable, demonstrating a rare understanding of biography's flawed contingency and its potential for daring experiment. And the netsuke? They live, as they have done for the past 150 years, in a vitrine, and de Waal's children sometimes play with them.

Times Literary Supplement, 3 September 2010

Homesickness

Christopher Benfey, *Red brick, Black Mountain, white clay: reflections on art, family, and survival*, New York & London: The Penguin Press, 2012

'I am homesick but for what home', wrote Lytton Strachey. Lost homes, lost ancestors, and lost objects have always been a subject for storytellers, but never more so than now. It is as though the diasporas, which our grandparents and great-grandparents bore so stoically during the confusions of the last century, have become more vivid, harder to bear. Hence books that read like pilgrimages in search of roots. The pioneer was W. G. Sebald, whose idiosyncratic *The emigrants* and *The rings of Saturn* remain the model for a new kind of hybrid narrative that mixes travelogue, cultural history, and autobiography. Three memoirs in the spirit of Sebald have appeared over the last year. All use objects to unlock the past. First up is potter Edmund de Waal's haunting *The hare with amber eyes*. Then there is the Australian art historian and lawyer Tim Bonyhady's *Good living street*, a recuperation of his grandmother and aunt's glittering artistic life in pre-Anschluss Vienna.

Now we have the English scholar Christopher Benfey's *Red brick, Black Mountain, white clay* which takes us on a tour of North Carolina, capturing its lush beauty and its alarming poverty. Benfey's mother's ancestors were brickmakers and folk potters from rural Piedmont, while his émigré great uncle and aunt – Josef and Anni Albers – held court as teachers and muses at the avant-garde Black Mountain College in the Appalachians in the late 1940s. The book ends with the extraordinary story of Josiah Wedgwood's search for pure white clay in the North Carolina outback, a quest in which one of Benfey's ancestors, William Bartram, had a walk-on part.

There are plenty of sideways diversions in *Red brick, Black Mountain, white clay* – Benfey's spell in a pottery in the Tamba region in Japan, his travails as an idealistic student working in a tiny village in Mexico, a conversation with the poet Randall Jarrell's widow, a disturbing visit to Berlin with his father, the extraordinary story of his ancestor Theodore Benfey, a German-Jewish Sanskrit scholar who provided a diffusionist explanation for the origin of fairy stories. The list goes on and on in a narrative that mixes geology with genealogy, modernism with the archaic.

Things do a lot of the memory work – 'a snuffbox, a stamp album, a rust-coloured pitcher, a handful of white clay'. Craft plays an important role too. Craft offers certainty, whether it be the skilful laying of bricks by Benfey's maternal grandfather or the resolved quietude of a North Carolina Jugtown pitcher made by Ben Owen or Anni Albers's construction of elegant necklaces out of paper clips and aluminium washers.

Craft abuts modernism in Benfey's discussion of Albers. If the Bauhaus had prepared her for a stripped down life, her mantra 'start from zero' also flowed from the experience of diaspora after a childhood of wealth and privilege. Benfey's biographical approach makes sense of the austerity and make-do qualities of her jewellery and weaving. As Benfey explains, even as collectors the Alberses were prepared for a nomadic life. They favoured pre-Columbian figurines made from the 'modest material of clay'. It was the kind of collection that could be 'held in two hands'.

Another kind of craft history floats up in Benfey's account of North Carolina's Jugtown pottery revival. The story is familiar enough and Benfey's thoughts on the tension between beauty and function, on the value of repetitive work, and on the alchemy of kilns are hardly original. But as part of a personal voyage of discovery his words read freshly and they are under-pinned by his erudition. Benfey has read the standard books on North Carolina folk pottery. But he also offers us the French poet Paul Valéry 'On the pre-eminent dignity of the arts of fire' and the sociologist Georg Simmel's thoughts on the aesthetics of vessels set out in his little essay 'The handle'. Benfey's picaresque search for origins turns out to be pretty much required reading.

Why biography?

Why biography? The case against can be easily marshalled. Where visual artists (designers and makers included) are concerned the work should always take precedence over the life. What is required is a catalogue raisonné. An elegant and detailed chronology can set out the biographical facts as known. Who needs psychological insights into schooldays and love affairs? In any case, biography often tells you less about the biographical subject and more about the appetites and prejudices of the biographer. And, however fully contextualised, isn't a single life too hermetic? If biography must be written at all it is surely better to look at a group, at networks rather than individuals.

But, on the other hand, if there is an extensive archive, stuffed with letters and regularly kept diaries, an individual comes alive and so does his or her period. At the moment I am writing a biography of the potter Michael Cardew. No one could fail to be captivated by the wealth of his papers, backed up by photographs, seemingly endless film footage, and a published autobiographical account of his life up to the age of 45. Then, of course, there are the pots, the objects that led me to him in the first place. The dangers of a biographical approach become evident. With someone as intelligent and well-read as Cardew, whose life takes the putative biographer into the thickets of national identity, the British class system, anti-industrialism, and postcolonial theory, the pots are in danger of being sidelined.

Perhaps what is needed is a succinct life followed by detailed examination of the work. That is what Alan Crawford provides in his majestic study *C.R.Ashbee: architect, designer and romantic socialist* (Yale University Press, 1985). About one third of the book is a life and two-thirds a survey of Ashbee's varied activities as an architect, interior decorator, designer of furniture, metalwork, jewellery, and creator of private press books. The division is not an absolute one. The 'life' section discusses 'work of the most important kind', not least the setting up of the Guild of Handicraft that gave an ideological framework to Ashbee's career as a designer. A similar, if more austere, life/work solution is provided by Robin Kinross in his two-volume *Anthony Froshaug* (Hyphen Press, 2000). In one volume we get a 47-page introduction by Kinross, examples of Froshaug's typography, and all his writings on typography. The second volume includes more personal writings and images. In effect, the reader is asked to construct the biography from a series of subtly juxtaposed texts, images, and footnotes. Both biographies put the work at the centre. We also end up feeling that we have breathed the same air, been in the same room as Ashbee and Froshaug. We know them.

That illusion, and it must be an illusion, is one of the intense pleasures of reading good biography. It seems sad, therefore, that there are not many living, breathing biographies of men and women, particularly women, in the craft world as it developed after the First World War. Only Fiona MacCarthy's *Eric Gill* stands out. Yet there are plenty of extraordinary lives to investigate. What about Phyllis Barron, Dorothy Larcher, Enid Marx, and Katharine Pleydell-Bouverie, just some of the remarkable women working in the crafts between the wars? They surely qualify for some kind of group biography. But anyone trying to do research in this area will encounter problems. The sources are very limited. We know a good deal about another inter-war figure, Ethel Mairet (and we have Margot Coatts's excellent short life). She seems to have made a conscious attempt to preserve her letters and papers, reminding us that on the whole archives are willed creations and that men (and their widows) appear more conscious of posterity in these matters. The material on Barron, Larcher, and Pleydell-Bouverie at the Crafts Study Centre concerns 'work' in the narrowest sense while Enid Marx's archive is not yet in the public domain. Only Pleydell-Bouverie has been properly memorialized in a brief book of essays, but these are so limited in scope that none, for instance, discuss the several rather interesting novels written by Pleydell-Bouverie as young woman.

All these upper-middle-class women would today be described as 'gay'. They made their lives with other women. They were also remarkably modest about their achievements. One can only assume that their personal papers were destroyed or sequestered. This is where biography becomes important however, for reasons that are far from prurient. Between the two World Wars, married women (with the magnificent exception of Barbara Hepworth) mostly found it difficult to pursue serious careers as artists. The 'single' status of these craftswomen was important. And while their lives are inherently interesting, mapping their careers fully would also do much to challenge our perception of craft and design in Britain then. They are the neglected modernists in that history. Someone needs to take on the challenge of documenting these networks of gifted women, giving us both the work and the life in full.

Crafts, no. 184, September / October 2003

The Enid Marx archive is now in the V&A's Archive of Art & Design.

People

William Morris in our time

'William Morris': exhibition at the Victoria & Albert Museum, 9 May to 1 September 1996

There have already been some notably sour previews and reviews of the major William Morris exhibition at the Victoria & Albert Museum, in which the great man has been held responsible for all kinds of nastinesses, from the savagery of the Khmer Rouge to the safe eclecticism of *The World of Interiors*.

Blaming Morris's designs retrospectively for Laura Ashley wallpaper and British cultural conservatism, or reading mass executions and totalitarianism between the lines of his utopian novel *News from nowhere*, is as misjudged as identifying Morris as a pioneer of the Modern movement. Yet there are problems. This is the centenary of his death but it is patently not quite Morris's moment. He stands four-square, devoid of the ironic, parodic, knowing ambivalences that appeal to postmodern sensibilities. If there is a postmodern hero of the exhibition, it is surely Dante Gabriel Rossetti, whose malicious little caricatures of Morris (often sent in letters to Morris's wife Jane) form a cruel subtext to all Morris's positive, innocent activities. But the fact that it is now unfashionable to feel enthusiastic about Morris's complex and endlessly creative life and works tells us more about the shallowness of design and art criticism in the 1990s than it does about Morris.

The young Morris emerges at the V&A as a touching but confused figure. The activities of his early years were both complicated and eased by his great wealth – he did not really have to stick at anything and he was surrounded by more talented men, with Rossetti as a towering figure who took both Morris and Edward Burne-Jones in hand, introducing them to a life of art and to a London that mixed glamour with squalor.

For Rossetti, 'art' meant painting, and for a while Morris laboured at it. But his marriage to a stableman's daughter, Jane Burden, gave a new focus to his developing creativity. At first he tried to paint her. But then he decided to create a home for her, in collaboration with the architect Philip Webb and drawing on the artistry of the men and women in his circle.

The Red House was a utopian haven, an alternative to the upper-middle-class Victorian milieu in which Morris had been brought up. It was an important project for two reasons. First, the Red House stands as the first interior created by an artist for a life of social and intellectual dissent. Its progeny includes Margaret and Charles Rennie Mackintosh's Glasgow flat of 1900, Charleston in Sussex decorated by Duncan Grant and Vanessa Bell from 1916 onwards, and the interiors made by artists like Duggie Fields, Andrew Logan, and Derek Jarman in the 1970s and 1980s. Such places were sanctums or what the architectural theorist Robert Harbison has called 'dreaming-rooms', expressing a rejection of every kind of convention, from conventional marriage to straight heterosexual society. Second, the Red House marks Morris's switch to applied art and to ambitions for 'a glorious art made by the people and for the people, as a happiness to both maker and user'. This withdrawal from fine art took Morris to the heart of all kinds of specifically modern anxieties about everyday objects and skills and materials employed to make them.

It is a new orthodoxy to dismiss Nikolaus Pevsner's identification of Morris as the harbinger of modernism in design. Nonetheless, his passion for intense research and development – only fully realized after he set up Morris & Company in 1874 – seems wholly modern. Morris sought to respond discriminatingly to the plethora of new materials and technologies that emerged during the nineteenth century. Many of his designs, like his range of carpets made on power looms, were mass-produced. On the other hand, some of his most luxurious productions were modern in a craft-revival spirit. These include the knotted carpets that are one of the glories of the exhibition and the marvellous high warp tapestries, mostly designed by Burne-Jones. These glamorous productions of Morris's last years raise questions about the relationship between Morris's thought and his art, not least because at the V&A they are in the same room as a small, timid display devoted to Morris's political activities as a revolutionary socialist.

The V&A curators, unlike the organizers of the 1984 ICA show, 'William Morris Today', are not putting Morris's politics centre stage. It is easy to understand why. The natural response might be to laugh at the juxtaposition of a monumental hand-knotted carpet made for the iron master Sir Lowthian Bell's mansion in North Yorkshire and Morris's copy of *Le kapital* (he read Marx in French), beautifully bound and tooled in gold by his fellow revolutionary socialist Thomas Cobden-Sanderson.

It is easy to mock Morris's politics, tempting to overlook them. It is likely that Morris's employees did not experience any real joy in labour as they sat for long hours on low benches knotting and cutting each double strand of an immense carpet. Morris liked to involve his women clients in embroidery projects but the wealthy Ada Godman probably tired as she slowly stitched the sequence of 'Artichoke' hangings Morris specially designed for her drawing-room in Northallerton. He had created a powerful repeat pattern, suitable for handblock printing but cruelly monotonous for an embroiderer to carry out.

And what of the Kelmscott Press, a project initiated in 1891 at the end of Morris's life? Morris spared no effort to create beautiful typefaces, engraved woodblock borders, fine inks and papers. But in 1899 the American economist Thorstein Veblen took Kelmscott Press books as prime examples of conspicuous consumption, less examples of honest workmanship, more trophies consumed by the leisure class to display their wealth and taste. Where was Morris's 'glorious art made by the people and for the people'?

In an unexpected way, Morris's exclusive productions did reach a wider public posthumously. Morris & Company work was sent by the Board of Trade to Ghent in 1913 and to Paris in 1914 to signify 'Englishness'. It was seen again at Burlington House in the 1916 Arts & Crafts Society exhibition, performing the same function at the height of the First World War. This transformation of Morris into the bearer of Edwardian national identity signalled that Morris was being depoliticized. For most of this century he has been associated not with radicalism or even design reform, but with a few pleasingly familiar wallpapers. And, it will be said, this was just as well, for Morris's politics were grotesque, an early example of champagne socialism.

In fact, it is wrong to set his politics aside. Morris, like many of his contemporaries, inhabited an intellectual universe that knew little of the actuality of revolution. Had he lived beyond 1917 he might well have recast his thoughts. But from the late 1870s onwards Morris began posing all kinds of uncomfortable questions. He learned to ask some of these questions from his beloved John Ruskin, from the passionately indignant passages of 'On the nature of Gothic' in *The stones of Venice*, and they concerned the relationship between art and work and pleasure in work. Perhaps that is why Morris is not a man for our time, for we have not even begun to answer any of those questions.

It is easier, therefore, to pass judgement on Morris for his inconsistencies than to wonder why ideas about joy in labour seem so embarrassingly remote today and why the contemporary workplace is more likely to be a site of anxiety and mistrust than of joy. And, looking at the bold scale of the late embroideries, tapestries, carpets, and books in the final room of this majestic exhibition, all criticism falls away. They were mostly made for a group of wealthy individuals but they go beyond the painting and sculpture of the age in their quiet grandeur. They do not look like a private art but more like a glimpse, an intimation of a new kind of unrealized public art of a humane and engaging kind. They make sense of all that Morris said and did.

The Spectator, 18 May 1996

T. J. Cobden-Sanderson and the meaning of life

'The Doves Bindery 1893–1921': exhibition at the British Library, London,
5 April to 7 July 1991

T. J. Cobden-Sanderson was one of life's late starters – having left Cambridge without a degree, he had a mysterious period apprenticed to a boat-builder and a spell at the Bar, followed by a nervous breakdown. In his early forties he married the Free Trader Richard Cobden's sprightly daughter Annie. That happiness did not alleviate a keen sense of ennui and the shame of living off his wife's income. He often felt suicidal, Oblomov-like, despite his charm, despite the endless sequence of idyllic holidays with Annie, despite the grand philanthropic circles in which he moved. But in 1883 he dined with William and Janey Morris. 'Why don't you learn bookbinding?' said Janey. 'That would add an art to our little community.' It might have proved rather pathetic – craft as therapy.

In fact Cobden-Sanderson's bindings, first entirely by his own hand and later from the workshop he set up in Hammersmith, were technically perfect and exquisitely decorated. Some 80 examples from his Doves Bindery are now on show in the British Library and they reveal his genius. There is apposite, well-arranged lettering, while the tooling ranges from an abundance of floral motifs to stark linear simplicity. Some of the decoration – like the receding panels aptly tooled on to Ruskin's *Elements of perspective* – looks startlingly modern, but many of his other designs were lush and complex. Constructionally the bindings were superb and they created an instant stir among bibliophiles and book-dealers. But Cobden-Sanderson did not simply rejoice in his unexpected practical gifts. Instead he dressed up and elevated the significance of his craft. Over the years he had developed a cloudy personal philosophy. He worshipped the Cosmos – the sun and stars and what he called the 'immutable universe'. He believed, therefore, that his bindings were a small part of this divine order and to create them was an act of divine worship.

Perhaps this consoled him for the occasional social slight his new profession brought him. 'I have heard of your bookbinding but, I own, with regret', wrote Lady Russell in a chilly note. Cobden-Sanderson turned to socialism; this too gave his artisanal activities meaning. He knew and admired the Marxist Henry Mayers Hyndman, the anarchist Prince Kropotkin, and of course Morris. 'I suspect I must give up a large selection of my old friends – the Howards, the Stanleys, the Russells. Preparing and hoping for a state of society which shall make their position impossible, how can I continue to be friends with them?' he wrote earnestly in his journal. Formerly he had filled his empty days paying calls. Now he became a passionate proselytizer for the Book Beautiful and a founder member of the Arts & Crafts Exhibition Society. He kept reminding himself of the true meaning of his new way of life. He was working, he explained in his journal, not just to please grand collectors, but to dignify labour.

In 1900 he extended the scope of the Book Beautiful, starting a private press in partnership with Emery Walker, whose vital contribution was to find the perfect typeface for the Press. As a result Doves Press books bound at the Doves Bindery are among the most beautiful private press books ever made. The grandest products of the Press, the Doves Bible and the Doves *Paradise lost*, embellished only with Edward Johnston's handsome calligraphic initials, were, as has often been pointed out, a devastating critique of the elaborate ornamentalism of Morris's Kelmscott Press. Stately simplicity was the Doves hallmark.

'I am greater than I know', wrote Cobden-Sanderson in 1901. 'I see things or try to see things in the light of the infinite.' There are many entries in the journals that suggest Cobden-Sanderson's increasingly manic identification with the Doves Press. In 1909 he quarrelled violently with Emery Walker, claiming the Doves typeface as his exclusive possession. He began to brood about closing the Press, fearing its continuance after his death. The First World War reminded him of the power of the printed word and in 1916 he rebelliously arranged an edition of Goethe's songs and poems in honour of Germany's past and with hopes for her future. It was his last and, in his view, most beautiful book. That year he started throwing the Doves Press fount of type into the Thames, paying nightly visits to Hammersmith Bridge till every letter had gone to the bottom of the river. Emery Walker did not attempt to seek redress.

Cobden-Sanderson was a paradoxical figure. He was a socialist, a pacifist, a vegetarian, and a pantheist. He supported his wife's activities as a militant suffragette. He greeted the Russian Revolution as a new dawn. Yet he created the epitome of luxury in book production that appealed and still appeals to the most discerning of bibliophiles. Like many middle-class men and women he found solace working with his hands. Nothing very socialist about that, you may say. But Cobden-Sanderson argued it differently. The Doves Press and the Doves Bindery were, he hoped, prophetic expressions of things to come – when a socialist state would transform daily life with guilds revived, with joy in labour, with seasonal festivals and pageantry.

Standing in the British Library looking at his finest of fine bindings it is difficult to see the connection with a coming utopia, but Cobden-Sanderson saw it plain and as a result died a happy man.

The Spectator, 18 May 1991

Picasso's ceramics

Each generation of artists and writers will construct their own Picasso from the immense range and richness of his oeuvre. Until relatively recently (despite Daniel-Henry Kahnweiler's recognition of their importance) Picasso's ceramics, along with a good deal of his post-war work, have been consigned to critical oblivion.[1] The tone was set by Clement Greenberg's magisterial and dismissive essay 'Picasso at seventy-five' which argued for the failure of Picasso's development and his decline into pastiche and diversification after the war.[2] By the 1970s this view was commonplace and Picasso's ceramic work was seen as a dissipation of his gifts: 'His arcadian thematicism thus came to its inglorious end'.[3] In the 1980s, with the collapse of a Modernist standard that focused on progression and the linear development of art, views were more generous. The reassessment of 'late Picasso' naturally called for a new look at the ceramics as one aspect of the rich allusiveness of his post-war art.[4]

Picasso's interest in ceramics can be tentatively traced back to his early days in Paris. There was his friendship with the jeweller, sculptor, and potter Paco (Francisco) Durrio, a Frenchman brought up in Bilbao and one of the circle of Spanish friends so touchingly described by Fernande Olivier in her memoir *Picasso et ses amis*. She recalled that Durrio had two heroes, the young Picasso, and Gauguin, whom he had known well before Gauguin left for Tahiti. It was Durrio's studio in the Bateau Lavoir that Picasso took over in 1904. Picasso acquired some of Durrio's own pottery, the anthropomorphic 'The mormons' and a *jardinière*.[5] Durrio's enthusiasm for Gauguin, and in particular for his ceramics, appears to have influenced Picasso. It has long been acknowledged that Picasso's sculptures carved in wood in 1906–7 resemble Gauguin's carvings in the same material. In addition a few small sculptures modelled in clay and cast in bronze at that time bear a distinct resemblance to Gauguin's ceramics. Two of these, 'Woman arranging her hair' and 'Head of a man' originated as ceramics made in Paco Durrio's studio.[6] But the earliest surviving pots associated with Picasso are simply applied art, two vases probably decorated by Picasso, possibly made by Jean van Dongen, and now in the Musée Picasso.[7] The interest continued. In 1932 Brassaï photographed the chimney piece in Picasso's studio; the photograph shows a largish vase which Picasso had overpainted with his own decorations.[8] And in the summer of 1936 Picasso visited the pottery town of Vallauris with the poet Paul Éluard. Éluard later dedicated a poem to Picasso with a few elegiac lines describing a potter throwing.[9] But Picasso's real involvement began in the years 1946–7 at the Madoura pottery at Vallauris.

The present splendid exhibition at the Barlow Gallery at Sussex University leads us to think again about Picasso's work at Vallauris, and to ask how close these ceramics bring us to the central concerns of Picasso's art. The exhibition is a small selection from Sir Richard Attenborough's extensive, lovingly assembled collection of the most beautiful of Picasso's *Éditions Picasso* and *Empreintes originales de Picasso*. It includes the anthropomorphic jug, 'Woman's head crowned with flowers' (which has something of Gauguin and perhaps of Durrio about it); the grand four-sided 'Figures and heads VII'; the pre-Columbian-looking vase 'Fishes and birds'; the lyrical pitcher 'La source', and a whole sequence of the oval platters which Picasso decorated with extraordinary inventiveness. The collection is crowned by two superb, unique pieces, the spouted jug, 'Visage de femme' and the oval platter 'Tête de Torero'.[10]

Both Jaime Sabartés and Françoise Gilot describe the mixture of chance and intention which brought Picasso to work at the Madoura pottery at Vallauris.[11] Suzanne Ramié – 'Madoura' – and her husband were hardly simple country artisans and Vallauris was in transition from a traditional pottery village to a centre for 'art pottery'. In fact it was a visit to a pottery show organized by the town's growing band of studio potters in 1946 that reawoke Picasso's interest in ceramics.[12] But the shapes and the quality of much of the pottery produced at Vallauris were reasonably close to the Mediterranean peasant pottery tradition. In the end, Picasso's active engagement in ceramics did not have much to do with Durrio or with Gauguin. What was more powerful was an influence which we can only guess at – Picasso's own memories of the peasant pottery of southern Spain, which had remained a rich and varied tradition long after country potteries had died out in England and had begun to decline in France. Zoomorphic shapes like the rooster jugs recorded in Llorens Artigas's survey of Spanish country wares were commonplace.[13] So too were full-bodied, almost crude vessels with big strap handles, which Picasso selected to decorate at Vallauris, or transformed into female forms; and of course, a whole range of generously shaped bowls and platters.

Picasso's interest in ceramics at Vallauris coincided with a period of extraordinary creative vitality – a kind of post-war expansiveness and celebration of life. Picasso was 64 when the war ended. For long periods in 1945 and 1946 he worked at Mourlot's lithographic studios. There he pushed the lithographic process to its limits and produced the eleven states of 'The bull' which allow us to share in his process of creativity. At Antibes he decorated the museum in the Château Grimaldi with arcadian subjects – nymphs, fauns, and satyrs. The following year, 1947, having filled the Grimaldi with work donated on permanent loan, he took up the Ramiés' invitation to work

Pablo Picasso painting 'Sphere decorated with a still life, including a bottle of wine', Vallauris, 1948.

at Madoura. There he appears to have quickly made arrangements for *Éditions Picasso* and later for *Empreintes originales*. Kahnweiler suggests that Picasso liked the lasting stability of ceramic, hinting that there was some question of immortality in his attraction to it, and noting that, in the late 1950s, most of his small paintings were executed as tiles, platters, etc.[14] Perhaps this is not as fanciful as it sounds: Picasso, intensely superstitious, never forgot a prophecy made in his youth that he would die in his sixty-eighth year.[15] His creativity in so many media, the beauty of Françoise Gilot, his fathering of her children, kept these horrors at bay. At Vallauris in 1950, in the sculpture studio there, he made the sculpture 'The pregnant Woman', an image of fecundity constructed partly out of vessels. The ancient idea of Pandora/Rhea, the divine mother fashioned from clay, the woman in the form of a jar, was thus given totemic reality.

Though there were moments of frustration – Gilot records Picasso saying of pottery, 'It's always an *object* but not always an *objet d'art*' – Picasso certainly did not regard ceramics as a mere diversion.[16] There were formal problems that engaged him and which he described to the sculptor Henri Laurens. In recording Picasso's conversation with Laurens, Kahnweiler provides us with a text to puzzle over, and one that recalls the *paragone* writings of the Renaissance.[17] Clearly Picasso saw in ceramics a chance to unite painting and sculpture. He told Laurens that, while painting should create a sense of space, he had found that by painting a ceramic form he was able to create the multiplicity of flattened viewpoints which he demanded from sculpture. As Kahnweiler astutely observed, some of the paradoxes he had first explored in the 'Glass of absinthe' of 1914 were again investigated in the unique ceramics.

Picasso decorated a series of spheres and found that the still-life image became elusive: *'Elle vous échappe elle tourne autour de la boule'*, he told Laurens. He decorated jugs so as to dissolve and dissect the jug wall. He continued to play with the ancient female/vessel metaphor. He never learned to throw, but he altered thrown pieces vigorously. He slab-built a few pieces – a bull and some doves. His love of transformation and metamorphosis led to his decoration of fragments of pottery and of tiles, kiln furniture, and hollow bricks. An important early group uses the standard press-moulded dishes made at the pottery as a painterly support. To these simple shapes Picasso brought the full range of his technical discoveries. (Gilot tells how he expanded the pottery's range of colours, while Sabartés records with some horror Picasso's mastery of potter's jargon.)[18] The powerful analogous thrust of his imagination led him to make the raised rim of the dish, variously, the leafy surround of the *Éditions* piece 'Visage gris', or the brown dust of the bullring and sparkle of the matador's tunic in the unique 'Tête de torero', both in the Attenborough Collection. Françoise Gilot was disapproving of the poor quality of the clays and workmanship at the Madoura pottery. But quality did not appear to be Picasso's intention, nor did he want to explore ceramics in the purely sculptural way that Miró did in collaboration with Llorens Artigas. He wanted to remain in touch with a very basic peasant tradition.

The most challenging pieces, like the spheres, were not selected for reproduction. In fact we know little about Picasso's attitude to the reproductions. Georges and Suzanne Ramié record that often Picasso could not tell the difference between a unique piece and an *édition*, but this, echoing his flattering remarks to his printmakers, seems unlikely.[19] The beauties of the Attenborough 'Visage de femme', the richness and complexity of the colours and the bold lines of the sgraffito could hardly be convincingly imitated. The *Empreintes* are closer to prints, being impressions in clay taken from plaster of Paris engraved by Picasso. But in the decision to make these reproductions there seems to have been an extension of the generosity and the desire for immortality which characterize 'late Picasso'. Only the very wealthy could afford Picasso paintings and sculpture, but at the Madoura pottery in the 1950s and 1960s it was possible to purchase *Éditions* and *Empreintes* for under £100 and little ashtrays for a few shillings. If in them the hand of the artist appears remote, the finest of the reproductions are impressive ceramics that animate and charge the space around them.

How do Picasso's ceramics compare with the best of studio pottery – the work of the designer's hand from start to finish? Certainly the studio pottery world's relationship to Picasso has been ambivalent. Bernard Leach, the doyen of studio pottery, found his admiration for Picasso severely tested by the ceramics: 'I cannot regard him as a good potter.'[20] But for other younger potters the first sightings of Picasso's ceramics after the war were a release. William Newland, Margaret Hine, Nicholas Vergette, and even Hans Coper, were all liberated by Picasso into exploring a Mediterranean rather than an oriental tradition. For a brief period in the 1950s the sober surroundings of the Crafts Centre at Hay Hill were enlivened with prancing bulls and anthropomorphic vessels. Curiously enough, the painters who took to decorating ceramics (from Pasmore in the 1950s to, more recently, John Hoyland, John Piper, and Bruce McLean) never developed the sculptural element of Picasso's ceramics: their contribution remains a timid one. But in the 1970s, when the crafts seemed an alternative to the increasingly remote concerns of the fine-art world, two potters in particular, Carol McNicoll and Alison Britton, carried on Picasso's researches into the special unity of painting and sculpture possible in ceramics. The beauty and profundity of their work form an honourable extension to the ideas that Picasso investigated at Madoura.

1. Daniel-Henry Kahnweiler, *Picasso-Keramik*, Hannover: Fackelträger, 1957.

2. Reprinted in Clement Greenberg, *Art and culture*, Boston: Beacon Press, 1961.

3. Tim Hilton, *Picasso*, 1975, London: Thames & Hudson, p. 270.

4. See Robert Rosenblum's essay in *The sculpture of Picasso*, New York: Pace Gallery, 1982.

5. Alan Windsor, 'Picasso's ceramics', *Ceramic Review*, vol. 81, May / June 1983, provides a valuable overview but lacks footnotes. See also Werner Spies, *Picasso sculpture*, London: Thames & Hudson, 1972, pp. 20–1; note 28, p. 266. On Durrio, see Crisanto de Lasterra, *En Paris con Paco Durrio*, Bilbao: Junta de Cultura de Vizcaya, 1966.

6. Spies, *Picasso sculpture*, note 28, p. 266.

7. Illustrated in *Musée Picasso catalogue sommaire des collections*, Paris: Ministère de la culture, 1985, p. 203.

8. Brassaï, *Conversations avec Picasso*, Paris: Gallimard, 1964, plate 3, pp. 34–5.

9. Roland Penrose, *Picasso: his life and work*, London: Gollancz, 1958, p. 263.

10. For a discussion of these pieces and for much else of use, see Marilyn McCully, Transformations in Picasso's ceramics' in *Original ceramics by Pablo Picasso*, Nicola Jacobs Gallery, London: Nicola Jacobs Gallery, 1984.

11. Jaime Sabartés, 'Picasso à Vallauris', *Cahiers d'Art*, no. 1, 1948, pp. 81–3; and Françoise Gilot & Carlton Lake, *Life with Picasso*, New York: McGraw Hill, 1964, p. 176.

12. Renée Moutard-Uldry, 'La Renaissance de la céramique à Vallauris', *Cahiers de la Céramique et des Arts au Feu*, June 1956, pp. 21–9.
13. J. Llorens Artigas and J. Corredor Matheos, *La Céramique populaire espagnole d'aujourd'hui*, Geneva: Les Editions de Bonvent, 1974.
14. Kahnweiler, *Picasso-Keramik*.
15. Leo Steinberg, *Other criteria*, New York: Oxford University Press, p. 121.
16. Gilot & Lake, *Life with Picasso*, p. 214.
17. Kahnweiler, *Picasso-Keramik*.
18. Sabartés, 'Picasso à Vallauris', p. 81, and Gilot & Lake, *Life with Picasso*, pp. 178, 181.
19. Georges Ramié, *Picasso's ceramics*, London: Secker & Warburg, 1975, p. 264; S. W. Hayter, *About prints*, London: Oxford University Press, 1962, p. 109.
20. Bernard Leach, *Beyond east and west*, London: Faber & Faber, 1978, p. 121.

Apollo, vol. 129, no. 327 (new series), May 1989

This was written as a preview of the Sir Richard and Lady Attenborough collection, shown at the Barlow Gallery, University of Sussex during May 1989. In 2007 the Attenboroughs gave their collection of Picasso's ceramics to the City of Leicester in memory of their daughter and granddaughter who died in the Asian Tsunami, 26 December 2004.

Eric Gill, workman

'Eric Gill: sculpture': exhibition at the Barbican Art Gallery, London,
11 November to 7 February 1993

In 1989 Eric Gill became infamous. Fiona MacCarthy's immaculately researched biography of the artist was reprinted three times that year. This was not because the British public had suddenly developed an interest in Guild Socialism and Distributism, or direct carving and typography, or joy in labour in an age of mass production. The reasons were rather more basic. Gill had meticulously recorded his sexual encounters – including excursions into incest and paedophilia – in his diaries. Earlier biographers had let these coded revelations pass, but MacCarthy discussed them in fairly elaborate detail. Gill's religious and political views and the extensive and varied corpus of his art suddenly seemed of little moment. For some, Gill's achievements were invalidated by his apparently obsessive preoccupation with familial sex.

It could be argued that Gill asked to be put under the moral microscope. For him art and life were one: his family and associates, with himself as patriarchal head, were intended to represent what he called 'a cell of good living' in a fallen world. Nonetheless MacCarthy's life of Gill seems to demonstrate that the narrative structures of biography, with its post-Freudian intimacy, can narrow rather than broaden our understanding – especially in the case of a visual artist.

The very full show of Gill's sculpture put together by Dr Judith Collins for the Barbican Art Gallery is therefore both a revelation and a rehabilitation. It fills the entire top floor of the gallery and while many architectural pieces had to remain *in situ*, Dr Collins has brought together more than 100 sculptures, associated drawings, engravings, and contemporary photographs. The sexuality, together with religion and politics, is generously represented, but it is given a context rooted in art. Looking at some of the early examples like the lovely 'Mother and child' (1910), we see Gill in the process of reinventing sculpture in the first decade of the twentieth century. The later work, including pieces of lyrical beauty, shows an artist going his own way determinedly blind to the activities of his peers. Perhaps that is why Gill is not now reckoned a sculptor of the first rank. Though by 1909 he had rejected his Arts & Crafts origins, he never abandoned one of the movement's central ideals – that life is best thought of as service. His overwhelming concern with content as opposed to form, his many religious commissions, his desire to be seen as simply another kind of workman doing a job, paid by the hour, are hardly typical of an ambitious twentieth-century artist.

In 1961 Henry Moore, just such an artist, recalled the sculptors who had influenced him in his youth. As a student he read Ezra Pound's life of Henri Gaudier-Brzeska (1916). He remembered with admiration the way Jacob Epstein dealt with the virulent attacks of his critics. But he felt able to dismiss Gill as a mere craftsman whose work could damningly be compared to knitting or polishing the silver. Gill had a way of distancing himself from the mainstream. For instance, Moore apparently never read Gill's seminal essay 'Sculpture' of 1917 (reprinted in Judith Collins's catalogue). Initially it appeared in the Workers' Educational Association journal *The Highway*, written for an audience of working-class men and women. Later, in 1924, Gill published a revised version with the fustian-sounding subtitle 'An essay on stone-cutting with a preface about God'. No wonder it passed Moore by.

Yet Gill was the first British artist to return to a method of carving in which the stone was attacked direct, not dependent on careful measurement and translation from a model. Gill made his first sculpture – now lost but represented in the show by a preparatory drawing – in 1909, just a year after Brancusi's early essay in direct carving, 'The kiss'. Direct carving was one of the practices which underpinned the energy and 'primitivism' of inter-war avant-garde sculpture; it was crucial to the achievements of Gaudier-Brzeska, Epstein, and Moore. Gill came to it through a training as a lettercutter and stonemason; it was natural for him to draw on stone and carve direct.

All in all Gill's relationship to modernism is a tricky and elusive thing.

Powerful archaic pieces like the solid little 'Rower' of 1912 – a work I've not seen before even in illustration – were greeted with excited recognition by Roger Fry, and Gill was included in Fry's second Post-Impressionist exhibition of that year. What could be more prestigious, more avant-garde? And Gill certainly shared a *musée imaginaire* with Fry and his circle. This encompassed sculpture from India, Mexico, and Egypt, all medieval European sculpture, all 'primitive' art. On the other hand such things were also icons of the Arts & Crafts movement in which Gill's early training was rooted.

Gill was an accidental modernist and his career and his account of it are therefore full of paradoxes. Epstein, whom Gill probably introduced to direct carving, was clearly influenced by Cubism. But for Gill the art of medieval England was more important – as the large relief for the Midland Hotel, Morecambe, reassembled at the Barbican, reveals. Gill's ideas about the superiority of carving over modelling came straight from Vasari's sixteenth-century treatise on technique, not an obvious modernist source. As a final confusion Gill claimed rather disingenuously that his initial impulse to carve was not primarily artistic but purely erotic: 'I just wanted to make in smooth stone round and smooth and lovely images of the round and smooth and lovely things that filled my mind.'

In 1913 Gill converted to Roman Catholicism and embarked on the 'Stations of the Cross' for Westminster Cathedral. At the same time he turned away from the fine-art world because people like Fry seemed 'essentially aesthetes'. Gill was painfully alert to issues that could not be encompassed by aestheticism alone – like mass unemployment and the relation of high finance to war. His political radicalism led him to write and to publish pamphlets. It also led him to carve the remarkable Leeds University War Memorial – represented in this exhibition by drawings, woodcuts, and a preliminary sketch in stone. Its subject, Christ casting out a crowd of top-hatted besuited money-changers, infuriated the burghers of Leeds. As a sculpture it is just a bit too much of an illustration, too eccentric. Yet it is worth pondering, being probably the only memorial to the Great War which makes a direct connection between conflict and plutocracy.

If Gill turned away from modernism, he certainly faced up to all the dilemmas posed by modernity. He had a toughly realistic attitude to patronage: the show includes preliminary carvings and drawings for many of his architectural commissions. The carvings of the East, North, and South Winds placed above St James's Park Underground station, the Sower 'broadcasting' in the foyer of Broadcasting House, the Morecambe relief of 'Odysseus saved by Nausicaa', are all works that are hard to categorize. Some of this public art testifies to Gill's sense of social responsibility, his desire to reach out to ordinary people. Other sculptures are ironic commentaries on the redundancy of the artist in an industrial age.

Gill's whole career confirms that a history of art that concentrates on formal developments and breakthroughs is of necessity limited. What we see from this exhibition is that his best pieces – 'Rower', his 'Small female torso' and 'Deposition' both of 1924, 'The sleeping Christ' of the following year – have a feeling for pure graphic form evident in his lettering and typography; their beauties are not strictly sculptural.

As a modern artist Gill had other problems brought into focus here. He had a high, almost disabling, level of skill and a calligraphic fondness for detail. He liked odd vulgar touches such as colouring the nipples of his carved torsos. His work was sometimes too highly finished to seem alive. As his friend and pupil David Jones pointed out, he was often better at making 'things' – holy water stoups, gravestones, a garden roller – than conventional sculpture. (On the gravestone he designed for himself and his wife, he describes himself modestly as a 'stone carver'.) Only his carved lettering, represented by one example in this exhibition, seems beyond criticism. But his sculptural achievement was substantial. When we encounter our hundredth free-standing Untitled, sited carelessly in front of a public building, Gill's awkwardness and bloody-mindedness suddenly look purposeful. Within limits – limits he well understood – he seems to have got the balance between his art and its context reasonably right. The life is a different matter, but this rich exhibition suggests that it would be sensible to set aside the life for a while.

The Independent on Sunday, 15 November 1992

Le Corbusier, craft-lover

In 1911 the young Charles-Eduoard Jeanneret embarked on what he was to call his *Voyage d'Orient*. Years later when he was a famous architect better known under the pseudonym Le Corbusier he set about editing his account of that journey – which took him from Vienna down the Danube to Budapest and Belgrade, over to Bucharest, on to Constantinople and then to Athens. The text was largely based on letters he sent to friends in his home town of La Chaux-de-Fonds in French Switzerland. Reading it today is an extraordinary experience. It might be thought that Le Corbusier had little time for craft or the vernacular. His influential plans for futuristic cities, in which high-rise buildings on pilotis loom over a landscape of parks and super-highways – the *Ville Contemporaine* for three million inhabitants of 1922, or his *Ville Radieuse* of

1930 – have been blamed for many of the ills of post-war urbanism. But Le Corbusier, like many early-modern twentieth-century figures, was at once progressive but also distinctly ambivalent about progress. Throughout his career his anti-modernism paralleled his love of technology.

On his journey of 1911, Le Corbusier was repelled by the modern cities that he visited and, correspondingly, deeply touched and moved by the vernacular art and craft which he encountered in villages and small towns. He became an ardent pottery enthusiast, buying traditional vessels wherever he went. He also studied local peasant costume and jewellery and made detailed sketches of traditional building techniques. He bought kelim rugs. And a sense of impending loss and sadness runs through all his writing at that time. He knew that the skills and the way of life he was witnessing were unlikely to survive untouched. He loved it all – the pottery, the textiles, the folk music, and the white-washed village houses – and reflected that 'we, we others from the centre of civilization, are savages'. But by the early 1920s, writing in his magazine *L'Esprit Nouveau* he decided that it was dangerous to be sentimental about these increasingly peripheral cultures. His caption beneath a photograph of a beautiful, complex Serbian pot which he bought in Baja in 1911 reads: 'Folk culture in its lyric power ... What about the immortal pose of Ruth at Jacob's well and the really beautiful industry of the potter which seems to have been the companion of civilization since time began? Finished! Replaced by a tin can.'

Le Corbusier came from a craft background. His father was a watch-face-enameller and as a student Jeanneret trained first as a watch-engraver. At the school of arts at La Chaux-de-Fonds his gifts were quickly recognized and he was given a richly regionalist Arts & Crafts training by his tutor Charles L'Eplattenier, embarking on his first architectural commission when he was only 19. By 1917, however, he had met all the significant modernist architects in Europe and was living in Paris, working on low-cost reinforced concrete housing systems, and was a self-invented Purist painter. But this did not mean the end of his interest in the vernacular, even if it was often excluded from his published rhetoric.

It has been pointed out that Le Corbusier had a markedly dichotomous, dialogic mind. Throughout his professional life he divided his day in two, one half devoted to painting and writing, the other to architectural practice. This schismatic tendency was apparent even in the context of his rendered, reinforced concrete villas of the 1920s. In the carefully constructed photographic records of their interiors, taken before clients moved in, Le Corbusier included kelim rugs and peasant pots alongside the industrial vernacular of Thonet chairs and Maples armchairs. His own furniture designs, in collaboration with Charlotte Perriand and his cousin Pierre Jeanneret, braided the

Amédée Ozenfant, Albert Jeanneret, and Edouard Jeanneret (Le Corbusier) with a favourite Serbian pot, August 1919.

industrial and natural. Their tubular and sheet steel chaise longue of 1928, upholstered with pony skin, combined function and poetry. Its frame could be tipped high and, lying feet in the air, Le Corbusier imagined himself a cowboy, smoking and relaxing after a day in the saddle.

Le Corbusier's technological ambivalence was further affected by visits to Spain in 1928 (where he bought more pots and discovered Gaudí), to South America in 1929, and by the impact of the Depression. A remote site dictated the plan of 1930 for an unbuilt house in Chile (the Maison Errazuris), with a pitched tiled roof, a framework of tree trunks and rough-cut stone walls. Many other low-tech designs were predicated on local French labour – the unrealized Maisons Locheurs scheme for workers' housing (1929), the Villa de Mandrot (1931) in the South of France, La Petite Maison de Weekend (1935) near Paris, and Le Corbusier's own Paris apartment (1934) with its rubble stone studio wall. It was there, with Louis Carré, that he held the exhibition 'Les Arts Primitifs dans la Maison Aujourd'hui' (1935) – a mix of African masks and sculptures, archaic classical sculpture, found objects, and his own and Fernand Léger's paintings. In the same year Charlotte Perriand included a simple wood and rush chair in the partnership's 'Young man's gym and study' shown at the Brussels exhibition.

The Second World War made the vernacular political. Pierre Jeanneret was to join the Resistance but in 1940, after the German occupation, Le Corbusier did not distance himself from the newly formed Vichy government. That year saw his plans for Maisons Murondins, self-build temporary housing made of rammed earth, timber and turf; by 1943, his ASCORAL group were researching folklore. The topic was a favoured one in National-Socialist circles but by then Le Corbusier was trying to distance himself from Vichy and when the war ended he had friends ready to give him both state and private commissions.

From the 1950s onwards Le Corbusier's use of the vernacular entered a complex monumental phase – with the expressive chapel Notre-Dame-du-Haut at Ronchamp, the dramatic monastery Sainte-Marie-de-la-Tourette outside Lyons, the Unité d'Habitation housing prototyped at Marseille, and in India, first visited in 1951, villas at Ahmedabad and a huge government complex at Chandigarh. His Maisons Jaoul (1952–5), two houses on a shared site in the Paris suburb of Neuilly, set the standard, puzzling young architects keen to see how their hero's work was developing after the war. As James Stirling observed: 'built by Algerian workmen equipped with ladders, hammers and nails, [the house] is technologically no advance over medieval building.' Not surprisingly Le Corbusier's friendships with artisans became increasingly important – with the builder Salvatore Bertocchi, with the cabinet-maker Charles Barberis, the enameller Jean Martin, the master glazier Jules Alazard, the weavers at Aubusson who translated his designs into tapestries under the direction of Pierre Baudoin, and the ceramicist Philippe Sourdive who made the brightly glazed leaves embedded in the concrete balcony tables at the Marseille Unité. Then there was the cabinet-maker Joseph Savina, first encountered in Brittany in 1935, who translated Le Corbusier's drawings into haunting wooden sculptures.

Le Corbusier's interest in detail, in imaginative use of materials and in the vernacular crafts did not mean that he believed in a generalized craft revival. He knew that the tin can had come to stay. But his final favoured retreat, Le Petit Cabanon, built in 1952, represented in a highly condensed way a rejection of certain aspects of modernity. It was made from a kit of parts clad with logs. It resembled a primordial hut, although it abutted his favourite restaurant. It was more evocative of his Swiss mountain childhood than the Provençal coast. It was from here, the simplest of simple dwellings, that he took his final swim in the Mediterranean, dying of a heart attack on 27 August 1965.

Crafts, no. 176, May/June 2002

Gordon Russell, English modernist

'Gordon Russell Centenary': exhibitions at Gordon Russell Ltd, 44–46, Eagle Street, London, 7 May to 12 June; Gordon Russell Museum, Broadway, Gloucestershire, 22 June to 3 July 1992

Was the Edwardian passion for old and reproduction furniture a symptom of England's social unease and decline? The Arts & Crafts architect and Guild Socialist A. J. Penty thought so. He pointed out that in 1851 Britain had had 'an insolent belief in her greatness' and, he incorrectly claimed, the antiques trade had not existed. It was a view echoed by most of the great and good in the early twentieth-century design world. The young William Rothenstein saw the antique shops of the Cotswolds as 'a disquieting sign of the times'. W. R. Lethaby, the most influential art educator of his day, believed the fashion for antiques and fakery was doing a great injury to a noble living craft. Antique collecting was 'mere infantile regression', wrote Noel Carrington disapprovingly.

Yet, confusingly, taste pundits like Carrington, John Gloag, and Roger Fry recognized that some antique furniture had a beauty and structural clarity which had never been surpassed. In fact the design establishment eventually took the applied arts of the eighteenth century to signify both the Englishness of English design and some kind of proto-Modern movement. We did not need instruction from Professor Gropius, the argument ran. We had experienced our design revolution over a century and a half ago. The serious, informed, Board-of-Trade-backed consensus went something like this: the English were a sturdy, island race and therefore impatient with the kind of grandiose furnishings that the French adored. Forget Art Nouveau and Art Deco. Plain, simple comfort based on eighteenth-century designs – fitness for purpose for hearts of oak – was what suited the British temperament. The craze for Victoriana in the 1920s – wax fruits under glass domes and Arundel prints – was dismissed as a fashionable upper-class aberration. Similarly, our fondness for crude, mass-produced reproduction furniture could be blamed on unscrupulous middlemen.

At the beginning of the twentieth century furniture that was regarded as quintessentially English was being designed by a handful of Arts & Crafts architects. Out of this limited if innovatory approach and out of the despised antique trade came Gordon Russell, a truly pioneering furniture designer who during the Second World War was able to test our supposed racial fondness for plainness and simplicity to its limits when he spearheaded the Utility furniture scheme. This year is the centenary of Russell's birth. A well-chosen exhibition at Gordon Russell Ltd's showroom at 44–46 Eagle Street and another at Broadway in Gloucestershire make plain his roots. Russell's early

A worker at the Gordon Russell factory at Park Royal, West London, polishes the veneer of a Murphy radio cabinet, late 1930s.

work was closely based on Ernest Gimson's much grander cabinets while Russell's first modern design, the legendary boot cupboard of 1925, singled out by Nikolaus Pevsner, was profoundly eighteenth-century in spirit. Perhaps Gordon Russell's greatest achievement was to make manifest the interwar design consensus as it developed and changed.

His story is a romantic one, a mixture of George Gissing and *News from nowhere*. As a young boy he lived in an 'ugly monotonous little suburban home' in Tooting. Thanks to his father's own romanticism he was transported from this desert to Broadway in the Cotswolds to be surrounded by beauty and tradition. His father was an artistic bank clerk turned artistic innkeeper and by 1914, when he joined the army, the son was a dabbler in antiques, turned furniture designer. Broadway and the remains of C. R. Ashbee's community at Chipping Campden educated him visually and between 1919 and 1929 Gordon Russell poured forth a stream of Arts & Crafts-inspired designs for furniture and metalwork. He employed local men and the business traded as The Russell Workshops – a picturesque name with an Art Workers' Guild flavour.

But in 1929 the firm was renamed Gordon Russell Ltd and the next decade saw a remarkable change. Chamfering and panelling were abandoned in favour of an English version of modernism. Much of the credit for this new direction must go to Gordon's brother, R. D. Russell. He had trained at the Architectural Association and he and his wife Marion Pepler moved in London's rather small circle of committed modernists. But Russell himself was certainly a driving force in the firm's boldest initiative – an extraordinary collaboration with Frank Murphy to produce a sequence of austerely handsome radio cabinets on a mass scale. In 1929 Gordon Russell Ltd opened a showroom in Wigmore Street and from 1936 to 1939 Nikolaus Pevsner was its buyer. It would be hard to think of a more absurdly distinguished choice. Up until the outbreak of war Wigmore Street was a mecca both for the firm's own modernist products and Modern movement design from Europe.

In his charming biography *Designer's trade* Gordon Russell drew a veil over his deficiencies as a businessman. In 1940 he was forced by the banks to resign as managing director of his own firm. This was hardly a setback. From 1943 to 1947 he was chairman of the Utility Furniture Design Panel and thus able to impose modernism with a Cotswold flavour on the nation. But did Utility furniture bear out the inter-war design consensus that fitness-to-purpose ideas came as second nature to the British? Unfortunately not: after the war, debased modernism and a tide of 'Jacobethan' and mock Tudor furnishing proved that as a nation we were both hard to categorize and – apart from the muted, unadventurous world of the country-house style – had an innate poor taste that at times bordered on the gloriously surreal.

And, as these exhibitions reveal, even Gordon Russell's own taste could be unexpectedly wayward. After two post-war decades in public life as President of the Council of Industrial Design, serving on countless committees, Russell started designing furniture again for his own private pleasure and use. By then he had real doubts about the Modern movement. He believed that the reintroduction of ornament to his late 1970s designs was a revolutionary step. But these late-flowering pieces – heavy yew tables and stools – lack the refinement of his designs of the 1920s and even bear an odd resemblance to the trade Jacobethan his influence did so much to combat. Ornament did return to avant-garde furniture even if it was employed in the ironic and self-mocking spirit we now call postmodern. In his earnestness and social purpose Russell was never to enter that fragmented, self-referential world. Despite all his contradictions, he remained a modernist to the end – of a particularly English kind.

Alexander Calder and his circus

'Alexander Calder: the Paris years 1926–1933': exhibition at the Centre Pompidou, Paris, 18 March to 20 July 2009

When we think of Alexander Calder we think of the mobiles – perfectly balanced, moving slowly in the ambient air, replacing sculpture with something lighter, plinth-free, just right for the atria of public spaces. The biomorphic sheet-steel shapes float like clouds, hung from graphic webs of wire. They often present twice-over: in themselves, and, if imaginatively lit, in shadow form. The mobiles (the name was dreamed up by Marcel Duchamp) stood for accessible modernism – they were a mixture of craft, engineering, and good design.

For the critic Clement Greenberg, Calder – 'wistful, playful, derivative' – was not a patch on his fellow American sculptor David Smith. As early as the 1940s Greenberg was condemning Calder's 'good taste already established by others' stemming 'entirely from the works of Picasso, Miró and Arp'. Calder mobiles were recognizable and safe. Even safer were his elegant painted sheet iron stabiles – all abstract, but evocative of birds, giant insects, farm tools, and of the cutting and bolting processes of heavy industry.

The big stabiles were the work of his post-war career – he died in 1976 just after his retrospective 'Calder's Universe', held at the Whitney Museum of American Art. It is the Whitney Museum that has put together the show 'Calder: the Paris years 1926–1933' at the Pompidou Centre in Paris. It is worth getting on a train to see this if only because it presents a much odder, more complex figure, whose art had a surprising trajectory.

Calder's parents were both artists but they encouraged him to take a less risky route through life and he studied mechanical engineering at the Stevens Institute of Technology in New Jersey. There he would have concentrated on statics – the strength and dynamics of materials – and kinetics or the geometry of motion. He graduated in 1919, took a variety of jobs, went to sea but finally began painting and enrolled at the Art Students League of New York. He became a good commercial illustrator, able to turn out entertaining lightning sketches for *National Police Gazette* and other magazines.

So far, so ordinary. But in the winter of 1926 he began playing with a toy circus, adding movement and articulation to the figures, so that the elephant could go round in a circle and a clown could climb on its back. Going back to a childhood fascination with wire, pliers, tools, and toymaking, seems to have unlocked something in Calder. From then on he began to express himself in wire, sometimes in combination with bits of wood and found objects.

Alexander Calder with the Cirque Calder, 1929.

By July 1926 he was in Paris and pursued his toymaking interests in combination with increasingly sophisticated sculptures, some powered by little motors, a return to kinetic mechanics.

He also began work on the 'Cirque Calder' – which was designed to be performed to an audience. Crouching on the floor, Calder would set up a circus ring complete with sawdust. There was a safety net for the trapeze artists. He would stick up circus posters and blow a whistle to announce the start of the show. He created a cast of miniaturized circus characters – clowns, trapeze artists, a belly dancer, ringmaster, sword swallower, lions and lion tamer – constructed out of bits of spool, elastics, cloth, cork, wood, and wire. Most were partly mechanized, animated by pulleys, wheels, wires, and pneumatics, but sometimes he would just push one of his 'actors' round the ring. The performances were strange and unforgettable. They made Calder famous in Paris in a cultish way, bringing him into contact with the leading School of Paris artists from whom he learned so much.

The 'Cirque Calder' was characterized by clumsiness, inspired ingenuity, and ritual. It managed to be both naive and scary – something the novelist Thomas Wolfe conveyed when he wrote a fictionalized account of Calder's staging of the circus at a fashionable party in New York in 1929. Wolfe describes a Calder pièce de résistance, a sword-swallowing act:

'He took a long hairpin, bent it more or less straight, forced one end through the fabric of the doll's mouth, and then began patiently and methodically to work it down the rag throat ... [he] kept working the hairpin with thick probing fingers, and when some impediment of wadding got in his way he would look up and giggle foolishly ... But he persisted – persisted horribly.'

Calder's fame rests with his mobiles but the 'Cirque Calder' and some of his early sculptures made in Paris are darker in mood. They chime with to-day's appetite for ethnographies and histories, reified in miscellaneous materials. Stuffed dolls, taxidermy, beadwork and embroidery, shadow play, and the poetic use of transferred technologies that characterize present-day art, craft, and design, were all being explored in Calder's circus back in 1926.

Crafts, no. 218, May / June 2009

Lucie Rie and reticence

'Lucie Rie': exhibition at the Crafts Council Gallery, London, 30 January to 5 April 1992

Lucie Rie is 90 in March. She is Britain's most famous living potter; even those completely ignorant of the beauties of studio ceramics will have heard of her. Over the past three decades she has been honoured in a sequence of large retrospective shows, the latest organized in 1989 by the fashion designer Issey Miyake for museums in Tokyo and Osaka. This week her birthday is being celebrated with an exhibition at the Crafts Council Gallery.

Yet all this is of small importance to her. She is an artist of extraordinary modesty and reticence. She has never written or given lectures. She has taught, but her standards were too high for this to be a particularly happy experience. Last year she had a stroke and since then has been living a life of even greater seclusion, seeing only a small circle of friends. There is no question of stopping making pots; making them is central to her life. No one could be more devoted to her art than Lucie Rie. In 1972 Linda Nochlin shook up the feminist and art establishments with an essay entitled 'Why have there been no great women artists?' Her answers were predictable enough – that women, until recently, had been denied access to the appropriate training and institutions. But another answer must be that few women have been able to operate with the extraordinary single-mindedness of a Lucie Rie – living alone, rising early, working late, day after day, year after year.

In the aftermath of her illness she sits peacefully, dressed as always in

Lucie Rie in 1986 at Albion Mews, London, with an array of her work and, on the left, Bernard Leach's Korean Moon jar, now in the British Museum.

white, in the first-floor living room of the tiny mews house off Hyde Park, which has been her home for over half a century. Her doctor and friend, Max Mayer, who took up pottery after he retired in order to work alongside her, sits with her. He tries to communicate what he believes to be her views during moments of silence. Sometimes she will agree, for example, that she sees herself as a craftswoman, not an artist. Sometimes she demurs, or echoes his remarks playfully and a touch ironically.

The austerity of her surroundings gives a clue to her background. She was born and trained as an artist in Vienna where she identified with the city's Modern movement rather than with the frivolously eclectic products of the once great Wiener Werkstätte. The stark furniture designed for her Vienna flat in 1926 by the young architect Ernst Plischke came with her when she fled from Austria in the year of Hitler's Anschluss. Once she had settled in England, a fellow refugee, the architect Ernst Freud, son of Sigmund, re-designed the mews house for her, incorporating Plischke's shelves, tables, and chairs. Today her home is a time capsule, a small monument to the heroic days of European modernism.

When Lucie Rie arrived in England in 1938 she was already in her late thirties and an eminent potter – her work had been exhibited the previous year at the Paris Exposition. Now she was a refugee in a country where, among a small circle of collectors and curators, studio ceramics had been elevated to the status of fine art – largely through the efforts of the potters William Staite Murray and Bernard Leach. But the springs of their inspiration were different from hers. Both men had been influenced by early Chinese and Korean pottery. Both believed in their own importance as proselytizers. Leach in particular had evolved a persuasive critical standard. He took his aesthetics from the Far East but mixed in cloudy socio-moral ideas about 'right-making'. He became her friend and, to some extent, her mentor.

For a while Lucie Rie's art faltered under these new influences. But the friendship of a younger refugee from Germany, Hans Coper, helped her remain true to her own way of working. With her help he was also to become a great potter in his own right and by the 1950s Coper and Rie were recognized as having evolved a ceramic style that looked urban and deceptively simple. Many of these early pieces were utilitarian – tea and coffee sets, salad bowls, cruets.

Of course there are limits to the amount of praise that can be heaped upon a coffee cup. But Lucie Rie's domestic wares are an unusually perfect marriage of form and function. In a more enlightened country she would have had a huge influence on mass-produced tableware. During the 1950s she was in fact commissioned to design a tea and coffee service for Wedgwood. Inexplicably, her prototypes were rejected. But if our industrialists proved unimaginative, the status of ceramics in Britain did act as a liberating force.

Among her loveliest pieces is a sequence of tall bottles. Their only function is to catch the light. They display that interplay of sculptural form and colour which is the particular strength of great ceramics. To explain objects like these it is tempting to talk in terms of skill. Lucie Rie's bowls and bottles have perfectly balanced but undulating rims which testify to her subtlety as a thrower. She is a mistress of the techniques of sgraffito and inlay and of staining the clay body to achieve remarkable colouristic effects. She can work with immense delicacy in porcelain or create majestic heavy pieces in stoneware with frothy volcanic glazes. Her range of white glazes alone seems infinite. She has extended the possibilities of glazing and the use of the electric kiln.

But skill is a red herring: many potters are technically skilful. The craft attracts practical minds that enjoy the unpredictable nature of its science. But this would not, I think, be true of Lucie Rie. She is more of an artist than most potters. She keeps a tight control on her materials and methods to achieve what she desires. The results could be lifeless – all that characteristic turning and finishing of the foot of each piece, the careful brushing-on of glazes and slips, the painstaking scratching of sgraffito lines. But in the act of creating a shape on the wheel, Lucie Rie has always worked with wayward ease. Her pots possess that 'nervous tremor of the creator' which Roger Fry, potter and critic, identified as crucial to great ceramics.

The Independent on Sunday, 26 January, 1992

Isamu Noguchi and his search for roots

Louise Allison Cort & Bert Winther-Tamaki (ed.), *Isamu Noguchi and modern Japanese ceramics: a close embrace of the earth*, Washington, DC: Arthur M. Sackler Gallery, Smithsonian Institution / Berkeley: University of California Press, 2003

The artist Isamu Noguchi worked in a remarkable variety of media and gen-res using traditional and technologically advanced materials to create light-ing, furniture, product designs, sculptures (ranging from portrait heads to large abstract public art projects), interiors, landscape designs (including some remarkable unrealized examples of land art), as well as set and costume designs for dance and theatre. In a fine-art world predicated upon authorial distinctiveness this accomplished versatility was viewed with suspicion. It was not until Nancy Grove's ground-breaking doctoral dissertation 'Isamu Noguchi: a study of the sculpture' (1985) that a serious attempt was made to see his oeuvre as a coherent whole. In 2001 the Vitra Design Museum's 'Isamu Noguchi: sculptural design' made that interconnectedness manifest in a haunting interdisciplinary exhibition imaginatively designed by the artist Robert Wilson. This new awareness of the visual unity of Noguchi's work frees us to return to specific areas of his practice, the most neglected being his ceramics.

Isamu Noguchi and modern Japanese ceramics: a close embrace of the earth, a book of essays and an accompanying exhibition, gives us for the first time a con-textualized insight into Isamu Noguchi's ceramics, made in Japan during intensive spells of activity in 1931, 1950, and 1952. In the late 1920s, inspired by Gaudier-Brzeska and by the experience of working for Brancusi, Noguchi had embraced ideas about truth to materials. He was therefore tempted to dismiss clay as 'too fluid, too facile', as a medium in which 'anything can be done'. But as Bert Winther-Tamaki explains in a biographical essay, in Japan, where ceramics were held in such high regard, these reservations were set aside.

Noguchi's relationship with Japanese culture was far from straightfor-

Isamu Noguchi with 'Metamorphosis' (1946, left)
and 'The queen' (1931, right), New York, late 1940s.

ward. Born in 1904, he was the illegitimate son of a cultivated Bryn Mawr
graduate, Leonie Gilmour, and of Yone Noguchi, a well-known Japanese
poet who had lived in the USA from 1893 until 1904. In 1906 Gilmour and her
2-year-old son went to join Yone Noguchi in Tokyo, but the relationship was
troubled, poisoned partly by Yone Noguchi's increasingly virulent nationalism. In 1918, aged 14, Noguchi was sent back alone to the USA. Like his close
friend the painter Arshile Gorky, Noguchi's youth was cut short and, like
Gorky, memories of his early childhood came to assume special importance.
On his first return visit in 1931, as a recognized young American sculptor on
a Guggenheim travel grant, Noguchi was therefore in search of his roots. But
he was also a young modernist hungrily seeking out inspirational non-European art.

Tang funerary sculptures seen in China were a predictable interest but
he also discovered the archaism and bold directness of Japanese prehistoric
haniwa figures. He may have been the first person from either East or West to
appreciate them as aesthetic objects rather than as archaeological evidence.
As Winther-Tamaki points out, in effect Noguchi was asserting his independence of his famous, unloving father whose taste, formed at the end of the
nineteenth century, did not encompass his son's primitivist vision. In 1931

Noguchi made a handful of portrait heads in terracotta and some remarkable slip-cast unglazed vessels and sculptural pieces, the most striking being the abstract stacked 'The queen', a piece that morphed his study of *haniwa* with Brancusian monumentality. But his real engagement with ceramics came on his return visit to a defeated, demoralized Japan in the early 1950s.

Isamu Noguchi and modern Japanese ceramics is of vital interest for those of us who have relied too heavily on English-language publications that foreground the activities of Hamada Shoji, Yanagi Soetsu, and Bernard Leach, ignoring the complexities of the post-war Japanese art and ceramics scene. For instance, essays by Niimi Ryu and Louise Allison Cort analyse the attitude of Japanese ceramicists towards authorship and originality, exemplified by a cult of the informed and explicatory copy. Noguchi immersed himself in Japanese ceramic practice and actually lived on the potter Rosanjin's estate. But, as Louise Allison Cort points out, even by the anarchic, irreverent standards of Rosanjin, Noguchi failed to use the historic vocabulary of clay and glaze in combinations that were meaningful to an elite Japanese audience.

Thus there was a profound irony at the heart of Noguchi's practice in ceramics. The work he made was innovative and extraordinarily beautiful. Within Japan he inspired radicals like the *Sodeisha* group led by Kazuo Yagi to work with greater freedom. But like many a Western modernist he was appropriating non-Western art for his own creative ends and, not surprisingly, the subtle associative aesthetic peculiar to Japanese ceramics eluded him. Meanwhile in the West the fine arts as mapped by figures like the paramount post-war critic Clement Greenberg excluded the applied arts and as a result Noguchi's ceramics were largely misunderstood or overlooked. *Isamu Noguchi and modern Japanese ceramics* is therefore an important contribution that recuperates a lost body of work and provides detailed insights into the uneasy context in which that work was made.

The Burlington Magazine, no. 1215, June 2004

Peggy Angus and flat pattern

This year Peggy Angus is 86 – the bravest, fieriest person you could hope to meet. She is a radical spirit with political ideals formed in the 1930s. She believes that art should have some sort of social responsibility, scorning what she calls 'scribbling to let off steam' and the kind of art only the critics can understand. Many of her ideas should be inscribed on tablets of stone – in particular her belief in what she calls 'creative patronage'. Angus argues that all the great art of the past was the result of a collaborative process and that all patrons – architects, the state, private individuals – should play an active part in the commissioning process. 'Art for life' is her motto.

Angus's interest as a schoolgirl and young student was in recording everyday scenes, particularly of life lived at the margins by the gypsies and travellers she came to know and draw near Barnet. In 1923 she won a scholarship to the Royal College of Art where she started in the painting department but soon switched to book illustration where her contemporaries and firm friends were Helen Binyon, Edward Bawden, and Eric Ravilious. It was an exciting time but after graduating she took a teaching certificate as a matter of duty. Nonetheless she was determined to be a painter and in all her teaching posts she has worked part-time only – sharing her job with fellow artists. This practice meant that on her retirement she received no teacher's pension.

In 1933 she found and rented Furlongs, a shepherd's cottage below the Sussex Downs, inspiring a whole series of paintings of the surrounding countryside and of country people. Furlongs, she has explained, was 'the matrix of much strange and inventive creation' and became a gathering place for many artists – Eric Ravilious and his wife Tirzah, Edward and Charlotte Bawden, Percy Horton, Maurice de Sausmarez, John and Myfanwy Piper, Olive Cook and Edwin Smith. Throughout the 1930s Angus played an active part in the Artists International Association. This was appropriate enough – her painting was firmly rooted in reality and occasionally sharply satirical. The injustices of the Spanish Civil War, the depression, and mass unemployment all combined to make her a political commentator.

But although Angus is a pleasing painter in an illustrational vein her real genius is for pattern design. Ironically it was through teaching that she discovered her extraordinary gift. After the Second World War, when materials were short, she got her pupils at the North London Collegiate School to work with potato and lino cuts. She invented a deceptively simple set of design rules for the children which produced startling results. The architect F. R. S. Yorke saw the work she was doing and immediately realized its potential for tile design. Yorke was her first creative patron. Encouraged by his interest she went on a short course in industrial ceramics at Stoke-on-Trent, experimented with tiles at the Royal College of Art with Professor Baker, and studied all kinds of abstract decoration. By 1950 she was working regularly with Carter of Poole, launching a series of designs which were silk-screened on to tiles.

The list of her collaborations with Yorke and his partners Rosenberg and Mardall, and with many other architects, is a long one. Among the earliest was a striking three-storey wall at the Susan Lawrence Primary School. The

Peggy Angus in her Camden Town studio in 1991 with her 'Twist' and 'Sun' wallpapers.

school was a showcase part of the redevelopment of Poplar in East London initiated by the Festival of Britain authorities in 1951 as a demonstration of planning and design. This was followed by projects for Warren Wood County Secondary School for Girls, Merthyr Tydfil College of Further Education, and many other major commissions. Angus's tiles did much to humanize and give colour to the rather cold unadorned interiors and exteriors of these quintessential buildings of the period.

Her patterns were inspired by all kinds of sources: the geometric framing of fifteenth-century frescoes, the patterning of Elizabethan damasks, details from medieval manuscripts, and the Polish paper cut-outs which she collected. Teaching was a constant inspiration. As she points out mischievously, she had a large workforce at her disposal and her long mural for the Brussels World Fair in 1958 had been developed from a large wall decoration made by her pupils for the school dining-room.

By the end of the 1950s Angus was moving into another medium – she invented a form of marbleized decoration which was silk-screened on to glass cladding and produced by the firm T. W. Ide under the trade name Anguside. This was used, and much praised, in the first stages of Gatwick Airport (another Yorke, Rosenberg, and Mardall project) but swept away in the expansion of the airport in the 1960s.

This same period saw a shift in emphasis. F. R. S. Yorke died and although Angus remained a consultant designer to Carter Tiles she began to work in a more craft-based fashion. In the late 1950s the painter Kenneth Rowntree had asked her to adapt some of her designs for wallpapers for his house. This she did and in 1960 she won the Sanderson Centenary competition for wallpaper design. It might have been thought that a new career as a designer for the wallpaper industry was about to open up, but although some of her patterns were produced by Cole and by Sanderson, Angus has always preferred the special effects of handprinting using a small lino block and household emulsion paint. By the 1970s she had largely cut her ties with industry. In fact these labour-intensive wallpapers made manifest her belief in creative patronage – clients were encouraged to have blocks specially cut for them with a design that seemed appropriate and, although she does fewer bespoke patterns these days, with a virtually unlimited range of colour combinations to choose from, the client still has to do some creative thinking.

Peggy Angus has invented an extraordinary variety of patterns over the years. Many are abstract while others make subtle use of leaves, birds and cherries, heraldic-looking dogs and dragons, corn stooks, stylized suns and winds, and grapes on vines, and they convey a vivid pastoral mood. Certainly her designs seem rooted both in the natural world and in the visual arts of the British Isles – from Celtic pattern to heraldry and the popular art of bargees and gypsies. The individuality of the place, whether Barra in the Outer Hebrides, Furlongs in Sussex, or the litter-strewn streets of Camden near her studio, is important to her.

Just how great a designer she is was recently demonstrated by an exhibition organized by the Silver Studio archive at Middlesex Polytechnic. 'A Popular Art' surveyed British wallpapers from 1930 to 1950, including Bawden and Aldridge's Bardfield papers of the late 1930s and the post-war Palladio range produced by the Wall Paper Manufacturers Limited. But Angus was easily the star. Her achievements have been recognized by fellow artists of all ages – not least because, unlike most papers, her designs form an ideal background for paintings. But it is hard to resist the feeling that she has not had the recognition she deserves. Perhaps this is because she has worked in a period when the language of ornament has, on the whole, been despised and forgotten. But it is never too late to state the obvious. When we look at her wallpaper and tile designs we really have to go back to William Morris to find anything quite so fresh and sylvan. Peggy Angus is surely one of the most inventive designers of flat pattern to have worked in recent times.

Crafts, no. 108, January / February 1991

Barbara Hepworth and the missing biography

'Barbara Hepworth Centenary': exhibitions at Tate St Ives, St Ives, 24 May to 12 October, and Yorkshire Sculpture Park, Wakefield, 31 May to 14 September 2003.

Barbara Hepworth was born in 1903 and her centenary is being marked by three exhibitions – at Yorkshire Sculpture Park, at the nearby Wakefield Art Gallery in Yorkshire, and at Tate St Ives in Cornwall. It all seems very appropriate. Wakefield was Hepworth's birthplace and she worked for over thirty years in St Ives, creating the home and studio that now form the Barbara Hepworth Museum and Sculpture Garden. But anniversaries do not always fall at strikingly propitious moments.

The 1990s saw fresh, imaginative reappraisals of Hepworth's achievements, largely initiated by Penelope Curtis, director of the Henry Moore Centre for the Study of Sculpture at Leeds. In 1994 Curtis co-curated the excellent Tate Liverpool retrospective out of which came a useful book of essays edited by the late David Thistlewood, *Barbara Hepworth reconsidered* (Liverpool University Press, 1996), to be followed by Curtis's succinct monograph *Barbara Hepworth* (Tate Publishing, 1998). But all this research was carried out with a significant restriction.

In her will Hepworth bequeathed 'all correspondence of historical interest' to the Tate Gallery. She died in 1975; since then her papers have been retained by one of her four executors, her son-in-law Sir Alan Bowness, while he worked on her biography. Twenty-eight years have passed and no biography has been forthcoming. Nor have scholars been granted serious access to her archive. Instead, they have had to work round it, and they have done so, imaginatively and diligently. Recently, part of the archive has been deposited at Tate Britain, but until it is catalogued it will remain unavailable. Hepworth valued her papers. They almost certainly include material from a host of interesting correspondents as well as her own thoughtful, fluent writings. We get their measure by reading her passionate, intelligent letters in other archives, to her second husband Ben Nicholson and to the critic E. H. Ramsden, to Herbert Read, and to the scientist J. D. Bernal. Yet here we are, in this special year, still only able to speculate about her archive's scope. This mysterious, sad story has clouded the Hepworth centenary celebrations.

Archives notwithstanding, the situation is salvaged by the fine show at Tate St Ives curated by Chris Stephens. His particular approach may not convey a career's trajectory – from the brilliant young woman showing small animalier pieces with her first husband John Skeaping in the late 1920s, to the member of an exclusive group proselytized in Herbert Read's writings of the 1930s, to the increasingly famous but isolated auteur of public sculpture for a welfare state. Instead Stephens illuminates formal connections within Hepworth's oeuvre, grouping motifs that she explored over many years – such as the series of vertical forms inspired by the human figure, and an array of sculptures that address the theme of maternity. In pursuit of these visual taxonomies he has tracked down sculptures that have not been seen for a long time.

Meanwhile, other sections of the show scrutinize precise creative moments. A room is devoted to the war years when Hepworth mapped her thoughts for future sculptures in exquisite, parabolic diagrams drawn on a softly painted gouache ground. The enclosed terrace of the museum is given over to a series of magnificent sculptures carved in 1954–6 from the seventeen tons of the Nigerian hardwood *guarea*, given to Hepworth by her friend and patron, the wealthy socialist collector Margaret Gardiner.

Stephens's curation reveals Hepworth's strength as a graphic artist and exquisite colourist, both on paper and in her use of colour on the inner surfaces of certain sculptures. But, more importantly, we get a sense of the visual ambiguity of her carved forms. Much of her best work turns out to be impossible to draw or to photograph, and demands to be circumambulated again and again. This quality of transcendent visual opacity is made evident in the first room devoted to the 'single form'. The earliest piece, 'Torso' (1929) carved from African ivory wood is figurative, but only just. It is a matter of subtle concavities and gentle swellings, made harder to read by the dark sheen of the tropical hardwood. The photograph in the fully illustrated catalogue gives no sense of its complexity.

It can be paired with another 'Torso' (1932) in which Hepworth has left tool marks just under the truncated raised right arm. Although this is a female form it has the stripped-down look of a medieval crucifixion, the kind of source that so inspired Eric Gill, the overlooked *fons et origo* of direct carving in Britain. Gill's name is never mentioned in the context of Hepworth's work but his career serves to remind us how limited our understanding of Britain's sculptural avant-garde has become. Figures like Gill or Ivan Meštrović, and, rather later, John Skeaping, were perceived to be 'modern' in the 1920s. By the mid-1930s, however, they had dropped from view.

Barbara Hepworth with the plaster 'Single form',
photographed at Morris Singer in May 1963.

Hepworth had belonged to this earlier avant-garde but after the 1930s her sculpture was exclusively framed by comparisons with Henry Moore, Ben Nicholson, and Naum Gabo.

As Penelope Curtis has demonstrated, this Moore–Hepworth–Nicholson–Gabo grouping does little to aid our understanding of Hepworth's work. Indeed it is quite easy to become passionately partisan on Hepworth's behalf, not because her work seems in any sense *retardataire* in that company but because of the relentless way in which her career from the 1930s onwards was analysed by male writers and artists. Thus for Herbert Read, Moore embodied power and vitality, while Hepworth stood for beauty and loveliness. For Patrick Heron, Hepworth's 'cold, calm, faceless' work was contrasted with Moore's 'human feeling and personality'. Innovatory practice became an issue – the first hole, the first oval form, and the first strung sculpture – and in this context Hepworth was often cast as an acolyte. By the 1980s, after Hepworth's death, we find Henry Moore claiming that without his benign influence as a fellow student at Leeds School of Art, Hepworth 'would have become a drawing teacher at a secondary school'.

Here, documentation provides a context. For instance, the quartet of wooden, coloured sculptures, three of them stringed, made by Hepworth in the mid-1940s, were in part inspired by nineteenth-century mathematical models. In 1935 Hepworth was writing to Ben Nicholson about plans to visit Oxford to look at some examples. It was an interest she shared with Moore and Gabo but her resulting sculptures also drew on the Cornish landscape and the classical world. The beautiful 'Pelagos' is at once the curved bay of St Ives and 'the arms and bosom of a goddess'. In a catalogue essay Sophie Bowness sees lyre-like stringed instruments as a further source. Hepworth was also interested in progressive design and her practice of painting the interior contours of these sculptures has a visual affinity with the way in which Alvar Aalto juxtaposed natural wood with painted passages in much of his furniture.

The St Ives exhibition includes few pieces made after the late 1950s. For later work we need to travel to Yorkshire. Wakefield Art Gallery has some fine early sculpture and drawings in its permanent collection. But it is currently showing a selection of Hepworth's highly polished, small, limited-edition bronzes cast in the last fifteen years of the artist's life. It is difficult to know what to make of these. They are seductively collectible, being accessible simulacra of her inter-war work. Yorkshire Sculpture Park, meanwhile, is showing some twenty carvings of the late 1960s and 1970s mostly in white Italian marble, a selection of bronzes from about the same period, including many maquettes and, outside in the park itself, an impressive seventeen public sculptures.

This northern show also introduces us to a sculptor working with a team of assistants. The white marble pieces all have that intelligent complexity of shifting planes so marked in Hepworth's sculpture from the late 1920s onwards, but they lack tenderness. Her craftsmen became almost too attuned to the kit of parts that made a 'Hepworth'. And of course the outdoor pieces remind us that at St Ives most of the work shown is table or at least room size.

Is there a problem here? We have to turn to the Liverpool retrospective catalogue and read Curtis's essay on 'The artist in post-war Britain'. 'You won't have a friend who thinks the same after the war as they did before it', Hepworth wrote to Ben Nicholson in about 1940. After the war Hepworth became a different kind of artist. From 1956 she began casting in bronze, and on occasion in aluminium, on a big scale. Some earlier large pieces were translated from wood into bronze. These sculptures and their context of New Towns, New Universities, and hopes for peace between nations are now the least researched part of her work. At the time Henry Moore was seen to have fulfilled that humanist role more effectively. The efflorescence of civic patronage after the war – epitomized for me by Hepworth's bronze 'Single form (antiphon)' placed outside the Music Centre at the newly built University of York in 1969 – all too quickly came to seem a series of paternalistic gestures. Hepworth, however, responded to the challenge in markedly varied and ambitious ways. Her thoughts on the role of public sculpture, and the social and political climate in which her ideas evolved, need now to be recuperated. Those archives again!

Times Literary Supplement, 27 June 2003

We are still waiting for the official biography of Barbara Hepworth.

Eva Zeisel's search for beauty: an obituary

Eva Zeisel, who has died aged 105, was one of the most respected post-war product designers in North America. Her specialism was ceramic tableware but she also designed furniture, textiles, glass, and lighting. Her remarkably successful career in the USA began soon after her arrival as an émigré in 1938. By the mid-1950s she had created an elegant, sculptural new look in ceramics that was partly inspired by the art of Jean (Hans) Arp, Salvador Dalí, and Henry Moore, and by Finnish and Scandinavian design. Together with Charles and Ray Eames, and Russel Wright, Zeisel offered an organic modernism that came to characterize informal middle-class living. She continued to design as a centenarian, still engaged in what she described as a 'playful search for beauty'.

Zeisel was born in 1906 in Budapest in the Austro-Hungarian Empire, grew up in Hungary under the right-wing regime of Admiral Horthy, took part in the cultural life of the Weimar Republic in Hamburg and Berlin, became a leading designer in Soviet Russia from 1932 until 1936, surviving Stalin's purges and narrowly escaping the Nazi holocaust.

Her family were wealthy, cultured assimilated Budapest Jews, her father a textile manufacturer, her mother, Laura Polanyi Striker, a historian and educationalist who ran a radical school. Eva's uncles were Karl Polanyi, the economic historian, and Michael Polanyi, the scientist and philosopher. Michael Polanyi was to write on the importance of 'tacit' or 'personal' knowledge and coincidentally Zeisel's greatness as a designer was in part based on her profound tacit knowledge of clay, rooted in Hungarian folk craft.

After studying painting Zeisel took the unconventional step of apprenticing herself to an artisan potter, treading out the clay with her bare feet and accompanying her master from house to house installing clay ovens. It was a training that gained her membership of the Guild of Chimney Sweeps, Oven Makers, Roof Tilers, Well Diggers, and Potters. She built a kiln in her parents' garden, sold pots in the market, designed for the Granít Earthenware factory, and represented Hungary at the Philadelphia Sesquicentennial Exhibition of 1926. In the tradition of medieval guildsmen Zeisel embarked on a modern version of a journeyman's travels, taking her to a pottery in Hamburg and to the Schramberger Majolikafabrik in Germany's Black Forest, where she had her first experience of designing for multiple production and learnt prototyping skills. By 1930 she had a design studio in Berlin where as a strikingly beautiful young woman she had a hectic social life. Curiosity, recklessness, and idealism took her to the Soviet Union in 1932 where she married the Viennese physicist Alexander Weissberg. Both became privileged foreign experts, Zeisel rising to become Artistic Director of the state-run China and Glass Industries, designing both for the mass and luxury market – her porcelain Intourist tea service was quietly classical, exquisitely hand-painted with views of Leningrad. In 1936 she was arrested in the wave of purges of 1934–9, accused of plotting Stalin's assassination. Freed after 16 months, mostly spent in solitary confinement, Zeisel found herself in danger again, as a Jew in Vienna. In 1938 she arrived in New York with her second husband, lawyer and sociologist Hans Zeisel.

She began teaching at the Pratt Institute in Brooklyn where she set up a pioneering ceramics design course. Using Emily Post's etiquette manual as a guide to American social mores, she created soft asymmetric forms,

From folk art to modern art: Eva Zeisel in her Budapest studio in 1926.

exemplified by her brightly coloured 'Town and country' earthenware for the Red Wing Pottery in 1946, with its memorable intertwining anthropomorphic condiment set. She designed a more formal but softly curvaceous all-white dinner service for Castleton China, put into production in 1946 and known as her 'Museum' service after being exhibited in her 'Modern china' show of that year – the first solo exhibition offered to a woman artist at the Museum of Modern Art. The 1950s were a period of great productivity for Zeisel and her designs directly inspired the British manufacturer Roy Midwinter whose 'Stylecraft' range was based on her nesting, asymmetrical designs. Zeisel was a modernist who resisted many modernist mantras, explaining that 'the designer must understand that form does not follow function nor does form follow a production process. For every use and for every production process there are innumerable equally attractive solutions.'

By the mid-1960s she turned away from design to write and to campaign against the Vietnam war. She was drawn back in the 1980s when a major retrospective 'Eva Zeisel: designer for industry' was organized by the Musée des Arts Décoratifs de Montréal and the Smithsonian. Honours crowded in and old designs were reissued. Her 'Tomorrow's classic' and 'Century' dinner service of 1950 for Hall China was produced in the UK by Royal Stafford in 2005, when Zeisel was aged 99. In 2000 she revisited the Lomonosov factory in St Petersburg, where she had worked as a designer in the 1930s, finding present-day Russia neither 'pleasant nor happy'. In her long productive life she experienced folk artisanship in Hungary, small-scale industry in Germany, Soviet mass production, design for the consumer boom of the USA in the 1950s, and, finally, the niche 'design classic' market from the 1980s onwards. Her husband Hans died in 1992. A daughter and a son survive her.

The Guardian, 22 February 2012

Sam Haile, a life unfinished

Barry Hepton (ed.), *Sam Haile: potter and painter*, London: Bellew Publishing, with Cleveland County Council, 1993

A brilliant career cut short is always tragic. Sam Haile died in a car crash in 1948, aged 38. Had he lived, Haile would surely have remained a meteoric presence in post-war ceramics. There is no book devoted to him, but now we have *Sam Haile: potter and painter*, which accompanies the travelling exhibition of his work initiated by Cleveland Crafts Centre. It includes a major essay by Paul Rice, a beautifully written and illuminating memoir by Haile's widow, Marianne de Trey, and a brief recollection by the artist Eugene Dana of Haile's time in the USA.

Rice writes perceptively about Haile, and suggests that his death and the premature retirement of William Staite Murray, his tutor at the Royal College of Art, meant that a whole school of potters who were producing technically simple, yet artistically daring work lost their way after the war. Certainly, if we compare the work of Haile, Murray, Margaret Rey, and Robert Washington with that of Hans Coper, the latter looks tight and careful. On the other hand, the 'Picassiettes' – as William Newland, Margaret Hine, Nicholas Vergette, and James Tower were dubbed by Bernard Leach – drew on similar, modernist sources to Haile's, but made work that was far more light-hearted and decorative.

The fact that the 1950s exemplified both light-heartedness and decorativeness in design and the applied arts might have been frustrating for Haile. My guess is that, post-war, he would have returned to the USA, where he

Sam Haile, slipware bowl, 1938.

would have been able to create increasingly ambitious ceramics in the positive and materially paradisical atmosphere of Ann Arbor or Alfred – two universities where he worked and taught in 1941–3.

Rice tells us a good deal that we did not know about Haile, but, in some ways, this book is a disappointment. For, although it accompanies an exhibition, it is not quite a catalogue and it does not compare with Malcolm Haslam's exemplary study of William Staite Murray (1984). It would have been good to have had a complete list of works by Haile, including lost or broken pieces and those known only from photographs. Because his oeuvre was relatively small, this should have been possible. A complete bibliography of writings, both by and about Haile, would also have been useful.

There are vaguenesses in the text. For example, Rice refers to 'The Second Surrealist Exhibition', which was probably the show, 'Surrealist objects and poems', put on at the London Gallery in 1937 (not 1936). More on Haile's membership of the Artists International Association, and contextualization of his involvement with the loose-knit group of British Surrealists, would have been helpful for the reader. In 1937, Haile showed a savagely satirical painting, 'Hitler must be overcome', in an Artists International Association exhibition. In view of the passionate debates which took place between Surrealists and Social Realists in 1936–7, a painting like this would have demonstrated the potential of Surrealism as a political tool.

Unusually among inter-war potters, Haile was politically committed. Did he join the Communist Party? Certainly, he thought about the relevance of handmade pottery to socialism and in an illuminating article in the Communist periodical *Our Time* (July 1946), he argued for the importance of the pottery of Bernard Leach to the present day. He wrote: 'The "realist" will cry that Leach is a devitalized reactionary, that he yearns for a mythical age long past. The "realist" is wrong.' Haile argued that Leach, as an artist, had influenced industrial design, and that he also had an affinity with 'the better constructivist sculpture'. As a socialist, he saw in Leach's St Ives workshop the germ of 'the freedom which is the only freedom – that of a vocational society voluntarily co-operating'.

Rice alludes to Haile's writings on painting and his rather obscure ideas on what he called 'the dimension k', which evidently represented for him some kind of tool with which to gain greater artistic autonomy. Haile was perhaps not a painter of the first rank, although, ironically, he apparently valued his paintings more than his marvellous pots. His pictures were, with a few exceptions, both illustrative and crowded. They lack a powerful, formal sensibility.

But as a twentieth-century potter Haile is a great formalist. His achievement, as Rice points out, was an ability to create remarkable ceramic shapes and then decorate them semi-figuratively, without in any way compromising the pot's intrinsic, sculptural presence. Indeed, the word 'decorate' seems inappropriate here. Haile employs some of the imagery of his paintings, but the process of painting on ceramic and the demands of a curved surface force him to simplify. And, while his paintings are often deeply melancholy, his pots are characterized by a kind of archaic merriment, which brings to mind the untroubled beauty of Minoan ceramics.

The career of Sam Haile demonstrates how uneasy the relationship between ceramics and painting tends to be. But, it also leaves us in no doubt that Haile's interest in aesthetics and in a narrative political art, mediated through Surrealism, helped make his pots exceptional.

Crafts, no. 123, July/August 1993

Marianne Straub, industrial artist

Between the ages of three-and-a-half and eight, Marianne Straub was treated for tuberculosis in a sanatorium. Nonetheless, it was a happy time, and she inadvertently had a rather advanced kind of education, to which we may attribute her powerful visual imagination. She was not taught to read or write, but she played instead at collage with scissors and paper. Instead of learning by rote, she spent her time making things. She remembers sharing her room with three little boys: 'We all had the same wonderful imaginative power: we could build our imaginary world, and I'm sure that was a great asset.' As a result, when she is given a commission she is able to visualize the interior, the colour scheme and her fabric vividly; she never thinks in terms of a sample, and does not need to put her ideas down on paper, but can quickly weave the prototype for the industrial looms which she understands so thoroughly. Her childhood misfortune gave her complete visual invention, and the ability (to use Donald Schön's eloquent phrase) to 'reflect in action', making and designing, in one craft-based process.

Other childhood influences were important, if less overwhelming. She was Swiss and Swiss girls were (and up to a point still are) brought up by their mothers to stitch, crochet, and knit well. She remembers that at school, until the age of 16, girls devoted half a day each week to needlework. Her mother encouraged a growing interest by giving her a narrow strip loom during a short illness. She was also conscious of the folk textile tradition in Switzerland: nineteenth-century countrywomen used to grow, spin, and weave their own flax. At the time of her girlhood, this tradition was dying and was only partly revived by the *Heimatwerk* network set up by Ernst and Agnes Laur at about the time Straub left for England. In addition there was Switzerland's premier position as a manufacturer of fine silks and of the most advanced industrial looms. By the time she was in her teens, she had decided to go to art school and study textiles.

The training at the Zurich Kunstgewerbeschule in 1928 was craft-based. She was taught by a 'real artist', Heinz Otto Hürlimann. He was something of a lone wolf, who, like many great teachers, instructed by letting his students work through their own mistakes. The key moment was when Straub's textile was pinned up and thoroughly discussed and analysed by her tutor. Hürlimann had trained at the Bauhaus but Straub recalls that he rarely spoke of his time there. His teaching emphasized making work for a contemporary environment, and eschewing any form of copying, either from the past or from other cultures.

Straub's decision to work for industry rather than as a handweaver was

Marianne Straub at home at Highsett, Cambridge, in 1989.
A Guatemalan textile hangs on the wall.

not, as has been suggested, directly influenced by Bauhaus thinking. She was a youthful idealist and she wanted to create work which could be enjoyed by the many, rather than by the wealthy few. As a student in Zurich she was a member of the Paneuropean Union, a high-minded organization founded in 1923 in response to the horrors of the First World War. She remembers that a prominent speaker at the meetings she attended was Walter Robert Corti, later the creator of the International Pestalozzi village for refugee children in the Appenzell. She was too individualistic to join a political party, but her membership of the Paneuropean Union, her admiration for Corti, and her involvement with the theatre at art school, suggest the diversity of those energetic student days.

The exclusive nature of the handweaver's work was distasteful to her in another way: her childhood illness had left her disabled, and she was all too aware that handweaving was regarded as an ideal occupation for women and men like herself. She was fiercely determined not to be categorized in that way. And it might be added that textiles, in the form of sewing and knitting especially, was seen as a female home-based occupation, and she hoped for broader horizons.

After leaving the Kunstgewerbeschule she took an unpaid job at the local mill in her home town of Amriswil. She became the technician's assistant – 'a handyman' – and discovered a liking and understanding of textile machinery. She was preparing herself for the industrial course run by the Swiss silk industry's Seidenwebschule. To her dismay, she was debarred from attending because she was a woman. If anyone should wonder why Straub has taken England so thoroughly to her heart, the answer must in part be that initial rejection in Switzerland. She came instead to Bradford Technical College, and this was our gain.

At Bradford she was given a thorough grounding in textile maths, weaving technology, industrial looms, cloth construction, and raw materials. Straub was soon a favoured pupil and she had enormous enthusiasm and a particular interest in mechanical matters. But the Bradford course was an industrial one, and even at the Kunstgewerbeschule she had not dyed or spun yarns. Her decision to work with Ethel Mairet at Gospels after leaving Bradford in 1933 was a wise one. There, her visual imagination was given an extraordinary boost. It is possible to make analogies between Gospels and Bernard Leach's St Ives Pottery. In both instances the students were immersed in constant discussion. Both workshops were remarkably primitive technically, but the aesthetic sensibility was elevated. Colour and yarn quality were revealed to Straub at Gospels. Ethel Mairet's eye for colour, and her gift for finding beautiful yarns from India, Africa, and Russia were a revelation. In return, Straub was able to pass on more complex weave structures to the Gospels workshop.

The relationship Straub had with the craft movement in Britain was interesting. She was quickly recognized as a major talent, speaking at the Dartington Conference of 1952 and organizing the textiles side of the conference. She was a close friend of key figures like Margaret Pilkington and Harry Norris of the Red Rose Guild. But she was not tempted to become a craftswoman. The early decision made in Zurich was not modified, and she found that the discipline and responsibility that were required of the designer for industry appealed to her. She was always careful, both at Helios and at Warners, to have control over the yarns and their dyeing, and always also to know the machines on which her designs were to be produced. In that sense she had a craft base within the industry, and was able to realize Ethel Mairet's frustrated hopes for industrial collaboration. She knew that only by completely understanding the machines she worked with could she have design freedom. As a result, her handwoven prototypes did not have to be adapted for power-loom production. She had none of that fear and distrust of complex technology that has so characterized the British craft movement.

When Straub reflects on influences, she has wise words to say about borrowing. The appropriation of designs horrifies her, as does the copying of weave designs for printed fabrics. She was recently delighted when one of her pupils was bold enough to take on a high street chain after her designs were plagiarized. On her travels abroad – to Mexico, to Guatemala, and to Mali – she examines yarns, colours, and techniques. But she is emphatic that 'you have to make your own contribution to your own culture: you don't lift designs from other cultures'. She notes with regret the worldwide destruction of ethnic craft traditions, just as she feels sad about the disappearance of the labour-intensive complex looms that were once used in the industry.

Marianne Straub's finest designs were created with modern architecture in mind. They fitted perfectly into the expansive projects of the post-war period: ocean liners like Caronia and new universities like York, where systems architecture and good landscaping created a civilized environment. That democratization of the arts lies at the heart of Straub's life as a designer for industry.

Crafts, no. 97, March / April 1989

Constance Howard, the embroiderer with green hair

This year Constance Howard will be 83. Still working, experimenting, learning, and teaching the art of embroidery, she is the pre-eminent figure in post-war embroidery for a multitude of reasons, but principally because of her creation of a pioneering course at Goldsmiths College. During the 1960s and 1970s this course became a byword for work that was radical, yet beautifully executed. In North America she is a revered figure who draws mass audiences. As well as teaching and practising her art, she has chronicled the history of British embroidery in this century. While Rozsika Parker's *The subversive stitch* treats the period after 1900 briefly and in mostly theoretical fashion,

Constance Howard's four-volume survey, *Twentieth century embroidery in Great Britain*, notes hundreds of individual embroiderers and vividly describes the art's changing aesthetic decade by decade. No other modern British craft has been recorded in such detail by a single writer.

By contemporary standards her early life was a struggle. When she was 10 she went one evening a week to the Northampton School of Art. At 14 she won a scholarship to attend art school full time, later becoming a student teacher, earning ten shillings a week. During that time she passed numerous Board of Education art exams (including embroidery which she disliked). By the age of 21, in 1931, she had won a free studentship to the Royal College of Art. But, although her local education department gave subsistence grants to three boys who were going to the RCA, it was argued that she was less deserving because she would probably marry. Before Howard went down to London she had to borrow money which took seven years to repay. It was an early example of sexual discrimination that still rankles.

At the RCA Howard studied illustration, producing an impressive body of white-line wood-engravings. She remembers she was painfully shy and worked fanatically hard, tackling all kinds of illustration as well as studying hard in the V&A. Embroidery was still of no special interest but she liked the embroidery tutor, Kathleen Harris, and made one large panel for her. She remembers Edward Bawden and Eric Ravilious as very shy young tutors, but otherwise 'we more or less taught ourselves'. In her fourth year she won a scholarship to do a teacher training course and discovered the pleasures of pedagogy at Wimbledon School of Art, where 'they made me do things I didn't enjoy, like giving criticism in antique drawing and plant drawing. They were marvellous to me and I really had a very good training.'

Howard's first job was at Cardiff School of Art from 1935 to 1937 where she taught a range of subjects and started a course in dress design. Dress design, theatrical costume, and millinery have always fascinated her, and she takes a lively interest in innovatory fashion. She particularly admires Vivienne Westwood and retains a special love for the work of the Spanish couturier, Balenciaga. She dresses elegantly herself, her clothes set off by beautifully arranged hair dyed a remarkable green, the colour she has boldly favoured since the early 1960s.

Howard stayed at Cardiff for two years but it was only during the war, while teaching at Kingston School of Art, that she started to explore the broad appeal and endless possibilities of embroidery. At Kingston her classes included Canadian soldiers and other ex-servicemen who came with embroidery kits, but whom she encouraged to work creatively. By 1945, in conjunction with the Arts & Crafts Exhibition Society, she was showing embroidery praised for its imaginative freedom, which built on the spontaneous verve of

Constance Howard pictured in 1998 in front of
a felted panel by Julia Hetherington.

pre-war pioneers such as Rebecca Crompton and Lilian Dring. She also contributed some work to the 'Pictures for Schools' show at the Whitechapel Art
Gallery in 1949 and her work was acquired by Stewart Mason, the discerning
Education Officer for Leicestershire, who during the 1950s assembled an impressive study collection for the county's schools.

Howard's embroidery of that time was indeed free, with a heraldic figurative style that suggested an interest in English popular art as well as Scandinavian and Russian illustration. During the 1960s she continued to develop
figurative ideas, but there was also a move towards abstraction, as in her
splendid altar frontal for a church in Kampala, Uganda. All her work featured a lively disjunction between line and blocks of colour. The effect was
similar to that employed by Lucienne Day in her textile designs and, probably, ultimately derived from the art of Paul Klee, Fernand Léger and Joan
Miró.

In 1947 Howard started teaching at Goldsmiths, giving classes in the history of costume once a week, and in 1948 she was invited to teach embroidery to trainee teachers there. She recalls: 'They had never actually done

250

embroidery before which was a great advantage. They were good artists –
painters, illustrators, and sculptors – and we got a good standard very quickly. Technique is nothing really; you learn that as you go along. It is the ideas
that count.'

For one student in particular, Christine Risley, the work of these trainee
teachers was a revelation and she persuaded Howard to give classes in the
main art school. Risley, a distinguished embroiderer in her own right, remembers that the painting school was narrow and old-fashioned in 1948,
while in Howard's classes 'you could enter a world of imagination – you could
use what colours you liked and whatever motifs you wanted personally.' She
recalls that Howard was strict about a proper understanding of stitches, fabric, and thread, and that she believed passionately in the importance of drawing. Margaret Hall, another former student, remembers her as 'a brilliant
educationalist who never failed to encourage you: she was quite critical, but
never destructive. She could intuitively work out where your strengths lay:
at times she seemed almost psychic.' Risley echoes this: 'She has this strange
intuition and rapport that endlessly encouraged and enabled you to bring
out unexpected things in your own work.' For women students she was a remarkable role model.

The embroidery course at Goldsmiths was very much Howard's creation.
It was one of only four such courses in the country and she was fierce in its defence, always pressing for new equipment and more space. By the early 1960s
the yearly exhibitions of her students' work had become famous, a must for
anyone interested in textile art.

Today she still works and experiments. Only the other day she attended
a day seminar held by the Council for the Care of Churches and felt a longing
to embark on an ecclesiastical commission. She is at the moment planning a
large banner based on a detail of a Docklands stairwell, an abstract sequence
of shapes and figures. In 1985 she began working in an entirely new fashion,
wrapping thread round card to create shimmering, abstract colour juxtapositions. But she is now doing a good deal of hand-stitching. Remarkably, as
she taught millinery to Mary Quant, she is also going to millinery classes to
perfect her technique. But, like many women designers, Howard is modest
about her achievements – tellingly she has the scantiest records of her own
work. Things somehow just get done; ideas somehow just happened. It is
easy to underestimate the iron will behind a lifetime of so much activity and
to forget that Constance Howard fundamentally changed the image of post-
war embroidery.

Crafts, no. 127, March / April 1994

Robin and Lucienne Day

'Robin and Lucienne Day: pioneers of contemporary design': exhibition at the Barbican Centre, London, 8 February to 16 April 2001

Think of someone over 70, educated and modern-minded. In their open-plan sitting room much of the restrained, beautifully made furniture is Scandinavian, but some will almost certainly have been designed by Robin Day, while the occasional flash of colour will surely be a textile designed by Day's wife Lucienne.

The Days have finally been honoured with a much-deserved retrospective marking over fifty years as designers of furniture and exhibitions and of textiles, wallpapers, and ceramics. Most of us will have experienced their work at some time – will have sat on one of Robin Day's classic stacking chairs or unconsciously taken in one of Lucienne Day's textile designs, steeped in graphic and painterly modernism. I use the word modernism advisedly because the Days were, and are, modern designers with a concomitant set of standards. They wanted their products to be low cost, they thought architecturally in terms of complete interiors, and they were informed by the best of continental fine art.

The first part of the exhibition at the Barbican displays all these hard-won values. Lucienne Day's textiles, characterized by complex, wiry draughtsmanship, extraordinary colour sense and a dash of Surrealism, translated School of Paris art into design. The most famous, like the prize-winning Calyx created for the Festival of Britain in 1951, now seem to exemplify all the New Jerusalem optimism of the period. Robin Day's early furniture has the same sense of democracy. Tellingly some of his finest early designs were initially intended for a public space – the humane interior of the Royal Festival Hall. There, his auditorium seats thankfully remain, but the rest – orchestra chairs, dining and lounge chairs - were disposed of in the early 1970s. This seems incredible now. At the Barbican an array of survivors of this blitz – with their spindly steel rod legs and curvaceous moulded plywood seat backs – look like sophisticated little domestic sculptures.

The Days would not thank me for being nostalgic about their early work. But their careers as designers chart the changing political economy of Britain. The 1950s saw an extension of war socialism, with an emphasis on good design for both public and private pleasure. Take the Days' joint contribution to the 1951 Milan Triennale. There they created an idealized domestic space, rich in hopes for an egalitarian future. Pots by Hans Coper and Lucie Rie, a handwoven rug designed by Gerd Hay-Edie, Lucienne's Calyx and Robin's handsome steel-framed storage system incorporating a bold abstract

Room setting at the 1951 Milan Triennale with Robin Day's chairs, tables, and a storage system incorporating a print by Geoffrey Clarke, and with 'Calyx' fabric by Lucienne Day.

print by the sculptor Geoffrey Clarke, all added up to what was then an affordable combination of art, craft, and design.

Over time the Days' portfolio changed. By the mid 1960s the relatively crude rusticities of early Habitat were to transform the mass market for domestic furniture. Undeterred, Robin turned to plastics with his extraordinary range of polypropylene injection-moulded chairs – forty million sold since 1964. Meanwhile Lucienne continued to design an impressive range of printed fabrics, wallpapers, and surface decoration for ceramics, putting sophisticated abstraction to functional use. (Only in the mid 1970s did she abandon industry and turn to the creation of a series of impressive one-off silk wall hangings.) Then there was a whole range of ambitious contract schemes, often carried out collaboratively: seating for Gatwick airport, interiors for BOAC VC10s, the entire furnishing of Churchill College, Cambridge, a design consultancy for the John Lewis Partnership.

What can we learn from the Days' remarkable joint career? First some gender politics, for here are a couple whose creative partnership has always operated on a basis of perfect equality – a rarer occurrence than one might think. Secondly, their work makes a lot of highly publicized current design look ill-thought-out and overpriced. Thirdly, we might conclude that the triumph of Habitat and of its successors and rivals spelled the end of fine craftsmanship in design. Finally, we learn that good design wins out in the end. Habitat are relaunching Lucienne's Graphica and Black Leaf textiles designs and a range of Robin's furniture. Rather more adventurously two adventurous firms – Twentytwentyone and SCP – have commissioned new work from Robin.

When I visited the show just before it opened the Days were there. Now both in their eighties, they were pleased with the selection – though Robin was a bit troubled by the bland layout (having created some brilliant exhibition designs himself) and Lucienne would have liked to see more of her recent wall hangings. Their appearance was impressive. I found myself thinking of the dress and demeanour of a well-known designer in his late forties – trainers, one-day stubble, dishevelled romper-like garments, odd headgear. The Days, on the other hand, looked quietly chic. This trivial thought stayed with me as I watched them supervise the arrangement of their most recent work. They operated, of course, as a team – polite, calm and professional emissaries from a lost world.

The Independent on Sunday, 18 February 2001

Ruth Duckworth, émigré

'Ruth Duckworth: new ceramics': exhibition at the British Crafts Centre, London, 11 October to 8 November 1986

The all-too-brief return of Ruth Duckworth to these shores last year again raised the question of serious sculptural ceramics in Britain. The post-war history of British studio pottery has in the past few years been presented in articles, exhibition catalogues, and reviews in a curiously abbreviated form. The only aesthetic to have emerged from a considerable body of writing and debate has been one based on the decorated vessel form of domestic size. This has meant that the revolution in ceramics here in the 1950s and 1960s has been neglected, while the analogous achievements of Voulkos and his followers in America have become part of ceramic history. (Perhaps this is yet another example of a characteristic lack of confidence in the best of our visual art.) The sculptural movement in British ceramics has a somewhat incoherent history, but it may be traced back to William Staite Murray and his followers; it reached a cul-de-sac in the Picasso-inspired efforts of Margaret Hine, William Newland, and Nicholas Vergette, was carried forward by James Tower, and, in the 1960s, by Ian Auld, Dan Arbeid, Gordon Baldwin, Hans Coper, Anthony Hepburn, Ian Godfrey, Gillian Lowndes, Bryan Newman, and Louis Hanssen. It was given a new vitality and adventurousness by Ruth Duckworth between 1958 and her departure for the USA in 1964.

It was in Britain that Ruth Duckworth developed as an artist. She arrived here in 1936, aged only 17, 'because there was nothing I could have done in Germany'. This was three years before Hans Coper and two years before Lucie Rie came; the painful background of flight from Nazism was common to them all. At first she studied at Liverpool School of Art. Youthful obstinacy and ambitiousness meant that she failed to follow the structure of the course: she studied painting, sculpture, and drawing in tandem, 'like Michelangelo', and left without a degree. The next few years were painfully hard – debilitating war work, learning stone-carving at Kennington School of Art, jobs as a puppeteer and as a monumental mason. She, like Coper, suffered deep depression as she struggled with her art and the business of survival: 'What is it, to start with, that makes me want to work? Originally the drive was an effort to alleviate anxiety – the anxiety that I might be destructive, damaging, undeserving of love.'

As a sculptor in wood and in stone, Duckworth faced the inveterate problems of patronage. Her 'Stations of the Cross' at St Joseph's, New Malden (1948–9), carved in collaboration with her husband Aidron Duckworth, were appropriately archaic in style, with echoes of Eric Gill's earlier reliefs of the Stations in Westminster Cathedral. Her torso of a woman in Hoptonwood stone, of the same period, showed the influence of the pre-war giants of British sculpture, Jacob Epstein and Henry Moore. Moore, whom she visited on several occasions, proved to be an important influence, as the free-standing porcelain pieces which she showed last year at the British Crafts Centre demonstrate. But, although she worked in many media in the 1950s, it would, I think, be true to say that she only found her uniquely memorable voice when she turned to clay.

Initially she simply wanted to glaze some clay sculptures. At Lucie Rie's suggestion, she went to Hammersmith and then to the Central School to study pottery. Of contemporary potters, Hans Coper was undoubtedly the biggest influence on Duckworth, but so were visits to the British Museum to look at pre-Columbian pottery: 'the first coiled pot made when I was a student at the Central School was entirely pre-Columbian in shape'. She went to the Central to learn the craft of a medium she had already worked with – above all to master throwing and glazing. In order to live, she made functional ware of great beauty and pure design. From the start, her work as a potter was characterized by immense variety in technique and mood. She swiftly developed a vocabulary of organic forms which she has refined continuously over the past twenty years. By the early 1960s she was making delicate pinched porcelain pieces, heavy stoneware cylinders, coiled ovoid pots with rough, partially glazed surfaces, and semi-figurative sculptures with a totemic air. Coiling, which was taught as a mere exercise at the Central, was to enter the repertoire of the modern potter largely because of Duckworth's instinctively sculptural way of working. So, too, were pinching and a particularly tender form of slab-building. For her, however, all these innovatory techniques were merely the means to achieve a sculptural effect. In contrast, those who were very clearly influenced by her (one might include Mary Rogers, Peter Simpson, Geoffrey Swindell, and many others) never quite freed themselves from technique.

In the early 1960s Duckworth was teaching at the Central. In 1964 she was invited to join the faculty of Midway Studios at the University of Chicago. With laconic detachment, Duckworth refers to a decision which has kept her in the USA ever since: 'I thought, well, I could look at this extraordinary country and it won't cost me anything – this country where they make such ugly things.' 'Although Chicago is a wild town, the States is as good a place as any other.' But her departure was perhaps timely. In 1961 she had published an article in *Pottery Quarterly* with her husband Aidron, entitled 'Pottery in a vacuum'. She argued that a period of post-war prosperity for potters was over. Just after the War, lack of competition from the commercial giants meant that tableware provided potters with a steady source of income and in many instances financed their more experimental work. By 1961, factory ware had won back its market and many potters began to suffer a major recession. Duckworth wrote:

> 'What is important, however, is that somewhere the will and skill to
> produce beautiful work are preserved and fostered. If he is left to work in
> a vacuum, the potter will dissipate his energies in the effort to survive, or
> be defeated by lack of money and interest. Perhaps we have never before
> had such a wealth of talent in this country as exists today. Whether it is to
> move forward in strength or whether it is to become debased and wither
> is in the hands of the new patrons – industry, the architect and the State.'

Duckworth particularly wanted to work on a large scale and the kind of architectural project she had in mind was only offered to her when she went to the USA.

For Duckworth, America was a land of opportunity – in 1968 she embarked on 'Earth, sky, and water'. This was more environment than mural, as it covered four walls and a ceiling in the Geophysics Building at Chicago University. In 1971 and 1974 she created two substantial murals for the houses

Ruth Duckworth with her newly completed (in 1969) ceramic mural 'Earth, sky and water', Henry Hinds Laboratory for Geophysical Sciences at the University of Chicago.

of private clients in the Chicago area, and in 1976 the beautiful 'Clouds over Lake Michigan' for the Dresdner Bank in Chicago. Her most recent project, 'The story of Creation' for a synagogue in Hammond, Indiana, is especially lovely. Planned as a gigantic spiral, the story unfolds from the abstract chaos of moon, sun, stars, and rocks, culminating in an innocent, fresh world in which Adam and Eve stand among the beasts and birds. This is a startling new figurative direction for Duckworth, though there are links with the New Malden carvings. It is true religious art of the kind that communicates with a Quattrocento directness of form and inscription.

Although there are striking continuities in Duckworth's work, these large-scale mural pieces were the direct result of her move to the USA. The porcelain pieces shown last year at the British Crafts Centre are also different from anything she made while in Britain. They are highly refined constructions that draw on the same sources – stones and bones – used by Henry Moore to create whole sequences of public sculptures. Rolled, scraped, and sanded, slowly created from the array of abstract shapes that litter her studio, these pieces are remote and cerebral. Though relatively small they have a monumental air, but because of the conviction with which the medium is manipulated they do not have the look of maquettes. Perhaps this is because Duckworth also includes details that could only work on a small scale – like the porcelain pins that hold some of these structures together.

They are entirely different in spirit from Duckworth's pinched porcelain work, where the hand of the artist is clearly present in the softly formed undulations of each piece. For also represented at the British Crafts Centre was the kind of work which I associate most with Duckworth. It cannot precisely be described as feminist, but it appeals to the feminine aspect of the psyche. Such work need not necessarily be made by women – for instance, Arshile Gorky made art of this sort – but its strength is made through tenderness, and its softness and unresolved air demand a very specific response. I am thinking of the large smoked earthenware sculpture with its semi-figurative look, of the wall pieces that appear to simultaneously veil and reveal forms of extraordinary softness, and a strange pair of twinned coiled vessels, all of which activate what can best be described as a visceral response. The British Crafts Centre show, which displayed Duckworth's characteristic range, was surely a landmark, an historic exhibition.

Duckworth is settled in the USA but she has had thoughts of returning to Britain. Her decision to mount a substantial show here was 'an experiment'. Before she left in 1964 she had concluded that ambitious large-scale work was virtually unsellable here, whereas in the USA she found that it was welcome. Today not much has changed; indeed, the cult of the vessel has made the areas in which ceramics can operate even more limited. The cautious boundary drawing of Peter Dormer's survey book *The new ceramics* may be taken as typical of the present conservative mood. Ruth Duckworth was born in 1919 but she is too ambitious and too youthful in spirit to accept that kind of restrictiveness. I imagine that she will not return permanently to Britain – which will be our loss – but will remain in the wild town which has allowed her to develop her art to its present brave scale.

Crafts, no. 85, March / April 1987

The British Crafts Centre is now known as Contemporary Applied Arts.

Ralph Beyer, direct and uncompromising

In 1937 a young German boy came to study at Eric Gill's workshop in Buckinghamshire. He was asked to draw an alphabet. Gill corrected it and then set him to carving inscriptions, tutored by Gill's assistant Laurie Cribb. Over 50 years later Ralph Beyer remembers Gill with affection and still puzzles over the artistic enigma of his first teacher.

Today Beyer is one of the most senior and distinguished lettercutters working in Britain – in the company of David Kindersley and John Skelton. He works alone, nowadays concentrating mainly on commissions that please him. But of his importance there can be no doubt, especially after seeing his work in the company of his fellow letterers in a recent touring exhibition, 'The spirit of the letter'. Beyer's two contributions – a heart-stopping quotation from Rabindranath Tagore cut in Ancaster stone, and a simple inscription modelled in plaster and clay and applied direct to the wall of the gallery – make one sit up. Neither example seems quite as eye-catching, quite as pretty, quite as self-evidently skilful and as highly finished as other things in the show. But both have that directness which gives all his work an essential quality. Lettering can appear decorative and it can look absolutely necessary. Beyer's work always seems the latter.

Lettercutting is one of those crafts which was done to death by a mixture of modernism in architecture and our gathering timidity about meaningful lasting inscriptions. Since the war lettering has largely been appropriated by architects and graphic designers and by trade monumental masons. And if we look at the lettering on major buildings like the Barbican or the South Bank complex we see that architects in particular deem the craft inessential. Letters can be tacked on as an afterthought. Usually the lettercutter is only

Ralph Beyer pictured with an inscription from Rainer Maria Rilke, 'Shatter me music' ('Bestürz mich, Musik', 1913), Ancaster stone, 1987.

called in to execute the dismal plaques revealed when the little curtains are whisked aside and the ribbon cut: 'This building was opened by ... .' But if Beyer is working at a craft that has largely been destroyed during the post-war years he is in fact heir to modernist ideas at their finest, experienced when they were newly minted in Europe in the 1920s and early 1930s.

That Beyer has about him an aura of that authentic idealistic modernism is hardly surprising considering his background. His father, Oskar, was an art historian whose eclectic book *Welt-Kunst* today looks like a source book for contemporary art. The young Beyer grew up with Erich Mendelsohn as a family friend and was inspired by the work of Rudolf Koch, the great calligrapher and typographer, whose expressive letterforms still have an unforgettably powerful impact.

When Hitler came to power the Beyer family left for Crete and Switzerland, and later Beyer was sent to train with Gill on the advice of Mendelsohn. Lonely and with imperfect English, Beyer found Gill a kindly taskmaster. But he also found him puzzling. Where did he stand in relation to the modernism that Beyer had lived and breathed in his childhood? Certainly there were Gill's friendships with Mendelsohn and Maxwell Fry and his involvement with plans for a modernist Académie in the South of France. And it was in Gill's household that Beyer came to read *Circle* and *Unit 1* and had his first encounter with the work of Henry Moore. Beyer observed and appreciated the modernism of Gill Sans and other Gill typefaces, and the way in which they were used in a radical fashion by René Hague, Gill's son-in-law. But at the same time his training was only in the rounded Roman that was the Gill letter-carving workshop style. Later, working with David Kindersley, he learned a more demanding Roman based directly on the lettering on Trajan's column. But neither letterform had much to do with modernism. So in a curious way Beyer's training and his ambitions were at odds.

In 1953 they came together when Beyer first saw David Jones's extraordinary painted inscriptions illustrated in *The Architectural Review*. He then thought back to his father Oskar Beyer's pioneering work on Christian catacomb inscriptions and he formed his own idea of their executants – ordinary men and women working in poor light and in secrecy. These images must have been in his mind when he carved his first commission in collaboration with the architect Keith Murray for the Royal Foundation of St Katharine in Butcher Row, and they are brought to fruition in his great 'Tablets of the Word' in Coventry Cathedral. Indeed his study of Roman catacomb art made Beyer sympathetic to that laudable post-war desire to clarify and simplify services and make arrangements in churches more accessible, taking the early church as a model.

At Coventry Beyer was inspired by the great early Christian symbols, the *Chi Rho* and the vine, and by the informal lettering found in the catacombs. Interestingly the commission was given to him because no sculptor could be found to carve suitable reliefs. (Matisse seems to be the only convincing twentieth-century relief sculptor.) It was a wise decision: lettering is both a means of communication and an abstract art which integrates gracefully with architecture.

The huge Coventry commission is only a part of Beyer's long career and is easily matched by his series of inscriptions for the Paul Tillich Park in New Harmony in the USA. And of course like all lettercutters Beyer has done routine work – though it is hard to think of an inscription he has cut which does not make you pause and think. And what of the future? Today it might seem that lettering's hour has come. Much postmodern architecture could accommodate carved inscriptions. But the benefits may be dubious: architecture which is pastiche and quotation will demand lettering in the same spirit. Nothing could be further from Beyer's approach, which is direct and uncompromising. So it seems likely that much of Beyer's future work will be private and will give eternal form to the beautiful texts which he selects from his wide reading. Oh for a lapidarium to house a sequence of such carvings!

The Spectator, 19 May 1990

Ralph Beyer (1921–2008) did not get his lapidarium but in 2009 his archive of drawings, rubbings, and prints, together with some carved stones, was bought by the Crafts Study Centre, University for the Creative Arts, Farnham, Surrey.

Ann Stokes, artists' potter

Most beautiful pots are essentially domestic. Their makers take up a position in a specific world and create objects that will be for general use and give pleasure. All traditional pots were made in this spirit. It is the very opposite of making high art, although a consciousness of high art need not be excluded. These wares, therefore, are functional because they communicate unselfishly. Within her world Ann Stokes has created an autobiographical domestic pottery that is little known outside it and intensely celebrated within it.

A measure of the affection felt for her work was the inclusion of some sixty side-plates in this year's Hayward Annual and warm appraisal by Nigel Greenwood in his catalogue. It gave potters a shock. Most of them had never heard of her. She does not exhibit regularly. She sells from home or works to commission. But here was a potter at the Hayward, admired by Nigel Greenwood, David Sylvester, and John Golding, yet working quite independently from what we might call the potting establishment. The side-plates are perhaps the key to her achievement. They are modest in form and decorated with a lyrical touch. She uses a small selection of glazes and coloured slips – copper manganese, a lovely white tin glaze, a glowing cobalt – gently brushed on.

Ann Stokes has always been in contact with the best of English art but, from the age of 17 until she married, she trained as a dancer. When Phyllis Badell's school was evacuated to St Ives during the war Ann Stokes stayed nearby with her painter sister Margaret Mellis. She danced in the morning, helped care for her nephew Telfer in the afternoon, and ate, as she remembers, from Bernard Leach plates. She carried on the dancer's routine as a Wren

Ann Stokes in her mirror, 2007.

in Paris and Aberdeen and returned to ballet school after the war, until a weak knee put paid to a professional career. In 1947 she married the man who had been her brother-in-law, the critic and painter Adrian Stokes. They lived in Ascona, Switzerland, for three years and there she would have seen plenty of simple earthenware, either undecorated in the form of huge garden pots or simply glazed with characteristic whites and greens.

Ann Stokes took up potting in the early 1960s, quite casually in order to amuse her son Philip. Once engaged she applied herself to the matter with all a dancer's perseverance. She learnt a good deal at the Well Walk Pottery near her home in Hampstead. She went to classes in Camden where the Sudanese potter Mohammed Abdulla taught her more. She read up glaze recipes. The first floor of her house was turned into her studio. The coal cellar housed her kiln. She chose to work with earthenware because stoneware, remote and transformed by high firing, never appealed to her.

John Fowler of Colefax and Fowler immediately liked her work and she made dinner services for him, and huge coiled terracotta garden pots. But over the past twenty years her range has been tremendous. Relief tiles, either modelled or carved, are built into the stairs of her house and into stately pier glasses. They decorate a restaurant in Henley and the bricked-in window of a Georgian house in Dorset. She narrates mythological tales – Odysseus returning to his father, the rape of Europa – or homelier scenes, a cat stalking peacocks or the Long Crichel goat. Like a latterday light-hearted Palissy she sends lizards crawling across the base of a mirror while frogs crouch on her ceramic boxes.

All the pieces that connect with food have a sensual charm. She makes a perfectly shaped bean pot. There are long platters and delicate coffee cups decorated with cream and brown slip and glazed inside with grey green. Then there are her great tureens, perfectly fishy on the outside and decorated inside with unexpected whites, yellows, and greens. When I visited her we hurried out into the garden to see a new delight – a recently completed fountain. Beside it crouched a great ceramic frog and a jet of water that issued from its mouth turned the winged top of the fountain – a fountain that both moved and sparkled with a dancer's poise. In the house another fountain gathered dust in her studio. A bird sits on its top basin and when the fountain is playing seems to beat up the spray with its wings. Many of her pieces – the lamps, the extravagant ceramic shades and mirrors – have an Islamic look. She has vivid memories of a trip to Turkey with the painter Derek Hill. All her travels, her visits to the British Museum, and her life in Italy have had a direct effect on her work.

Roger Fry once wrote: 'Pottery is of all the arts the most intimately connected with life, and therefore the one in which some sort or connection between the artist's world and the life of his contemporaries may be most readily allowed.' This was strikingly true of the products of the Omega Workshop and it is equally true of the work of Ann Stokes. Omega suggested a way of life and a rejection of certain aesthetic standards. These were summarized by Lytton Strachey in his Memoir Club essay 'Lancaster Gate' in which he recalled the barren appearance of his parental home. By a curious coincidence Adrian Stokes has also given an account of his childhood in the same part of London with its visual desert of railings and dusty park grass. But he contrasted Bayswater with a counter landscape, an anticipation of Italy, a

264

Virgilian scene that as an adult he came to know well: 'the family mid-day meal under a fig tree, with a fiasco of wine on the table, olives, cheese and bread.' He always felt that the decorative was underprized in our culture. His widow continues to elaborate on the Virgilian theme. Ann Stokes's work has much to do with playful metamorphosis, with feasting and with a peculiarly British love affair with the Mediterranean.

Crafts, no. 77, November / December 1985

Ann Stokes (1922–2014) is memorialized in *Ann Stokes: artists' potter* (London: Lund Humphries, 2009).

Tadek Beutlich, weaver: an obituary

Tadek Beutlich, who has died just before his 89th birthday, was a strikingly innovative post-war textile artist, an inspired teacher and a gifted print-maker. He was born in Lwówek in Poland on April 19, 1922. His father ran a delicatessen and a confectionary factory but when Beutlich was eight financial problems forced a move to Poznań where Beutlich eventually enrolled at the Academy of Fine Arts on a scholarship. He had a thorough Arts & Crafts training in ceramics, stained glass, weaving, and sculpture (to which he was particularly drawn). After the Nazi invasion of 1939, as a Pole of German origin, he was made a German national, studying art for a term in Weimar and subsequently at Dresden Art Academy before being drafted into the German army in 1941, aged 19. Training as a radio operator he listened into BBC broadcasts, confirming his doubts about the regime he was serving. He was sent to the Russian front and then to Italy. He was captured by the Allies, detained in a POW camp and released to join the Second Polish Corps, part of the British Eighth Army. Before demobilization he studied at the Academy of Art in Rome and was able to visit museums in Italy.

In England he took up a government grant offered to all ex-serviceman and initially studied painting and drawing at the Sir John Cass School of Art. He transferred to Camberwell School of Art after visiting an exhibition at the Victoria & Albert Museum of French tapestries that included demonstrations of weaving, which he returned to watch again and again. This and a subsequent exhibition of Finnish *rya* rugs, also at the V&A, inspired him to abandon painting for textiles. In his small bedsit he started to weave on a simple frame using the limited colour range of cheap darning yarns available

Tadek Beutlich: a weaver without a loom, 1997.

just after the war – white, grey, and black. At Camberwell Barbara Sawyer, a former pupil of the great weaver Ethel Mairet, arrived to teach in Beutlich's second year. Sawyer took her students to meet Mairet at Ditchling and to the firm of R. Greg & Co in Manchester, where Beutlich met the ex-Bauhaus designer, weaver, and yarn specialist Margaret Leischner. Both women's imaginative treatment of yarns had a profound influence on Beutlich.

Initially Beutlich made flat-weave tapestries, inspired by folk art and continental modernism. An important catalyst was 'Modern American Wall Hangings' toured by the V&A Circulation Department from 1961 to 1963. This had an impact on Beutlich similar to British painters' responses to the 1956 Tate Gallery exhibition 'Modern Art in the United States'. By 1965 when Beutlich made 'Moon', he was experimenting with weavings that included charred wood, seed pods and x-ray film. His book *The technique of woven tapestry* of 1967 is still considered indispensable by weavers all over the world.

Beutlich was in touch with fellow Polish exiles, as a key figure in the Polish Group 49 and through exhibiting at Mateusz Grabowski's eponymous gallery in Chelsea. There he saw the remarkable post-war weaving coming out of Poland, by figures like Magdalena Abakanowicz and Wojciech Sadley, which had caused such a stir at the First International Biennale of Tapestry at Lausanne in 1962. He soon began to work on a monumental, three-dimensional scale, using flowing hanks of sisal and jute with results that, in the case of 'Archangel' (1969), proved perhaps too powerful for British sensibilities. He was nonetheless patronized by local councils buying for schools and civic centres and by a range of private clients, including the Neal Street Restaurant, where 'Archangel 11' hung for several years.

He took part in the third (1967) and fourth (1969) Lausanne Biennales (one of the few British exhibitors apart from tapestries sent by Dovecot Studios in Edinburgh) and was included in 'British Artist Craftsmen' toured by the Smithsonian in 1970 and in 'Deliberate Entanglements' organized by Bernard Kester at the University of California at Los Angeles in 1971. This brought him an American audience and he was the only British artist seriously represented in Mildred Constantine and Jack Lenor Larsen's seminal book *Beyond craft: the art fabric* (1972), where he was described as 'Britain's greatest artist in fibre'. Admired abroad, Beutlich felt isolated at home, with only Peter Collingwood and Ann Sutton matching his originality with textile. His work was never to be purchased by the newly formed Crafts Advisory Committee (now Crafts Council), a situation he found 'like Kafka and *The castle*'.

Beutlich was a visiting lecturer at Camberwell School of Art from 1951, where he met and married his wife Ellen (*née* Eadie) in 1952, and in 1967 he bought Gospels, Ethel Mairet's house and studio at Ditchling. Gospels was expensive to maintain and in 1974 Beutlich resigned from Camberwell, moving to near Alicante in Spain with his wife and young son. He took no loom to Spain, experimenting with local esparto grass and brightly coloured acrylic wools bought in the local market to make what he called 'free-warp' tapestry, weaving and wrapping organic wall hangings and free-standing pieces that looked like living organisms and which anticipated aesthetically projects like Christine and Margeret Wertheim's 'Hyperbolic crochet coral reef'.

These off-loom works link to some of his exquisite, biologically inspired wood-block prints published by Editions Alecto.

Beutlich's last works, made on his return to England in 1980, refer back to the trauma of his wartime experiences, using his off-loom techniques to create figurative groups whose collective helplessness recall Goya or Bosch, both artists he admired. During the 1980s he was rediscovered by younger weavers and curators, and was included in Michael Brennand-Wood's 'Fabric and Form' of 1982, in 'Influential Europeans' of 1992, and in Pennina Barnett and Pamela Johnson's show 'Under Construction: exploring processes in contemporary textiles' of 1996. His career was celebrated in a touring solo retrospective in 1997–8 and he was appointed MBE in 1993.

The Guardian, 25 June 2011

Peter Collingwood, weaving for walls

Next year Peter Collingwood is having a major retrospective exhibition that will go on a world tour. It is a fitting tribute to a great artist who is also one of the most scholarly writers on weaving techniques. The introductory catalogue essay will be written by the Japanese Junichi Arai, whom Collingwood regards as 'probably the world's greatest weaver'. And it was through his friendship with Arai that Collingwood was given his most challenging commission to date – a major hanging for the newly built Cultural Centre in the textile city of Kiryu. The hanging was unveiled on 11 May this year. But first some background.

Collingwood experimented with weaving as a medical student and while working for the Red Cross with Palestinian refugees in Jordan he encountered a people for whom weaving was a way of life and he began to buy Palestinian and Bedouin textiles. He subsequently gave up medicine to train with Ethel Mairet in 1950–1, moving on to work with Barbara Sawyer and with Alastair Morton of Edinburgh Weavers. Morton, who designed odd interesting warps for Collingwood to weave experimentally, became a role model: 'He showed me how the technical approach to weaving, so often the dominant one in a male weaver, can be linked to aesthetics.' Collingwood touches here on an interesting point. In the view of Hilary Bourne, one of the most successful weavers of the 1950s, men tend to weave like machines, with the difference exemplified by the Ditchling workshops of Mrs Mairet and that of Valentine KilBride. Collingwood, thanks to Mrs Mairet and Morton's influence, was to combine technical perfection with artistic innovation.

Collingwood soon developed a clear vision of what handweaving should aim for and from 1953 his ideas started appearing in *The Journal for Weavers, Spinners and Dyers* – a modest publication full of fiery and interesting debate among textile artists. Some of Collingwood's values clearly derived from Mairet – for instance that it was pointless to do weaves that could be effectively accomplished on a power loom. He differentiated between what he termed 'craftsman weavers' (a reservoir of sound knowledge) and the 'artist weaver' – who would be 'alive to contemporary trends in fashion, decoration, painting and all the arts; he reacts sensitively to the spirit of the time. He is the contemporary weaver.' Collingwood, who by 1955 had an editorial role on the Guild's *Journal*, recommended a clutch of design magazines to broaden the outlook of British weavers – *Kontor, Form, Ornamo, Kunsthandwerk*, and above all the Italian journal *Domus*.

Collingwood was determined to survive as a full-time handweaver. This has led him to experiment with techniques that allowed for swiftness and economy of effort in pieces like his yellow double corduroy pile rug bought by the Victoria & Albert Museum in 1957 or his large double cloth wall hanging of 1960 for Gordon Russell, commissioned by the Council of Industrial Design. This was a major project for which, Collingwood explained, time and money precluded true tapestry techniques. In addition the scale, originality and daring use of unorthodox materials by American weavers proved inspirational. Peter Collingwood visited the United States in 1963, teaching and meeting weavers. He found much to admire. A piece like Lenore Tawney's 'The flame' which he used to illustrate his account of his US trip in the *Journal*, with its linen thread disciplined with curved brass rods and folded brass and steel ribbon, was an undoubted influence. By the end of 1963 he had made a comparable 3D hanging in linen, brass, and wire using the sprang technique (a method of making fabric using only warp threads). By 1964 he had created his first macrogauze wall hanging by adapting his loom to allow the warp threads to create angled crossings. Fine steel rods hold these warps in position and rods can also be used to open out the textile into a three-dimensional structure. The macrogauzes are quick to weave and hold the attention through their structural logic (and ambiguity).

Collingwood's 'Macrogauze 1' was shown in 'Weaving for Walls' (1965–7), a V&A touring exhibition organized in association with the Guilds of Weavers, Spinners and Dyers. This important show took a determinedly fine art direction, revealing the powerful influence of North American practice. All the weavers involved, including older figures like Gwen Mullins, pushed their art to its limits. Collingwood and his liveliest contemporaries – Tadek Beutlich and Ann Sutton – went furthest. Peter Glenn, one of the V&A curators, argued that Ann Sutton's 'Sunspot' 'could well be a modern abstract

Peter Collingwood installing his 3D macrogauze in stainless steel yarn
at the Kiryu Performing Arts Centre, 1977.

painting'. Constructivism was a natural ally for innovatory weaving. The same year as 'Weaving for Walls' Sutton first met the constructivist sculptors Kenneth and Mary Martin at the Barry Summer School. They had started out as weavers and Sutton ran a course at Barry which she had renamed 'Textile construction'. Sutton's other contribution to 'Weaving for Walls' was 'Pendant 10' – a piece that was more mobile than weaving, with plastic tubing, 'machine-sculpted' blocks of wood and mirrors inserted into a handwoven double cloth. Tadek Beutlich also eschewed traditional tapestry techniques for this show with 'Moon' (now in the V&A) a transparent linen and ramie wall hanging, which, rather in the American mode, incorporated all kinds of 'found' materials – charred wood, x-ray film, and honesty seeds.

By the mid-1960s Beutlich, Collingwood, and Sutton were aware of each other's work and conscious that they represented a new ambitiousness in textiles. Collingwood's work developed steadily and inventively, exploring all the possibilities thrown up by altering and adapting handlooms, creating macrogauzes, rugs, and abstract strip-woven hangings using rug techniques. Architects and designers instinctively admired the logic of his work and pieces were commissioned for all kinds of interiors from offices to conference centres. A comparison can be made with the work of Hans Coper with whom in 1969 Collingwood shared an exhibition at the V&A. In the catalogue

Collingwood noted: 'Whose hand throws the shuttle is often immaterial; what are vital are the weaver's decisions as he controls the semi-mechanical process.' Both Coper and Collingwood were handworkers but the pots and weavings had a coolly rational look and developed formal ideas in elegant sequences. Both were minimalist colourists, whose spectrum was dominated by creams, charcoals and greys. In 1965 Collingwood was included in a Design Council show that examined the relevance of handwork to industrial design and, indeed, his work suggests all kinds of industrial possibilities on the brink of being realized. The fact that he has never actively collaborated with industry somehow seems beside the point.

Collingwood began to demonstrate that he could work on a monumental scale. His macrogauze for the W. H. Smith headquarters in Swindon (1977) and a splendid 3D hanging for the Wellesley Park Office in Boston, Mass. (1976) – measuring 26 by 19 feet – are works of art that function perfectly in the massive atria characteristic of corporate architecture. Paintings on such a scale rarely succeed, while conventional tapestry would require years of toil. Collingwood's macrogauzes have a natural affinity with architecture. Indeed with their suggestion of harmonic ratios they look like diagrammatic propositions for good proportion.

The Kiryu macrogauze is Collingwood's most ambitious piece to date. But this is chiefly because of the extraordinary material from which it is woven. I have said that Collingwood's work looks as if it might serve as an inspiration to industry even though he has never worked industrially. In the case of the Kiryu macrogauze he has entered the industrial field by taking on an extraordinary new material and working with it successfully. The yarn, manufactured by Bridgestone Metalpha Inc., is made of drawn stainless steel filaments, 6,800 microfilaments made into the equivalent of a 2-ply yarn. It looks exactly like silk thread, but, because it is disturbingly heavy, holding it comes as a shock. Heat treatment yields a range of colours and Collingwood worked with grey, golden brown, and dark reddish brown yarns. The steel microfilaments were first made for use in industrial filters, but Collingwood is the first person, apart from Junichi Arai, to have used the new yarn creatively.

Collingwood kept a diary while working on the Kiryu piece during January–May 1997. It is a harrowing account in which the weaver records a daily battle to overcome a problematic material. It is difficult not to feel that steel yarn is peculiarly unpleasant stuff and that only someone with Collingwood's tenacity and inquiring mind would have seen the project through. Liable to graze your hands, difficult to cut, only to be handled wearing a face mask, the steel yarn sounds like a triumph of technology over good sense. In addition the dead weight quality of the yarn made the facture of the macrogauze especially taxing physically. The justification for its use was purely aesthetic. Collingwood persevered because the yarn looked wonderful – both as he struggled with it in his studio and finally when it was hoisted into position – a glittering three-dimensional hanging of awesome size, made of 9 strips each 32 inches wide and 5 metres long and weighing 90 kilos. I have only seen photographs of the hanging but it looks like a supremely resolved collaborative venture – between the imaginative Arai and Collingwood, working thousands of miles away in East Anglia. But it was a taxing experience. As Collingwood, a profoundly knowledgeable weaver, wrote wearily on 31 January after nearly a week struggling with the yarn, 'Many discoveries today'.

Quilters' Review, no. 24, 1997

Norman Potter, dissenter: an obituary

The designer Norman Potter liked to quote Rilke's command 'Hold to the difficult', alternating it with the sombre maxim of his fellow poet and friend Denise Levertov: 'We are living our whole lives in a state of emergency.' His presence was uplifting, even electrifying. He was a free spirit of great charm, wit, and integrity, with deeply engrained habits of dissent, whose thinking, like the layout and content of his typed lectures and letters, tended to be 'ranged left and open-ended'.

Potter's childhood was not an extended one. His background, gentility fallen on hard times, took him to a semi-charitable militaristic school. Aged 14 he turned to Rational Press Association books for comfort, taking in Joad and Huxley. Still in his teens, living in a commune, he read Herbert Read's *Poetry and anarchism*, finding in Read a mentor he never ceased to admire and an intellectual home in anarchism. He thus came to know the scholarly, sophisticated circle of men and women associated with the journals *War commentary* and *Freedom* – Mary Louise Berneri, John Hewetson, George Woodcock, and Vernon Richards.

During the Second World War he spent a month in Chelmsford Prison (still a teenager) for refusing to carry an identity card. This was followed, in 1948, by six months in Wandsworth and Wormwood Scrubs, after an unsuccessful attempt to initiate a moral debate on the nature of war with a military tribunal. He found prison educative and thereafter saw himself as outside the class system, duty-bound to question any kind of institution.

Norman Potter in his Corsham workshop in the early 1950s.

In solitary confinement for non-cooperation he scratched some lines by W. H. Auden into the wall with a bent pin – 'look shining at / new styles of architecture, a change of heart'. These words proved prophetic. By 1949 Potter had begun his life as a designer, teaching himself skills, investigating hand- and power-tools and evolving a design philosophy which took in figures from the Arts & Crafts movement like C. R. Ashbee and W. R. Lethaby, together with younger members of what he saw as an intellectual family – Lewis Mumford, Herbert Read, E. F. Schumacher, and Colin Ward.

Like his hero W. R. Lethaby he loved sailing boats, lived on them in hard times, and regarded their interiors, when well fitted, as perfect design statements. He immersed himself in a study of the Modern movement, visiting its key sites, starting with Wells Coates's Lawn Road flats, where he felt instantly at home. He was buoyed up by his friendships with the typographer Anthony Froshaug, with the designer Geoffrey Bocking, and with a lively group of Architectural Association students editing the magazine *Plan*.

After secondary school Potter had no further formal education. Such a thing was hardly necessary. A spacious mind, a marvellous feel for accuracy and precision in language, and a sense of the high seriousness of the designer's calling took Potter to the books, buildings, and objects which he needed to know. This provided the basis for the workshop that he ran during the 1950s in Corsham, Wiltshire, in partnership with George Philip. This was intended to be as accessible as a local garage and offered undiluted modern design. Though interested in handwork, Potter abhorred the craft furniture movement as it had developed since the 1920s; his own furniture and fittings, recorded with a Brownie box camera by his wife Caroline, were closest in spirit to the Dutch cabinet-maker and architect Gerrit Rietveld. In siting a modernist workshop in a small West Country town, Potter was creating something that was in the best sense marginal and quietly disruptive.

At the end of the 1950s, at the invitation of Hugh Casson, Potter went to teach in the Interior Design School at the Royal College of Art. Conscious that art schools provided 'a useful education frequently offered to the wrong people at the wrong age for the wrong reasons', he made his contribution there as 'grimly undecorative as our subject matter would allow', bringing in a 'modernist monoculture and methodological underpinnings'. There were Bauhaus precedents for Potter's pedagogic style. He demanded a wholehearted commitment from students. Those able to take the heat and fire found themselves embarking on an invigorating, far-reaching, occasionally unsettling dialogue with their tutor.

In 1964 Potter and a group of like-minded designers migrated to form a Construction School at the West of England College of Art in Bristol, beginning what Potter described as 'a long, long struggle against the grain of English design education'. The intention was to re-examine and readdress the modernist project. At Bristol Potter emerged as an indispensable (if dangerous) man to have in an institution. In 1968 he largely abandoned teaching to join the disaffected students at Hornsey and Guildford. He resigned from Bristol, returning in 1975 to work out a radical non-hierarchical structure for the Construction School, with students working in 'families' and awarding their own degrees. Potter's last foray into teaching, in 1989–90, at Plymouth School of Architecture took his ideas to their natural conclusion. He soon came to see the school as over-restrictive and his so-called 'counter-course' interventions eschewed assessments. His writing at that time had a darkness at its philosophical core, as he encouraged students to face up to 'extreme situations'.

The conventional sites of post-war British art education were unable to accommodate Potter's bold intellectual range, but out of his first period at Bristol came a classic work. *What is a designer* first appeared in 1969 and was enlarged and republished (in 1980 and 1989) by Robin Kinross's Hyphen Press. The book is an update of the early modern (and Arts & Crafts) project, which puts the workshop (and a moral sensibility) at the heart of the design process. It is an intense, practical book, a combination of vision and good sense. Potter's friendship with Kinross led to a close collaboration on an edition of his collected writing, which appeared in 1990 as *Models & constructs*. This extraordinary book (designed on the purest modernist principles in collaboration with Kinross) contained snatches of autobiography, poetry, illuminating writing on music, and philosophical and practical thoughts on design, construction and the workshop.

Potter's aversion to compromise in public and private life did not make for material ease. Those who loved him were tested to their limits. Things were always difficult on a day-to-day basis, although his combination of practicality and wisdom meant that he could transform any interior into a Modern movement statement of pellucid beauty. This was dramatically demonstrated by his refashioning of his final home, a sheltered housing flat in Falmouth. He left four children, the eldest, Sally, a film-maker, and the youngest, Charlotte, still a schoolgirl. In their company the essential sweetness and humour of his character became movingly manifest.

The Independent, 16 December 1995

Eileen Lewenstein and a sense of duty

Just after the war, when rationing was still in effect and daily life seemed relentlessly drab, Eileen Lewenstein and Brigitta Appleby started Briglin Pottery. They had first met at the Central School of Arts & Crafts in London. Eileen was then taking an art teacher's diploma at the Institute of Education and in 1945 went to teach at Derby High School for Girls. She had read Bernard Leach's *A potter's book* and she introduced pottery into the school's art classes. She was already committed to ceramics and during the evenings she went to pottery classes run by Robert Washington, one of William Staite Murray's liveliest pre-war pupils.

By 1946 she was back in London and met Brigitta Appleby again at the Donald Mills Pottery, just south of the river in the Borough. She stayed there for two years making slipped earthenwares, reduction fired stoneware, and refractory elements for electric fires. In 1948 with all the confidence and recklessness of youth Eileen and Brigitta decided to go it alone.

Today Briglin is less known that it should be, but its wares were well documented in the *Studio Yearbook of Decorative Art* throughout the 1950s and 1960s. Its visual identity was far stronger than that of the Donald Mills Pottery. Briglin's functional earthenware and handsome vases took design inspiration from Scandinavia and also from the work of two urban émigré potters, Hans Coper and Lucie Rie. Eileen and Brigitta were young modernists. While a wartime student of drawing and painting at the West of England College of Art in Bristol, Eileen found Gropius's account of the Bauhaus (published

Eileen Lewenstein working in her last studio in Portslade, East Sussex, 1989.

in 1939) in the city's central reference library and she gradually built up a collection of books on modern design, art, and architecture. Unlike some of the potters inspired by Leach's neo-oriental work and ideas, she was not anti-commerce nor anti-industry in her outlook.

From the start Briglin operated as a profitable efficient business at a time when numerous small potteries were set up, flourished for a while and then failed. Astonishingly Briglin was to continue as a successful pottery for a further 40 years, giving employment to scores of young potters. Eileen remembers the early years at Briglin with intense pleasure but in 1958 she left to work on her own, inspired by the hand-built work she saw in the American magazine *Craft Horizons* and by the example of Helen Pincombe who was then hand-building. A couple of years later Eileen saw the idiosyncratic work of Catherine Yarrow, a painter, printmaker, and a self-taught creator of mysterious totemic forms in clay. Eileen's friendship with Catherine Yarrow further encouraged her desire to stop designing and making functional pottery and instead to explore its sculptural possibilities. It was a bold step to take.

For ten years Eileen taught at Hornsey School of Art and took to working in stoneware – hand-building, throwing and altering, constructing and slab-building screens, and from the early 1970s creating more delicate forms in porcelain. A sequence of bold abstract grid forms shown at the Eva Hauser Gallery in 1966 led to a large-scale architectural commission for the Convent of Our Lady of Sion in West London. This handsome example of public art can be glimpsed if you drive down Chepstow Villas and demonstrates that makers and architects can work fruitfully together – and that an atheist can sensitively interpret an ecclesiastic brief.

Eileen has always had a strong sense of duty about her art and her craft. She was co-opted onto the Council of the newly formed Craftsmen Potters Association in 1957 and played an active part in making that organization a success. In 1970 she and Emmanuel Cooper launched *Ceramic Review* which for the past twenty-eight years has provided a unique documentation of the ceramics scene in Britain and worldwide. These days *Ceramic Review* is a handsomely produced glossy magazine but it has not lost sight of its original intention – to publish articles by and for potters (as well as writing by scholars, polemicists and collectors). The responsibility of running *Ceramic Review* inevitably had its effect on Eileen's output as a potter. There were the demands of editorship, of teaching, of bringing up two sons, and living with an intensely creative partner, her husband Oscar Lewenstein, whose work as a theatre impressario and as a film producer brought Eileen into contact with many of the leading actors and playwrights of the post-war period.

In 1975 Eileen and her husband moved to live permanently in Hove. Her studio there led onto the beach and a windswept garden of sea kale. This new setting marked a turning point in her work and gave a fresh focus for her natural taste for abstraction. Her regular walks along the beach (often with camera in hand – she is an excellent photographer) enabled her to build up a new vocabulary of forms. These celebrate the action of the sea on the groynes and the concrete sea defences, on the flotsam and jetsam thrown up on the beach, subtly altered by the ceaseless motion of the waves.

I am lucky enough to own a stoneware piece that reveals the flexibility and beauty of Eileen's sea-inspired imagery. It consists of two thrown but altered and flattened vessels. Each has an iregular profile, and the two shapes gently interlock. The effect suggests that the two vessels were once joined but were subsequently worn apart by the pounding of the waves or some other natural force. This is just one reading of the piece; there is also a tenderer anthropomorphic one. The two pieces suggest honed down figurative sculpture and a memory of Brancusi's 'The kiss' comes floating up – two vessels transformed into two lovers.

The sea imagery in Eileen's work operates in different ways. There is the grand sequence of press-moulded dishes which carry an abstracted sea language and which combine all the translucent freshness of water-colour with the permanence conferred by the firing process. Then there are the tough-looking abstract modules that can be arranged in an infinite number of sequences and which are directly based on the great concrete breakwaters that once littered the coastline to the west of her house. Above all, the smooth eroded quality of many of her shapes and the pale beauty of her colours evoke the special ambiance and bright lightness of the seascape she has come to know so well.

Eileen espouses a particularly British form of modernism which is best exemplified by the paintings, pots, sculptures, and *objets trouvés* collected by Jim Ede at Kettle's Yard in Cambridge. Her own home is filled with the fruits of those long walks along the shoreline – pieces of driftwood, pebbles, and pieces of transformed plastic and glass.

Eileen's husband died last year after a long illness. Nursing him stretched her energies to the limits and she eventually had no time to make pots. Now that she is leaving *Ceramic Review* we can only hope that she will start making again – for our pleasure and for hers.

Published as a leaflet by Aberystwyth Arts Centre, November 1992

Eileen Lewenstein is in danger of being forgotten. She may not have been on the level of the ceramicists Ruth Duckworth or Gillian Lowndes (also in danger for being overlooked), but her work at its best had great clarity. She was a good friend to me, *inter alia* showing me the manuscript of Michael Cardew's autobiography, setting me on the way to writing his biography. At one point we exchanged hundreds of letters and I still have hers, in her exquisite hand, full of wise advice. She and her husband Oscar Lewenstein introduced me to the good life lived according to socialist principles.

Patrick Reyntiens, data reprocessor

Just after the Second World War was an optimistic moment for all the arts. It was a period that proved energetic and generous enough to accommodate a renaissance in stained glass, which, despite gifted practitioners like Evie Hone, Harry Clarke, and Douglas Strachan, was in decline in the 1920s and sidelined in the 1930s. The late 1940s, however, saw a host of commissions, mostly funded by the government to repair war damage and to celebrate peace.

This renaissance shaped the life of Patrick Reyntiens, a painter fresh from art school who today must be counted the senior figure in British stained glass. Reyntiens trained with E. J. Nuttgens in the early 1950s, received a grant to study glass in French churches, and in 1952–3 was introduced by Penelope Betjeman to John Piper. A remarkable partnership began. There was an instant rapport, for the young Reyntiens combined craft skills in glass with an intimacy with and understanding of avant-garde art.

Piper himself had been interested in glass in an antiquarian spirit since

1929 and he was conscious of the work of Rouault and a post-war Parisian figuration which made free with bold black outline, reminiscent of the lead-lines of stained glass. Throughout the 1950s there was a happy coincidental visual reciprocity between much innovatory French and British painting and the potential of stained glass for colour intensity and semi-abstraction. It was a timely moment for the creation of a shared language and for the Piper / Reyntiens partnership and for subsequent Reyntiens collaborations with Cecil Collins and Ceri Richards.

Reyntiens initially translated a Piper gouache of two heads which led on to a magnificent series of joint works – the hieratic nine windows in Oundle School chapel, the reckless beauty of the Parables and Miracles at Eton College Chapel, and the abstract Baptistery window at Coventry Cathedral. As Reyntiens explains: 'Piper's designs were made with all the freedom and franchise of a painter and I had to take them into my very spleen and liver and reinterpret them, very much as Rimsky-Korsakov re-orchestrated Mussorgsky. And that to me is not an illicit occupation.'

These are generous, expansive thoughts about co-authorship. But then Reyntiens argues that it is only the recent marginalization of painting which has forced the artist to renounce the role of interpreter – or as Reyntiens puts it, priest – and take up a new role as originator or solitary prophet: 'Until the eighteenth century artists were priests; they reprocessed data which society laid at their feet and reclothed it in an aesthetic wonder. Even someone as original as Michelangelo or Raphael was reprocessing very old facts, very old data.' For Reyntiens, stained glass will always be a priestly occupation, not a prophetic one.

Almost at once as a stained-glass artist Reyntiens was conscious of a paradox: 'On the one hand you had the old cultural vision which was the history of art and the history of the Catholic church (of which I am a member) going back for 2,000 years and on the other hand you had the Modern movement. The one was decorative, figurative, didactic, historiated, allusive, reinforcing. The other believed in a tabula rasa, scientific fact, reason, no decoration, political collectivism of one kind or another.'

Nonetheless, despite his consciousness that the decline of stained glass coincided with the coming of age of the modern world, Reyntiens's own glass has always reflected developments in contemporary painting – from his semi-abstract 'Still life' shown in the Smithsonian 'British Artist Craftsmen' exhibition of 1959–60, to his return in the 1980s to figurative work inspired by a whole range of resonant visual and literary sources, above all Ovid's *Metamorphoses* which have inspired a dazzling sequence of expressive small-scale panels.

Reyntiens is a strikingly learned artist, at home with classical literature but also one of today's finest commentators on contemporary art. His reviews for *The Tablet* are notable for their sensitive visual insights and openness to the new. Characteristically, he is equally familiar with the language and lore of the cinema, seeing it as replacing stained glass as the major public communications system after the Great War. Indeed Reyntiens can make out a persuasive case for late nineteenth-century and Edwardian glass functioning as a form of visual propaganda throughout the British Empire. If necessary he can create glass that employs that Victorian vocabulary – his glass for the Great Hall at Christ Church, Oxford deliberately set out to honour and employ the language of the nineteenth century.

Though Reyntiens has written a key handbook on glass, as well as an elegiac history, technique in itself is not something he enjoys discussing. 'People think of glass as a mechanical thing. But it isn't. That is why a fine art education is so terribly important. Fine art refines the feelings and if you do not have feeling it is absolutely no use at all. A fine art degree is a sine qua non for any live design situation – the government policy of downgrading fine art in the interests of the applied arts and design is fatal nonsense, I'm afraid. '

Reyntiens speaks from bitter experience. For ten years – from 1976 until 1986 – he was head of Fine Art at the Central School of Art and Design. He also put much of his energy into a joint educational project run with his wife, the painter Anne Bruce. Burleighfield in Buckinghamshire was an alternative art school with workshops for stained glass, tapestry design, printing, print-making, and ceramics, and a commitment to training both local adults and children as well as young artists from all over the world. It ran from about 1964 until 1979 and anticipated numerous later community arts projects. One of the major disappointments of both their lives was the experience of being excluded from their own foundation by trustees who failed to understand what was being achieved beyond the logic of financial profit and loss.

Reyntiens, as his most recent book, *The beauty of stained glass*, makes clear, has a deep, historical understanding of the practical function of religious glass. At present he is working on a major window for the Southwell Minster in Nottinghamshire. A building of such beauty and antiquity presents an enormous challenge. His design combines interpretative iconography with a poetic response in which sources as diverse as Dante's *Paradiso*, Alasdair MacIntyre's *After virtue* and Tarkovsky's *Nostalghia* throw up images. Today, when religion is either ignored or is turning towards fundamentalism, Reyntiens can talk with wit, erudition, and happy conviction about angels. For him, art and education are issues with a religious component.

The synthesis of reality and imagination is no easy matter in a technocratic society. Reyntiens believes that only artists instinctively possess the necessary moral imagination to achieve this synthesis. Then again he argues that the task of the educator is to introduce the young to the world in its most vivid primary form. 'What is teaching? Asking someone to love something that you love yourself. That is all teaching is and ever was. Teaching is not the conveyance of a commodity.'

As both artist and educator, through thick and thin, Reyntiens has remained optimistic and idealistic. His art mirrors the man – with stained glass that pays homage to the theatre, to erotic art, to Greek mythology as well as to abstraction and the central mysteries of Christianity.

The Spectator, 18 / 25 December 1993

Gordon Baldwin and games of chance

'Gordon Baldwin': exhibition at Contemporary Applied Arts, 24 February to 2 April 1989

As a schoolboy, Gordon Baldwin was warned off the life of an artist. A well-meaning master showed him a reproduction of a work by Paul Klee, explaining. 'It's very dodgy being an artist – they're very poor – look, Klee had to paint on newspaper.' Baldwin never forgot this naive remark but he also recalls that he found Klee immediately accessible and moving, unlike the Old Masters he had been taught to admire. Determined to become a painter, he took an Intermediate Course at the art school in Lincoln, his local town. The course required him to take a craft and he chose pottery; it was his first encounter with clay. As an aspiring painter Baldwin knew that he needed to study in London, but the grant system was designed to keep most students in their local area. In the autumn of 1950 Baldwin joined a suitably obscure course in industrial ceramics, at London's Central School. His mild interest in ceramics was transformed by circumstance.

Baldwin remembers his time at Central as marvellous. Painting came to seem less important. Technical training in ceramics was provided by Dora Billington and Gilbert Harding Green, and by visitors like Bill Newland, Kenneth Clark, and the department's technician Nicholas Vergette. But the ceramics department was also alive with other less expected figures. Victor Pasmore, Eduardo Paolozzi, Robert Adams, William Turnbull, Alan Davie, and Richard Hamilton were all at the Central, and from 1952 a Basic Design course was being evolved there. Recently the Basic Design movement has been much criticized, but when taught by these inspirational figures it was vital and stimulating.

Gordon Baldwin in his studio at Eton College in 1988, surrounded by his work.

Baldwin had also enrolled for the studio pottery course. At the Central, Leach's ideas were kept in perspective. Dora Billington looked to a European rather than to an oriental tradition, and perhaps, romantically, to some lost English tradition. He remembers an early book on English studio pottery, probably George Wingfield Digby's *The work of the modern potter* which came out in 1952. He was struck by Hans Coper's work, mainly because he seemed the only true twentieth-century artist in the book, and Baldwin instinctively felt himself 'a modern artist as opposed to anything else'. He also recalls a Coper show at the Berkeley Galleries – probably in November 1950 – and a visit to Cambridge to see Picasso's ceramics: 'very interesting and a little surprising'. But the real excitement came from sculptors visiting the department: William Turnbull's course on Basic Design, and above all Paolozzi, taking a lump of clay and prodding and poking it with his fingers, oblivious to 'pottery quality and feeling for clay and all those sorts of concepts that hung around, undefined but important'.

Baldwin was excited by the intensity with which Turnbull and Paolozzi did things: 'I was going round seeing their exhibitions: they were like gods'. During the 1950s, an openness prevailed in avant-garde sculpture. Many leading sculptors had received no formal training in that discipline and came from other fields: Reg Butler from ironwork and architecture, Lynn Chadwick from architecture, Geoffrey Clarke from glass at the RCA. And despite their training as fine artists, the new wave – Hamilton, Paolozzi, and Turnbull – were concerned to break down barriers about 'right' materials and 'correct' method.

By the late 1950s there had been a renewal of interest in Brancusi, with a major retrospective at the Solomon Guggenheim Museum in 1955 and special homage paid at both the 1959 Documenta and the 1960 Venice Biennale. Baldwin, like many sculptors, was deeply affected by Brancusi's rediscovery. His interest in the base as an important part of sculptural form derives from Brancusi, as does his love of a certain inelegance and awkwardness. Brancusi worked with a craft tradition at the back of his mind, but it took a leap of the imagination to reveal that an everyday object could function as high sculpture. Baldwin was very attuned to the achievements of early twentieth-century sculpture. Boccioni's 'Development of a bottle in space' was similarly a key work for him, inspiring a series of 'Developments' on the bottle and bowl theme.

In 1970 Baldwin organized a Surrealist fortnight at Eton College which involved his pupils and himself in the creation of Surrealist objects. He had been teaching there and at the Central School for over a decade. Baldwin's deeper reading of Surrealist texts for the fortnight was a creative release. In particular he was attracted to the succinct dreamlike prose and poetry of Jean Arp: 'Art usually shows an absurd resemblance to the aspect of something else.' Arp's search for non-high-art materials, his wise words on decoration, his observations on abstraction, amplify our understanding of Baldwin's work. Most of Baldwin's black pieces were generated by the 'laws of chance' so revered by Arp, who wanted his own art to develop naturally, entitling one sculpture 'Stone formed by a human hand' and another, 'Sculpture to be lost in the forest'.

In the 1970s Baldwin gradually moved from dark to light, making pieces coated with layer upon layer of white slip. Mark-making and painting became more important. 'I've always tried to avoid a really comfortable relationship between the marks and the piece.' It is this 'uncomfortable' tension which gives his current works such strength and beauty. Nudged along by Paolozzi as a student, he came to realize that you did not have to devise a decoration; you could quite simply do it, letting the line roam at will. Chance plays its part: raindrops might provide the basis for patterning, and the changing nature of light is a continual source of wonder.

His fascination with the minimal changes which occur at his studio window explain his love for specific kinds of art: Klee's fine ragged line, William Scott's daring way with an empty canvas, certain Sung ceramics, and in music, the minimalists, the systems composers, the 'wandering sound' of the *shakuhachi* flute and the sitar. He loves art 'in which not very much happens': no Wagner, no Old Masters. And those painters, sculptors, and musicians whom he admires, he regards as colleagues: 'all artists are struggling to make sense of themselves with the few tools they have at their disposal wherever they happen to be.'

But he reckons that a few basic things are peculiar to ceramics. He regards the vessel form as crucial, even though many of his pieces barely reveal themselves to be containers. However, he has no particular regard for Leach's vocabulary of foot, belly, and lip. He recalls a visit from William Staite Murray, a potter whom he admired: 'Our idols destroy themselves when we meet them.' Murray was quite old, and acting the part of a dandified old buffer. 'I suppose he likes Picasso', Baldwin heard him mutter as he left his studio.

At odd moments Baldwin reflects, without too much sadness, that none of the really big inventions and breakthroughs in contemporary art have taken place in ceramics. Status and reputation mean little to him, even when critics turn to ceramics only to suggest that pots are acceptable so long as they are decorative. Gordon Baldwin stands aloof, proving that pottery can share the profundities of painting and sculpture. Now, more than ever, the particular beauties and purities of his art and the art that he admires repay our attention.

Crafts, no. 96, January / February 1989

The still lives of Gwyn Hanssen Pigott

On 10 July 2013 a group of friends gathered together at the London gallery Erskine, Hall & Coe to celebrate and mourn the fine and remarkable life of Gwyn Hanssen Pigott, one of the world's greatest contemporary potters. Many were fellow ceramicists, some were collectors, while others were simply friends. Some were followers of Prem Rawat, known as Maharaji, whose teachings had inspired Gwyn since 1972. Matthew Hall spoke first, movingly recalling her solo show that had ended on 8 July, three days after her untimely death, and the pleasure Gwyn took in setting it up. Then two distinguished fellow potters spoke. Jennifer Lee read out telegrams from all over the world. Alan Caiger-Smith stood in the centre of the room and spoke with eloquent humour, recalling Gwyn when he first met her in the late 1950s, soon after her arrival in England. He went on to explain just why her mature work was so majestic and serene. Finally her sister Beverley Larwill recalled Gwyn as a child in Australia, part of a household of clever sisters. To stand together, raise a glass and remember Gwyn was the best that we could do in sad circumstances.

Perhaps it was fitting that Gwyn died here in England – where in earlier years she became an admired and revered teacher and friend. But wherever she had fallen ill in the world – in her homeland Australia, in Europe, in the USA, in Japan and Korea – a group would have assembled to mourn her passing and celebrate her life. She was a world citizen. It was not just her genius as a great potter – perhaps the greatest of this present time – that made her loved. It was her gift for making a connection with people of all ages and cultures, a kind of energized innocence mixed with intense sensitivity and extreme sophistication. Her last few weeks, spent in Europe, were characteristically full – with visits and plans and of course her marvellous exhibition.

She was born Gwynion Lawrie John in 1935 in the former Australian mining town of Ballarat, south of Melbourne. She was to take the names of both her husbands – of the late Louis Hanssen (who committed suicide in 1968 and whose later life was the subject of Nicholas Wright's play *The reporter*, 2007) and of her second husband John Pigott, from whom she separated in 1980. To do that as an ardent feminist may seem paradoxical, but it was part of Gwyn's graciousness, loyalty, and modesty that in turn was born of an absolute integrity.

Her upbringing was both strict and privileged. Her father, of Welsh descent, was the director of a large engineering firm while her mother, who had trained as an arts and crafts teacher, worked in an eclectic range of media, from water-colours to tapestry weaving to earthenware pottery. During her last year at secondary school Gwyn took classes at the School of Mines art college but had thoughts of studying architecture. She was good at mathematics and science.

At the University of Melbourne she majored in art history and paid regular visits to the National Gallery of Victoria, going down a long corridor that housed the Kent collection of Chinese ceramics. It was 'these seductive objects' that increasingly fascinated her. She met the first Australian exponent of stoneware, Harold Hughan, who introduced her to Bernard Leach's *A potter's book* – which singled out early Chinese ceramics as exemplary, under the rubric 'the Sung standard'. Joseph Burke, the head of her department and an authority on English eighteenth-century painting, allowed her to write on contemporary Australian ceramics for her final year thesis.

When she met Ivan McMeekin, an artist and potter who had served as a

First Mate on the Yangtze River, she realized (to her father's dismay) that she wanted to devote her life to ceramics. McMeekin and his young apprentice embarked on an exploration of local materials as they sought to create the dense almost porcellaneous qualities of Sung wares through raw glazing and wood-firing. She translated the Jesuit priest Père d'Entrecolles' *Lettres édifiantes et curieuses* on porcelain manufacture in early eighteenth-century China for McMeekin and they pored over A. D. Brankston's *Early Ming wares of Chingtechen*. It might seem like a strange life for a young woman in her early twenties but it was a time of intense happiness.

In 1958 Gwyn arrived in England, took part in the first Aldermaston march in protest against nuclear weapons, and rode a push-bike to all the major ceramic workshops, working at Winchcombe Pottery with Ray Finch, and with Harry and May Davis, discussing oriental ceramics with Sir Alan Barlow, visiting the potter Katharine Pleydell-Bouverie, working at the Leach Pottery at St Ives, and assisting Michael Cardew with his historic summer course 'Fundamental Pottery with an emphasis on geology and raw materials'. In 1960 she set up a pottery in West London, teaching her poet husband Louis to make pots, working for Alan Caiger-Smith, and attending classes given by Lucie Rie at Camberwell School of Art. Both Gwyn and Louis exhibited to acclaim at Liberty, at Heal's, and at Primavera, London's premier craft and design shop.

In 1964 she bought a house in Achères, near Bourges, inspired by the traditional stoneware of the Haut-Berry area. She had worked at Cardew's Wenford Bridge Pottery during 1964–5 and was now committed to wood-firing and digging her own clay. Her long apprenticeship was over and in France she went on to make some of the finest functional stoneware and porcelain of all time. There are good examples in British collections – at Bristol Museum and Art Gallery, at Paisley Museum, in the former ILEA collection housed at Camberwell College of Arts, and at the V&A. But in 1973 she walked away from her rural idyll and a varied teaching career.

She briefly joined the Bread and Puppet Theatre, returning to Australia in 1974, setting up a pottery in Tasmania, and marrying her assistant John Pigott in 1976. By 1980 she was working in the Jam Factory Workshops in Adelaide (a difficult period when she considered abandoning ceramics) and in 1981 she moved to Brisbane as Potter-in-Residence at Queensland University of Technology, where she also taught for the Australian Flying Arts outreach programme, travelling in small planes all over north Queensland. In 1989 she moved to Netherdale, a sub-tropical sugar-cane region west of Mackay in north Queensland, and in 2000 set up her final pottery near Ipswich in south-east Queensland.

By the early 1990s she was exhibiting worldwide and her work had taken a decisive turn away from production pottery. In 1971 she had been

Gwyn Hanssen Pigott, 'The Listeners', wood-fired porcelain, 1998.

profoundly affected by a large retrospective exhibition of paintings by Giorgio Morandi at the Palais de Tokyo in Paris. In the early 1980s she was using the Japanese-Korean potter Heja Chong's Noboragama kiln, a method of firing where glaze is redundant. New shapes seemed required, memories of Morandi floated up, and she began making bottle forms that were to develop into the still-life groups for which she became renowned. These groups were given a further beauty by her subtle glazes, which made her arrangements both painterly and sculptural. It was a move in the direction of fine art, seen at its most ambitious in her fifty-five-foot installation 'Caravan' shown at Tate St Ives in 2004.

Their beauty and haunting titles – 'Waiting', 'Breath', 'At the gate' – led to invitations to create similar atmospheric groupings using pots from the oriental ceramics collections at the Freer Gallery of Art, Washington (2008) and, subsequently, objects from the ethnographic collections at the Museum of Anthropology, Vancouver (2012). In 2002 she was awarded the Order of Australia Medal, and in 2006 the National Gallery of Victoria staged a major retrospective of her work. At the time of her death she had plans to work in Japan and Spain and to show her work at Chatsworth House, Derbyshire.

That she was a towering figure in the field of ceramics and indeed art of any kind goes without saying. Her work is strong but exquisite, with a classical rightness and clarity; her's are Ur-pots, Platonic forms, the beginning and end of pottery. She elevated domestic pottery – by the post-war period a large, democratic movement – and made it utterly timeless and pure. In 1988

she explained of her pots: 'They are about themselves, and al̩
needing them that are behind them. Sometimes they are beau.
all the trouble. They sustain me. I have to make them; they are aɔ.
sustains me.'

In the terrible hours of Wednesday 3 July, when Gwyn succumbed to a stroke, her doctors at Charing Cross Hospital, who were luckily the best, had to make decisions. That they were right was certain – especially if we return to her words about her pots: 'They sustain me. I have to make them; they are about what sustains me.' Her pots were what she called her 'daily pleasure mines' that brought, out of the chaos of life, silence and calm.

Crafts, no. 244, September/October 2013

Sam Herman and free glass

Some craft movements are younger than others. We can roughly date the beginnings of studio pottery to a period just before the First World War. But the studio glass movement is of much more recent origin. The possibility of working with hot glass in studio, as opposed to designing for factory production, only became a reality after the famous Toledo seminars of 1962, when Dominick Labino and Harvey Littleton developed the small studio-sized tank furnace and a suitable glass formula for studio use. And we owe the introduction of hot glass in studio in Britain to Littleton's pupil Sam Herman, who came to study in Edinburgh in 1966 and the following year moved to London as a research fellow at the Royal College of Art.

Herman was born in Mexico in 1936. His uncle was a gifted amateur artist who let the young boy embellish his drawings and generally gave him an aesthetic grounding. In retrospect it seems that those early years in Mexico made Herman the kind of colourist in glass that we know him to be – fiery rather than tasteful. He left Mexico when he was 10 years old and after secondary schooling in the USA he went to college to study sociology and anthropology. His intention was to go on to do a Masters and a Doctorate in that area but the broad-based American university system allows for surprising changes of direction. It was his tutor in his subsidiary area in art who suggested that his talents might lie elsewhere and he then applied to do postgraduate work in sculpture.

Herman joined a course at Seattle but his time there was brief – just three days. He left after being reprimanded for drawing in an abstract fashion in a

Sam Herman at the Royal College of Art, late 1960s.

life class. He had a family to support so he took a job as a management trainee but after a year he went to the University of Wisconsin to study under Leo Steppat, a Viennese-born sculptor he particularly admired. Sculpture was his major subject, but when he heard of a new glass course being set up by Littleton he took it as a subsidiary. Almost by chance Herman found himself involved in an entirely new discipline that had grown out of the Toledo seminars.

'Once I'd tried it, glass became my first love', Herman recalls of his initial experiences on the course. Littleton was a pioneer. As in the early days of studio pottery the level of knowledge was basic. Students and staff learned together and together they built their studio from scratch in a hut allotted them by the university. 'In terms of learning to blow the glass we had to teach each other – everyone helped each other – there were no secrets.' When it comes to sources for Herman's art there is no doubt that glass itself is a crucial inspiration. But Herman is aware of the dangers of a material-based vision: 'People get sucked into the material and enjoy it, but what they make has nothing to do with art.' Nonetheless glass is a material that makes pressing and extremely physical demands. 'Glass is like a dance between you and the material – it requires immense attention and foresight to handle a material that has what amounts to a life of its own in a molten state.'

Behind this passionate response to the material (which has made Herman such an exceptional glass artist and such a good teacher) lies a study of the best in art. His taste is perhaps not unusual for his generation but it is elevated; it encompasses contemporary sculpture – including Kenneth Armitage and Henry Moore. It takes in the old masters, archaic Kouroi figures, child art, and a great swathe of so-called primitive art. For Herman the key word is vitality – a Bergsonian *élan vital* which he looks for in a whole range of art.

Perhaps another key to Herman's art is his determination to avoid safe situations. For instance he left a secure job at the Royal College in order to set up a glass project in Australia, at the Jam Factory Workshops. 'In terms of money and prestige it was a total loss; in terms of something exciting it was a great experience.' Part of this adventurousness is a determination not to restrict himself to one material. He has always continued to make sculpture and has recently started painting seriously. He collaborates with the glass industry – at the moment with the Belgian firm of Val-Saint-Lambert. Then there is an unselfish care for younger practitioners. With the help of Graham Hughes, Herman set up the Glasshouse on Long Acre in London's Covent Garden.

Herman is an optimistic man but when he meditates on the way art schools are going at present he feels a sense of outrage. When he arrived in Britain he was greatly impressed by the standards and equipment in our art colleges. Now all this is in violent reverse – staff–student ratios in particular – and Herman has taken early retirement from teaching. Since then he has been working on a broad front – painting, making sculpture, and designing. Soon he will be opening a new hot-glass studio in Camberwell, South London. This above all is to be welcomed. To study a piece of glass by Herman is to become conscious of a free spirit translating his ideas into a uniquely suitable medium. Influences on Herman are subtle and they arrive circuitously. To unlock them is a task he leaves to us. All of which suggests that an exhibition showing the whole range of Sam Herman's work might be a rewarding tribute to an artist who has played such an important role in establishing glass as an art form in Britain.

Crafts, no. 105, July/August 1990

Gillian Lowndes's strange transformations

Some six years ago Gillian Lowndes began to make the most remarkable pieces of an artistic career which has extended for a quarter of a century. 'New Ceramic Sculpture' is devoted to Gillian Lowndes's most recent work, but also includes some key earlier pieces; these were selected so that certain unities were not overlooked in an oeuvre which at first sight seems so various in style and technique.

Lowndes's formal training as an artist began in 1957 in the sculpture department of the Central School. Her time there was brief: she switched to ceramics 'because there seemed to be more possibilities'. The life modelling which had dominated the first weeks of her classes was replaced by abstract work – for pottery is invariably an abstract discipline. The training emphasized throwing. Ruth Duckworth recalls that the processes which were to become so important to the potters of the 1960s – coiling and slab-building – were taught there as exercises. Lowndes remembers a free atmosphere and an unstructured course. At the Central, she came into contact with the key ceramicists of the period – all, sadly, to be frustrated in various ways by the sharp divisions between the fine arts and the crafts in this country. Ian Auld, in a joint interview with Lowndes, observed that he, Ruth Duckworth, Dan Arbeid, Gordon Baldwin, and Bryan Newman were breaking away from the older established figures in ceramics: he named Leach, Coper, and Rie. These three may seem strange bedfellows, but of course all were dedicated to majestic vessel forms, so in that way they appeared to be conservative figures.

By 1960 Lowndes was working in a studio in Bloomsbury shared with Robin Welch. The pieces made in the decade that followed were extraordinarily varied. Throwing did not give her great pleasure, but she made some memorable bowls incised with a dark, ragged, Klee-inspired line. She employed coiling to build up industrial-looking pipe forms and voluptuous curved vessels. Other pieces showed the influence of Ruth Duckworth who, before her departure for America in 1964, had created some of the most purely sculptural and beautiful pots in British ceramics. A series of undulating wall-like containers made by Lowndes in 1969 anticipated the current vocabulary of several ceramicists. But Hans Coper was struck by how 'she will make a shape which is more drainpipe than anything else, yet somehow it is a pot'. A particularly striking work was a hollow drum with a softly curving interior which had formal affinities with the interests of contemporary sculptors like Phillip King, Tim Scott, and William Tucker. Some of the shapes, rhythms, and contours which they were exploiting were inspired by materials like moulded plastic which were clearly also influencing Lowndes at that time. But as a potter she was excluded from that frame of reference and official discourse.

In 1969 Lowndes had indicated her impatience with the artist-crafts-women label. 'It was only when I started sculpting clay that I realized how limited the boundaries were. I hate any technical process and I find glazing dull and tedious.' Heretical words from the recipient of the 1964 Geneva medal for glaze excellence. For all her technical expertise, the limitations imposed by making art through craft seemed burdensome at that time. The next year she accompanied Auld to Nigeria, where he took up a two-year fellowship at Ife University. In retrospect, Lowndes realizes that this was a crucial time for her. From that experience and her subsequent sustained contact with African art flowed the work which she values and which she continues to develop. She did not make much out there – some cloth sculptures and some bonfired pots which she did not keep. On her return she made wall reliefs – odd, unhappy pieces that played with European decorative motifs like bead moulding and claw feet, and with ideas of decay and dissolution. It took some time before she could create work which drew on her particular response to what she had seen in Nigeria.

In Nigeria, surprisingly, the pots which Lowndes must have seen did not make a great impact on her. Instead she was particularly drawn to non-ceramic materials and intrigued by their range and curious juxtaposition. Her Africanism is not easily understood by looking at her subsequent work but it is principally to do with the unsettling effect of diverse materials – cowrie shell coats, iron assemblages, the leather, cloth, wood and beadwork of masks. African expediency and improvisation appealed to her. But the poetic content of these artefacts was important too. For example, the Yoruba have a cult of twins, Ibedji. They are 'children of the gods' and the way in which they are posthumously commemorated by tenderly cherished wooden figures has a troubling resonance, even if we barely understand the impulse behind such ancestor worship.

After her return from Nigeria, Lowndes reasserted an impatience with clay. In an interview of 1977 she spoke of switching to metal, glass, or plastic – in short of joining the then mainstream of sculpture which put the concept before the material. This was not to be, but from about that time she gave up using many of the techniques conventionally associated with building ceramic forms. First there came a series of pieces made up of laboriously rolled strips of clay, which recall some primitive architecture based on a system of palisades. These were perhaps the first pieces to have that now characteristic look of some cult object which draws on our unconscious mythic imagination – our sense of archetypes. This palisade group was followed in 1978 by similarly architectural-looking pieces made up of fibreglass dipped in

Gillian Lowndes, London, 1986. Behind her are two collage pieces and she is surrounded by her husband Ian Auld's collection of African art.

porcelain slip. Their fragile structure was held up by a wire armature and the folded pieces secured by steel pins. At the back of Lowndes's mind was a desire to recreate in clay the Samoan bark cloths which she and Auld were collecting.

By 1980 Lowndes had developed her use of fibreglass dipped in slip to make porcelain bags containing bricks held together with pieces of looped wire. It was the start of her career as a bricolage sculptor. The problem of sculptural scale was solved by the inclusion of found materials. When Anthony Caro first made table pieces, he incorporated details like handles so as to suggest that the sculpture might be lifted and was therefore not a maquette for a larger project. Similarly Lowndes's use of an actual brick or tile in a piece leaves the spectator in no doubt as to its intended scale.

The found materials which Lowndes employs are poor, low-status ones – old bricks, clinker, granite chippings, mild steel strip, cheap industrially made cups and tiles. In this basic materiality she had an affinity with the new sculpture of the 1980s and with artists like Tony Cragg, David Mach, and Bill Woodrow. She is only limited by the demands of the firing process. For instance, she has tried to use foam rubber dipped in slip, but was defeated by the toxic fumes. Lowndes has exhibited an impatience with what might be called the craftsmanly side of her art. But her bricolage approach has made sense of her commitment to ceramic processes. Her work undergoes a uniquely strange transformation in firing; her mastery of underglaze and glaze, and her understanding of the metamorphosis of disparate elements enable her to create work of rare strength – quite simply, there is no other sculpture like it.

In his curious book *The psychoanalysis of fire*, Gaston Bachelard notes 'that which has gone through the ordeal of fire has gained in homogeneity and hence in purity'. Until recently, it was a point of honour for Lowndes that the various materials that made up a piece were actually united by the firing process. Now she fires and assembles her work. This has allowed her to build upwards and in general to work on a larger scale. Her pieces have become more three-dimensional; they no longer invariably lie on a supporting surface. The wire she uses has a more vigorous draughtsman-like quality as it curls round its central core to end in a graphic scribble on a tile. The elements of each piece are less recognizable because they are coated or disguised with spots of underglaze – 'a device someone who is not very fluent with the brush can use'.

However, Lowndes's work cannot be written about as a series of formal problems solved, although ceramics lends itself to discussions of 'how?' as opposed to 'why?' She herself points out, 'any art can narrate ... if it wants to.' Much recent debate has withheld this function from ceramics. Nonetheless, narrative is central to Lowndes's ambitions, which is why the kind of beauties which we may expect to find in ornament are not present in her best pieces. For example, the 'Tail of the dog' series, named by her after the roughly L-shaped patterning on Congolese cloths, has that combination of industrial skin and interest in the irrational and subconscious that typifies the narrative sculpture of our time. From the Renaissance onwards, narrative was defined as *istoria* and it is that sense of history in its widest sense which animated the collage pieces of 1985 and made explicit use of the very fabric of London in decay. Her latest works, springing up or reclining with elegant ease, are Lowndes's *paragone* pieces in that they examine intuitively the relationship between painting, sculpture, and ceramics.

Published in the catalogue of the exhibition 'Gillian Lowndes: new ceramic sculpture', Crafts Council Gallery, London, 28 January to 29 March 1987

Carol McNicoll, slip-caster

Since the early 1960s British colleges of art have offered students a strongly theorized and compulsory dose of art and design history. It is no accident that British artists and designers have a sharply attuned historical sensibility. This partly explains why British visual culture tends to the literary, the mannered, and the subtly parodic. Students who have been introduced to the writing of semiologists like Roland Barthes, or who are immersed in the wordplay of James Joyce or Samuel Beckett, or who admire Marcel Duchamp, are unlikely to approach creativity innocently. Many art students who graduated in the late 1960s and early 1970s made Marcel Duchamp their hero. Crudely interpreted his art seemed to suggest that 'anything' could be art. But in fact Duchamp's magus-like reordering of categories was a response to a crisis of representation in the visual arts. One of the many questions he posed goes something like this: 'Why produce when there is so much to consume?'

Carol McNicoll was born in 1943 on Christmas Eve in Moseley, Birmingham. She was the only child of David McNicoll, a Scottish engineer, and Bridget O'Keefe McNicoll, an Irish Catholic nurse from County Waterford. Her father could draw beautifully, was good at making things and gardened obsessively. Her mother had wanted to be a clothes designer before a sense of duty took her into nursing. She taught Carol to sew and was always elegantly dressed herself. McNicoll's sense of *habitus* – a framework of judgement and taste – was subtly readjusted by Catholicism. In Birmingham the localized reinvention of Catholicism, which had come out of revived nineteenth-century religiosity, was 'like a lens into European baroque'. This aesthetic was reinforced on visits abroad with her parents, when her mother, guidebook in hand, took her into churches. Those dark incense-laden interiors in which high art objects of great beauty jostled with gaudier offerings brought in by worshippers became part of McNicoll's visual vocabulary. Catholicism worked on her in narrative ways too. She learnt about the lives of the saints. These exemplary figures saw visions which, worryingly, in her every-day world, would have been dismissed as signs of madness. It then seemed to McNicoll that those best able to combine the visionary and the functional were artists. Evidently not all artists had an easy time of it but 'artists provide themselves with rituals which make life meaningful'.

Growing up a Catholic in post-war Britain brought McNicoll closer to a European sensibility. And her childhood home in Solihull mapped a remoter culture in the form of engraved brasses, carved furniture, and good carpets brought back by her father from India. McNicoll used to pore over G. Griffin Lewis's *The practical book of oriental rugs* with its chapters on 'Designs and their symbolism'. Years later, in 1972, she went to the great Islamic carpet exhibi-tion at the Hayward organized by David Sylvester. It was a prescient show, put on at a time when decoration / decorative were damning words in the art world. A year later McNicoll began to use pattern, starting with some bowls which looked like *trompe l'oeil* rugs folded into shape.

Convent schooling was followed by one term of science at university, but McNicoll became more interested in making costumes for the Birmingham Rep and for Joan Littlewood's theatre at Stratford East. The Birmingham art school world had seemed promising and in 1967 she arrived at Leeds Poly-technic to study Fine Art. She and three others directed a film called *Musical*, involving the whole art school in a send-up of the genre. This was followed by her own shorter film in an 'unknown foreign language' shown three times in succession with different subtitles. It was 'about ambiguity'. Painting and sculpture were not central to her tutors' practice nor to her course. McNi-coll turned to making ceramics, inspired by a former model maker who had worked for Spode and by one of her tutors, Dave Seeger, who had cast a witty crab pattern teapot. Her work was given a context by the eighteenth-century ceramics McNicoll saw in the V&A – from faience asparagus plates, the lacy beauties of Meissen porcelain, to English softpaste porcelain formed into shell jugs, leafy teapots, and plaice sauceboats. At her degree show at Leeds in 1970 she showed slip-cast pieces like 'Chops, chips and peas with tomatoes' – a set of containers whose lids imitated the food they contain.

At the Royal College of Art McNicoll collaged casts from found moulds rescued from an old pottery factory. Quotidien objects like tea sets were given a surreal twist – three-spouted teapots, upside-down jugs, cups cast in stacks of three. This work was in a memorable solo show 'China my China' put on at the College in 1974. The critic William Feaver wrote a generous review in which he noted 'The tapping of Surrealist sources and the admixture of old china devices – concepts like the Toby Jug, the cottage teapot and the fish-shaped plate – results in a series of objects that stand halfway between art and utility' and which 'restore wit and expression to a field dominated in re-cent years by the well-meaning Council of Industrial Design'.

Carol McNicoll at home, London, 2014.

That McNicoll's ceramics were extremely fashionable in the 1970s was no accident. At the College she was one of a group of women – including Alison Britton, Jacqueline Poncelet, Jill Crowley, Glenys Barton, and Elizabeth Fritsch – who transformed the ceramics scene in the late 1970s. But McNicoll was a bit different from the rest of this loose group. Like her friend Janice Tchalenko, she preferred production to the one-off craft object. By the late 1970s her vases, jugs, cups, and plates had an almost iconic status, appearing on record sleeves and starring in a *film noir* commercial for Maxell tapes. They were cast from folded pleated foil or from fans and leaves, or appeared to unfurl, or had corrugated sides. In those early years she was more a designer than a craftswoman with her work being produced in quantity for Lawrence Dumaire's Paris shop Axis and Christopher Strangeways' shop on the King's Road, followed by designs produced in Tokyo and in 1985–6 for Next Interiors.

Since arriving in London in 1970 McNicoll has moved among a group of fellow creative spirits. Between Leeds and going to the RCA in the autumn of 1970 she worked as a machinist for the fashion designer Zandra Rhodes. Rhodes bought McNicoll's work from the start and Rhodes's 'massive talent for textile design' was to be an influence, as was her extraordinary shaping and cutting of clothes, influenced by non-European dress. Through Zandra Rhodes she met the architect Piers Gough who first bought and later commissioned work including 'The architect's teaset' of 1984. He was to design McNicoll a remarkable flat, completed in 1983, with curving walls, gleaming flexible exposed ducting, monumental cast-iron Victorian radiators, pastel bathrooms suites and eclectic tiling. Throughout her time at the College she was close to Brian Eno. His glam-rock band Roxy Music was very much a product of the art school ambiance and its members were intellectual, obsessively stylish, and, in the case of Eno and Andy McKay, wearing clothes made by McNicoll.

During her childhood visits to Ireland McNicoll witnessed her uncles and aunts abandoning their old farmhouses for spotless new bungalows. This did not make sense to her and she mourned the loss. The interiors she has created in recent years reject that kind of cautious functionalism. Every surface is treated: walls are painted with free lyrical patterns while eclectic mixtures of tiles clad cast-iron columns. A stair wall is covered with cut up olive oil cans. Her idea of home is a triumph of bricolage, improvisation, and salvage – an industrial cooker, marble shelves on salvaged iron brackets, screens made of Indian textile posters of long-gone politicians, her own drawings printed onto heavy velvet. This ceaseless creativity extends into every area – cooking, clothes, gardening, and, of course, ceramics. McNicoll is a classic subculture consumer, active, creative, and critical in her appropriation and transformation of material artefacts. She spends a lot of time remaking objects.

In her ceramics McNicoll's interest in improvision is taken a step further. She has always slip-cast. A body of work from the 1980s included in this exhibition reveals her ingenuity as an expressive mould-maker. Functional but extravagant forms were combined with a highly evolved language of surface decoration. Like many of her fellow ceramicists she evolved a fiercely individual visual language based on an invented set of procedures. But over the last couple of years McNicoll has gone far beyond her work of the 1980s and early 1990s. Like contemporaries working in the fine arts, she is addressing the old Duchampian problem of making art in a full world. In this context her invariable use of slip-casting has a powerful resonance. The sculptor Richard Deacon reflected on this in a catalogue essay on her work of the 1980s:

'All cast forms are borrowed or derived from something else – there is the pattern from which the mould is prepared and out of that mould a cast is taken. The pattern, the source, can be almost anything, another object, a designed form, a part, a surface, etc. The cast apes the source object and is capable of multiple production. While that capacity for multiplicity has enabled Carol to work as a production potter, it seems to me that it is the notions of derivation, borrowing and replication inherent in casting that constitute continuity, coherence and the means of progression in Carol's work.'

Deacon was writing presciently. Derivation, borrowing, and replication are at the heart of imaginative art practice now, together with investigations into the oddness and the instability of objects.

We are now seeing immense change in the way people frame categories and in the way things are made. In the Hayward exhibition 'Material Culture: the object in British art of the 1980s and 90s' (1997) the curators observed that the artists included had turned to object-making because 'the category of sculpture had of itself little appeal'. In the context of another significant show, 'Loose Threads', held at the Serpentine Gallery in the summer of 1998, its curator wrote of using work made with thread to 'unpick the seams between painting, sculpture and drawing … high art and craft, masculine and feminine'. The late 1990s have seen artists become increasingly interested in what anthropologists have termed 'the social life of things'. It is an approach which informs much of the work in the current 'British Art Show 5' touring Britain until January 2001. Pre-existing objects, poeticized, dominate the exhibition.

In this spirit McNicoll's new work powerfully conflates two traditional opposites – production and consumption. She consumes to produce – not simply through selecting so-called 'found objects' but by the transformation of objects through the process of slip-casting. Part of her genius lies in her choices of meaning-bearing objects. They come, of course, singly and innocently – a ceramic carthorse redolent of a lost England of whistling ploughboys, a bit of wooden tourist art in the form of a statuesque giraffe, an ornamental bird from the 1960s whose mannerist elongation suggests vague Brancusian influences. But they are cast in multiples and then they are grouped to perform tasks – carrying bowls or grapes or teapots, acting as bearers of objects as well as bearers of meaning. They are made stranger by their surface decoration. McNicoll has collected transfers, or decals as they are known in the USA, for years. Most are made for 'trade' use – vine leaves, the Indian tree pattern, horses' heads for instance. Here they are wrenched out of context and paradoxically become powerful diagrams of national obsessions and forgotten colonial ambitions.

A fine example of this new body of work (now in the Fitzwilliam Museum) multiplied a plastic figure of a turbaned Indian, which once held a box of tea in a shop window, into a group of three holding a mass of cast grapes. This 'bowl' is a haunting object – the figures appear to dance and move. They are covered in a vine leaf transfer – they hold the grapes and they are the vine. They belong in the domestic interior but all the familiar tropes of the bourgeois souvenir are confusingly mingled – the vine leaf, the colonial memento, the grapes, the grape dish. These irregular transactions between objects and ornament and pattern are wonderfully developed in the new bowls. McNicoll is, if anything, bored by consumption theory, by the semiotics of taste, and by debates over the difference between a commodity and a gift. She has lived alongside these theoretical discussions since her student days and her way of life – the way she consumes and the way she travels – comments on these sociological and philosophical attempts to make sense of late capitalism. But what she has done with these recent 'knick-knacks' is casually and precisely twitch all these teeming ideas into art.

Published in the booklet *Carol McNicoll: knick-knacks*, accompanying her exhibition at Yorkshire Sculpture Park, Wakefield, 2000

Svend Bayer and the aesthetics of denial

Svend Bayer lives in a thatched house by a narrow road outside Sheepwash in Devon. There he has his workshop, his showroom, and two cross-draught wood-fired tunnel kilns. Behind the house is a beautifully planted wood. Between the wood and the house there is a curved beech hedge. Anyone seriously interested in ceramics will be aware of this pottery and will have seen the

Svend Bayer unloading his kiln, Sheepwash, Devon, 1982.

series of photographs taken by Graham Portlock in 1982 of Bayer unloading his kiln, carrying his work out into the sunlight, a solitary figure surrounded by the majestic large garden pots that then exemplified the most demanding, even heroic, side of his work. Bayer is charming, erudite, and approachable, but his career has often been characterized as one of renunciation and sacrifice. Michael Cardew, who believed Bayer to have been 'easily my best pupil', saw him as 'a force of nature'. His friend the potter Mark Hewitt has written of the 'aesthetics of denial' and of 'a life of almost monastic rigour'.

Svend Bayer lived and worked with Michael Cardew at Wenford Bridge for three and a half years, from 1969 to 1972. He was the ideal student – self-sufficient and driven. Cardew did not teach in a conventional way but he provided a set of standards and an intellectual framework. Bayer knew that he was with 'the best potter in Britain; I was like someone who had been starved their entire life and suddenly had been given food.' But there were things about Cardew's approach that never appealed to Bayer – chiefly his fondness for ball mills and grinding machines, his choice of kiln, his use of saggars, his romantic respect for science, his interest in glaze chemistry.

Quite early on Bayer knew that he was 'going to be far more purist and use materials just to hand, using the firing process to glaze the pots'. So while working at Wenford Bridge was a crucial influence, a journey made in 1973 to Japan, South Korea, Thailand, and Burma was perhaps even more important. It was a trip rich in epiphanic moments. Bayer saw kilns bigger than houses, elegant water-powered hammer mills used to prepare clay and pots produced on a huge scale. In Thailand he saw barges stacked high with jars floating down from Ratchaburi, a wood-firing Stoke-on-Trent dominated by dragon kilns. It made the practice of studio pottery in the West seem insignificant and artificial.

But the great kiln complexes of the Far East were operated by extended families and by whole villages. Bayer set out to replicate that generosity of scale on his own. He did so triumphantly but at a certain cost. His first 600 cubic foot kiln built at Sheepwash in 1975, the model for all future kilns, was based on what he had seen in Thailand. In those early days he fired nine times a year, with each relatively rapid (and stressful) firing producing about a thousand pots. He covered the whole range of ceramic forms: decorated plates, bowls, mugs, and pitchers filled the front of the kiln, while the garden pots were stacked rim to rim at the back. This demanding routine, which included the building of two further kilns, one of 800 cubic feet, was carried on until the mid-1990s.

The mid-1990s was a time of creative and personal crisis. Bayer grew to hate decorating pots and to dislike fulfilling orders for a round of shops and galleries. Cheap imports from the Far East have meant that his plain, handsome garden pots no longer make the same economic sense. He wanted to work in a different, more meditative way. The change of pace was made manifest in his adoption of much lengthier firings in which the decoration of his pots depended only on an interaction with wood ash. He began to share his deep reservoir of knowledge and experience, giving workshops on making big pots and on kiln building, principally in the USA. He lists his kilns on his curriculum vitae as creative objects in their own right. Their organic beauties stand as the antithesis of the rigid structure of Cardew's circular Bourry kiln, imprisoned in its steel banding.

Now, in 2005, there is no doubt that Bayer's aesthetics have changed over the past fifteen years. He destroys more pots while simultaneously seeing a beauty beyond function in apparently damaged pots. In that same spirit he has decided to stop making specifically domestic wares. Instead he has returned to his roots, studying a group of remarkable stone axes which had been excavated in Denmark by an uncle and given to him when a small boy. These have inspired a handsome series of abstract forms that will 'sit on a base and just be objects'. He has started to take enormous risks with his big pots, not least because he is no longer quite the same kind of ceramicist.

Bayer now makes less and fires as daringly as he can. The results are subtle and demand our complete attention, for these are some of the most arresting pots of our time. They are essentially non-functional but have been inspired by the world's greatest vernacular traditions, seen by Bayer as a young man. This exhibition, therefore, stands for formal beauty, for an accumulation of experience, and for a culture of work that has all but vanished in our globalized world.

Published in a Rufford Crafts Centre leaflet, 2005

Ron Arad: reinventing the wheel

'Ron Arad: before and after now': exhibition at the Victoria & Albert Museum, London, 12 June to 1 October 2000

It is unusual for the V&A to honour a living designer with a major retrospective, and the museum has certainly never staged such an exhibition which involves its historic collections quite so dramatically. Ron Arad's furniture is presented on a series of mirrored ramps which snake from the museum's Cromwell Road entrance through the Mediaeval Treasury and out into the Pirelli Garden. Old and new collide to some effect – Arad's 'Infinity' bottle rack climbs like ivy over the case which houses the twelfth-century Eltenberg Reliquary. This may seem crass, and it has annoyed the kind of art critic who knows nothing about the applied arts but enjoys attacking the V&A. In fact the juxtaposition has the odd effect of refocusing attention on that extraordinary twelfth-century work of art and craft, and on other objects of great beauty in the Treasury. Nonetheless, this is a tough exhibition to get to grips with. There is no catalogue and nothing is labelled, making interactivity with the new technology an imperative. Computer screens in each section provide important insights into the work and suggest some of the problems facing a creative designer in Britain today.

Famously, Arad started out making things himself, inhabiting in the 1980s a borderland typical of the period, emblematic of the collapse of British industrial production in the Thatcher years. Some of the early work was a species of ad hoc-ism. Take the Rover chair made from salvaged leather seats from the Rover 2000, mounted on scaffolding tubing. This captivatingly narrative object manages to suggest both insouciant chic and, for the target audience born like Arad in 1951, childhood moments in the family car. Other chairs like 'Big easy' and 'Tinker' were literally hammered into shape by panel-beating and welding in Arad's workshop.

In the early 1980s Arad seemed to be part of a fashionable group – including furniture makers Tom Dixon, André Dubreuil, and Danny Lane – creating neo-primitive objects, roughly factured using low-level industrial techniques. It was a reversion to low-tech which aptly reflected the unsteady, febrile mood of the time, in which the bubble of affluence always seemed about to burst. And Arad had a genius for creating an ambience for his work through his series of One-Off shops. The final one, in Shelton Street, Covent Garden, was a triumph of irrational design, being lined with pieces of sheet steel haphazardly collaged into a gleaming metal cave. It was filled with mocking critiques of good taste and good design – most memorably Arad's widely copied brutalist turntable and speakers embedded in concrete, a punk response to Bang & Olufsen.

Arad has come a long way since those early, inspired bricolage days. Today he bypasses British manufacturers' indifference and lack of flexibility by taking his designs to major firms all over Europe – to Vitra, Kartell, and Cassina – and by establishing a collaboration with Marzorati Ronchetti, the famous family-run firm in Italy which now makes up his one-off pieces. (That Britain lacks the small, flexible family firms which made the European postwar design boom possible is one of the sad lessons of this exhibition.) Arad is clear-headed about how his work divides up and about the myriad processes currently available to designers. These are neatly summarized by Arad as wasting (cutting away material), moulding, forming, assembling, and, less familiarly, growing – Arad's poetic way of describing processes like fusion deposition modelling or stereo lithography, in which a computer model on screen is translated into an actual object by a 3D printer. These are used as a matter of course in industry, but Arad manages to go beyond their use for rapid prototyping and employs 3D printing processes to create short runs of odd, magical lamps, bowls and vases in resins and polymides. They are, in

Ron Arad in his London drawing room with a prototype
steel spring bookcase, seated on a prototype cantilever chair, 1993.

Arad's own words, 'not made by hand, not made in China', and they suggest a
new blurring of boundaries between art and production.

Is Arad a good designer? By all the standards of early twentieth-century
design the answer must be no. But the values of modernism mean little to
consumers under 50 and, in any case, Arad manages to operate imaginatively
as a quasi-Surrealist on the borders of architecture, fine art, and design. (His
architectural practice, growing in interest, is not really covered in this exhibition.) Thus 'Paparelle', a chair made from woven stainless steel held in
tension, can seem wildly overblown or pleasingly sculptural, depending on

whether the context is one of design or fine art. Only one object in Arad's body of work actually makes me angry. This is his 'Bookworm', which in both its tempered steel and plastic versions seems dedicated to breaking the spines of books – it is the ultimate bookshelf for a non-reading culture and makes one nervous about his role as professor of design products at the Royal College of Art.

But there are plenty of remarkable, even haunting, objects in this exhibition. Often a one-off idea will translate into manufacture – like the foam-upholstered versions of his welded steel chairs. This ability to move between one-offs, short runs, and mass production accounts for the freshness of Arad's designs. Some of the best designs are generated because here is a designer who plays constantly with materials and techniques. The FPE chair (Fantastic Plastic Elastic) is made of a flexible plastic sheet inserted into a pair of split aluminium tubes. When the tubing is bent it bites into the plastic, holding it firm, and lo! a chair is born. Then there are his extraordinary BOOPs (Blown Out Of Proportion) in which super-plastic aluminium is heated, inflated with air and subsequently cut and joined to create organic low tables and upscaled vases. Here the process – blowing up metal like a balloon – accounts for the visual strangeness of the object. Arad is also ingenious with more quotidian technology. Two wheels and ball-bearings, and we have his range of mobile storage units known as RTWs (Reinventing The Wheel). These look heavy and industrial but can be rolled about with ease, the inner wheel and the unit's shelving remaining stationary.

In fact reinventing the wheel is an activity that Arad has made his own – going over old ground, forgetting about functional perfectibility, and injecting poetry into everyday objects. And sometimes he comes up with a design which would please the modernists too – like his flat stack chair for Kartell, which folds so thin that 200 stacked chairs stand only 1.6 metre tall. Indeed, everything about Arad's development suggests that the next ten years will be even more varied and creative.

The Spectator, 16 September 2000

Philip Eglin, memory-traces

I am lucky enough to own a small 'Madonna and child' made by Philip Eglin in the early 1990s. It is a complicated object although it only stands 28 centimetres high. It recalls Northern Renaissance painting and the playfulness of small-scale Italian bronzes of the same period – made to be handled and studied. It is also part of the extended tradition of the ceramic figurine in Europe, from eighteenth-century porcelain table decorations which reified the cultural capital of the elite, to more provincial work, shading into folk art. In Eglin's Madonna, high art is embodied in the complex formal relationship of the mother and child, while his use of splashed and poured brown and green pigments suggest the homeliness of lead-glazed Staffordshire wares. On many of his early pieces Eglin roughly scrawled graffiti-like inscriptions, taking this interplay firmly into the present. Studying my 'Madonna and child' reminds me of how learned good artists invariably are.

The assurance of Eglin's figurative work has not diminished. A recent series of porcelain Madonnas inspired in part by one of the V&A's most majestic publications – Paul Williamson's *Northern Gothic sculpture 1200–1450* – are among the best things he has ever made. I first saw them in Denmark last year and I was awed by their melancholy beauty. But Eglin's work always operates on many levels and these Madonnas continue his interrogation of opposites – high art and low art, treasure and rubbish. There is the power of the iconography, the hieratic pose, the references to thirteenth-century French sculpture and the translation of battered wood into porcelain. But a closer look reveals that these Madonnas are constructed using moulds taken from the packaging dross of the supermarket – from discarded milk cartons and the dimpled bases of polystyrene trays. Eglin's porcelain Madonnas test out our taste and disrupt our efforts to create taxonomies.

In 1998 Eglin's genius hit upon a new form – oddly-scaled cylinders that he calls 'buckets'. These may have surprised admirers of his figurative work but they are remarkable objects whose surfaces carry complex layers of imagery and text. The 'buckets' have many memory-bearing functions, some of them reparative. Eglin drew beautifully as a child but few of his drawings were kept. So he uses the buckets to carry simulacra of his children's pictures and writings. On a scrap of paper in his studio he writes: 'Our memories of childhood fade. Ensure my own children's images are kept.' These innocent productions keep company with images of Napoleon, the Pope, Christ crowned with thorns, a photograph of a Japanese bath-house, an erotic Indian miniature, Eglin's own fine drawings, and bold painterly passages of colour. The data may have been arbitrarily chosen. Indeed the way in which

Philip Eglin, two Madonnas and a Pietà in the kiln awaiting firing, 2009.

these pieces are constructed suggests chance. Eglin translates and prints his visual material onto sheets of soft clay, using these to build his vessel. He works, in effect, with a series of decorated surfaces that he collages together. But each bucket tells a different secret story and has its own visual logic. I say secret because there is a hermetic quality about these extraordinary pieces and I am not sure that even Eglin himself could entirely explain all of these haunting juxtapositions.

The activities of copying, replicating, collaging, and synthesizing have always been central to the visual arts. And in all kinds of ways the copy has always been important to ceramics. For one thing, ceramic, as a relatively humble material, has often drawn on more highly regarded arts such as architecture, precious metalwork, and sculpture. The tedious and seemingly endless late twentieth-century debates about the relationship between art and craft have made much of this, arguing that ceramics have always been a step behind the breakthroughs and developments in the fine arts. But as we come to understand the narrowness of the idea of an evolutionary avant-garde, the tendency of ceramics to draw on what Philip Rawson has called 'memory-traces' becomes its great strength.

The place where memory is most powerfully reified is, of course, the home and the world of objects we find inside the home. The rhetoric of modernism affected to despise the home, surely in part out of fearfulness. In the domestic space objects, and people, lead unstable existences – treasured and admired one minute, cast out the next. Perhaps it is no accident that Eglin's ceramics are made in his front room rather than in a distant studio. I suspect that despite his complaints about lack of space and the problems of standing back from finished pieces, Eglin needs the complexity of home – the piles of papers, the shelves of admired objects, his wife and children, whose presences are intertwined with his creativity. Eglin is dealing with problems that particularly face artists now – why make and on what terms in this very full world of goods? Home, with its attendant safeties and dangers, is a good place in which to do his kind of memory work. It is a place for boundaries to be blurred and a space in which to reconfigure the past and to enact the future.

Published in a leaflet accompanying 'Philip Eglin: new work', exhibition at the Barrett Marsden Gallery, London, 29 June to 28 July 2001

Robin Wood, traditional radical

Robin Wood travels light; but strapped to and covering his rucksack there is a traditional Cumbrian basket known as a swill, made from split oak by his friend Owen Jones. Out of the rucksack comes first a pocket knife with a rosewood handle made by Trevor Ablett, a self-employed specialist craftsman, one of the last of Sheffield's 'little mesters', and secondly a pair of dressmaking shears made at Ernest Wright & Son, one of the last Sheffield scissor-makers. (Scissor-making has sunk to a deplorable state: these are the real thing and as beautiful as a small sculpture.) Finally Wood produces a work of his own, a quaich – a small two-handled drinking bowl with a silver rim. He is appropriately named – as a wood-turner and -carver and the author of a scholarly study of the wooden bowl.

In 1995, while working for the National Trust as a warden, he discovered the work of George Lailey, famous for his nesting bowls cut from a sin-

Robin Wood in his workshop, turning the exterior of a large bowl using a pole lathe.

gle block. With Lailey's death in 1958 the skill died too. Inspired, Wood researched the subject and went on to forge his own tools and build his own foot-powered lathe. He is now the last professional pole lathe bowl-turner in this country. Erudite and charming, he looks more like a rock musician than the practitioner of an ancient craft.

Wood takes his skills lightly. His instructive 'Front room spoon carving' in which he chops, cuts, and whittles at speed in his living room to the accompaniment of 'Born to be wild' is on YouTube, as is 'Battle of the bowls' in which he takes on a power lathe wood-turner and wins. His blog (www.robin-wood.co.uk) reveals his remarkable range of interests – most importantly that he is as interested in industrial crafts as in rural ones. The skills within steel mills interest him just as much as those of swill basket making.

Back in 2008 Robin started developing plans to set up a body that could identify and support traditional and industrial crafts on the brink of disappearing. It would be, as he put it 'a cross between CAMRA and the Rare Breeds Survival Trust'. At the moment there is no organization to protect and encourage such crafts – they fall outside the Crafts Council's remit to support the innovative. But for most of the twentieth century rural crafts at least had representation. From 1921 the Rural Industries Bureau (RIB) worked to preserve certain country crafts and to modernize others. They had a staff of expert advisors, a shop, and a journal. From 1968 the Council for Small Industries in Rural Areas (CoSIRA) carried on the valuable work of the RIB. But in 1988 CoSIRA became part of the Rural Development Commission and by 1999 the Rural Development Commission's responsibilities were transferred to the Countryside Agency. The picture becomes confused but at some point traditional craft skills lost an advocate. By 2006 it was all change again with the formation of Natural England – chiefly devoted to environmental conservation.

The obvious home for traditional craft skills (both rural and urban) might appear to be the Department for Culture, Media, and Sport. But traditional craft is not recognized within the DCMS arts and culture area overseen by the Arts Council, nor by English Heritage which is restricted to buildings and monuments. Robin Wood cites the example of English Heritage's decision to acquire J. W. Evans, a family-run silver and plate manufactory in Birmingham. They have saved the building, the equipment, tools, and pattern books, but, as Wood points out, 'all the skill, tacit knowledge, and "living heritage" walked out the door the day it closed'. These closures destroy a sense of place and part of Wood's vision is to restore a sense of regional difference – to enable children in Cumbria to experience swill basket making, children in Sheffield to forge a knife and spoon, children in Stoke-on-Trent to make a clay pot.

In early 2009 Wood formed the Heritage Crafts Association. Six months later there was a debate on traditional crafts in the House of Commons initiated on 25 June by Wood's MP Tom Levitt (find it at www.theyworkforyou. com/debates). The Heritage Crafts Association will be holding its press launch at the Victoria & Albert Museum in late March and has a website (www.heritagecrafts.org.uk) that explains its goals. To protect and ensure the transfer of skills and knowledge is reminiscent of the Japanese Law for the Protection of Intangible Cultural Properties passed after the Second World War. It is an idea that was taken up by UNESCO in 2003 in its Convention on the Safeguarding of Intangible Cultural Heritage – signed by 107 countries, though not by the UK. The Heritage Crafts Association is (despite its name) a radical organization, set to do battle just in time.

Robin Wood's HCA can be seen as part of a movement which has broadened our understanding of craft – taking it beyond the studio crafts of pottery, textiles and so on, to a more general idea of process. As process, craft can happen in any area – in a factory, in the home, in architecture, fine art and design. Wood's intelligence and catholic range of interests make him an inspiring advocate of craft without boundaries – craft for the twenty-first century.

Crafts, no. 223, March/April 2010

Two essays

'For love and not for money':
reviving 'peasant art' in Britain 1880–1930

Late nineteenth- and early twentieth-century philanthropic projects to revive what was variously called 'peasant art' or 'home industries' or 'village
industries' touch on a surprising range of social, economic and political
issues.[1] For instance, it may seem strange that what amounted to a network
of rural reconstruction schemes in Britain should have been centred on artistic activity – as opposed to, say, agricultural reform. The peasant art movement was in part inspired by the anti-industrial writings of John Ruskin
and William Morris. But in practice only lip-service was paid to these radical
Victorian thinkers. Class interests were not to be compromised. Peasant arts
were initiated chiefly by the aristocracy and landed gentry in a spirit of stasis,
stressing self-help rather than social change in the countryside.

What were 'peasant arts' and who sought to introduce them and why?
The term implies the existence of a peasantry – a social grouping which can
barely be identified in late nineteenth-century Britain. The model was the
independent smallholder in the remoter parts of continental Europe, whose
rich regional dress and impressive array of vernacular craft skills impressed
adventurous British travellers up to and during the Second World War.[2] It
was understood that vernacular crafts from wood-carving to lace-making
flourished in France, Germany, Austria, and Switzerland because 'the conditions of land tenure have given the people an interest in the soil ... conse-
quently the country districts are not depopulated'.[3] In contrast the British
(and particularly English) countryside was emptying from the mid nineteenth century, the exodus peaking during the agricultural depression of the
1880s.[4] Britain's transformation from a rural to a largely urban nation was
an occasion for upper-class cultural pessimism characterized by fears of a politicized urban working class who would know nothing of rural cultures of
deference.[5]

Set against these anxieties were idealizations of 'peasant' life and creativity. Crucially, peasant art or industry was defined as 'made for love not
money' and 'not to sell to another, but to keep or at most to give'.[6] A series
of special numbers of *The Studio*, appearing from 1911 to 1913, documented
'peasant art' in Europe. As the issue devoted to Italy noted, peasants carved
or embroidered 'not for the sake of bartering and money. It is work done for
themselves, their homes and families'.[7] Implicit in this kind of writing was
an ambivalence towards a key aspect of modernity – the intense commodification of goods and by extension human relations in an industrialized

society. In *Das Kapital* Karl Marx had provided a sophisticated historical summary of the process in Britain. Drawing on a range of sources from Thomas More to William Cobbett, Marx describes the disappearance of an independent British peasantry and notes that the extirpation of rural crafts formed part of this process because 'only the destruction of rural domestic industry can give the home market of a country that extension and stability which the capitalist mode of production requires'.[8]

As Marx made clear, this process of commodification was inexorable and had taken place early and with particular ferocity in Britain. Not surprisingly, therefore, the peasant art revival had its critics among the more politically aware members of the Arts & Crafts movement who may not have read Marx but knew his most accessible source material. Some like A. H. Mackmurdo and C. F. A. Voysey were keen supporters of peasant arts but, for instance, C. R. Ashbee perceived its weaknesses from the perspective of his own attempts at urban and rural regeneration in London and Chipping Campden. Writing in 1899, William Morris's biographer H. W. Mackail saw the movement as being of 'little value' and as 'a mixture of charity and patronage' which served to 'multiply the productions of amateur incompetency'.[9] This sounds like Morris's own view. In 1889 he had given a muted, hostile interview to the secretary of the Home Arts and Industries Association (HAIA).[10]

This organization, founded by Eglantyne Louisa Jebb, takes us to the heart of the peasant art movement. According to the painter G. F. Watts the HAIA had sprung 'from the work of one lady whose love of the beautiful had led her to share it with a poor crippled boy, teaching him to carve beautifully instead of doing the ugly work she had found in his hand'. Subsequently 'the boys of all the village round came to her asking to be taught too'.[11] Other accounts fill out the story. The boy was found by Mrs Jebb weeping over some worsted work.[12] In a variant version he was discovered sobbing as he cleared stones from a field.[13] There is no reason to doubt the good intentions of Mrs Jebb who initially began an organization called the Cottage or Home Arts Association, renamed in 1884 the Home Arts and Industries Association at a meeting chaired by Lord Brownlow.[14] Jebb was Anglo-Irish, had attended art school in Ireland and in 1871 married a distant cousin, Arthur Jebb of the Lyth, Ellesmere, Shropshire. She started teaching wood-carving in the servants hall, later expanding into chair-carving, carpentry, mosaics, and painting. She knew passages from Ruskin and Morris by heart.

The HAIA got off the ground through a series of social networks and became the umbrella for most of the existing projects designed to encourage craft in country places. A surprising number, for example the Keswick School of Industrial Art and the Langdale Linen Industry, got under way at about the same time as the HAIA. In 1884 there were already 40 affiliated branches giving classes with 320 students. By 1889 there were 450 classes, 1,000 managers and teachers and 5,000 students.[15] Instruction was mostly free and work was sold.[16] Although the principal aim was to reach country people there were many affiliated classes in cities and towns such as Mabel de Grey's wood-carving and inlay classes in Pimlico and Stepney in London. Some classes taught the disabled, the blind, and the simple-minded.[17] There were annual exhibitions, the first (1885) held at Lord Brownlow's London home at Carlton House Terrace, but from 1891 until at least 1933 they were held at the Albert Hall where from 1887 the HAIA had an office and studio. These exhibitions were important social events. Exhibits were catalogued and arranged geographically. Regional identity was thought important, although few of the products were indigenous to the areas where they were made.[18] Some ordinary Arts & Crafts workshops like the Della Robbia Pottery of Birkenhead chose to exhibit with the HAIA. Awards were given for exceptional work.

Favoured crafts taught in classes affiliated to the HAIA included wood-carving ('by far the most important class'), metal repoussé work and embossed and stencilled leatherwork.[19] These were hardly traditional country crafts though some of the carving, chip carving for instance, was indebted to continental peasant examples. Mrs Jebb's mentor was Charles Godfrey Leland, an expatriate Philadelphian of old New England stock and a propagandist for craftwork in education. He had published a craft guide, *The minor arts* (1879) inspired by his contact with William Morris and by studies at the school of art at South Kensington. Present at the HAIA's first committee meetings, he was interested in the artistic interior and he envisaged the poor creating 'Pompeian floors, carved dadoes, stencilled walls and ceilings' for their homes.[20] His influence partly explains the historicist nature of the HAIA's design sources, necessitating a budget for exemplary casts, electrotypes and other reproductions for distribution to classes.[21] But the HAIA's interest in wood-carving was also indebted to Ruskinian and Morrisian visions of idealized work which invoked the image of some kind of artisan, neither artist nor labourer, invariably carving, letting fancy roam, with a mind stocked with images of birds and bees and flowers, and able to translate them into ornament freely and at will.[22] The reality of HAIA wood-carving classes was probably more circumscribed.[23] Repoussé work, invariably in copper, had a different virtue. It was easy to teach, though in time it came to stand for all that was limiting about the peasant art movement. In 1933 George Marston of the Rural Industries Bureau dismissed repoussé work as 'futile and meaningless. What a pitiful sight it is to see a student using his skill and intelligence to bump up dragons, flowers and ships – pictures which are the province of the painter rather than the craftsman.'[24]

The nature of the objects made reflected the background of the leaders of the peasant art movement. Mrs Jebb's Ellesmere neighbours Lord Brownlow and his wife were important figures. He was a considerable landowner and one of the few men to be directly involved, setting up wood-carving classes at his estates at Ashridge Park in Hertfordshire and at Belton in Lincolnshire and creating designs to be used in these classes.[25] But his grandeur was matched by that of the women involved. At the top of the social hierarchy was Alexandra, Princess of Wales, who visited an early exhibition, bought a corner cupboard made at Ellesmere as well as brasswork and a spindle, and subsequently set up a technical school at Sandringham in Norfolk specializing in carpentry and cabinet-making.[26] Then there was Maria de Rothschild who held carving classes at Ascott Wing in Buckinghamshire, and the Countess of Warwick who, after a dramatic conversion to socialism in 1895, set up needlework classes at Easton in Essex.

The HAIA was dependent on voluntary support and it was recognized that gentry women had the will and time to introduce crafts to countryfolk. 'Is there a daughter of the squire who can do fretwork, bent ironwork, embossed leather?' asked one writer in 1915.[27] This raised gendered debates about standards. As one critic pointed out, 'There are thousands of ladies who can paint nicely in watercolours and atrociously in oils', but 'when these ladies undertake to form and teach country classes they are often completely at sea and are in need of direction from the outset'.[28] In the late 1920s two researchers from the Oxford Agricultural Economics Research Institute gave a negative account of the involvement of women in the small businesses which came out of the peasant art movement: 'Very low rates of payment are, unfortunately, sometimes a characteristic of small village industries run from so-called "philanthropic" motives, and the promoter of such an industry is sometimes able to impress the workers so forcibly with the idea of her philanthropy that they will toil uncomplainingly for a wage which would arouse the most passive of employees in a commercial industry to strong protest.'[29]

But the peasant art movement provided opportunities for a number of creative (if privileged) women like the Countess of Lovelace and the Honourable Mabel de Grey, who were both active designers within the movement. Other gifted women were the wives and widows of successful artists, like Elizabeth Waterhouse, the wife of the architect Alfred Waterhouse, who ran a thriving repoussé copper workshop in the basement of her home at Yattendon Court in Berkshire and whose designs were regularly singled out for praise by reviewers, and Mary Watts, the wife of G. F. Watts, whose terracotta work at Compton near Guildford was widely admired.[30] Both these women started ed classes which developed into successful businesses.[31] Significantly, other highly praised groups which exhibited at the HAIA shows used designs provided by trained artists – for instance metalwork designs supplied by John

Pearson and J. D. Mackenzie at Newlyn, by John Williams and Temple Moore at Newton, Cambridgeshire and at Fivemiletown in Ireland, by Harold Stabler at Keswick School of Industrial Art, and designs for carving at Leigh in Surrey by William Aumonier, and by Arthur Simpson for classes at Windermere.[32]

The aims of the peasant art movement and of the HAIA reflected national anxieties. In Mrs Jebb's view the HAIA classes exercised 'good influence' and resulted in 'happier lives and lighter hearts, tidier children, cleaner cottages, and a better moral tone all round' while another early committee member spoke of the need to create rural prosperity in the wake of an exodus to the cities.[33] In 1896 the editor of *The Studio* Gleeson White argued that an important purpose of the peasant art movement was to encourage overlooked latent genius for 'one in a million may be a new Grinling Gibbons'.[34] There was a general consensus that the countryside was a healthy gene pool for the national stock, with sturdy countryfolk being contrasted with 'white-faced workmen living in courts and alleys'.[35] Godfrey Blount, whose Peasant Arts Society (later the Peasant Arts Guild) based in Haslemere exhibited regularly with the HAIA, believed that in an ideal society nine out of ten people should be agriculturalists working at handicrafts in their leisure time.[36] The model was continental Europe and by 1908 the Society had been given the extensive exemplary collection of woodwork, work in metal, horn, and bone, and textiles chiefly from Scandinavia, Russia, and the Baltic, amassed by the Revd Gerald Davies.[37] The collection complemented the Scandinavian-inspired pattern weaving and 'Russian' lace produced by the Peasant Arts Society. The Society's annual reports and its magazine *The Vineyard* (1910–22) devoted to tales of 'peasant' life and Blount's numerous books, suggest the political background. In Blount's book *The blood of the poor* of 1911 the city and its politicized working class are regarded as the enemy. Blount envisaged a deferential peasantry watched over by an enlightened aristocracy. State welfare and socialism were dismissed in favour of voluntary altruism in which the rich would employ a workforce making 'wholesome things in simple ways'. Interaction between social classes was an important motivating force for peasant art activity. Hermann Muthesius, in a report of 1900 on the movement for the German government, had noted the gulf between the social classes in Britain. For a member of the Association's committee, Alfred Harris, the peasant art movement was a way of combating incipient socialism, calling 'into play the exercise of charity and self-denial among an army of cultured persons' and acting as 'a great social lever for bringing into closer sympathy, and uniting by stronger bonds, wealth with poverty, culture with ignorance, refinement with coarseness'.[38]

As we have seen, it is striking how little attention was paid to existing, if endangered, country skills such as wheelwrighting, spoon and bowl turning, chair bodging, small-scale quarrying, and the production of utilitarian earthenware and slipware. These were to become the focus of valedictory study rather later, signalled by the furniture designer Ernest Gimson's interest in vernacular joinery and wheelwrighting and his plans of 1917 for an 'Association of Architecture, Building and Handicraft', a scheme for a network of craft villages of 200 craftsmen apiece 'making in quantity things of common use at prices within the reach of average incomes'.[39] Things of 'common use' were not typically made in Victorian and Edwardian peasant art classes. That lacemaking received sustained encouragement is suggestive. It was a craft with a vernacular historic background but it was its association with luxury dress which attracted aristocratic and royal patrons from the 1880s until the Great War.[40] The same went for the quilting revival orchestrated by the Rural Industries Bureau and the Women's Institutes in the late 1920s. In this instance quilters were provided with high quality silks and satins to work with, turning a traditional thrift craft into a luxury product.[41]

After the First World War the HAIA carried on its work but its exhibitions were less discussed. Its ethos must have seemed paternalistic. The government-backed Rural Industries Bureau (RIB, set up in 1921) and the Women's Institutes represented a more realistic approach to country crafts in the inter-war years. The impetus for the founding of the RIB came from the Ministry of Reconstruction formed during the Great War.[42] In 1918 the Ministry commissioned a special report on rural reconstruction which was complemented by a document submitted in 1918 by the progressive Design and Industries Association. This highlighted 'the philanthropic taint' that characterized poorly paid village industries and the dangers of sweating in cottage and home industries and recommended rural factories such as food processing plants as offering the best solution for rural employment.

The tendency to artiness which had characterized the HAIA classes was, however, to affect the policies of the RIB. The first two directors of the Bureau, John Brooke and George Marston, had trained as fine artists. Although Marston, as we have seen, dismissed the popular philanthropic village craft of repoussé work, the kinds of rural activities which were encouraged by the RIB tended nonetheless to have aesthetic appeal.[43] Large rural firms and businesses in country towns were excluded in favour of small-scale village enterprises. Activities integral to the agricultural economy like hurdle-making or food processing were ignored at the expense of wrought ironwork, furniture making or quilt making.

One craft, blacksmithing, received the lion's share of the RIB's attention. The livelihood of the blacksmith, who had previously made most of his living through farriery, was being threatened by the introduction of complex agricultural machinery backed up with an efficient after sales service. The

RIB helped introduce oxyacetylene torches to enable smiths to repair this new machinery. But the Bureau also encouraged the creation of wrought ironwork as a 'sideline' and from 1928 provided patterns for gates, weather vanes, and outside lamps, which were markedly picturesque and remote from the essentially functional nature of the farrier's work. In effect country crafts were being reinvented for consumption by a new kind of country dweller whose ties to the land were purely recreational.

The National Federation of Women's Institutes was inspired by a Canadian model with a branch in Anglesey in 1911 and a constitution by 1917. It soon became a powerful network in which women of all classes collaborated and in which the crafts were to play an important role. Its spirit was rather more democratic than the HAIA. Alice Armes was its handicrafts organizer between the wars and important craft exhibitions were held in 1917, 1918, 1920, 1921, and 1922 (this last at the V&A). The Women's Institutes found an ardent ally in W. R. Lethaby, the Arts & Crafts architect and educator. Several of his articles for the WI magazine *Home and Country* survey surviving country crafts with the help of research by WI members. In general the WI emphasized regional vernacular women's crafts – glove-making, mat-making, knitting – and high skill.[44]

In the 1920s and 1930s interest in country crafts was no longer dominated by rural philanthropy administered by the landowning classes. An abstract idea, that of a lost 'organic community', became an intellectual middle-class concern, vigorously set out in the pages of *Scrutiny*, the small circulation literary magazine first published in May 1932 and edited by L. C. Knights and Donald Culver, joined in 1933 by F. R. Leavis and Denys Thompson. The phrase 'organic community' also peppered the pages of Leavis and Thompson's book *Culture and environment* of 1933. This was an attack on mass advertising, the mass media, and 'Levelling-Down', intended for use in schools as a primer to train 'taste and sensibility'.[45] That a thinker as rigorous as Leavis should respond to the encroaching barbarism of popular magazines and music, television, cinema, and radio with invocations of the land and the past, suggests a stasis amounting to a crisis in English cultural life which worked to sustain interest in country crafts.[46]

The popularity of 'country writing' went far beyond the rarefied pages of *Scrutiny*. A torrent of books appeared, mostly published by Batsford and Longmans, on rural life and customs. But the recorders of country crafts like Dorothy Hartley and H. J. Massingham had no interest in the artificialities of the peasant art movement. In her *Made in England* (1939) Dorothy Hartley surveyed and illustrated quarrying, mining, brickmaking, and all crafts relating to woodlands and excluded 'arts and crafts' and 'studio' items from her 'plain record of country work written as simply as possible'.[47] Massingham also took up an extreme purist position. His dreams of rural regeneration led him to collect old tools and 'by-gones', adzes, axes, augers, and lace bobbins. These were housed in his thatched summer house for future revivals: 'They would be of service to posterity should England again recolonize with small farming communities.' Tools were links with an older England: Massingham wrote emotionally of seeing breast ploughs being used in the northwest Cotswolds, 'uncouth' implements that appeared to antedate the Anglo-Saxon plough drawn by oxen.[48] A wooden seedlip or box used to broadcast seed evoked 'an unenclosed England ... an organism of independent workers who, if poor, were not paupers, if labouring all their lives, had their feasts and plays and processions, if only living for subsistence, knew nothing of the the worse-than-bestial embitterments of 'economic man' nor of the diabolical philosophy of Hobbes nor of the horrors of industrialism'.[49]

The response of artist craftsmen and women to the fast disappearing vernacular between the wars was more pragmatic. The intricacies of HAIA wood-carving and repoussé work seemed as irrelevant as the Arts & Crafts movement. Inter-war artist craftsmen and women travelled to the margins of the British Isles. Their modernism sought an authentic vernacular but the models which appealed tended to be functional and unadorned. Wales drew craft weavers – Ethel Mairet, Elizabeth Peacock, Margery Kendon, Marianne Straub, Heremon Fitzpatrick – who individually 'discovered' the yarns mulespun in the small Welsh water-powered wool mills. Makers and designers alike were struck by the 'economy and purity of form' of traditional spoons and axe hafts made by carvers and turners like William Rees of Carmarthen and James Davies of Abercych in Pembrokeshire.[50]

In Ireland a privileged aristocracy and intelligentsia had began to anthropologize the margins of their own country at the turn of the century.[51] Visitors from England found the same authenticity. Margery Kendon, whose researches were compared by Thomas Hennell to Cecil Sharp's recovery of English folk song, visited County Mayo in Ireland in 1935 and 1936 to record techniques such as spinning on a traditional big wheel and spindle, and the craft of indigo dying.[52] Ireland was also a place of pilgrimage for Eric Gill and Michael Cardew, providing a less specialized but nonetheless authentically 'primitive' experience. The Highlands and Islands of Scotland offered similar experiences. May Morris, writing in 1919, recalled how moved she was by the unforced beauty of an Orkney Island spinning room and by the colours and patterns of Fair Isle knitting: 'the design is just that of a remote people handling material and process with surety – almost one's idea of Phoenician borderings or Peruvian.'[53] As late as 1938 the design writer Amelia Defries described how in the Shetlands a girl will 'spin, dye and weave' a plaid 'to give her husband on his wedding day, to cover and keep him from all weathers for the rest of his life.'[54] But in Scotland aristocratic and philanthropic patronage and maintenance of craft, particularly weaving and embroidery, had a longer life than in England.

But the European continent remained the place to see authentic work (together with, increasingly, the Far East, the Indian sub-continent, and Africa). Elizabeth Peacock went to Brittany in 1939 to study flax spinning and linen weaving. According to Ella McLeod three days spent with two Brittany weavers 'revolutionized Elizabeth Peacock's handling of linens'.[55] Ethel Mairet visited Eastern Europe in 1917 to study traditionally created yarns, textiles and embroidery. In Scandinavia and Finland, which she visited on four occasions in the 1930s, she saw handweaving of a high standard based on tradition and encouraged and supported by the state.[56] Macedonian embroidery seen in Belgrade in the early 1920s turned sculptor Jean Milne into a textile artist.

The inter-war years witnessed a more democratic attitude to the countryside and the creativity of its inhabitants. Instead of groups of boys summoned to the big house to be instructed in artistic activity we have figures like Hartley and Massingham getting to know individual country people and respectfully recording their skills.[57] There were aristocratic figures like Lady Plymouth who in the 1920s designed furniture, which was made in workshops on her husband's estates at Hever near Redditch. And during the Depression craftwork was on offer at the Vountary Occupational Centres. This provoked criticism, particularly on the left: 'we have this preposterous paradox: in the most industrialized country in the world, with huge factories idle, the unemployed workers are offered charity work at petty handicrafts'.[58] But the 'peasant art' movement had come to an end while the objects which came out of the movement – from the straightforwardly crude to the eclectically historicist – gradually began to turn up in country salerooms and in antique shops. Hardly examples of 'people's art' nor strictly classifiable as 'Arts & Crafts movement' they posed problems of taxonomy and they remain embarassingly ambiguous objects, emblems of an intricate set of cultural tensions and confusions.[59]

1. For useful accounts of the early movement see Geoff Spenceley, 'The lace associations: philanthropic movements to preserve the production of hand-made lace in late Victorian and Edwardian England', *Victorian Studies*, June 1973, pp. 433–52; Anthea Callen's groundbreaking *The angel in the studio: women in the Arts and Crafts movement 1870–1914*, London: Astragal Books, 1979; G. E. Mingay (ed.), *The Victorian countryside*, 2 vols, London: Routledge & Kegan Paul, 1981; Jan Marsh, *Back to the land: the pastoral impulse in Victorian England from 1880 to 1914*, London: Quartet Books, 1982; Jessica Gerard, 'The lady bountiful: women of the landed classes and rural philanthropy', *Victorian Studies*, winter 1987, pp. 183–210; Pamela Horn, *Ladies of the manor: wives and daughters in country house society 1830–1918*, Stroud: Alan Sutton, 1991; *William Morris: questioning the legacy*, Whitworth Art Gallery: Manchester, 1996, pp. 53–8; Pamela Horn, *The Victorian country child*, Stroud: Sutton Publishing, 1997.

2. See Tanya Harrod, *The crafts in Britain in the 20th century*, New Haven & London: Yale University Press, 1999, pp. 199–201.

3. Mrs Ernest Hart, 'Art and technical teaching of the Donegal Industrial Fund' in *Transactions of the National Association for the Advancement of Art and its Application to Industry, Edinburgh meeting 1889*, London, 1890, p. 435. (Hereafter: *National Association*.)

4. W. A. Armstrong, 'The flight from the land', in G. E. Mingay (ed.), *The Victorian countryside*, vol. 1, p. 129.

5. See Howard Newby, *The deferential worker: a study of farm workers in East Anglia*, London: Allen Lane, 1977.

6. 8th Annual Report, Peasant Arts Fellowship, 1924; Gerald Davies, 'The Peasant Arts Museum in Haslemere', *The Vineyard*, vol. 1, 1910, p. 9.

7. Elisa Ricci, 'Women's crafts' in Charles Holme (ed.), *Peasant art in Italy*, London: The Studio, 1913, p. 17.

8. Karl Marx, *Capital: a critique of political economy* (1867), vol. 1, Harmondsworth: Penguin Books, 1976, p. 911.

9. J. W. Mackail, *The life of William Morris* (1899), London: Longmans, Green and Co, 1922, vol. 2, p. 210.

10. Minutes Book of the Home Arts and Industries Association, 6 November 1889, British Architectural Library, RIBA. My thanks to Alan Crawford for this reference and for much other help with this article.

11. G. F. Watts, 'The national position of art', in *National Association*, p. 50.

12. Alfred Harris, 'Home arts and industries', in *National Association*, p. 422.

13. Francesca Wilson, *Rebel daughter of a country house: the life of Eglantyne Jebb, founder of the Save the Children Fund*, London: George Allen & Unwin, 1967, p. 29.

14. Minutes Book of the Home Arts and Industries Association, 20 November 1884, British Architectural Library, RIBA.

15. Peter Stansky, *Redesigning the world: William Morris, the 1880s and the Arts and Crafts*, Princeton, NJ: Princeton University Press, 1985, p. 106.

16. *The Builder*, vol. 48, 1885, p. 859.

17. See, for instance, *Art Workers' Quarterly*, vol. 3, 1904, pp. 137–8.

18. See H.-L. Alphonse Blanchon, 'The revival of the lesser arts in foreign countries', *The Craftsman*, vol. 3, 1902, p. 80.

19. *The Builder*, vol. 49, 1885, p. 44.

20. On Leland, see Eileen Boris, *Art and labor: Ruskin, Morris and the craftsman ideal in America*, Philadelphia, PA: Temple University Press, 1986, pp. 84–5, 123–4.

21. For the historicist nature of HAIA exhibits, see the review in *The Builder*, vol. 49, 1885, pp. 44-5, and Grace Johnson, 'Provincial arts and crafts', *The Studio*, vol. 4, 1894, p. 51.

22. See, typically, William Morris, 'The art of the people' in William Morris, *Selected writings* (ed. G. D. H. Cole), London: Nonesuch Press, 1934, pp. 528–9.

23. For an amusing account of a wood-carving class, see H. G. Wells's novel *Kipps* (1905).

24. G. E. Marston, 'Educational value of handicrafts', *Rural Industries*, winter 1933.

25. See *Building News*, vol. 50, 1886, p. 1029 for Lord Brownlow's frieze designed for his Belton class and 'carried out in hardened chalk'.

26. Francesca Wilson, *Rebel daughter*, p. 29.

27. J. L. Green, *Village industries: a national obligation*, London: Rural World, 1915, p. 94.

28. G. Baldwin Brown, 'Presidential address', *National Association*, p. 268.

29. Helen E. Fitzrandolph & M. Doriel Hay, *The rural industries of England and Wales: decorative crafts and rural potteries*, vol. 3, Oxford: Agricultural Economics Research Institute, 1927, p. 112.

30. On Yattendon Court, see Rev. J. E. Smith-Masters, *Yattendon and its church*, London: The Cornwall Press, 1929, pp. 70–2. Classes ran from 1885 to 1918. Work was made up by Henry and Harry Smith, the local blacksmith and his son. Wooden blocks were prepared by the estate carpenter A. Aldridge, who also ran a wood-carving class.

31. On this point, see 'Art handiwork and manufacture', *Art Journal*, vol. 68, 1906, pp. 211–2.

32. A point made by Gleeson White, 'The Home Arts and Industries Association at the Albert Hall', *The Studio*, vol. 8, 1896, pp. 91–101.

33. Mrs Jebb, 'The Home Arts and Industries Association', *The Magazine of Art*, 1885, p. 298.

34. See Gleeson White, 'The Home Arts and Industries Association at the Albert Hall', and Jane Wilgress, 'Alec Miller: guildsman and sculptor in Chipping Campden', *Campden and District Historical and Archaeological Society*, 1987. Miller discovered his talents when employed aged 12 by Miss Anstruther to help with her Glasgow HAIA wood-carving class. Interestingly her pupils were upper-middle class or aristocratic.

35. W. A. Armstrong, 'The flight from the land', in Mingay (ed.), *The Victorian countryside*, vol. 2, p. 131.

36. 'In admiring memory of Godfrey Blount', Arthur Fifield, Coulsdon, c. 1937.

37. *A country museum: the rise and progress of Sir Jonathan Hutchinson's Educational Museum at Haslemere*, Haslemere: Educational Museum, 1947, p. 112; Greville MacDonald, *Reminiscences of a specialist*, London: George Allen & Unwin, 1932, pp. 380–1.

38. Alfred Harris, 'Home arts and industries' in *National Association*, p. 430.

39. 'The Association of Architecture, Building and Handicraft', 9 July 1917, typescript, Henry Wilson Archive, London: Royal College of Art.

40. See Spenceley, 'The lace associations' (note 1 above).

41. See Holly Tebbutt, 'Industry or anti-industry? The Rural Industries Bureau: its objects and its work', London: V&A / RCA MA thesis, 1990, pp. 108–9.

42. For a good overview, see Tebbutt, 'Industry or anti-industry?'.

43. G. E. Marston, 'The educational value of handicrafts', *Rural Industries*, autumn 1933, p. 71.

44. See Simon Goodenough, *Jam and Jerusalem*, London: Collins, 1977, and Pat Kirkham, 'The inter-war handicrafts revival' in Judy Attfield & Pat Kirkham (ed.), *A view from the interior*, London: Women's Press, 1989, pp. 177–9.; also W. R. Lethaby, *Home and country arts*, London: National Federation of Women's Institutes, 1923, especially the essay 'Village arts and crafts'.

45. F. R. Leavis & Denys Thompson, *Culture and environment: the training of critical awareness*, London, Chatto & Windus, 1933, p. 1.

46. See Iain Wright, 'F. R. Leavis, the Scrutiny movement and the crisis', in Jon Clark, Margot Heinemann, David Margolies, & Carole Snee (ed.), *Cultures and crisis in Britain in the Thirties*, London: Lawrence and Wishart, 1979.

47. Dorothy Hartley, *Made in England* (1939), London: Century Hutchinson, 1987, p. 172, p. xi.

48. H. J. Massingham, *Country relics*, Cambridge: Cambridge University Press, 1939, p. 103. See also Massingham's *Shepherd's country: a record of the crafts and people of the hills*, London: Chapman and Hall, 1938, pp. 103–5, for more lyrical meditations on the breast plough.

49. Massingham, *Country relics*, p. 108.

50. Michael Cardew, *A pioneer potter*, London: Collins, 1988, p. 74.

51. See for instance J. M. Synge, *The Aran Islands* (1907), Harmondsworth: Penguin Books, 1992.

52. Margery Kendon, 'Newport in County Mayo' (1936), manuscript (collection of Ditchling Museum).

53. May Morris, 'Weaving and textile crafts' in *Handicraft and reconstruction: notes by members of the Arts & Crafts Exhibition Society*, London: John Hogg, 1919, p. 44.

54. Amelia Defries, *Purpose in design: a survey of the new movement seen in studios and factories and at the 'Exposition internationale des arts et techniques appliques à la vie moderne'*, London: Methuen, 1938, p. 59.

55. Ella McLeod, 'The diary of visit to Brittany summer 1938', typescript (collection of Margaret Bide) p. 46.

56. Margot Coatts, *A weaver's life: Ethel Mairet 1872–1952*, London: Crafts Study Centre / Crafts Council, 1983, pp. 84–93.

57. Hartley, *Made in England*, p. xi.

58. Allen Hutt, *The condition of the working class in Britain*, London: Martin Lawrence, 1933, p. 185.

59. See Emmanuel Cooper, *People's art: working-class art from 1750 to the present day*, Edinburgh: Mainstream Publishing, 1994.

Published in David Crowley & Lou Taylor (ed.), *The lost arts of Europe: the Haslemere Museum Collection of European peasant art*, Haslemere: Haslemere Educational Museum, 2000

'Visionary rather than practical': craft, art, and material efficiency

Emotional responses to materials and manufactured objects have a long history, but they provoked vivid writing during the design reform debates of the nineteenth century and were carried forward into the twentieth century. In particular, nineteenth-century anxieties about plasticity and about composite materials are still with us. Wood continues to represent sustainability, 'truth to materials', emotional durability, and an assumed reassuring contact between material, tools, and maker. By contrast, the facture offered by new media, in the form of self-replicating rapid prototyping machines, appears disembodied while also offering the possibility of homesteader-making. The desirability of recycling and up-cycling is currently central to our emotional responses to materials, with the world's waste dumps becoming sites of horrified fascination and inspiration. Symbolic moves in the direction of autarchy and reverse engineering by artists and designers register doubts about sustainability and seek to uncover the hidden impact of individual materials. This survey of historic and current attitudes towards materials and making processes by makers, artists, and designers sheds light on anxieties familiar to us all, concerning technological development, authentic experience, agency, a sense of selfhood, and the often bruising experience of modernity itself.

Victorian values[1]

In 1858, John Ruskin spoke on 'The work of iron in nature, art and policy'.[2] He began with a personal vision of the chemistry of iron, which he described as taking its oxygen from the air 'as eagerly as we do' and of its virtuous role, for, without iron oxides, the Earth would be 'the colour of ashes'. Iron, Ruskin observed, was also responsible for colouring our blood so that 'we cannot even blush' without its help. Through the process of rusting, iron makes the 'ochreous dust' that gives warmth to bricks and tiles. This, Ruskin contrasted with iron put to the service of man to make 'hard, bright, cold, lifeless' knives and swords. Ruskin wanted worked iron's qualities to be honoured and respected as strength and ductility, 'tenacious' iron being best shaped at speed under a hammer into decorative scrolls and leaves. The central part of his talk contrasted worked iron with cheaper cast iron, then widely used for ornamented railings and gates. Cast-iron railings were brittle imitations of wrought iron and, unlike stone and brick walls, 'shelter nothing, and support nothing'. They were emblematic of a 'sophisticated, unkind, uncomfortable, unprincipled' society.[2] Ruskin gave his talk at Tonbridge Wells, and his sophisticated audience, taking the waters in the spa town, cheered him to the echo.

This intertwining of ethical and emotional responses to materials has a long history. The idea that mankind's transformation and commoditization of the physical world carries a moral charge had traction in the ancient world. Pliny the Elder devotes two books of his *Natural history* to metals and one book to stone, where he laments 'the prodigality of our inventiveness! In how many ways have we raised the price of objects! Man has learnt to compete with nature'.[3] In the sixteenth century, Michelangelo and Vasari developed the idea that the sculptor, in particular, needed to respect his raw material. In a sonnet, Michelangelo modestly defined sculpture as a process of subtracting what was superfluous to reveal what already existed:

'To break the marble spell
Is all the hand that serves the brain can do.'[4]

The belief that the pact between man and the natural world is an uneasy one disrupted by man's greed, as Pliny suggests, also runs like a seam through European folklore. Mining and minerals offer easy abundance but often at a terrible price in the fairy tales collected in the early nineteenth-century by the Brothers Grimm.[5] It is not surprising that in 1851 Ruskin himself wrote *The King of the golden river*, a cautionary tale for children with a strong ecological message centred on the mining of precious ores.[6]

Ruskin's poetic, idiosyncratic attitude to materials (in which he identified the individual characters of iron, blown glass, marble, precious stones, wood and stucco) was replicated in many nineteenth-century debates about authenticity. We tend to think of plastics as the first group of new materials to excite popular anxiety.[7] But in the nineteenth century, papier mâché and rubber anticipated the plastics family in their quality of malleability and their capacity to stand in for other materials.[8] These were materials that were poured and moulded, and, like cast iron, effaced the role of the craftsman while imitating craft effects. As the architect and designer A. W. Pugin observed in 1836: 'All the mechanical contrivances and inventions of the day, such as plastering, composition, papier mâché, and a host of other deceptions, only serve to degrade design, by abolishing the variety of ornament and ideas as well as the boldness of execution, so admirable and beautiful in ancient works.'[9]

Pugin deplored 'pressed putty ornaments' as opposed to 'bold execution', while, in a similar spirit, the designer and design theorist Gottfried Semper noted in 1852 that: 'Rubber and gutta-percha are vulcanized and utilized in a thousand imitations of wood, metal and stone-carvings, exceeding by far the natural limitations of the materials they purport to represent.'[10]

For Semper, it was only the 'uncivilized nations' that were able to make good work because they designed with the logic and resistance of natural materials in mind. Semper wrote sorrowfully: 'We . . . are masters of enormous means and it is this abundance of means which is our greatest danger. Only by reasoning are we able to get some kind of order into this matter, since we have lost our feeling for it.'[11]

The designers and educators Richard Redgrave and Owen Jones, in the context of the Great Exhibition of 1851, concurred. Jones urged visitors to go to the exhibition to study and learn from the products from the Indian subcontinent,[12] whereas Redgrave chose the past tense to write dramatically of the Indian craftsman: 'His hand and his mind wrought together. He worked, not to produce a rigid sameness, but as Nature works. But this is not possible with the stamp, the mould, the press, and the die.'[13]

If a handful of design reformers raised doubts about plasticity's disorderly tendencies and about the loss of control of the means of production, then it is important to stress that most nineteenth-century descriptions of new materials and processes were positive, even celebratory. Writing on papier mâché in 1889, James Carruthers noted its usefulness in simulating ceiling beams and in covering columns of iron and brick to imitate stone or wood. He concluded triumphantly that 'there are no forms, however intricate, to which it is not equal'.[14]

Why should we attend to the negative responses of the design reformers, a loose grouping of architects, artists and designers, some associated with the Arts & Crafts movement? They were hardly at the centre of industrial production in Victorian Britain. But the products they designed and wrote about operated at a domestic level, and, as a result, their discussions of the proper use of materials reached a non-specialist audience. In particular, John Ruskin's and William Morris's writings on the environment, on materials, on threatened crafts in the colonies and on our consumption tastes were very widely read. Observations from William Morris's lectures – 'Have nothing in your houses that you do not know to be useful, or believe to be beautiful' – became well-known aphorisms.[15]

A lost domain

By the twentieth century, such design reform views had become naturalized and simplified under the rubric 'truth to materials', a term implicit in Herbert Read's discussion of form in his *Art and industry* of 1934, and central to ambivalent twentieth-century responses to a variety of new materials such as plywood and, rather later, plastics.[16] In the early twentieth century, part of being modern was to be anti-modern. There was, as the social historian Jose Harris observes, 'a lurking grief at the memory of a lost domain – a sense that change was inevitable, in many respects desirable, but that its gains were being purchased at a terrible price'.[17] Harris is writing about Britain, but the sense of loss was Europe-wide. The German poet Rainer Maria Rilke observed in 1925: 'Even for our grandparents, a "house", a "well", a familiar tower, their very dress, their cloak, was infinitely more intimate: almost everything a receptacle in which they both found and enlarged a store of humanness ... The animated, experienced things 'that share our lives' are running out, and cannot be replaced. We are perhaps the last to have known such things.'[18]

Wood as evidence

In the area of the artistic crafts in Britain in the first half of the twentieth century, responses to materials continued to match Ruskin's heightened, visceral reactions. All the craft disciplines, from silversmithing to bookbinding, had something to say about materials and how to use them and how not to use them. Taking furniture and joinery as a test case, here is the furniture maker Arthur Romney Green discussing doors: 'the cheapest and softest kinds of wood are chewed up by machine saws into small pieces which are glued together again between two sheets of cheap veneer under great steam presses ... this filthy compound is then veneered, say with oak and walnut not so thick as notepaper; and so you have the modernist door, looking like that which it cannot possibly be, a solid board of oak or walnut.'[19]

Plywood, like papier mâché, is made using glue. What might be called a 'glue culture' was associated with the East End furniture trade with its intensive division of labour using outworkers in ill-ventilated rooms assembling fiddly needlework and jewellery boxes, using glue as a cheap alternative to dovetails, mortising and pegging.[20] Glue, malodorous and made from animal substances, came to symbolize incorrect making among Arts & Crafts furniture makers, who insisted on revealed construction and an avoidance of veneers.

This might seem fanciful and unprogressive. But wood compounds are still with us in the form of ubiquitous medium-density fibreboard. Here, a negative, apparently emotional response to a composite wood product turns out to have a basis in science. Medium-density fibreboard is recognized as posing a health risk when cut and machined because it contains formaldehyde, one of the ingredients used to bond the wood particles into a solid board.[21]

Many early twentieth-century craft furniture makers also argued for the beauty of native timbers. Between the wars, the ethics of furniture making and joinery braided with a nativist sense of loss regarding British woodlands and landscape. This fear of erasure of familiar materials and places floats up in the Cambridge literary critic F. R. Leavis's writings about a lost 'organic community'.[22] The text that most inspired Leavis was George Sturt's classic *The wheelwright's shop*, published in 1923. Sturt had inherited the two-century-old wheelwrighting business from his father. As an educated man, he felt an outsider, but as an outsider, he set out to describe the indescribable – the tacit skills involved in building horse-drawn waggons. His task was difficult because his employees' knowledge was, as Sturt explained:

'set out in no book. It was not scientific. I never met a man who professed any other than an empirical acquaintance with the waggon-builder's lore . . . The lore was a tangled network of country prejudices, whose reasons were known in some respects here, in others there, and so on. . . . for the most part the details were but dimly understood; the whole body of knowledge was a mystery, a piece of folk knowledge, residing in the folk collectively, but never wholly in any individual.'[23]

The design process described by Sturt was highly flexible, a characteristic that came to fascinate members of the 'design methods' movement in the 1960s and 1970s. Inspired by the vernacular trial-and-error methodology recorded by Sturt, figures such as John Chris Jones argued in favour of flexible, interdisciplinary teamwork as against the individual designer working with a drawing board, remote from craft and process.[24]

Sturt was attempting to explain a deep understanding of a specific material. He was setting out to describe what Michael Baxandall, in the context of the limewood sculptors of Germany, has called the chiromancy of wood.[25] Sturt explained that farm waggons were made of tough slender pieces of wood 'with just the right curve'. These were natural curves, not steam bent, and the wheelwrights selected their material from woodlands that they knew intimately. Indeed, everything was done on an intimate scale. By the 1920s, Sturt's wheelwright's shop, which he had inherited in 1884, had become a motor repair shop. Any attempt to go against this apparently inevitable flow would be, Sturt reflected, small-scale. The recuperation of centuries of woodcraft knowledge would inevitably be limited. Timber, Sturt wrote, had turned into 'a sort of enslaved and humiliating padding for steel'.[26]

Sturt witnessed the passing of a whole world of knowledge. Today, it is possible to consider a return to wood as a substitute for steel, albeit as a remote 'back to the future' possibility. As David Edgerton points out in *The shock of the old: technology and global history since 1900*, in the case of aircraft the initial shift from wood to metal was more a matter of ideology than necessity, indexing progress.[27] Edgerton argues that during the inter-war years the continuing use of wood in aviation, while perfectly practical, came to appear eccentric and *retardataire*. Wood in the context of aeroplanes ceased to be an emotionally durable material even if it was still practically durable.

Emotional durability, a useful phrase coined by the designer Jonathan

Chapman, is another way of describing an emotional response to materials.[28] Chapman regards emotional durability as a goal for sustainability, if consumers can be educated to bond with their possessions, valuing the imperfections of goods as they age. Our ideas about the effectiveness of goods and materials are skewed in favour of newness, of material and of technique. For instance, seeing bamboo scaffolding encircling high-tech skyscrapers under construction in Hong Kong can be a shock. Yet what appears counterintuitive makes perfect sense in a Far East context where bamboo is readily available and its qualities understood. Bamboo bends in high winds, whereas steel scaffolding breaks.[29] In the West, however, bamboo appears less emotionally durable than steel.

In the world of craft, Sturt's *The wheelwright's shop* has remained inspirational. Books such as Herbert Edlin's *Woodland crafts in Britain: an account of the traditional uses of trees and timbers in the British countryside* (1949) and Oliver Rackham's *Trees and woodland in the British landscape* (1976) have led present-day furniture makers such as Richard La Trobe-Bateman and David Colwell to use wood locally and sustainably. In 1983, the furniture maker John Makepeace set out to revive the ancient woodland craft of sustainable coppicing at Hooke Park in Dorset, and this lapsed project remains the most promising British initiative in the area of sustainable wood. Makepeace put coppiced roundwood thinnings to an architectural use in collaboration with the German architect and structural engineer Frei Otto, the structural engineer Sir Edmund Happold and Richard Burton of Ahrends Burton Koralek. Two substantial buildings were constructed in the late 1980s built from thinnings combined with innovative joints using epoxy resin and steel cables developed by material scientists at Bath University. In addition, freshly felled timber was used to create compressed arches.[30] The Architectural Association, having owned Hooke Park since 2002, have recently (in 2010) opted to develop Makepeace's pioneering collaborative use of sustainable forestry, technology and vernacular craft knowledge. Material efficiency using wooden architecture remains a promising area to be explored.

Partly because of anxieties about the UK's small manufacturing base and our translation into a service economy nation, the idea of products coming out of sustainable woodland has considerable emotional durability at present. For example, in 2010, nine leading British designers chose to publicize a fortnight they spent learning the craft of bodging or green wood-turning in Clissett Wood in Herefordshire. They cleaved logs and used bow saws, pole lathes, and drawknives. Working in this setting, designing through making, instead of using three dimensional software, gave them a new freedom. As the craftsman and thinker David Pye observed, there is a flexibility about a craft approach (the workmanship of risk) that can breathe new life into design for multiple production (the workmanship of certainty).[31] Working in Clissett Wood gave all the participants a new respect for an 'old' material. Gareth Neal is a furniture designer who uses new media tools to cut complex shapes and to create intricate marquetry veneers. He observed of the experience: 'What a valuable commodity timber is because every bit you split is used. One bit becomes a rail, the next becomes a spindle, even the shavings go on the fire to keep you warm. You get so much product out of a small piece of wood.'[32]

New media

Going back to the woods is not a prospect all designers would relish. Arguably, the software that designers use may also be regarded as a kind of material. The digital artist Casey Reas believes that different software has different qualities or, as he puts it, 'atmospheres', analogous to the differences between oak and limewood or between rigid and flexible materials.[33] Each piece of software has different properties that combine an 'atmosphere' and a set of tools. But what is more relevant to material efficiency is the way in which three-dimensional software can help designers reconsider and reposition traditional materials and traditional techniques. In a project at Harvard Design School in 2002, thin sheets of plywood were laser cut into small panels using a three-dimensional computer modelling program. By borrowing cutting strategies from the tailoring of clothing and using tailoring darts, each panel was dry bent and joined to form a cloth-like construction, a decorative wooden membrane letting in light and air.[34] A relatively 'old' material, the plywood so despised by Romney Green, took on a new appearance. As well as allowing a reconsideration of materials, three-dimensional software appears to promise flexible production. An extreme example would be the exploratory work that the artist Annie Cattrell has carried out with scientists, combining magnetic resonance imaging (MRI) scanning with rapid prototyping. She has had MRI scans made of her heart that have been printed out using a rapid prototyping machine to create a sculpture entitled 'Centred 1 and 2' (2006). A further series of sculptures, 'Seeing, hearing, smelling, touching and tasting' (2000–4), rendered brain-scan data recording different sensory functions of the human brain in resin.[35] Cattrell has created a series of extraordinary works of art exploiting rapid prototyping machines.

The general public too have been captivated by the idea of rapid prototyping. Adrian Bowyer's RepRap open-source, self-replicating rapid prototyping machine makes it possible, in our living rooms, to print out spare parts for appliances.[36] We can become homesteaders all, no longer in thrall to the dark satanic mills of anywhere. No more imports. Make your own pliers. Make the children toys for Christmas. Make your own destiny. The exhibition 'Power of Making', at the Victoria & Albert Museum in 2011, was hugely popular partly because of the presence of rapid prototyping machines. Crowds of people watched with fascination as objects 'grew' as the printer head moved back and forth.[37] But if three-dimensional printers follow the expanding trajectory of home computers or mobile phones, then we should be worried. Rapid prototyping is not rapid, as a production process. In fact, it is a method of production best suited to customized miniatures such as hearing aids or as forming the basis for a mould for casting. Adrian Bowyer's claim that RepRap production can be deemed carbon-neutral or carbon-negative needs to be examined closely, together with the question of energy use by all three-dimensional printers in comparison with factory-based multiple production.

The taxonomy of the dump

The current popular interest in three-dimensional printers is revealing, underlining that many of us feel that the production of goods is out of our control. The success of Matthew Crawford's book *The case for working with your hands or why office work is bad for us and fixing things feels good* (2009) is symptomatic of this reaction against passive consumerism. So, too, is the current tendency for artists, designers and craftspeople to make work through recycling. Artists' interest in the sheer volume of stuff is not necessarily a comment on overproduction, rapid obsolescence and waste. But artists certainly take inspiration from the most dramatic site of recycling – the world's rubbish dumps.

All round the globe (though not in the so-called First World), marginalized men, women and children are making their own contribution to material efficiency. The city waste dump at Olususun in Lagos, Nigeria, is, as the documentary film-maker Gavin Searle discovered, a surprisingly ordered environment.[38] The scavengers help each other out. Theft is frowned upon. Troublemakers are banned from the dump. Each scavenger is busy categorizing his or her specialism. Some collect glass, some collect copper wire, some collect rags and so on. In order to make a living, the scavengers have to work systematically, creating taxonomies of objects. The scavengers on the world's rubbish dumps lead lives that embody a form of creativity, albeit in extreme conditions. Of course, there are dumps and dumps. Some are pretty much off limits; the southern Chinese city of Guiyu is where the USA (and probably the UK) sends thousands of tons of electronic waste each year. Our nice clean computers and neat mobiles are full of poisons in the form of lead, cadmium and polyvinyl chlorides. If Gavin Searle were able to celebrate the power of the human spirit on the Lagos dump, then there is surely nothing to celebrate at Guiyu, where covert photography and filming have recorded primitive and dangerous recycling in one of the unhealthiest places on the Earth.[39]

The dump, as evidence of our limitless desire for goods and the sheer monumentality of stuff, the goods that surround us, has become a subject. Artists have transformed rubbish into large-scale monuments that aspire to a new kind of sublime.[40] For example, the British artist Michael Landy's installation 'Breakdown' examines overconsumption from the perspective of an individual's own possessions. In 2001, Landy assembled all his possessions in a former London department store. He found that he owned over 5,000 objects – from pencils, to scraps of paper, to a car. These were catalogued as art-works, clothing, equipment, furniture, kitchen, leisure, motor vehicle, perishables, reading material and studio material, and placed on a moving production line. In a strange reversal of manufacture, all Landy's possessions were dismantled by a group of white-coated technicians. The process took one week. Breakdown was a huge popular success. Young people flocked to see objects being taken apart, sorted, shredded and crushed for recycling.[41]

Landy's 'Breakdown' underlined the scale of our consumer needs. But we need further reminding that the centres of manufacturing are constantly on the move, chasing economic efficiency, apparently careless of the effect on lives and communities. The artist Neil Brownsword's 'Salvage series' (2005) reflects on UK de-industrialization. It is an installation made up of hundreds of items associated with the industrial production of ceramics – drip trays and trivets, props and spurs used to support objects in the kiln, tangled strips of clay left after turning, collapsed and fused saggars and the ghostly residue left by the process of plaster-lining damaged moulds. Industrial by-products are put to the service of memory, of a shrinking culture of making at Stoke-on-Trent as factories make workers redundant and relocate production to the Far East.[42]

Waste is subject and object in the sculptures of the British artist Phyllida Barlow. She writes: 'We are competing with materialism that is on such a gigantic scale. There is a giant global industry of objects and how does one compete with that?'[43]

Her sculpture is in part a resistance to the glamorous art object – she cites disparagingly the work of Jeff Koons. She uses only cheap discarded materials to make objects. 'Untitled DIY 2006' was made on the spot in Seoul, Korea, out of freely available packing materials. Most of her art is subsequently dismantled and recycled. Barlow's improvisatory approach is often inspired by random relationships between objects she sees on the streets or beside railway tracks.

Streets of invention

The streets of Rio de Janeiro in Brazil are rich with Barlow's kind of inventiveness with humble materials, but driven by urgent practical requirements. The artist Gabriela de Gusmão Pereira has documented this everyday creativity. If Barlow uses impoverished materials deliberately, then the poor of Rio have no choice. They live on what Gusmão calls 'Invention Street', making do as best they can. Gusmão has photographed and drawn a whole series of 'inventions': a sound system with a cardboard box speaker; a resting place made of two broken seats; a portable sound system on a tricycle with its own light show; a portable bed for a homeless person. People who live on the streets have to adapt and appropriate. Artists can aspire only to the integrity of these improvisations.⁴⁴

The kinds of objects and arrangements that Gabi Gusmão photographed come close to what are known in Brazil as *gambiarra*, a term meaning contraption, gadget, making do. *Gambiarra* may be defined as an improvised amendment to an object, normally combining another object. They are comparable to prototypes but they are both provisional and final, an unlikely mend, almost an illustration of a problem. If Gusmão captured a needs-must economy, there is now a whole world of *gambiarra* images on the internet that travel like memes and, I suspect, are more to do with competitive playfulness than dire necessity: a soup spoon is made from a fork and the base of a polystyrene cup; an electric drill is combined with a handwhisk; a bike is adapted so that its front wheel incorporates a shopping trolley; gaffer tape is used to make countless rough but inspired mends. Some *gambiarra* have no real usefulness but make a political point about consumerism as visual contributions to a contemporary luxury debate. A child's globe is taped to a car dashboard as a joke Satnav. An apple is taped to the lid of a cheap PC.⁴⁵

Gambiarra culture has had an impact on design in general. For instance, the Spanish designers El Ultimo Grito create handsome tables made from waste cardboard and sticky tape coated in brightly coloured fibreglass. The Campana Brothers' Favela chair made of hundreds of pieces of waste wood is, as its name suggests, directly inspired by improvisatory shantytown construction in Brazil. Ironically, the Favela chair is now produced commercially in short runs by the furniture company Edra, retailing at £4,500 a chair. Both these two delightful objects – El Ultimo Grito's 'British racing green table' and the Campana Brothers 'Favela' chair – reek of romanticism concerning poverty and the improvisations that poverty inspires. There is something troubling about a design situation where the poor of the globe become source material for high-end design rather than designers devoting time to designing low-cost products for the poor.

From scratch

No wonder some young designers think of starting from scratch. 'Starting from scratch', 'beginning with zero', 'a tabula rasa', 'the Robinson Crusoe syndrome' – these are all phrases that suggest a new dynamic. The idea of beginning again – and maybe failing – recalls Robinson Crusoe's boat in the novel by Daniel Defoe. Alone at that point on his island, Crusoe painstakingly hollowed a canoe out of a great trunk of wood, taking three months over the task. But the boat was too heavy to drag down to the sea. It was made, Crusoe concluded philosophically, 'as a *Memorandum* to teach me to be wiser next Time'.[46]

The reality of taking control of the means of production, as Crusoe was forced to do, has been tested in various recent projects that are deliberately more visionary than practical. Thwaites's reverse-engineering toaster project presented at his RCA degree show in 2009 suggests the byzantine complexity of even the simplest objects we consume – and highlights the poisonous materials out of which they are made.[47] Thwaites attempted to make from scratch an Argos electric toaster costing £3.95 using materials only from the British Isles. He made some startling discoveries in his autarchic quest. To make workable iron, he found his best guide to be *De re metallica*, a sixteenth-century treatise. His iron ore came from a 'heritage' mine in the Forest of Dean, his copper from polluted standing water in disused workings in Anglesey, his mica was cut with a penknife off rocks in the Scottish Highlands. He melted Canadian coins for his nickel, discovering something of the horrendously polluting nature of nickel smelting. Plastic's complexity defeated him. His toaster ended up costing £1187.54 and it was a hilariously abject object – 'a kind of half-baked, handmade pastiche of a consumer appliance'.[48] What he learnt was the hidden environmental cost of goods that appear as if by magic in our shops. He discovered that, as sovereign consumers, we are technologically frighteningly ignorant.

The designer Tomáš Gabzdil Libertíny has also tackled the paradox of living in a world of goods whose origins are barely understood. He describes his Honeycomb Vase made for the Dutch design group Droog as an example of slow prototyping. It is not made by hand nor made by machines. It is made by bees, by 40 000 bees at work for a week.[49] This essentially absurd object made people smile, but did it make them think? Perhaps Libertíny had in mind Karl Marx's famous passage in *Capital*, chapter 7 on the architect and the bee:

'A spider conducts operations which resemble those of a weaver, and a bee would put many a human architect to shame by the construction of its honeycomb cells. But what distinguishes the worst architect from the best of bees is that the architect builds the cell in his mind before he constructs it in wax.'[50]

Marx was talking about the sanctity of work and the distinctiveness of human labour. We are not bees. We need to remember that we are craftsmen and women, designers and artists, and scientists gifted with imagination and foresight. In a full world that means making anything at all is a responsibility. In the context of providing material services with less material production, visionary rather than practical responses to materials and processes should not be ignored. The activities of artists and experimental designers can offer alternative value systems and new ways of approaching sustainability and material efficiency.

I thank Glenn Adamson for allowing me to read part of his *The invention of craft* in manuscript and my former student Catharine Rossi for lively discussion. Jorunn Veiteberg of Bergen School of Art, Norway, and Professor Jianxiong Mao of South China Normal University invited me to test some of these ideas at conferences they organized.

1. The phrase 'visionary rather than practical' in the title of this paper is taken from Julian M. Allwood, Michael F. Ashby, Timothy G. Gutowski, Ernst Worrell, 'Material efficiency: a white paper', *Resources, Conservation and Recycling*, vol. 55, no. 3, 2011, pp. 362–381 (at p. 370).
2. John Ruskin, 'The work of iron in nature, art and policy' (1858), in E. T. Cook & Alexander Wedderburn (ed.) *The works of John Ruskin*, vol. 16, London: George Allen, 1903–12, pp. 375–411.
3. James Hall, 'Material facts', *Times Literary Supplement*, 27 May 2011, p. 3.
4. Giorgio Vasari, *Vasari on technique* (1550), ed. G. Baldwin Brown, New York: Dover, 1960, pp. 179–180.
5. Esther Leslie, *Synthetic worlds: nature, art and the chemical industry*, London: Reaktion Books, 2005, pp. 25–47.
6. E. T. Cook & Alexander Wedderburn (ed.) *The works of John Ruskin*, vol. 1, London: George Allen, pp. 305–54.
7. Roland Barthes, 'Plastic', in his *Mythologies* (1957), London: Jonathan Cape, 1972; Jeffrey L. Meikle, *American plastic: a cultural history*, New Brunswick, NJ: Rutgers University Press, 1995.
8. Glenn Adamson, *The invention of craft*, London: Bloomsbury, 2013, chapter 2.
9. A. W. N. Pugin, *Contrasts: a parallel between the noble edifices of the fourteenth and fifteenth centuries, and similar buildings of the present day, shewing the present decay of taste*, London: [Published by the author], 1836, p. 35.
10. Gottfried Semper, 'Science, industry and art: proposals for the development of a national taste in art at the closing of the London industrial exhibition', in Gottfried Semper, *The four elements of architecture and other writings* (ed. Harry Francis Mallgrave), Cambridge: Cambridge University Press, 1989, pp. 134–8.
11. Gottfried Semper, *Kleine Schriften*, Berlin: W. Spemann, 1884.
12. *A catalogue of the articles of ornamental art selected from the exhibition of the works of industry of all nations in 1851 and purchased by the government*, London: Department of Practical Art, 1852.
13. Richard Redgrave, 'Class xxx: supplementary report on design', *Reports by juries on the subjects of the thirty classes into which the exhibition was divided*, London: Royal Commission for the Great Exhibition, 1852.
14. James Carruthers, 'Papier mâché', *The Decorator and Furnisher*, vol. 15, no. 1, 1889, p. 10.
15. William Morris, 'The beauty of life', in William Morris, *Selected writings* (ed. G. D. H. Cole), London: Nonesuch Press, 1934, at p. 561.

16. Herbert Read, *Art and industry: the principles of industrial design*, London: Faber & Faber, 1934.

17. Jose Harris, *Private lives, public spirit: Britain 1870–1914*, Harmondsworth: Penguin Books, 1994, p. 36.

18. Rainer Maria Rilke, *New poems*, translated by J. B. Leishman, New York: New Directions, 1964, p. 17.

19. Artifex (A. Romney Green), 'Work and play: the autobiography of a small working master in prose and verse', National Art Library, London: manuscript MSL/1974/14203, c. 1942, vol. 11, ch. ix, p. 26.

20. Pat Kirkham, Rodney Mace, & Julia Porter, *Furnishing the world: the East London furniture trade 1830–1980*, London: Journeyman, 1987.

21. For a British response, see *Medium density fibreboard: hazard assessment document*, London: Health and Safety Executive Books, 1999.

22. F. R. Leavis & Denys Thompson, *Culture and environment: the training of critical awareness*, London: Chatto & Windus, 1933.

23. George Sturt, *The wheelwright's shop*, Cambridge: Cambridge University Press, 1923, pp. 73–4.

24. C. Thomas Mitchell, *Redefining designing: from form to experience*, New York: Van Nostrand Reinhold, 1993, pp. 38–60.

25. Michael Baxandall, *The limewood carvers of Renaissance Germany*, New Haven, CT, 1980 Yale University Press, pp. 32–8.

26. Sturt, *The wheelwright's shop*, p. 74.

27. David Edgerton, *The shock of the old: technology and global history since 1900*, London: Profile Books, 2008, p. 10.

28. Jonathan Chapman, *Emotionally durable design: objects, experiences & empathy*, London: Earthscan, 2005.

29. Saif Osmani, 'Material of resistance: contesting the cultural and aesthetic ownership of bamboo', talk given at Chelsea College of Art and Design (unpublished), 28 March 2011.

30. Jeremy Myerson, *Makepeace: a spirit of adventure in craft and design*, London: Conran Octopus, 1971, pp. 148–64.

31. David Pye, *The nature and art of workmanship*, London: Studio Vista, 1971.

32. Grant Gibson, 'The bodgers' parade', *Crafts*, no. 224, 2010, p. 41.

33. Tanya Harrod, 'Otherwise unobtainable: the applied arts and the politics and poetics of digital technology', in *NeoCraft: modernity and the crafts* (ed. Sandra Alfoldy), Halifax, Nova Scotia: The Press of Nova Scotia College of Art and Design, 2007, p. 229.

34. Toshiko Mori (ed.), *Immaterial / ultramaterial: architecture, design and materials*, New York: George Braziller, 2002, pp. 1–4.

35. Marius Kwint, 'Cosmic dust: the work of Annie Cattrell', in *Annie Cattrell: arresting*, London: Anne Faggionato, 2006, pp. 9–11; Cathy Gere, 'Thought in a vat: thinking through Annie Cattrell', *Studies in History and Philosophy of Science, Part C: Biological and Biomedical Sciences*, vol. 35, 2004, pp. 415–36.

36. Rhys Jones, Patrick Haufe, Edward Sells, Pejman Iravani, Vik Olliver, Chris Palmer, & Adrian Bowyer, 'RepRap: the replicating rapid prototyper', *Robotica*, special issue 01, 2011, pp. 177–91.

37. Daniel Charny (ed.), *Power of making: the importance of being skilled*, London: V&A Publishing / Crafts Council, 2011.

38. 'Welcome to Lagos', episode 1, BBC2 TV, 15 April 2010. Director: Gavin Searle; producer: Will Anderson.

39. Xia Huo, Lin Peng, Xijin Xu, Liangkai Zheng, Bo Qiu, Zongli Qi, Bao Zhang, Dai Han, & Zhongxian Piao, 'Elevated blood lead levels of children in Guiyu, an electronic waste recycling town in China', *Environmental Health Perspectives*, vol. 115, no. 7, 2007, pp. 1113–17.

40. Johanna Drucker, *Sweet dreams: contemporary art and complicity*, Chicago: University of Chicago Press, 2005, pp. 112–24.

41. Michael Landy & Clive Lissaman, *Breakdown inventory*, London: Ridinghouse, 2001.

42. *Neil Brownsword: collaging history*, Stoke-on-Trent: The Potteries Museum and Art Gallery, 2005.

43. Mark Godfrey, Jon Wood, & Phyllida Barlow, *Objects for … and other things: Phyllida Barlow*, London: Black Dog Publishing, 2004, p. 66.

44. Gabriela de Gusmão Pereira, *Rua dos Inventos / Invention Street: a arte da sobrevivência / the art of survival*, Rio de Janeiro: Ouro sobre Azul, 2004; Gabriela Gusmão, 'Looking is a way of touching', *The Journal of Modern Craft*, vol. 2, no. 2, 2009, pp. 201–9.

45. Gabriel Menotti, 'Gambiarra and the prototyping perspective', talk given at Rewire: the Fourth International Conference on the Histories of Media Art, Science and Technology, Liverpool, 2011.

46. Daniel Defoe, *Robinson Crusoe* (1719), Oxford: Oxford University Press, 2007, p. 116.

47. Thomas Thwaites, *The toaster project, or a heroic attempt to build a simple electrical appliance from scratch*, New York: Princeton Architectural Press, 2011.

48. Thwaites's own words, at: < www.thetoasterproject.org >

49. Jennifer Hudson, *Process: 50 product designs from concept to manufacture*, London: Laurence King, 2008.

50. Karl Marx, *Capital: a critique of political economy* (1867), vol. 1, Harmondsworth: Penguin Books, 1976, p. 284.

Philosophical Transactions of the Royal Society, A: Mathematical, Physical and Engineering Sciences, no. 1986, 13 March 2013

Afterword

Some of the articles in this book were written as obituaries. Textile artist Tadek Beutlich (1922–2011), potter Gwyn Hanssen Pigott (1935–2013), designers Norman Potter (1923–95) and Eva Zeisel (1906–2011) are commemorated in this way. But other individuals have died since my article about them appeared. This category includes the Ghanaian politician Reginald Reynolds Amponsah (1919–2009); the artist Ian Hamilton Finlay (1925–2006); the designers Peggy Angus (1904–93), Lucienne Day (1917–2010), Robin Day (1915–2010), and Marianne Straub (1909–94); the embroiderer Constance Howard (1910–2000); the lettercutter Ralph Beyer (1921–2008); the potters Ruth Duckworth (1919–2009), Ray Finch (1914–2012), Ewen Henderson (1934–2000), Eileen Lewenstein (1925–2005), Gillian Lowndes (1936–2010), Lucie Rie (1902–95), and Ann Stokes (1922–2014); the textile artist Peter Collingwood (1922–2008). It was a privilege to know them.

Index